THE WORLD ENCYCLOPEDIA OF

MEAT, GAME AND POULTRY

THE WORLD ENCYCLOPEDIA OF

MEAT, GAME AND POULTRY

LUCY KNOX AND KEITH RICHMOND

HERMES HOUSE

This edition is published by Hermes House, an imprint of Anness Publishing Ltd, Blaby Road, Wigston, Leicestershire LE18 4SE; info@anness.com

www.hermeshouse.com; www.annesspublishing.com

If you like the images in this book and would like to investigate using them for publishing, promotions or advertising, please visit our website www.practicalpictures.com for more information.

Publisher: Joanna Lorenz
Managing Editor: Linda Fraser
Copy Editors: Bridget Jones and Susanna Tee
Indexer: Dawn Butcher
Designer: Nigel Partridge
Photographers: Craig Robertson (recipe section) and Janine Hosegood
Stylist: Helen Trent
Food for Photography: Joanna Farrow and Bridget Sargeson, assisted by Victoria Walters (recipe section); and Annabel Ford (reference section)

A CIP catalogue record for this book is available from the British Library.

PUBLISHER'S NOTE

Although the advice and information in this book are believed to be accurate and true at the time of going to press, neither the authors nor the publisher can accept any legal responsibility or liability for any errors or omissions that may have been made nor for any inaccuracies nor for any loss, harm or injury that comes about from following instructions or advice in this book.

NOTES

For all recipes, quantities are given in both metric and imperial measures and, where appropriate, in standard cups and spoons. Follow one set of measures, but not a mixture, because they are not interchangeable.
Standard spoon and cup measures are level. 1 tsp = 5ml, 1 tbsp = 15ml, 1 cup = 250ml/8fl oz. Australian standard tablespoons are 20ml. Australian readers should use 3 tsp in place of 1 tbsp for measuring small quantities. American pints are 16fl oz/2 cups. American readers should use 20fl oz/2.5 cups in place of 1 pint when measuring liquids.
Electric oven temperatures in this book are for conventional ovens. When using a fan oven, the temperature will probably need to be reduced by about 10–20°C/20–40°F. Since ovens vary, you should check with your manufacturer's instruction book for guidance.
Medium (US large) eggs are used unless otherwise stated.

CONTENTS

INTRODUCTION

Meat is probably our favourite food. In every meat-eating culture in the world, it is the food for a feast, a celebration or any special occasion. Every one of our festivals – Christmas and Easter in Britain, Thanksgiving and Mardi Gras in the United States, Hanukkah in the Jewish calendar, not to mention anniversaries and feast days – centres around a special meal, and in each one meat, game or poultry is almost always the central component.

However, meat is more than just a festive food. All those who enjoy meat do so because it not only tastes superb served in large joints or as whole birds, but also because it is delicious when cooked and served in more modest portions. Meat above all is versatile. It can be fried, grilled, poached or stewed, served alongside pasta, rice, grains or vegetables or cooked with just about anything. There is really no limit to the ways that meat can be used.

Above: The meat of the wild buffalo has been eaten since ancient times, but these huge, strong animals were also used in the past by farmers to pull their carts and ploughs.

Below: Game birds are hunted both for food and "sport" in many countries. However, nowadays, most species are protected by laws that forbid hunting during breeding times to allow the stock to grow in number again.

The first domesticated animals

Meat has been eaten for as long as man has been able to catch the animals. At first the animals were wild, but it wasn't long before ancient man began to domesticate animals such as cows, sheep, goats and pigs, and birds such as chickens, geese and ducks. The animals were reared for their milk, skins and wool as well as for their meat or, in the case of buffalo and oxen, for their ability to pull the first ploughs and early carts. Chickens, ducks and geese were kept for their meat and for their eggs.

Sheep were first domesticated by the tribesmen of Central Asia 10,000 years ago, and by 2000 BC, farmers in China, Egypt and the middle and near East had learnt to domesticate cattle, goats, pigs and sheep for their meat. Eight hundred years later, it was Chinese farmers again who learnt to domesticate chickens and ducks.

The tradition of hunting

Birds and animals that are eaten, but not domesticated and reared on farms, are referred to as game. Our ancestors ate far more game than is consumed nowadays, and some once popular birds such as swans and peacocks have so diminished in number that they are no longer eaten, while other birds and animals such as quail and wild boar are now reared for the table in farms. Nowadays, most game is protected by strict laws and can only be killed at certain times of the year.

Above: Geese have been domesticated for thousands of years, but they have defied all attempts at intensive rearing, so fresh birds remain a seasonal treat.

The historical importance of meat

Meat has played a central role in the development of agriculture, industry and commerce in almost every country in the world, and it is often referred to in historical texts. The Old Testament is full of references to eating meat, from Genesis onwards. In the New Testament, too, there are countless stories where meat symbolizes worship and celebration. When the Prodigal Son returns to his home, his father cries, "bring the fattened calf and kill it. Let's have a feast and celebrate."

Elsewhere in literature, whether calf, lamb, oxen, poultry or game, meat features regularly, symbolizing wealth, prosperity and good living. Conversely, poverty and need is regularly symbolized by a lack of meat at the table. People would calculate their position in society by how frequently meat was served. For the greater part of history in Britain and most parts of Europe, meat was a luxury food for all but the well off. Kings and queens may have dined on all sorts of wonderful roasts and meats, but for ordinary people, meat was eked out to add much sought-after flavour and protein to broths and stews that otherwise were made up of meal, and vegetables if they were lucky.

Above: Sheep were the first animals to be domesticated and are now farmed all over the world often in small mountain flocks.

Until very recently meat was far and away the most expensive component of a meal and, in times of shortages, it was inevitably the first ingredient in which to cut back. Throughout history people have made the most of meat by serving it with economical starchy ingredients and accompaniments such as pastry, dumplings or Yorkshire puddings to eke it out and make a little go a long way.

Left: Free-range chickens have access to the outside and plenty of room to wander about – a far cry from the tiny cages in which intensively reared hens are cooped.

Below: Farmers have realized that well-cared-for cows produce better meat.

In fact, it is thanks entirely to the less affluent members of society that we have so many different recipes for cooking meat. Stews, casseroles, tagines, hot-pots, pies and cassoulets are among the hundreds of ways devised by ordinary people for using the poorer, less tender cuts of meat.

The influence of religion and custom

It is not only cost that determines how much meat is eaten; consumption also varies according to religion, custom and taste. Beef is one of the most popular meats in most countries except in India where Hindus do not eat the flesh of the cow, which they consider to be sacred, and Muslims and Jews will not eat pork or any meat that hasn't been killed in a specific ritual way. British people will not eat horsemeat or dogmeat, although the former is much enjoyed in the rest of Europe and the latter in much of the Far East.

Right: After years of being farmed intensively indoors, many pigs nowadays are being reared in the traditional ways and enjoying a far more pleasant life outdoors in the fresh air.

Better farming

In most countries there are no religious laws underpinning meat preparation, and consequently the meat available in our shops continues to change, as methods of breeding and butchery improve. Meat today is vastly superior in flavour and texture to that available even 20 years ago. Farmers have responded to concerns about healthy eating, and are breeding animals that provide leaner meat. In addition, they are realizing that the more care lavished on cows, pigs or poultry, the better the meat. Customers in turn are demanding this too, both because of concern about the welfare of animals and birds and because of a desire for good, lean meat.

There is no doubt that free-range chicken tastes better than its intensively reared equivalent, or that free-range pork tastes far better than the meat

Above: Kangaroo is hunted in every state in Australia, and the lean, flavourful meat is becoming more widely available in supermarkets and butchers' in Europe.

Above: Alligator is popular in the southern states of America. These animals are now reared in farms to protect the wild species from extinction.

Below: Ostriches, whose natural habitats include Australia and Africa, are now reared in farms in Scotland.

from pigs reared on factory-like farms. As a result, more and more farmers are reverting to traditional, often organic, methods where animals are allowed to graze freely outdoors, free from both chemicals and pesticides.

Organic and traditionally reared meat and poultry is becoming increasingly available from specialist butchers' and many supermarkets. It costs a little more than intensively reared meats, but is considered to be superior in every respect, being healthier, with better flavour and a leaner and more tender texture. Most of us are happier knowing that the meat we are eating comes from an animal that was properly treated when alive.

This is especially true of calves. Veal was considered a delicacy in Medieval Europe and has remained a popular premium meat ever since. In the 1990s, though, consumption of veal declined in Britain and North America because of concerns over the methods used in raising the animals. But a commitment by farmers to more humane farming methods has seen veal come back into fashion and nowadays a wide range of cuts are available from good butchers'.

New meat varieties

Other meats have also become newly fashionable both in their country of origin and elsewhere. Meats from animals such as alligator, crocodile, emu, kangaroo, ostrich and wild boar can nowadays be bought in butchers' shops and supermarkets almost as easily as beef, lamb, pork and poultry. These new meats appeal not only because they taste very good but also because they are lean and tender. Like some of the traditional "game" animals and birds, such as deer and quail, many of these animals are no longer hunted in the wild, but are bred for the table in special farms.

Preserved and cured meats

Meat was once butchered at home and cut into convenient portions for eating there and then, or it was preserved by drying, salting or smoking for eating throughout the year. Nowadays of course, thanks to modern transportation and refrigeration, fresh and frozen meat is widely available throughout the year from butchers' and supermarkets. However, despite the availability of fresh meat, many of the cured meats such as bacon and ham, which our ancestors preserved out of necessity, are still produced and eaten today simply because they taste very good.

Other meat products, which were once made to preserve meat, include fresh, smoked and cured sausages. These were originally produced to use up the scraps of pork left after home-reared pigs had been butchered. They are still made throughout the world but nowadays sausages are more likely to be produced in a factory than in the home. There are thousands of regional varieties and types available.

Below: Although dried and cured meats are no longer produced out of necessity, they remain popular throughout the world. This butcher's shop in Normandy, France has a wide range of dried sausages and cured meats for sale along with fresh meat, game and poultry.

Right: Buy from a traditional butcher who will offer a wide range of lovingly prepared small cuts and special joints.

Butchery methods and laws

In the West there are some minor differences in the butchering of meat from country to country, but in some other cultures there may be significant differences in the slaughter, aging and preparation of the carcass.

In Muslim countries, animals are ritually slaughtered in accordance with Islamic tradition, a method that involves cutting the throat of the animal and suspending it so that the blood drains out. The meat is known as halal meat, the word meaning "legal and allowed". This and other Islamic food customs have existed since the 7th century, taught by the prophet Muhammad, and strict Muslims will take care to only buy meat from halal butchers.

Traditional recipes such as Roast Beef with Yorkshire Puddings (above) are included in the recipe section along with contemporary ideas such as Marinated Alligator Steaks with Cajun Vegetables – a Louisiana speciality (right).

In Judaism too there are numerous food laws. Only animals that chew the cud and have cloven hooves can be eaten. All others, including rabbit, pigs and horses are considered unclean and are forbidden. All meat must be koshered before it is eaten, which means that it must be slaughtered by cutting the animal's throat to let the blood drain. For this reason, game that has been hunted and shot is also not allowed. Meat and dairy products may not be eaten at the same meal, and in most countries only meat from the forequarter of the animal can be eaten.

Cuts of meat

The way that a butcher prepares a carcass to produce cuts of meat varies not only from country to country, but also sometimes from region to region, and identical cuts often have a variety of different regional names. As a rule of thumb, the best joints come from the hindquarter and loin of an animal; in other words those parts that have the least exercise. However, it is worth remembering that the tougher cuts are not only cheaper to buy, but they are also often extremely flavourful.

Using this book

The first part of this book gives a detailed guide to all the different types of meat, game and poultry, with useful information on buying and storing as well as instructions on preparation and cooking methods.

The recipe section includes classic dishes from around the world as well as a range of modern recipes. You will find something here for every type of meal, whether it's a recipe for a romantic supper for two, something quick and easy to cook for the family, or an impressive roast for a big occasion.

Left: Coq au Vin, which is just one of the classic, traditional dishes included in the recipe section.

EQUIPMENT

Personal experience is the ideal guide to buying equipment. The novice cook or first-time kitchen owner is best advised to begin with a few basic items for preparing, cooking and serving, and then buy more equipment as required. Sophisticated appliances should be planned purchases. The important rule to remember is that the finest equipment is not a cure for bad basic cooking, but using the right tool often makes the job easier and quicker.

Usefulness

If the decision to buy is a difficult one, make a list of all tasks the equipment eases, then tick off tasks you already carry out by hand or with inferior tools. Next, tick off the things you want to do, but cannot because you do not have the right equipment.

Working space

With so many affordable large items of kitchenware readily available, it would be easy to fill the entire kitchen work surface, leaving barely enough space for a chopping board. Measure the equipment, then think about the space available and whether it is something that has to be left out permanently to be useful. Look at the availability of electric sockets. Check fittings, such as clamps or wall-mounting brackets – for example, is the surface suitable for a mincer to be clamped on it or is there a suitable space for a wall-mounted tool?

Storage

Cupboards, drawers, shelves, hanging racks, tool trolleys or tool boxes are all useful. Every storage option has good and bad points. Covered or closed storage (drawers or cupboards) are cleaner than open shelves or hanging racks, particularly in a small kitchen or near a hob where steam and splashes from cooking can be a problem.

Above: A steel for sharpening (top) is essential, along with a range of good-quality knives.

Below: Measuring cups and spoons

Over-filled drawers are not only very irritating, but they are also damaging to equipment and dangerous when sharp or pointed items, such as knives and skewers, are kept in them.

Equipment used frequently should be easily accessible – a hanging rack near the hob can be practical for small tools, such as draining spoons, graters and sieves, that are used and washed regularly.

Large, awkward or heavy items should be easy to lift and move, if necessary. Bad stacking causes damage, chipped edges and scratched surfaces. A tool box can be a great way of storing rarely used items, such as sausage-filling nozzles, mincer, pie funnel, individual pie tins or moulds.

PREPARATION EQUIPMENT

Kitchen scales

There is a wide choice, from spring scales that are not particularly accurate to balance scales with weights (these can be precise) or digital scales, which vary in quality, but can be excellent, particularly for small amounts.

Measuring cups

American measuring cups are also available in other countries. They come in sizes from ¼ cup = 50ml/2fl oz to 1 cup = 250ml/8fl oz.

Measuring spoons

A set on a loop will not be lost as easily as separate spoons. These are essential for accurate measuring as they are calibrated in sizes from 1.5ml/¼tsp to 15ml/1 tbsp.

Knives

Select knives that are comfortable to hold and well balanced. Blades of high-grade stainless steel, fully forged and with the tang running through the handle are strong and durable. It is better to have one good knife than 12 poor implements. Pay a premium price for a blade that will sharpen well. **A cook's knife** (sometimes called a chopping knife) with a blade about 20cm/8in long and **a paring knife**, with a 10cm/4in blade, are good basic choices. With these you will be able to carry out most techniques.

Knife sharpening and storing

A sharpener is essential for keeping knives sharp and useful; sharpen them regularly to keep the blade fine and smooth. A steel is the usual choice and better than many of the inexpensive sharpening devices. Electric knife sharpeners are available.

A stone is inexpensive and excellent for keeping knives sharp – available from hardware stores or Chinese supermarkets, look for a stone with a fine and coarse side. Start by sharpening on the coarse side, then grease the fine side with a little cooking oil to finish sharpening the blade.

Always wash and dry knives thoroughly after sharpening and before use. A knife block is useful for storing knives safely, it also helps to prevent damage caused when knives are jumbled together in a drawer.

A boning knife has a narrow, flexible blade, which bends easily for cutting around curved bones.

A carving knife (slicing knife) with a 20–25cm/8–10in blade is useful for carving joints, and **a ham knife** with a 25cm/10in ridged blade is useful for carving thicker slices of meats, such as ham and pork.

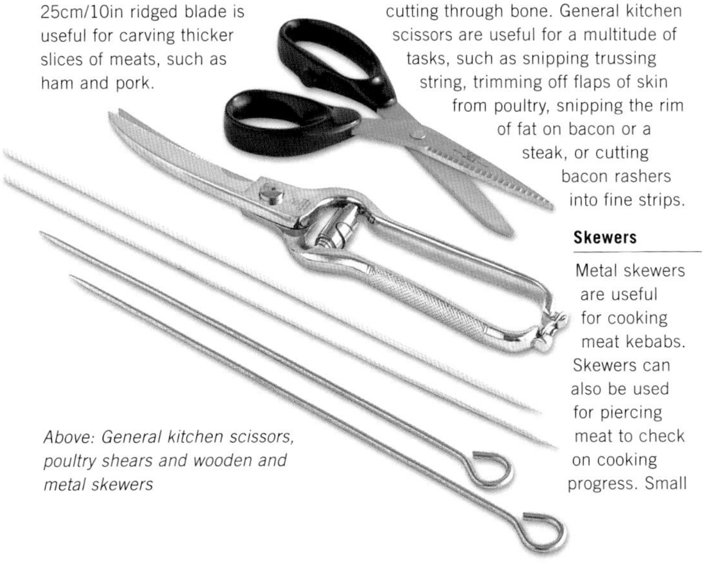

Above: General kitchen scissors, poultry shears and wooden and metal skewers

Above: Plastic chopping boards

Meat cleaver

This heavy, wide-bladed knife is used for chopping meat bones and preparing Asian ingredients by authentic methods. It is also useful for finely chopping meat.

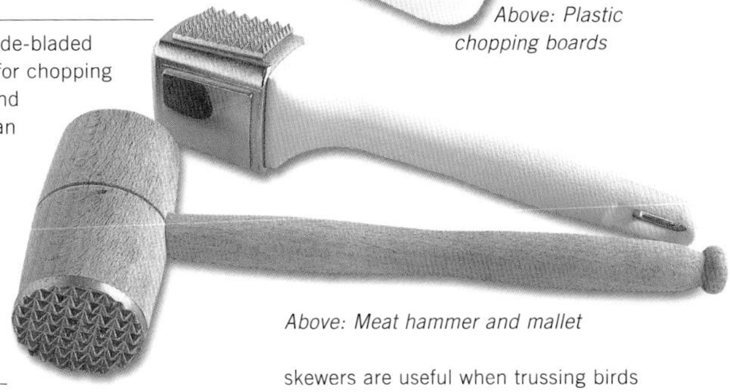

Above: Meat hammer and mallet

Scissors

Poultry scissors or shears are useful for cutting through bone. General kitchen scissors are useful for a multitude of tasks, such as snipping trussing string, trimming off flaps of skin from poultry, snipping the rim of fat on bacon or a steak, or cutting bacon rashers into fine strips.

Skewers

Metal skewers are useful for cooking meat kebabs. Skewers can also be used for piercing meat to check on cooking progress. Small skewers are useful when trussing birds or joints. Wooden or bamboo skewers are used for some kebabs.

Meat hammer or mallet

Usually wooden, sometimes with metal ends, this is used to tenderize meat or to thin slices or steaks. Choose one with one flat side for beating and one dimpled side for tenderizing meat. A steak mallet is smaller than a meat hammer. It is made from metal and used to tenderize steak.

Chopping board

Wooden chopping boards are the traditional type. Sturdy plastic composite boards are more hygienic as they are not absorbent; however, they still need thorough scrubbing as the surface becomes scored with use. Sturdy plastic composite boards can be put in the dishwasher.

Above: String, clear film, aluminium foil and polythene bags

Mortar and pestle

This is used for crushing spices and grinding flavouring ingredients.

String

Buy fine string for cooking, to truss birds and tie joints. Cook's shops sell high-quality, smooth string that does not leave tiny threads on the meat, but good string is available from stationers. Avoid "fluffy" string or coarse twine. Store the ball of string in a polythene bag with cooking equipment to keep it clean and avoid having it handled by dirty hands from gardening or similar messy tasks.

Kitchen foil

This is useful for covering meat to keep it moist and also to prevent it from becoming too brown during cooking.

Clear film

Useful for covering raw or cooked foods.

Polythene bags

Available in a variety of sizes, these are useful for storing raw and cooked meat and meat dishes in the freezer.

Plastic boxes with lids

These are invaluable for storing cooked dishes and individual portions of raw meat in the fridge or freezer.

Salt and pepper mills

For freshly ground black pepper and sea salt. Look for a pepper mill with a metal grinding mechanism (rather than plastic, which does not wear well). A pepper mill is also useful for favourite spices that are good coarsely ground, such as coriander.

Food processor

For chopping, grating, blending, slicing, beating, mincing and many more culinary tasks. Select a processor with a bowl to suit your requirements, big enough to prepare the quantities in which you normally cook and not too big to be of use for every-day amounts. Try to buy a food processor that will sit on your kitchen work surface, rather than one that has to be taken out of a cupboard every time you use it. Some large food processors have smaller bowls to fit inside the main container when processing small amounts. Look for an appliance that has a powerful motor, particularly when planning to mince or chop meat.

Mincer

Several types are available, from the traditional hand-cranked metal mincer, which clamps on to a work surface, to an electric mincer. All mincers come with blades of various sizes, so that meat can be passed through a coarse blade first, then through a finer blade if required.

Left: Mortar and pestle

Above: Food processor

Right: Mincer

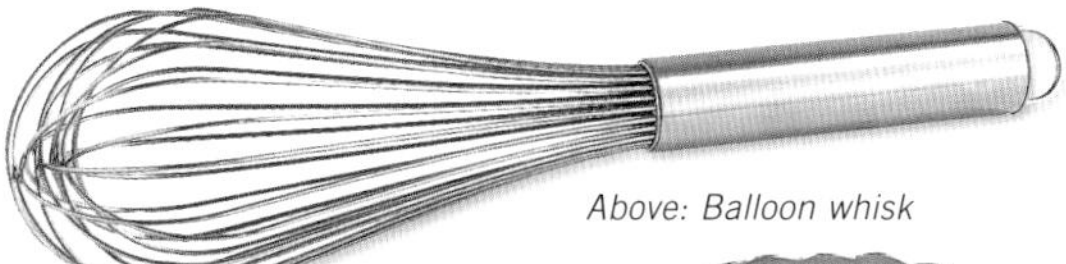

Above: Balloon whisk

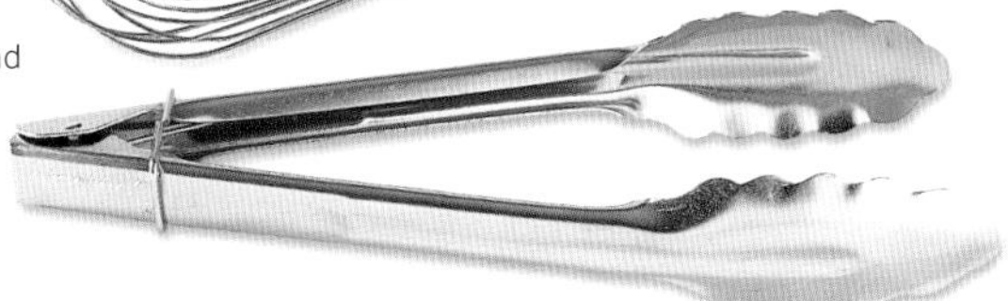

Above: Metal tongs

COOKING EQUIPMENT

Balloon whisk

Useful for whisking gravies and sauces, smoothing out lumps and bringing a gloss to the liquid.

Timer

This is useful for accurately timing cooking.

Oven gloves

Buy heavy cotton mittens or the longer gauntlet type of glove. Use to protect your hands when handling hot dishes, tins and pans.

Metal tongs

Useful for lifting and turning small cuts of meat when cooking. The tongs shown above have a useful spring action.

Basting spoon

A large metal spoon for basting roasts and baked dishes during cooking.

Balloon baster

A huge plastic or metal dropper, with a heatproof balloon end for expelling air and squeezing in cooking juices, which can be squirted over the top of the meat to baste. A balloon baster is also useful for transferring the excess fat from a roasting tin to a dish, for example, as when roasting fatty birds such as goose or duck.

Skimmer

A round, perforated, metal skimmer is ideal for skimming scum from stock.

Metal spatula or fish slice

These can be bought in various sizes and are useful for turning large pieces of meat during cooking.

Draining spoon

Perforated or with slots, this large, metal spoon is mainly used for removing meat from a saucepan or frying pan when browned, leaving the fat behind for cooking the next batch.

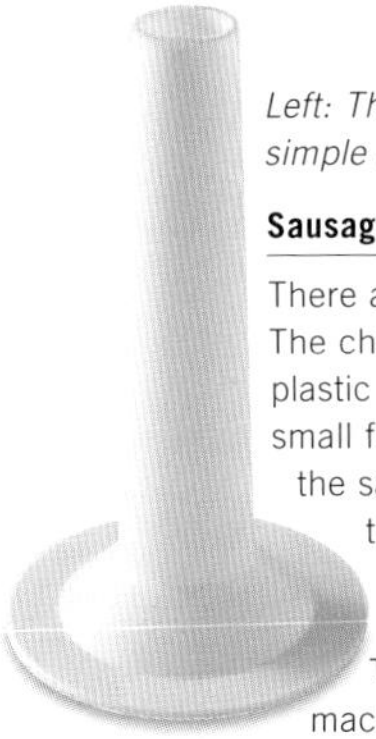

Left: This funnel is a simple sausage maker.

Sausage maker

There are several types. The cheapest are made of plastic and consist of a small funnel for passing the sausagemeat into a tube for casing and a plunger to push the meat through. The more expensive machines are electric, but they work on the same principle. You can also make sausages using a piping bag and plain nozzle.

Meat hook

This is a specialist item that is used for hanging meat and aging furred and feathered game.

Larding needle

A large, long needle with a ridged gripper at one end, used for threading strips of fat through lean joints of meat to ensure that the meat remains moist during cooking.

Trussing needle

This metal needle with a large eye is used for threading fine string through meat, game and poultry to keep it in shape during cooking.

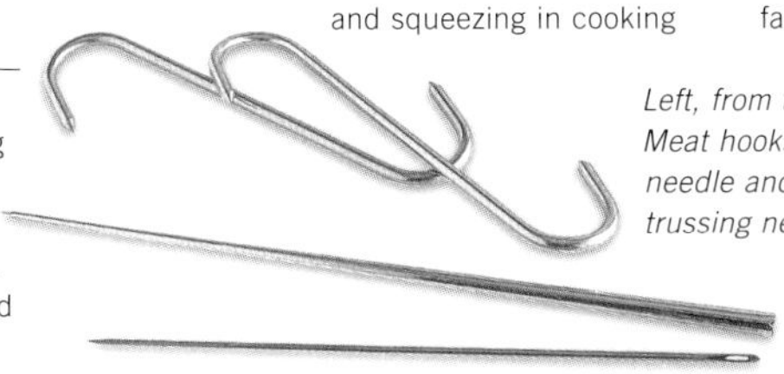

Left, from top: Meat hooks, larding needle and trussing needle

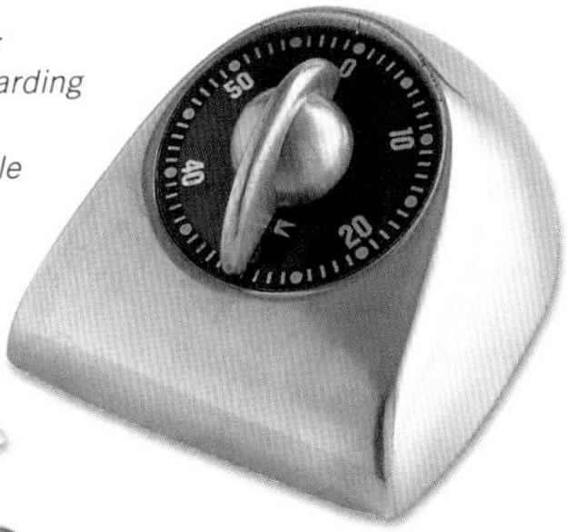

Above: A clockwork timer is inexpensive, yet extremely useful.

Below: Basting spoon and fish slice

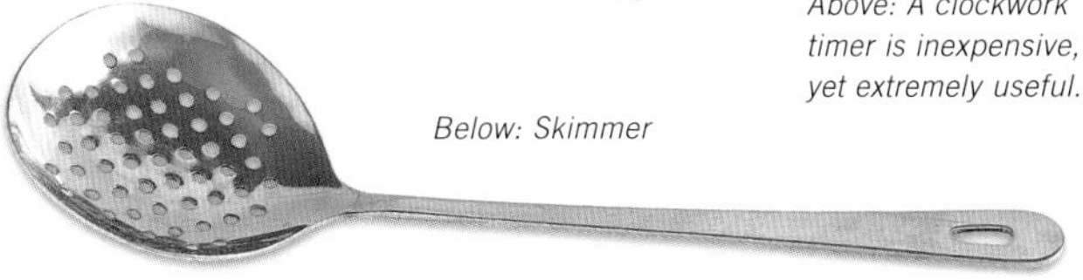

Below: Skimmer

Left: Frying pans come in a range of sizes.

Griddle

These cast-iron cooking pans may be flat or, more commonly, ridged and are used for cooking on the hob. Griddling, especially on a ridged pan, provides a healthy and attractive alternative to frying. The ridges keep the meat above fat that drips off, and they sear attractive marks on the surface of the meat as it cooks.

Left: Flat and ridged griddles

Saucepans

Three sizes of pan are useful, typically 16cm/6¼in, 19.5cm/7½in and 23cm/9in. Look for heavy, durable pans that distribute heat quickly and efficiently. The best are heavy stainless steel, with a core of copper and silver alloy in the base. Look for strong handles that do not conduct heat well and reinforced rims designed to pour cleanly. Look for a long guarantee from a reputable manufacturer and remember that high-quality, expensive pans will give a lifetime's service.

Non-stick coatings do not last as long as stainless steel. All-metal pans, which can be used in the oven as well as on the hob, are useful if you have a large oven. Buy the wrong pans and you will curse them every day, so it is worth taking plenty of time over the choice. Ask friends who share your cooking habits, read consumer reports and try out one pan before investing in the set.

Below: Saucepans

Above: Preserving pan

Frying pan

A good-quality, heavy-based frying pan with a non-stick coating is vital. Use for sealing joints and cooking small cuts.

Preserving pan

A traditional large and deep preserving pan can be useful for boiling ham.

Left: Stock pot

Roasting racks

Good roasting tins come with a rack. Place in a roasting tin to allow heat to circulate around a joint or bird and fat to run off. Useful when cooking fatty meat or poultry, such as duck.

Below: Roasting rack and tin

Casserole

An ovenproof cooking dish with a lid. Flameproof casseroles can be used on the hob, for browning ingredients as well as braising and stewing in the oven.

Stock pot

A large, deep pan for making stock and cooking large cuts of meat. Heavy-duty stainless steel will last a lifetime. Look for a pan with small metal handles on both sides, then it will double as a huge ovenproof casserole, ideal for baking ham as well as boiling it.

Grill pan

A good-quality grill pan will not buckle under fierce heat.

Roasting tins

Choose two heavy, deep tins to cook birds or joints of different sizes. They should be tough enough to withstand high heat and hob-top cooking as well as long, slow cooking without buckling and they should not rust. High-quality, heavy stainless steel or enamel tins are a good choice. Handles are a bonus and make lifting tins with heavy roasts much easier. Covered roasting tins, with dimpled lids to encourage steam to condense and drip back into the tin, are useful instead of having to use foil.

Roasting trays

The best roasting trays are made from heavy-duty aluminium. Again, select trays of different sizes for different tasks.

Right: Oven and meat thermometers

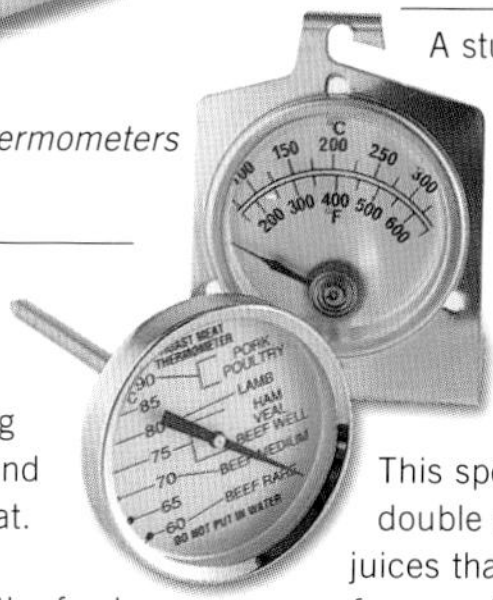

Roasting bags

These are clear, ovenproof bags in which to roast meat. They are good for cooking poultry and game birds and small, rolled joints of meat. They not only keep in moisture, but also baste the food as it cooks. In addition, roasting bags help to keep the oven clean by preventing splashing and spitting.

Meat thermometer

This is very useful for checking the cooking progress when roasting a joint of meat. Follow the manufacturer's instructions for use. Some thermometers are inserted into the raw joint, then placed in the oven with it. Others are inserted at the end of cooking, once the meat is removed from the oven. The point of the thermometer should be inserted into the middle of the thickest part of the joint.

Oven thermometer

Temperature gauges on ovens can be inaccurate. So it is a good idea to invest in a small, neat thermometer that will hang on the oven shelf and give an accurate reading.

SERVING EQUIPMENT

Ladles

Useful for serving sauces and gravies as well as moist casseroles and stews.

Spiked meat platter

Metal platter, with short spikes in the middle to hold a joint in place while carving and (usually) a sunken rim into which fat or juices run and collect.

Carving fork

A sturdy, long-handled fork that is useful for holding joints of meat in place while carving birds or joints.

Gravy skimming jug

This special jug has a double spout, so fat juices that form on the surface can be poured off before the gravy is poured out. This type of jug is also useful for skimming stock.

Sauceboat

Designed for serving gravies and sauces at the table. Make sure that it has a saucer to catch drips.

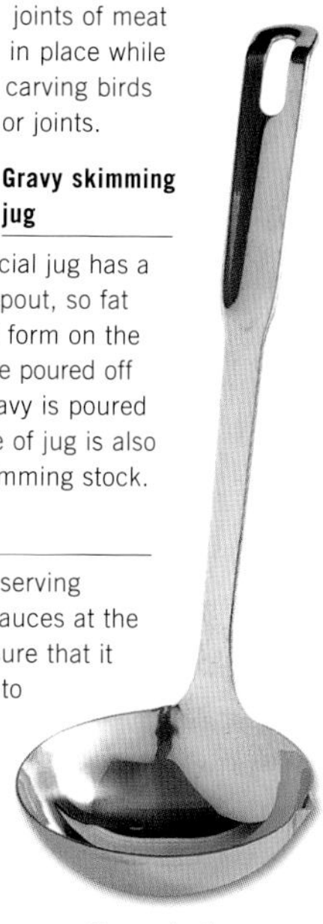

Above: Ladle

MEAT

This chapter includes essential information on meat from domesticated animals: beef and veal from cows; lamb from sheep; pork, bacon, gammon and ham from pigs; as well as meat from animals and birds, such as kangaroos, llamas, alligators, wild boar, ostriches and emus. Sausages – both fresh and cured – and cured meats are included, as is offal, from traditional types such as liver and kidney to more unusual meats, such as sweetbreads and lights. Each section covers basic cuts and types, with information on nutrition, buying and storing. There are essential step-by-step techniques giving detailed instructions for preparation techniques, such as boning and tying, as well as information on every type of cooking method, from frying and grilling to roasting and stir-frying.

BEEF AND VEAL

Among the most varied of meats, beef provides a full-flavoured ingredient for stewing, succulent joints for roasting and tender steaks for grilling. In humble broths and peasant-style stews or extravagant dishes fit for banquets, the carcass includes cuts for all types of cooking, making it as good a choice for economical everyday meals as for dinner-party dishes.

Beef is eaten all over the world. From the British Sunday roast or the classic American burger to Russian Stroganoff, every country has its specialities. Even though food and cooking are now multi-cultural, many traditional dishes have endured to become international favourites. Beef Wellington, succulent fillet dressed with pâté and encased in puff pastry, also known as *boeuf en croûte* in France, stands out as one of the great dishes. Similarly, while the fashion for serving simple stews may fluctuate, some casseroles will always have a place on good menus. *Boeuf Bourguignonne*, made with little onions and mushrooms in red wine, or *osso bucco*, the Italian casserole of veal on the bone, are two good examples.

The same is true of Indian and South-east Asian cooking. Many curries, stir-fries, salads or pots of noodles based on beef feature not only in their home countries but also in high-class dining rooms worldwide.

There are exceptions, and beef is not acceptable among all meat-eating cultures. For example, the cow is regarded as a sacred animal by Hindus. It is appreciated for its milk and as a working animal, but not killed for its meat. In many African communities cattle are prized possessions, given as a dowry with marrying daughters and accumulated rather than being reared for their meat.

Cattle have long been regarded as a source of milk or even for their blood, taken from the veins of the live animals and drunk as a source of nourishment, particularly by nomadic communities. Having a suitable temperament for herding and existing primarily on a diet of grass, these strong, useful animals were first domesticated in ancient Macedonia. They were inexpensive to buy and easy to keep, they provided milk and, ultimately, meat that was very good to eat.

Above: Some breeds, like these Highland cattle, are reared in only a few countries.

The beef we know today is far removed from the tough, stringy product from the carcass of an aged, working animal. Specific breeds have been developed over generations in different countries for the quantity and quality of meat they yield. For example, Aberdeen Angus and Hereford are well-known British breeds, and Charolais and Limousin are traditional French breeds. Although young dairy cows are used for meat, male cattle are the primary source, often castrated and always slaughtered young to yield a tender product. Breeding, rearing methods and environment, and ultimately the process of slaughtering and immediate management of the carcass all influence the quality of the meat.

Veal is not as universally popular as beef. In some countries it was at one time regarded as bland by comparison by some, then avoided because of general disapproval of rearing methods. In spite of a change of attitude and broader acceptance of veal, it is still not as popular as other meats. More humane rearing methods adopted in recent years are influencing choice, and veal is now available in supermarkets as well as from specialist butchers.

Left: New breeding methods for calves have made veal more acceptable, but it is still not as popular as other meats.

Nutrition

Not only does beef bring flavour to a meal, but it also makes a valuable contribution in terms of food value. Eaten in moderation, meat plays an excellent role in a healthy, well-balanced diet. Modern breeding has reduced the fat content of beef and meat is now sold trimmed of excess fat. It is worth remembering that the body needs some fat, so the aim should be to balance it with plenty of starchy foods, fresh fruit and vegetables.

Beef and veal are sources of high-quality protein. They provide all the essential amino acids required for growth as well as maintaining the body. Beef is an excellent source of iron in a form that is easily absorbed by the body. It also provides zinc and other minerals and is an important source of many of the B vitamins.

Buying

Beef that is properly hung, for weeks rather than days, allowing time for the muscle to mature and the fat to develop, has a full flavour and becomes succulent and tender when cooked. Well-matured meat is a deep, rich, burgundy brown in colour, not bright red, and the fat is creamy rather than white. The best roasting joints are those from cuts with an even marbling of fat, which provides flavour and keeps the meat moist and juicy.

Look for meat that has been well butchered. The signs are cleanly cut meat, which is neat and evenly trimmed, with meat that follows the line of the muscle and bone. Bones should be smooth, without any sign of splinters. Smaller cuts, such as steaks, should be of uniform thickness so that they cook evenly in a similar length of time.

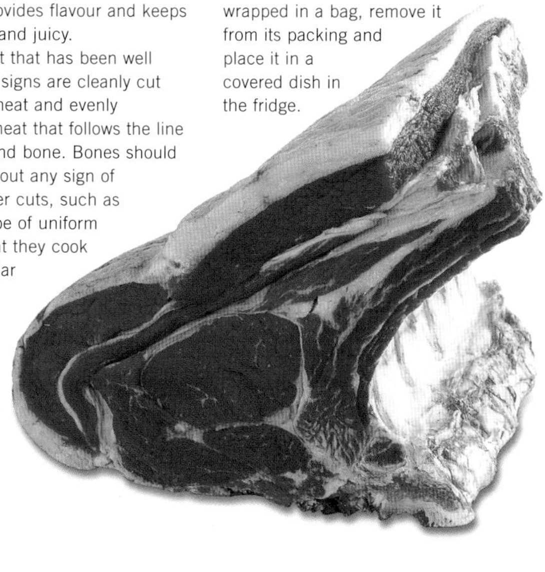

Right: Large roasting joints like this forerib of beef will keep in the fridge for up to five days before cooking.

Veal can be judged by its colour: the whiter the meat, the greater the proportion of milk in the diet of the calf. Pale meat is tender, with a delicate flavour. Older veal is pink or rosy pink, rather than white, and it often has a layer of creamy-white fat. If it is brown, veal is either very old or very stale. Veal has little fat and joints are often larded before roasting to keep them moist.

Above: Loose minced beef is best cooked and eaten on the day it is bought.

Storing

Beef and veal should be kept on a low shelf in the fridge, below and away from cooked foods and ingredients that are to be eaten raw.

As a general rule, when buying pre-packed meat, always check and observe the use-by date on the packet. Pre-packed meat, which is securely sealed, should be stored in its packaging. If the packaging is damaged and there is any danger of meat juices escaping, or if the meat is bought loose and wrapped in a bag, remove it from its packing and place it in a covered dish in the fridge.

The dish must be large enough to contain any juices and the lid should cover it completely.

As a guide to buying meat that is not pre-packed, minced meat and small cuts of veal are best eaten on the day you buy them, but joints, chops and steaks will keep for up to three days and larger joints for up to five days.

Beef and veal freeze well, particularly smaller pieces. Store tightly wrapped, individual portions of veal for up to six months and beef for up to one year. Thoroughly thaw the meat before cooking. Put the meat in a large dish to catch drips and thaw slowly in the fridge overnight. Never re-freeze raw meat that has been frozen then thawed.

Beef and BSE

Bovine spongiform encephalopathy, a disease found in cattle in the 1980s, is thought to be the result of feed manufactured from sheep and cattle carcasses. The growth in the number of cattle with the disease resulted in a review of cattle rearing, slaughtering and butchering, and the use of cattle food generated from animal carcasses has now been banned. Some types of offal and beef on the bone were withdrawn from sale in some countries, but it is likely that these bans will be lifted.

Right: Sirloin can be roasted or cut into steaks for frying or grilling.

THE BASIC CUTS OF BEEF

There is a wide choice of beef, the result not only of basic butchering techniques, but also of advanced preparation. As well as the traditional small cuts and large roasting joints, boned, sliced, diced and trimmed meat is also available.

Check the labels on packed meats, as they include a guide to cooking or the method for which the meat is best suited. The butcher or person weighing meat at the loose meat counter in the supermarket will be trained to provide information on the joints or particular prepared meats on offer. It is worth asking their advice, especially as they will be aware of particularly good buys.

Butchering techniques differ according to country and regional traditions. Many larger supermarkets or good butchers offer a wide selection of international cuts. Cuts from the top of the animal, along the middle of the back, are tender because they are from muscles, that perform comparatively light work. These include the most expensive cuts, which can be cooked by grilling and frying as well as by roasting.

Cuts from the neck, shoulders and lower legs – the parts of the animal that work hardest – are tougher, coarse in texture and less expensive than the prime cuts. For tender results, they require longer cooking by moist, gentle methods. However, when well cooked, these cuts have an excellent flavour. The following is a guide to the basic beef cuts.

Sirloin

Also known as best end loin, the sirloin can also be cut into steaks, including entrecôte, porterhouse or T-bone. This is a lean, tender cut from the back of the animal for roasting in joints or grilling and frying when cut into steaks.

Entrecôte steak

A steak cut from the sirloin.

Above: Entrecôte steaks are cut from the sirloin.

Below: Chateaubriand is a prime cut from the centre of the fillet.

Left: New York steak

Porterhouse steak

Traditionally a large steak cut from the sirloin, but sometimes used for steaks cut from the rib of beef.

Forerib

A high-quality cut available on the bone or boned and rolled for roasting as a joint or cut into thick slices (steaks) for grilling or frying.

Above: T-bone steak

Below: Rump is good for roasting.

T-bone steak

Cut from the end of the sirloin, this steak takes its name from the T-shaped bone it contains.

New York steak

Also known as New York strip or shell steak, this cut is taken from the prime eye of meat from either the sirloin or porterhouse area.

Fillet

Taken from the centre of the sirloin along the back of the animal. This is a particularly lean and tender cut. It should be larded for roasting or cut into steaks for grilling and frying. It is also cut into thin strips or fine slices for stir-frying or brief poaching.

Chateaubriand

Cut from the centre of the fillet, this is a very lean and tender cut that is ideal for roasting or grilling.

Rump

This is not as tender as fillet, but it is another good-quality cut for roasting or quick, dry-cooking methods. Rump steaks are delicious grilled, fried, barbecued or braised. Cut into thin strips, rump can also be stir-fried.

Topside

Also known as top rump, this cut is taken from the round of beef. Available boned and rolled for roasting, it is also good braised or pot-roasted. Topside is quite lean so it is best larded or barded with fat before cooking and basted frequently during cooking.

Below: Topside, which is also known as top rump, is a lean joint that is best braised or pot-roasted.

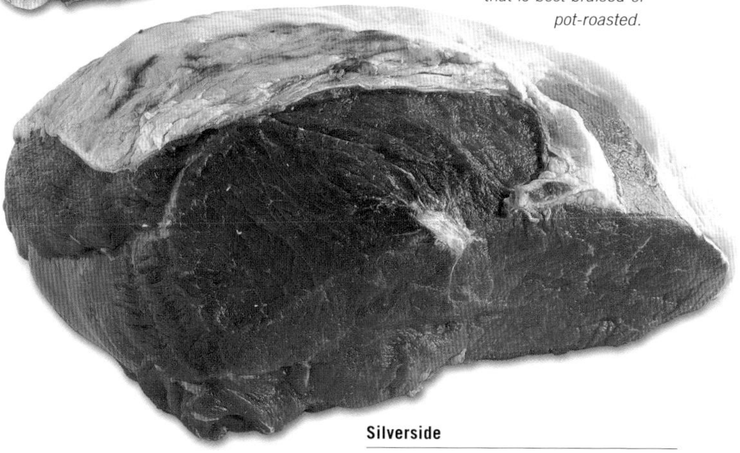

Silverside

Taken from the hindquarter round of beef, this is better suited to pot-roasting than roasting. Silverside is a lean cut that should be larded or barded with fat and then basted frequently during cooking. It is also the traditional choice for boiling.

Below: Silverside is often sold barded with a thin layer of fat and tied into a neat, cylindrical joint for roasting or pot-roasting.

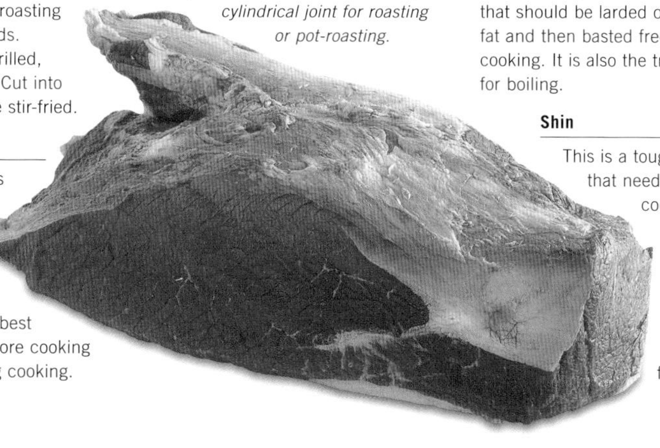

Shin

This is a tough cut of beef that needs long, slow cooking, preferably stewing. It is a lean cut with a good flavour and is often sold boned and cut into pieces for stewing.

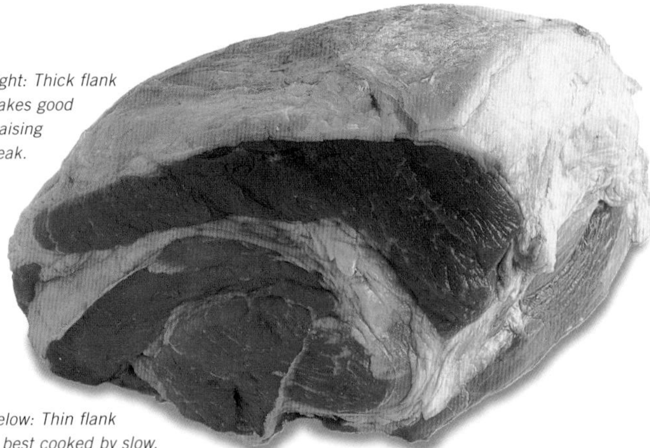

Right: Thick flank makes good braising steak.

Below: Thin flank is best cooked by slow, moist methods of cooking. It produces rich-flavoured stews.

Left: Skirt is lean, but needs moist, slow cooking.

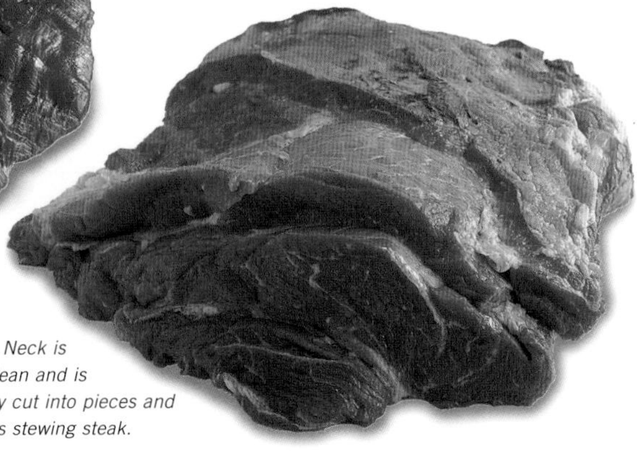

Above: Onglet is a thick, juicy cut that is best braised.

Right: Neck is fairly lean and is usually cut into pieces and sold as stewing steak.

Thick flank

Usually sold thickly sliced as braising or stewing steak, this lean cut requires slow, moist cooking. Left whole, thick flank is more suitable for pot-roasting than roasting.

Thin flank

This rather fatty cut needs long, slow cooking, and is best suited to cooking methods such as braising and stewing. It can be cut into pieces or minced.

Skirt

This is a thin, braising cut that can also be pot-roasted. It is taken from behind the flank. Skirt is lean but fairly coarse in texture.

Onglet

A French cut of beef that is taken from the skirt and flank area.

Neck

This is one of the less tender cuts and is good braised or stewed. It can be used for making minced beef.

Clod

A cut for long, slow stewing, this is from the neck area and is also used for making minced beef.

Chuck and blade

These two cuts are often sold together as braising steak or separately. Both chuck and blade are lean cuts, which have little fat surrounding them, but are well marbled with internal streaks of fat.

These cuts benefit from long, slow cooking to develop the flavour of the meat and give tender results.

Thick rib

Also known as top rib, this cut is taken from beneath the chuck and blade above the brisket. It is often boned and rolled, but it is best roasted with the bone in. It can also be cut into steaks and either pot-roasted or braised.

Thin rib

Also known as flat rib, this comes from behind the thick rib, below the forerib and above the brisket. It is a cut for pot-roasting or braising.

Brisket

Taken from the fore end of the animal, just below the shoulder. This is a fairly tough cut that has a comparatively high proportion of fat. It is a well-flavoured cut that tastes best when pot-roasted, braised or stewed, but may also be salted or spiced.

Leg

This tough cut comes from the back legs of the animal. It is usually sold cut into thick slices cut horizontally through the central bone and needs long, slow cooking, such as stewing or braising. When cooked, the meat is richly flavoured and gelatinous.

Minced beef

The paler the mince, the higher the fat content, so look for dark mince, which will have a higher proportion of lean meat. Use for burgers, meat sauces and meatballs.

Above: Chuck steak is one of the best meats for stewing.

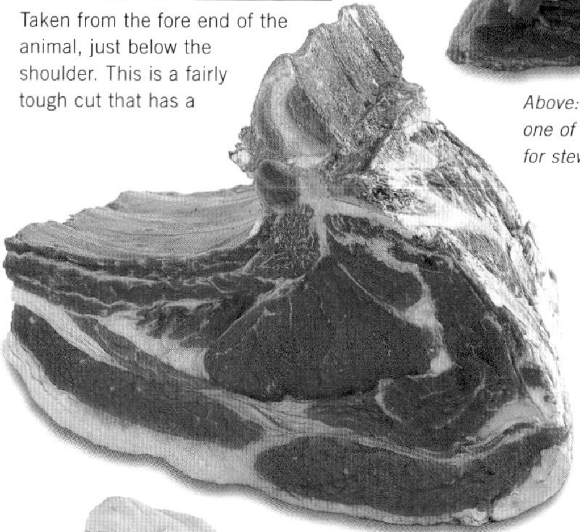

Above: Thick rib is sold with and without the bone.

Above: Blade is usually boned and cut into thick slices. It is well marbled with fat and, cooked slowly, produces rich-tasting stews.

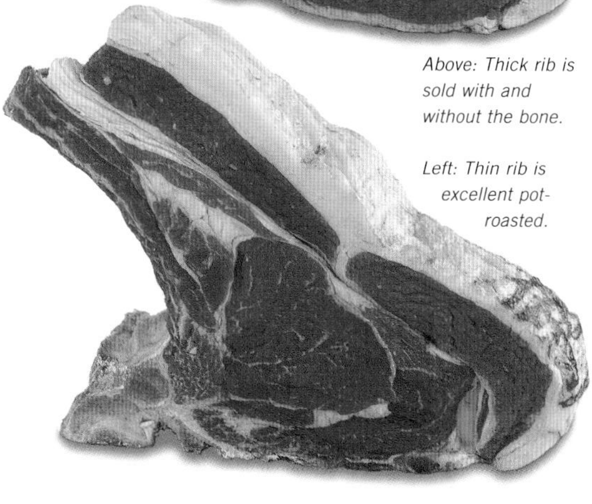

Left: Thin rib is excellent pot-roasted.

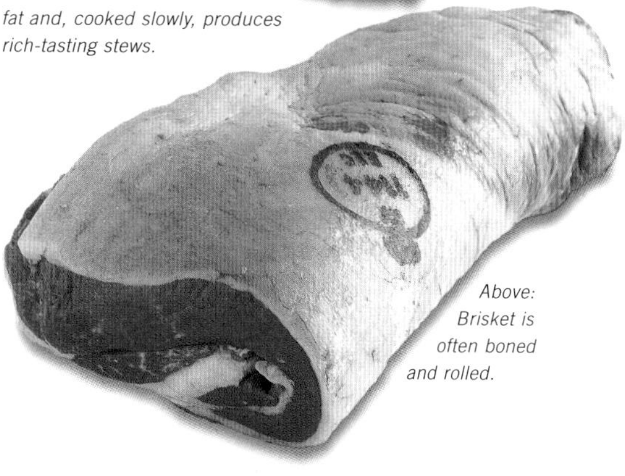

Above: Brisket is often boned and rolled.

THE BASIC CUTS OF VEAL

There is an increasingly wide range of veal cuts available from specialist butchers and larger supermarkets. There are large cuts suitable for roasting and braising and smaller cuts for the quicker cooking methods of frying, griddling and grilling. The following is a guide to the basic cuts of veal.

Above: Fillet is usually cut into escalopes.

Right: Breast has an excellent flavour.

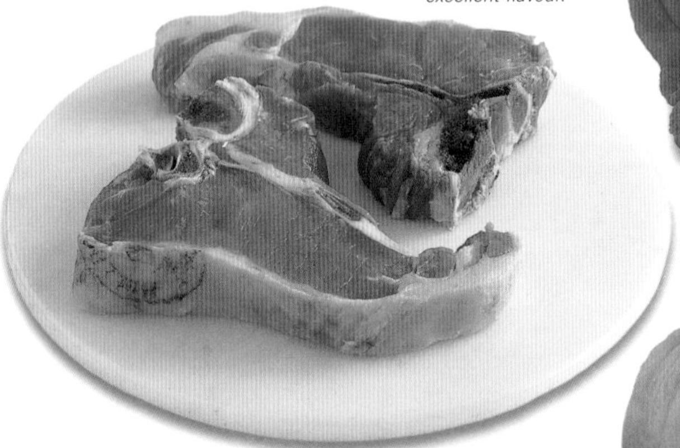

Above: Veal chops, which resemble T-bone steaks, are good for grilling or frying.

Right: This large, prime veal joint for roasting is a combination of loin and fillet and is available from specialist butchers.

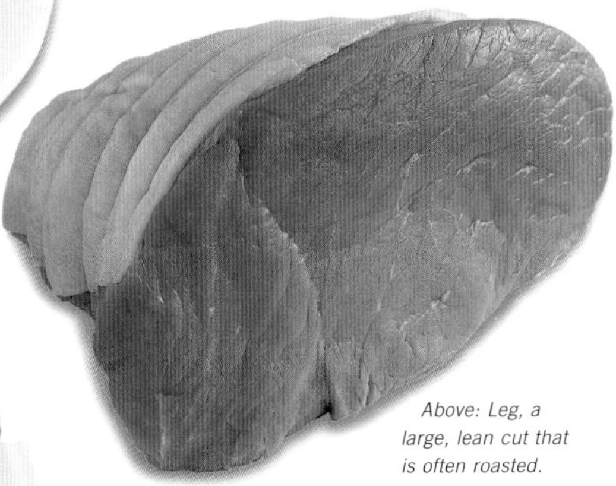

Above: Leg, a large, lean cut that is often roasted.

Fillet

This is a lean, boneless cut taken from the hindquarters. It is usually sliced crossways into thin escalopes and then sautéed in butter or olive oil, but it can also be roasted whole.

Breast

This cut can be roasted on the bone, or boned, stuffed, rolled and roasted, or cut up into riblets for grilling.

Chops

Taken from the loin, these are on the bone, and they are usually grilled, griddled or pan-fried.

Left: Knuckle is the bonier end of the hind leg and is often cut into thick slices and used to make the rich Italian stew, osso bucco.

Knuckle

The end of the hind leg, this is very bony and used mainly for boiling or stewing, but can also be braised. It is usually sold cut crossways into thick slices.

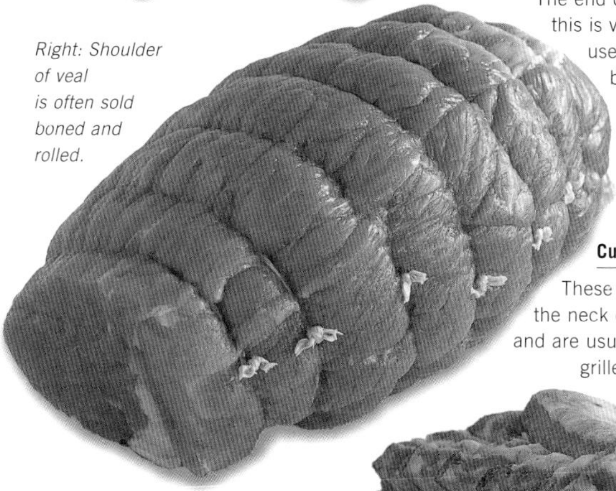

Right: Shoulder of veal is often sold boned and rolled.

Cutlets

These are taken from the neck end of the loin and are usually griddled, grilled or pan-fried.

Leg

A good-quality cut for roasting. This large, tender cut is often boned and stuffed.

Loin

Taken from the back of the animal and available either on the bone or boned and rolled. This lean, tender cut is ideal for roasting.

Right: Best end of neck is one of the tougher cuts of veal and so is better pot-roasted, braised or stewed.

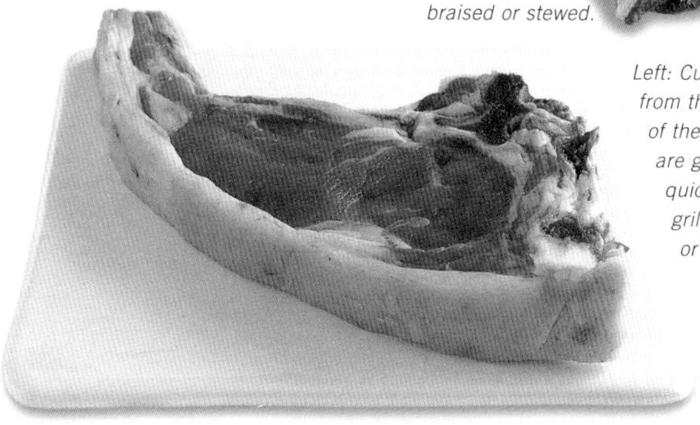

Left: Cutlets are cut from the neck end of the loin and are good cooked quickly by grilling, griddling or frying.

Shoulder

Also called the oyster, this can be boned, stuffed and rolled and makes an excellent, not-too-expensive joint for roasting. Shoulder can also be cut into chunks for stewing or as a pie filling.

Best end of neck

This is usually sold on the bone for roasting and is juicy and tender. Ask the butcher to remove the chine bone so that it can be carved more easily. Best end is also sold in cutlets for frying.

Wines to serve with beef and veal

Beef is a big powerful red meat that will stand a big powerful red wine. The classic clarets of Bordeaux – made mainly from Cabernet Sauvignon, Cabernet Franc and Merlot grapes – complement beef perfectly. Try a smooth St Emilion or Margaux with a roast or the heavier reds from the Médoc or Graves with a robust stew.

Full-bodied Italian red wines are also good with beef stews. Alternatively, try the smooth Merlots from Bulgaria and the Australian reds made from Cabernet Sauvignon, Shiraz, Grenache and Pinot Noir grapes.

The complex Cabernet Sauvignons from the Napa Valley, Sonoma County and Santa Cruz go well with beef and veal. The soft, fruity reds made from Merlot and Cabernet Sauvignon in Washington State are a good choice for pan-fried veal.

South Africa's traditionally burly reds made from Pinotage, Pinot Noir, Merlot, Shiraz and Cabernet Sauvignon stand up well to beef.

The sophisticated Cabernet Sauvignons from Chile and the earthy reds – made from Malbec, Merlot and Cabernet Sauvignon – from Argentina are also worth trying with beef and veal.

PREPARING BEEF AND VEAL

Boning

Depending on the cut, beef and veal can be cooked on or off the bone. As with other types of meat, boneless joints are easier to carve and serve. They can also be stuffed or cut up, for example into cubes or dice. Butchers are always ready to bone meat given notice and they are best equipped for the task, with equipment and specialist skills.

However, it is useful to know how to tackle the task. Whatever the cut, there are a few basic principles to follow: use a sharp knife, preferably one with a fine, flexible blade as it will follow the contours of the bones easily. Follow the shape of the bone, removing the maximum amount of meat and cutting around it, rather than slicing into it.

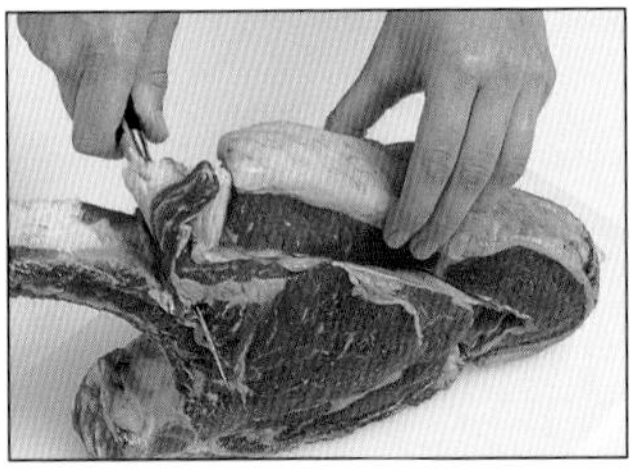

1 To bone a rib of beef, follow the rib bones, working down from the tops of the bones. Follow the curve of the bone with the knife, easing the meat away from the bone as it becomes free.

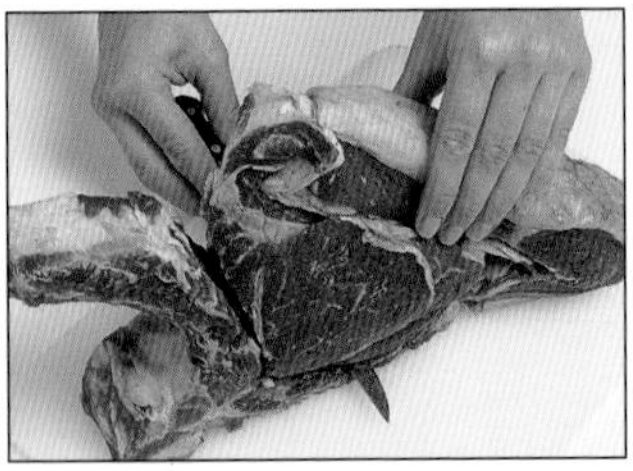

2 Carefully cut through the cartilage around the base, keeping the eye of the meat as whole and neat as possible. Then remove the bone. Finally, trim off any excess fat from the boned joint.

Barding and larding

These are methods of introducing fat to very lean joints, to keep them moist and succulent during the cooking process and also to add flavour.

Barding

This is simply wrapping fat around or over lean meat; thin slices of pork or beef fat can be used. This is often obvious on lean, rolled joints bought from the supermarket where the meat is wrapped in a separate coating of fat. Streaky bacon can also be used for barding. The outer covering of fat bastes the meat, preventing it from drying out before it is cooked through.

Larding

This involves more preparation and is the technique of threading strips of pork fat through lean meat to keep it moist from the inside as the fat melts during roasting. The strips of fat, or lardons, can be rolled in herbs or spices before being threaded through the meat to add extra flavours to the meat.

A larding needle is used; with some less tender cuts or if the needle is blunt, it may be necessary to pierce holes through the meat with a skewer first before inserting the strips of fat.

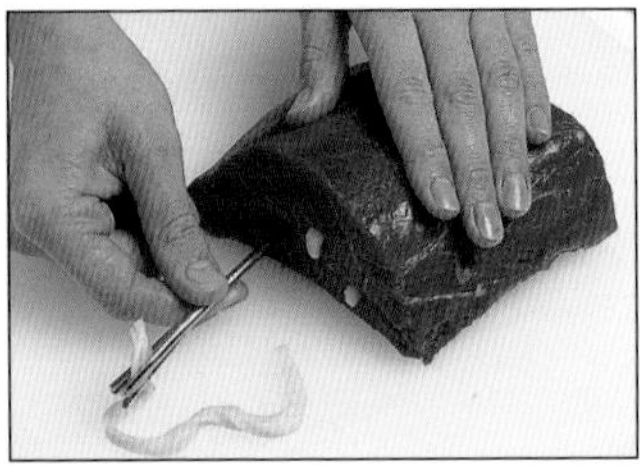

A larding needle has a gripping device, instead of a hole, to hold the fat. For meats that will be cooked by slow, moist methods, insert the needle, following the grain of the meat. Attach a strip of fat to the needle, then push the needle through the meat. Lard the meat at regular intervals to keep it evenly moist during cooking. For meats that are to be roasted, thread the strips of fat into the outside of the meat in long stitches.

Tying a boneless joint

A boneless joint, such as sirloin, silverside or topside is best tied before roasting. This helps to keep it in shape and promotes even cooking. The joint may be stuffed first, if required – make sure that the cavity is large enough to contain the stuffing so that it is not squeezed out when the joint is tied. Fine string is used for tying – this is available from good cook's shops and larger supermarkets, or alternatively fine parcel string can be used. It is a good idea to use special cooking string and store it in a polythene bag or box so that it is kept clean.

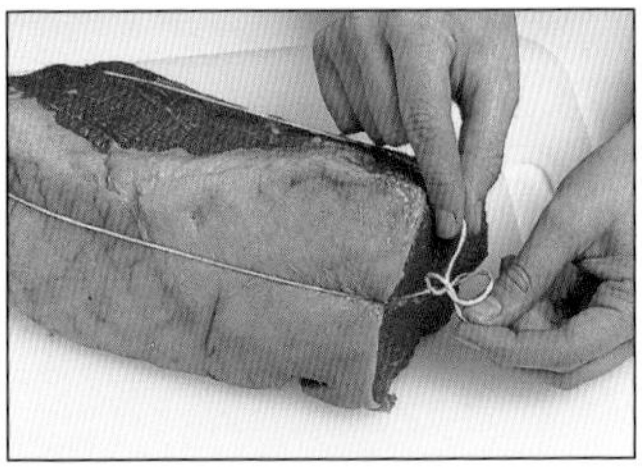

1 Roll, fold or arrange the meat into a neat shape, then tie a piece of fine string lengthways around the joint. Pull the ends tightly (it needs to be fairly tight as the meat will shrink during cooking) and secure the string with a double knot.

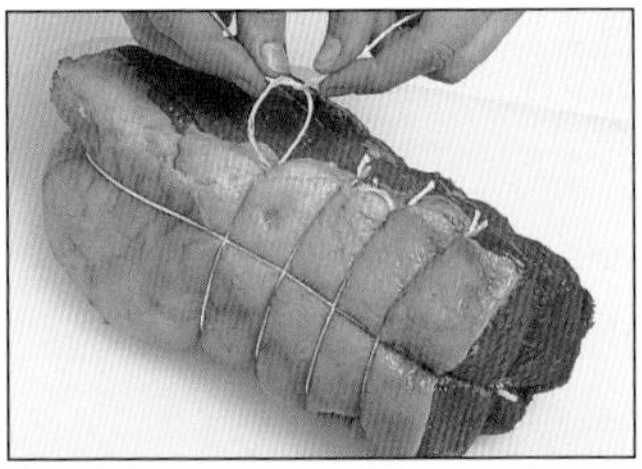

2 Tie more string around the joint at regular intervals, about 2.5cm/1in apart, knotting and trimming the ends as you go. Try to ensure that you apply even pressure when tying each length of string to keep the meat in a neat, even shape and to avoid squeezing the meat more in some places than others.

Trimming and slicing fillet

Before cutting fillet into steaks, to create a neat eye of meat, remove the chain muscle running along the side.

1 When the small chain muscle has been removed, cut away the sinewy membrane that held it in place.

2 Cut the fillet into 2cm/¾in thick slices. At the narrower end of the fillet, cut slightly thicker slices and pound them with a meat mallet to flatten them to the same size as the wider slices.

Trimming steak

Although a little fat gives good flavour, a thick rim of fat does not cook well in the time it takes to grill steak.

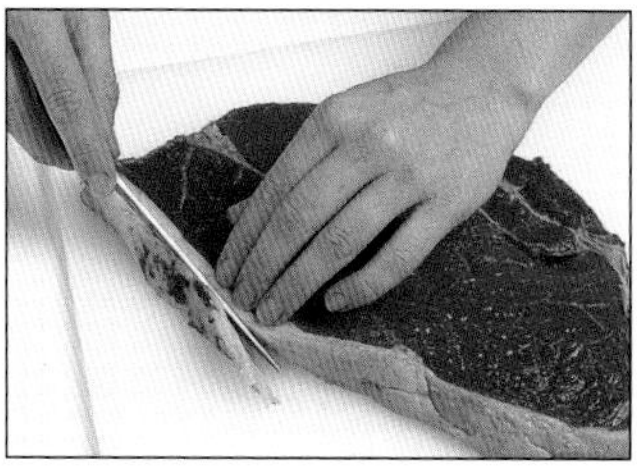

1 Trim the outer layer of fat, leaving no more than 5mm/¼in next to the meat.

2 Use sharp, kitchen scissors to snip the fat around the steak at 2.5cm/1in intervals around the edge. This helps to prevent the steak curling up during frying or grilling.

Cutting meat for braising or stewing

Tougher cuts of meat, such as braising or stewing steak cook evenly and more quickly if they are cut into thick slices or small even-size cubes for cooking.

1 Trim the meat, cutting off the excess fat and any gristle, membranes or sinew from the meat.

2 Cut the meat across the grain into 2.5cm/1in thick slices, using a large, sharp knife. Slices of braising steak can be either braised or casseroled. Braising or stewing steak can also be cut into cubes (see below).

3 To cut the meat into cubes, first cut the slices lengthways into thick strips.

4 Cut the strips of meat crossways into 2.5cm/1in cubes.

Tenderizing steak

Pounding meat breaks down its tissues and helps to give a tender result.

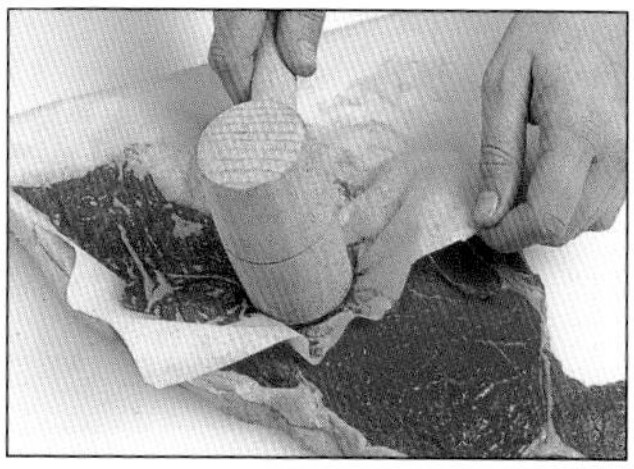

Place the steak on a chopping board and cover it with greaseproof paper. Alternatively lay the meat between two sheets of greaseproof paper. Pound the meat evenly with a meat mallet.

COOK'S TIP

Pounding meat is especially important with thicker pieces of tender cuts. If you don't have a meat mallet, use the base of a heavy pan, or a wooden rolling pin. Ensure that you beat the meat evenly.

Mincing

When you mince meat at home, it means you can select the cut required and trim off excess fat first. Stewing or braising cuts are ideal, especially for making long-cooked meat sauces, but rump or fillet steak can be minced for making burgers and similar dishes. A food processor can be used for mincing meat: this gives ground meat, rather than the coarser minced texture. Trim the meat and cut it into small cubes, then process it in small batches for even results, pulsing the power on and off. Take care not to over-process.

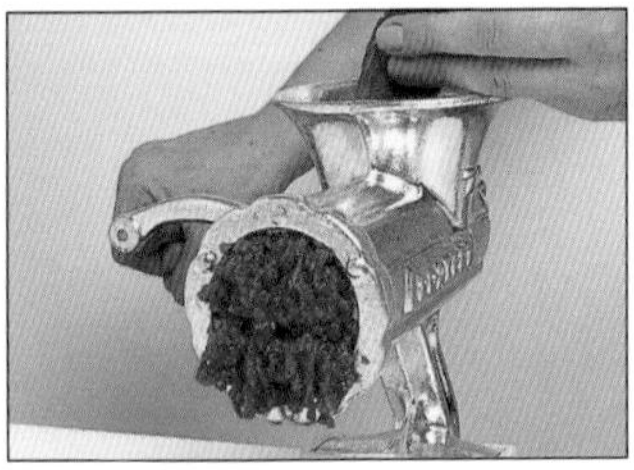

To use a traditional mincer, trim the meat and cut it into pieces, then feed it into the top of the mincer, while turning the handle. Use a coarse or medium blade, the former for long-simmered sauces and the latter for meatloaves or meatballs. For fine mince, pass the meat through a coarse blade first, then pass it through a fine blade.

Alternatively, cubed steak can be chopped finely. This is particularly good for tender frying cuts. Use a pair of very sharp knives, one in each hand, and a rhythmic chopping action. Use the flat blades to bring in the meat from the sides so that it is all evenly chopped.

Steak tartare

This is a dish of uncooked, hand-minced steak, seasoned and flavoured to individual taste and served with a raw egg yolk. It is vital that both meat and egg are perfectly fresh and bought from reliable suppliers. The meat must be minced at home to avoid any risk of cross-contamination.

1 Finely mince 450g/1lb fillet steak by chopping it using a pair of very sharp knives.

2 Stir in 1 finely chopped small onion, 30ml/2 tbsp chopped fresh parsley, salt and black pepper.

3 Arrange the steak in mounds on four chilled plates. Make a hollow in the middle of each. Place 1 egg yolk in each hollow and serve.

COOKING BEEF AND VEAL

Pan-frying

This is the traditional cooking method for steaks such as sirloin and fillet, and is also good for veal chops. Use a heavy pan, preferably non-stick. Cook steaks or chops in the minimum of fat, then add flavoured butter when serving, if you like. Butter burns easily, so heat the oil in the pan first and add the butter just before the meat, to avoid this.

1 Use kitchen paper to grease the frying pan with a little sunflower oil.

2 Heat the pan until it is very hot before adding a knob of butter.

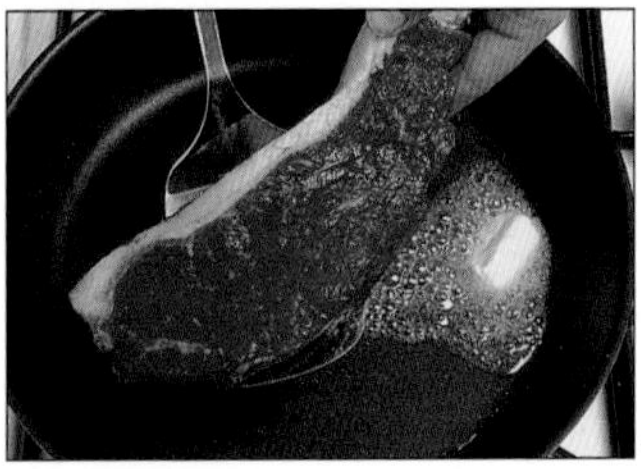

3 The butter should melt immediately. Add the steak or chop and cook for the required time (see right).

4 Use a draining spoon or fish slice to transfer the steak to a warm plate.

Cooking times for pan-fried beef
The cooking time depends both on the cut and on how well cooked you like it. **For very rare fillet steak**, cut about 2.5cm/1in thick, allow 1 minute on each side; for rump allow 2 minutes on each side.
For rare steak, allow 2 minutes each side for fillet; 3 minutes for rump.
For medium fillet steak, allow 2–3 minutes; allow 2–4 minutes for rump. **For well-done steak**, allow 3 minutes, then reduce the heat and allow a further 5–10 minutes.

Dry-frying beef

The method varies according to the meat. Lean beef such as steak is cooked in a very hot pan smeared with a little oil. High-fat meat is fried over a high heat so that the fat it contains melts and seeps out. The fat can then be discarded or used for cooking.

1 Preheat a frying pan or flameproof casserole. Add the meat and cook over a high heat; stir-fry mince; separate strips as they cook; or turn steaks once.

Steak *au poivre*
This classic dish is made by coating fillet steak with crushed black peppercorns, which flavour the meat, protect it as it is pan-fried and give a crunchy texture.

1 In a small mortar using a pestle, coarsely crush 30–45ml/2–3 tbsp black peppercorns.

2 Tip the crushed peppercorns on to a plate and press each piece of steak firmly into them to coat both sides evenly.

3 Grease a frying pan with a little oil, then heat until very hot. Add a knob of butter, followed by the steak as soon as the butter has melted. Cook until the steak is well browned and cooked (see cooking times for pan-frying, left).

Pan-frying veal

There are many tender cuts of veal suitable for pan-frying. Escalopes, which are cut from the fillet, are the classic cut for this method.

1 Place the veal escalope between two sheets of clear film or greaseproof paper, or on a chopping board, and cover with clear film. Use the flat wooden side of a meat mallet or a rolling pin to firmly, but gently, beat the veal out thinly and evenly. Repeat with the remaining escalopes.

2 Use a heavy frying pan, preferably non-stick, and heat it until it is very hot. Smear with enough butter and oil to prevent the meat from sticking. Add the veal escalopes when the fat is sizzling and cook for 1–2 minutes.

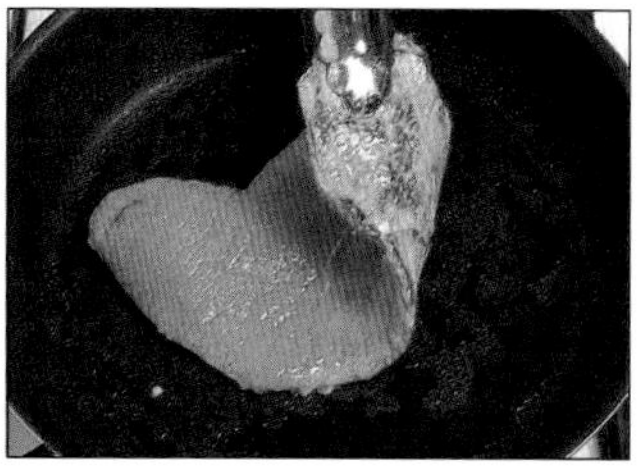

3 Turn the escalope over and cook for 1–2 minutes on the second side. Serve immediately, with the pan juices poured over, or make a sauce with the pan juices (see the Cook's Tip below).

COOK'S TIP
To make a simple sauce, remove the veal and keep warm. Add a splash of sherry, simmer to reduce by half, then add double cream and season to taste.

Stir-frying

This is a fast method of cooking tender meat. The meat should be cut into thin slices across the grain, and then the slices cut into fine, long strips. Use rump, fillet or thinly cut "minute" steak. Also look out for steak sold prepared especially for stir-frying.

1 Heat a wok or large, heavy frying pan to smoking point and then add a little oil.

2 Add the meat in batches and cook over a high heat, stirring all the time to cook the meat evenly.

3 Remove the first batch before adding more meat. If too much meat is added at once, the temperature drops, the strips of meat do not cook quickly and their juices seep out, then they braise in the juices.

Griddling

This is a fashionable, healthy method of cooking, suitable for steaks, such as rump, sirloin and fillet. A ridged, cast-iron pan is used, allowing the fat to drain away from the meat into the grooves while the meat cooks. The meat is seared with the pattern of the hot ridges. A non-stick griddle is useful for cooking with the minimum of extra fat.

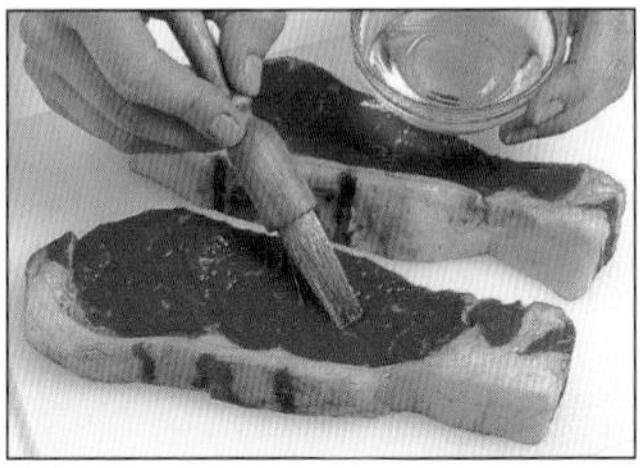

1 Preheat the griddle until it is almost smoking. Brush the meat very lightly with a little vegetable or sunflower oil, which are very light and will not flavour the meat.

2 Lay the meat on the hot griddle and cook following times for grilling (right).

3 Metal tongs are useful for turning steaks halfway through cooking.

Grilling beef

This is a quick, healthy way of cooking lean meats, such as rump, sirloin or fillet steak because the fat drips away during the cooking process. Preheat the grill for 5 minutes, until very hot before cooking the meat. The fierce heat quickly cooks the surface of the meat to seal in the juices. If the grill is not hot enough, the meat cooks slowly, allowing the juices to seep out. Cooking the meat quickly keeps it moist and tender. The steaks should be cut to the same thickness to ensure even cooking.

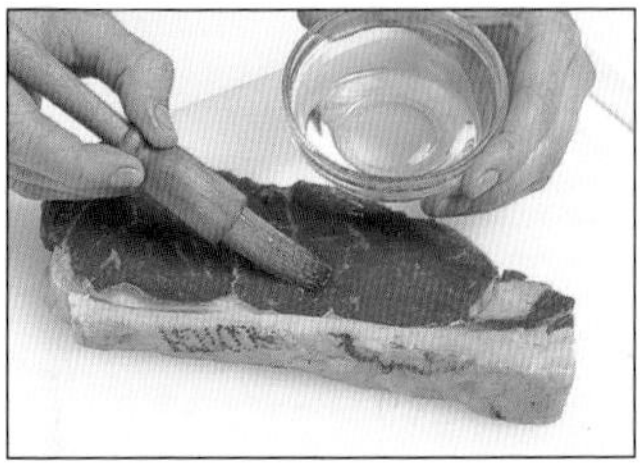

1 Brush the steak with a little light vegetable oil or melted butter on both sides to keep it moist during cooking. Season the steak well with salt and freshly ground black pepper, then place the steaks on the grill rack.

2 To cook the steak until very rare *(bleu)* using fillet steaks cut 2.5–3.5cm/1–1¼in thick, allow about 1 minute on each side; for rump steaks allow 2 minutes on each side.

COOK'S TIP

Use a light oil, such as vegetable or sunflower oil, for brushing the steak. If you use a heavier oil, such as olive oil, it detracts from the flavour of the meat.

3 For rare steak *(saignant):* increase the time for fillet to 2 minutes each side; 3 minutes each side for rump.

4 For medium steak *(à point):* allow 2–3 minutes each side for fillet and 2–4 minutes each side for rump.

5 For well done steak *(bien cuit):* allow 3 minutes on each side, then reduce the grill setting and allow 5–10 minutes more, turning the steak once or twice during cooking, until the meat is firm and brown.

Barbecuing

The barbecue should be lit about 30 minutes before cooking. The coals are ready when they are grey and ashen on the surface – this is when they are hot, but not flaming. They will cook the meat quickly and evenly. The rack must not be too near the coals. If the coals are too hot or the rack too near them, the meat will burn on the outside before it is cooked to taste in the middle. Brush the barbecue rack lightly with a little sunflower oil before laying the food on it.

Marinating is a good way of bringing flavour to meat before grilling, griddling, pan-frying or barbecuing, and it helps to keep very dry cuts moist during cooking. Lengthy marinating also helps to tenderize the meat. Kebabs can be marinated once threaded, as here, to save time when ready to cook, or the cubes of meat can be marinated separately for an hour or two before threading on to skewers.

The marinade can be used to baste the kebabs or meat before and during cooking. Regular basting promotes even cooking and prevents the meat or other ingredients from drying out.

Flavoured butters

One of the simplest ways of dressing grilled, griddled, pan-fried or barbecued steak is by adding a pat of flavoured butter. Beat one of the flavouring ingredients below into 225g/8oz softened, unsalted butter. Chill until fairly firm, then roll into a cylinder shape in greaseproof paper and wrap in clear film. The flavoured butter can be stored in the fridge for up to 2 days. Slice the butter and place on the hot steak before serving.

Garlic butter Add 2 plump finely chopped garlic cloves.

Parsley butter Add 30ml/2 tbsp chopped fresh parsley.

Mixed herb butter Add 30ml/2 tbsp chopped fresh herbs.

Lemon butter Add 30ml/2 tbsp lemon juice and the grated rind of 1 lemon. Lemon juice and rind also go well with garlic or fresh parsley or a mixture of both.

Chilli butter Add ½–1 red seeded and chopped chilli.

Shallot butter Sauté 1 chopped shallot in butter, add 15ml/1 tbsp red wine and cook for 5 minutes. Cool, then beat into the butter.

Right: Flavoured butters are excellent for serving with steak – the pats of butter melt on the hot steak to form a simple, yet delicious sauce.

Stewing, braising and casseroling

These are long, slow and moist methods of cooking either in the oven or on the hob. The meat is simmered slowly at a low temperature in liquid – wine, water, beer or stock. This is ideal for tough, inexpensive cuts, such as shin, leg, brisket, thin flank, or chuck and blade. Stewing steak is tougher and needs longer cooking than braising steak.

1 Trim off any excess fat and cut the meat into 2.5cm/1in cubes.

2 Toss the meat in seasoned flour, shaking off any excess. This coating browns to give the casserole a good flavour and thickens the cooking liquid.

3 Heat 30ml/2 tbsp sunflower oil in a flameproof casserole. Add the meat in batches and cook over a high heat.

4 When the meat is well browned on all sides, use a draining spoon to remove the meat before adding the next batch to the casserole. If necessary, heat a little extra sunflower oil in the casserole before adding more meat.

5 Add the sliced or chopped onions and other vegetables to the remaining fat and juices in the casserole and cook, stirring occasionally, for 5 minutes.

6 Return the meat to the casserole, add herbs, then pour in the cooking liquid. Stir to loosen all the cooking residue from the base of the pan and heat until simmering. Simmer gently on the hob or in the oven until the meat is tender. The casserole may be covered for the entire length of the cooking or uncovered towards the end to allow excess liquid to evaporate and the sauce to thicken.

Pot-roasting

This long, slow method of cooking is ideal for slightly tough joints such as brisket, thick flank, topside and silverside. The meat is cooked in a covered pot on a bed of vegetables with a small amount of liquid, which creates a moist environment. This produces succulent results.

1 Heat a little sunflower oil in a large, flameproof casserole until very hot. Add the meat and cook over a high heat, turning frequently, until browned on all sides. Remove the joint from the pan.

2 Stir in the onions, leeks and root vegetables, then cook, stirring, for a few minutes. Replace the joint on top of the vegetables and pour in a little liquid, such as stock, wine or beer. Cover and cook gently on the hob or in the oven until the meat is tender.

COOK'S TIP

One of the easiest ways of coating cubes of meat evenly in seasoned flour is to put the seasoned flour in a large plastic bag. Add a couple of cubes of meat at a time and shake gently until the meat is evenly coated in flour. Remove the coated cubes of meat and transfer to a plate before adding the next batch.

Roasting beef

Large joints give best results, allowing time for the outside of the meat to brown and the fat to melt and become crisp before the centre of the joint is overcooked. Forerib (either on or off the bone) or sirloin are good cuts for roasting. Fillet of beef can be roasted, but it is very lean and should be larded first, then basted well during cooking.

Roasting times for beef
Weigh the joint and calculate the cooking time as follows:
On the bone
For rare beef: 20 minutes per 450g/1lb at 180°C/350°F/Gas 4, plus 20 minutes.
For a medium result: 25 minutes per 450g/1lb, plus 25 minutes.
For well-done beef: 30 minutes per 450g/1lb, plus 30 minutes.
Off the bone
For rare beef: 15 minutes per 450g/1lb at 180°C/350°F/Gas 4, plus 15 minutes.
For a medium result: 20 minutes per 450g/1lb, plus 20 minutes.
For well-done beef: 25 minutes per 450g/1lb, plus 25 minutes.

Roasting times for veal
Allow 25 minutes per 450g/1lb at 180°C/350°F/Gas 4, plus an extra 25 minutes, for veal on or off the bone.

Roasting techniques

There are two methods: either place the cold joint in the oven or sear it first. When cooking a very large joint, it is easier to place it in a roasting tin, fat-side up, and roast for the calculated time. The comparatively long cooking allows plenty of time for the fat to melt and brown.

Alternatively, with a medium-size joint, browning the fat first on the hob gives a better result, as the cooking time is not long enough to cook the fat thoroughly. This method helps to prevent uneven shrinkage, which can make a joint irregular in shape.

1 Preheat the oven to 180°C/350°F/Gas 4. Heat a little oil in a frying pan and sear the joint of beef on all sides, particularly the fat. Season well and place on a rack in a roasting tin, fat-side up, then transfer to the oven.

2 Roast the meat for the calculated time. A meat thermometer is useful for checking progress and to determine when the joint is cooked. Heat the spike of the thermometer in very hot water, then insert it into the thickest part of the joint to check the temperature: 60°C/140°F indicates that the meat is rare, 70°C/158°F is a medium result and 75°C/167°F is well done.

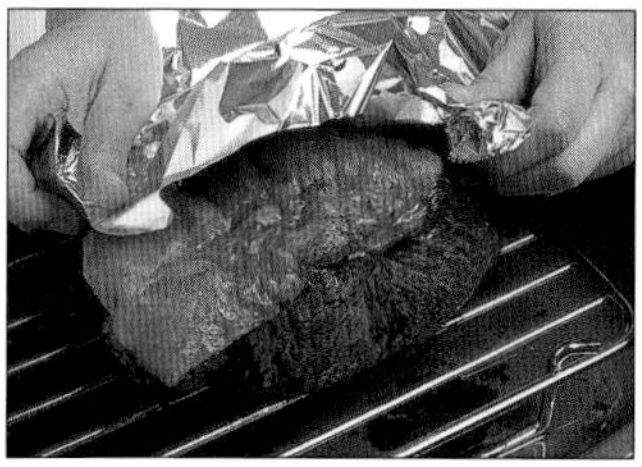

3 Cover with foil; leave for 10 minutes before carving. This allows the temperature to even out and the fibres to relax, making the meat easier to carve.

Carving a rolled joint

When the cooked joint has been allowed to stand and relax for 10 minutes, remove the string before carving.

Use a carving fork to hold the joint firmly in position, then cut the meat into slices using a gentle sawing action. When carving this type of joint, the meat can be cut into even, thin slices.

Carving rib of beef

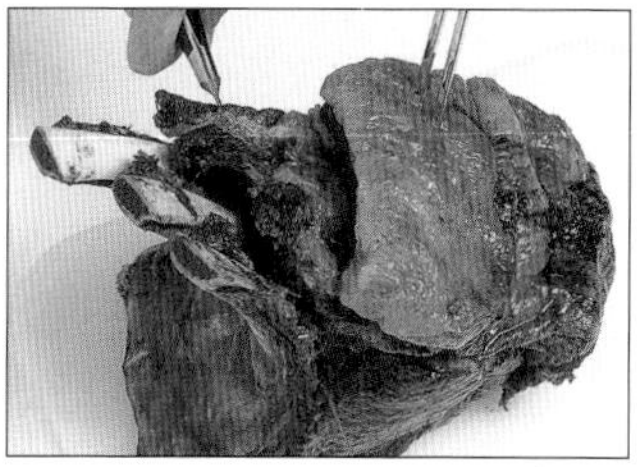

1 Allow the cooked joint to stand for 10 minutes to relax, then place it on a board or spiked meat platter and hold it firmly in place with a carving fork. Cut down between the meat and the ribs to remove the meat from the bones.

2 Set the bones aside. Turn the joint on its side and carve even slices across the grain of the meat.

LAMB

This rich meat is savoured as succulent roasts, delicious on chargrilled kebabs and inimitable in full-flavoured stews or casseroles. Matched by robust herbs or aromatic spices and served with piquant or zesty accompaniments, lamb features in all cuisines. From Morocco there are spicy tagines of lamb cooked with fruit and served with couscous; throughout the Middle East lamb is cooked with rice or other grains and fruit to make intense pilaffs; Indian cooks prepare koftas using minced lamb or saffron-soaked roasts and cream-enriched kormas from tender cuts. Humble potato-topped pies, dainty cutlets or noisettes are typical Western favourites.

These and other lamb dishes span all cultures and occasions. The meat from sheep has always been a democratic food, found on the plates of the poor and rich alike. In countries where many peasant populations rely on vegetables, grains and pulses for their meagre diet, lamb is often the sacrificial animal, offered by the rich on festive occasions and shared with the less wealthy.

Historically, sheep were mainly reared for their products – milk and wool. Sheep were central to the whole way of life of many early communities, and they were considered so vital for wool production in Elizabethan England that there was a ban on killing them. In Asia, however, where sheep were first domesticated, the meat was also eaten.

Left: *Different countries have their own specialist breeds. These dark-coated sheep are from the Hebrides.*

Above: The meat of sheep from New Zealand is internationally renowned.

Modern breeds and types

Farming and modern rearing have introduced breeds that are well removed from the scrawny animals that would have provided modest amounts of tough, strong-flavoured meat centuries ago. Tastes have changed comparatively recently and the mutton that was a choice meat in Victorian times is too strong for contemporary palates.

Countries have their specialist breeds, for example fat-tailed sheep are reared in the Middle East for their long tails (usually docked from other breeds and in other countries). Wales is famous for flavoursome lamb and the South Downs in England is an area of excellent grazing and produces high-quality meat. The salt marshes of Brittany in northern France are home to *pré-salé* lamb, which has a distinct and tasty flavour. New Zealand and Australia are internationally known as excellent sources of lamb, with New Zealand exporting high-quality meat.

Young lambs, killed before they are weaned, yield delicate, pale meat known as sucking lamb or *agneau de lait* in France, where two categories are produced depending on maturity. Milk-fed lamb is also appreciated in Italy. Meat from grazing animals is more common, usually from four months old and up to one year. Mutton comes from older sheep, over a year and onwards. Just as sucking lamb is not widely eaten, old-fashioned mutton is not readily available and popular, but it can be purchased from specialist butchers. Before refrigeration and modern storage methods, lamb and mutton were salted in the same way as pork. Now a gourmet "find", salted lamb or mutton ham is available from specialist suppliers. Smoked lamb is not widely available, but it is prepared when good lamb is available and small specialist smokers have space available for its preparation.

Flavour enhancers

Just as Yorkshire pudding and similar starchy puddings were served to satisfy hunger and make a little beef go a long way, so thousands of years ago, bitter herbs were first added to lamb in the hope that this would make it less palatable, such that a little would be eaten in modest amounts. However, the sharp flavours were found to enhance and complement the lamb. Over the years, mint or other herbs combined with vinegar, were sweetened with sugar to become an appropriate condiment.

Sweet, sour and sharp flavours are long established seasonings for rich or fatty meats. While mint sauce is a classic accompaniment for Western-style roast lamb, tangy, natural yogurt is popular for marinating the meat of older animals before cooking it with spices, Indian style, or combining it with fresh herbs for Mediterranean dishes. Marinating in yogurt, vinegar, lemon juice or tamarind juice also helps to tenderize sturdy mutton before cooking.

Nutrition

Although lamb is traditionally a fatty meat, particularly from some of the mountain breeds, notably Welsh lamb, the fat content depends on the breed and the rearing methods. The meat available now is no longer as fatty as it was in the past, and sheep farmers are rearing leaner animals that still have excellent flavour.

Along with other meats, lamb is primarily a high-quality protein food. It is an excellent source of iron in a form that is readily absorbed by the body and it is also a good source of zinc. Meat, including lamb, also provides an important source of the B vitamins and minerals, including copper, manganese and selenium.

For a healthy balance, serve modest portions of meat for everyday meals, adding plenty of starchy foods such as potatoes, bread, rice and pasta, and lots of vegetables and fruit. Lamb is splendid in casseroles with vegetables and pulses, such as pumpkin, green beans, potatoes, chick-peas and haricot beans. Flageolet beans, the small, pale-green pulses, are delicious with roast or grilled lamb.

Below: Lamb noisettes and cutlets are examples of good lamb, with their fine-grained pink meat and creamy-white, firm fat.

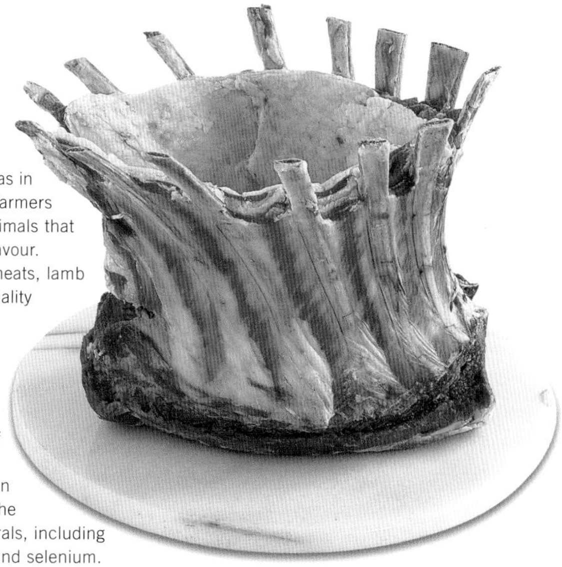

Above: Joints, like this crown roast, will keep in the fridge for up to five days.

Buying

Meat from milk-fed baby lamb is very pale and looks rather like veal; meat from sheep less than one year old has slightly darker pink flesh; meat from sheep more than one year old is known as mutton and it has darker flesh with a stronger flavour. Prime lamb is taken from five to seven month-old animals and it is known as spring lamb.

Look for firm, slightly pink meat with a fine-grained, velvety texture. The fat should be creamy white, firm and waxy.

Avoid meat that looks dry or dark and grainy, surrounded by yellow fat.

Storing

Lamb should be stored on a low shelf in the fridge, well away from other foods, in a covered dish large enough to contain any drips. Leave pre-packed meat in its packaging and use by the date given on the packet. When buying loose meat, chops and steaks should keep for two to four days, larger joints for up to five days. Minced lamb should be eaten on the day it is purchased.

Lamb freezes well. Wrap it in freezer bags and seal tightly. Store small cuts in the freezer for up to three months, larger cuts for up to six months. Thaw meat overnight in a dish in the fridge.

THE BASIC CUTS OF LAMB

Prime cuts are taken from the top of the lamb carcass, along the middle of the back. They are from the muscle least used during the life of the animal and yield the most tender meat. These are the cuts to cook quickly, by grilling and frying as well as roasting; these cuts can also be cooked slowly by moist methods such as stewing and braising.

Cuts from the neck and lower legs, parts that worked hardest when the animal was alive, are cheaper, and they need slower, gentle cooking in a casserole or stew until tender.

Loin

Usually sold as a joint, sometimes boned, stuffed and rolled, this prime cut is good for roasting. Loin chops can be griddled, grilled, pan-fried or barbecued. Loin chops have a small T-bone (part of the backbone from which they are cut). *Côte d'agneau* is the French term for a chop taken from the loin or rack (best end).

Above: Chump chops are good for pan-frying and grilling.

Below: Saddle of lamb, or double loin, is a huge roasting joint taken from both sides of the carcass.

Noisettes

Boned and rolled loin, tied with string, then sliced into small rounds. Noisettes are very good to pan-fry, sauté, griddle or grill.

Double loin chops

Sometimes called Barnsley chops or butterfly chops, these are cut from a saddle of lamb. They are suitable for grilling, frying or braising.

Chump chops

These chops are cut from between the leg and the loin, and they have a small round bone in the middle.

Saddle

This large roasting joint is the whole loin taken from both sides of the carcass and is sometimes called a double loin of lamb.

Leg

A tender cut, often divided into fillet and shank, which is sold both on the bone or boned.

Below: Leg and leg steaks are tender and good for roasting and barbecuing.

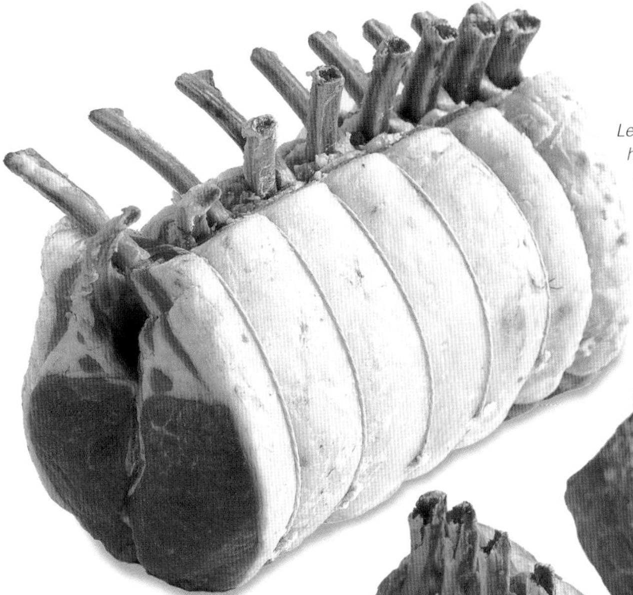

Left: Guard of honour is made by tying together two racks of lamb.

Guard of honour

This consists of a pair of racks of lamb interlinked with the fat on the outside.

Crown roast

This joint is made by tying two racks together in a circle to resemble a crown.

Shoulder

A tender joint, which can be roasted on or off the bone. It can also be braised or stewed. Boneless shoulder can be cubed for stews, kebabs and pies, or minced.

Leg is ideal for roasting, or the cubed meat can be used in a wide variety of braised or casseroled dishes. It can also be grilled or barbecued.

Leg steaks

Cut across the leg, with a small round of bone in the middle, these can be pan-fried, grilled or braised. They are sometimes called gigot chops.

Rack

The French *carré d'agneau* is taken from the best end. This can be roasted on the bone or boned, stuffed and rolled. It is a good joint for two or three people. Also sold as small cutlets or chops, each with one rib bone, which are good for grilling or frying.

Above: Racks of lamb can be sold trimmed and chined (left) or with the chine bone still intact. The chined joint is easier to carve.

Breast

This long, thin cut is fairly tough and fatty. When boned, stuffed and rolled it can be roasted slowly or braised.

Scrag end and middle neck, and fillet

Inexpensive and ideal for stewing, braising and casseroling, these are the traditional cuts for Irish stew and Lancashire hot pot. The lean eye of meat from the middle neck is sold as fillet, and is good for grilling.

Shank or knuckle

An economical, yet flavourful cut, best stewed, pot-roasted or braised.

Minced or cubed lamb

Quick and convenient, these can be used for pies, bakes or kebabs.

Left: Minced and diced lamb

PREPARING LAMB

Boning a shoulder

Removing the blade and shoulder bones from a shoulder of lamb means that the joint can be rolled and tied or stuffed (see below right). Boning the joint means that it is much easier to carve uniform slices of meat.

1 Using a sharp knife, carefully scrape back the flesh to reveal the wide end of the blade bone.

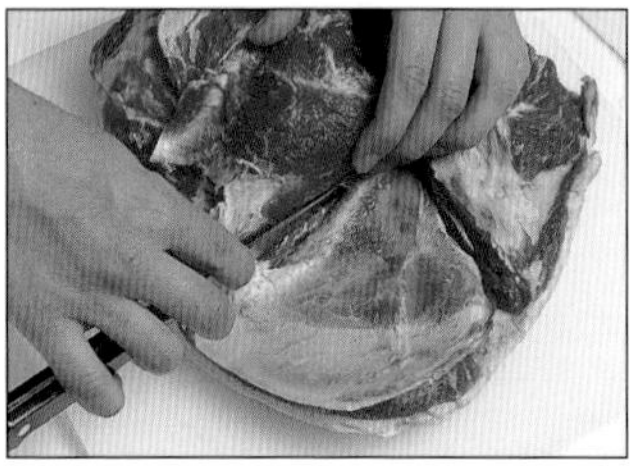

2 When the edge of the bone is free, follow the shape of the blade to cut the meat carefully off the bone. Do this on both sides of the large, flat bone.

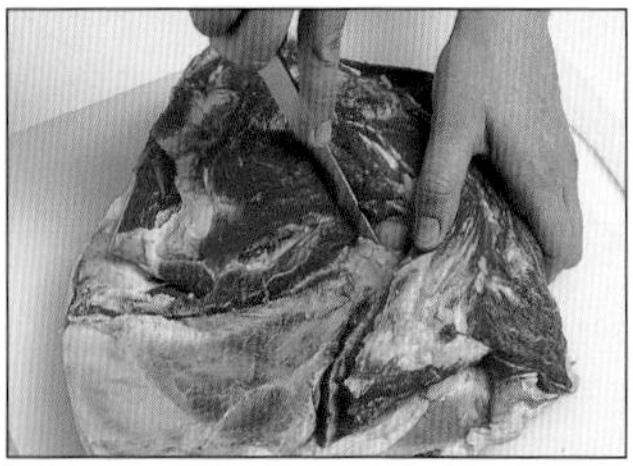

3 Cut right through the ball and socket joint to separate the blade and shoulder bones.

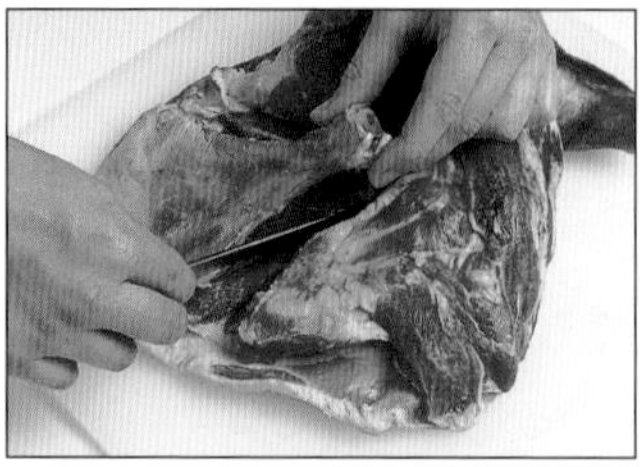

4 Hold the joint open, then pull the blade bone away from the meat, scraping off any meat from the narrow end of the bone (reserve this to include in stuffing, see below).

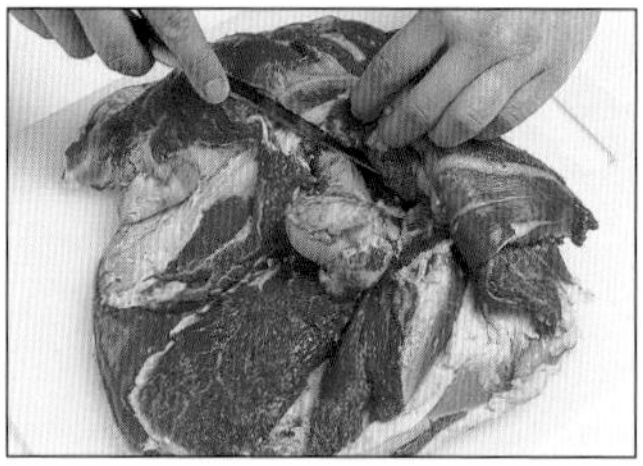

5 Cut and scrape the meat away from the shoulder bone and then pull the bone free. The joint is now ready to be stuffed and rolled or just rolled.

Stuffing a boned shoulder

1 Finely chop any meat trimmings left over from boning the shoulder. Mix with 30ml/2 tbsp chopped fresh herbs (any Mediterranean herbs work well – try a combination of rosemary, thyme, oregano and basil), 2 crushed garlic cloves, 1 finely chopped shallot, 115g/4oz fresh white breadcrumbs, and then season with plenty of salt and freshly ground black pepper.

2 Open out the boned shoulder and spread the stuffing evenly over it, leaving a space all around the edges of the meat. Carefully fold the meat back into its original shape ensuring that all of the stuffing stays in place or, alternatively, roll the meat. Tie the joint neatly with string to keep the stuffing in place and to keep the joint in shape during cooking.

Boning a leg

Removing the bone before roasting makes space for stuffing the leg, if required (see below left for a simple stuffing), and the roast joint is easier to carve than a joint with the bone in.

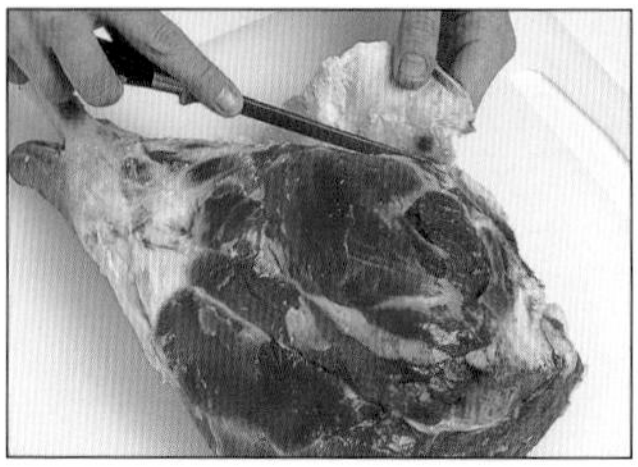

1 Using a sharp knife, carefully trim off all the excess fat from the outside of the joint and carefully cut through the tendons at the bottom of the shank.

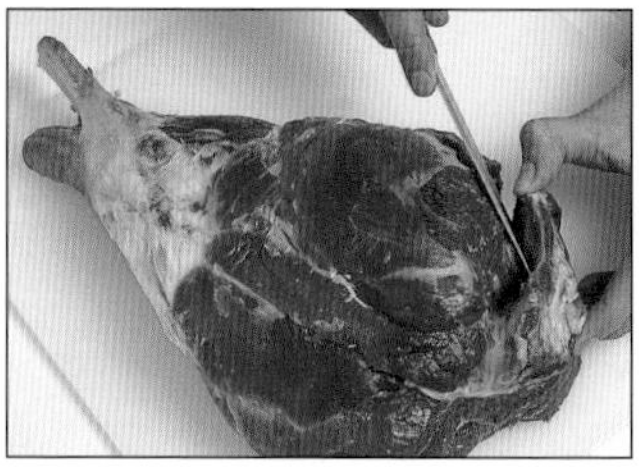

2 Cut around the pelvic bone and through the tendons, then remove the pelvic bone.

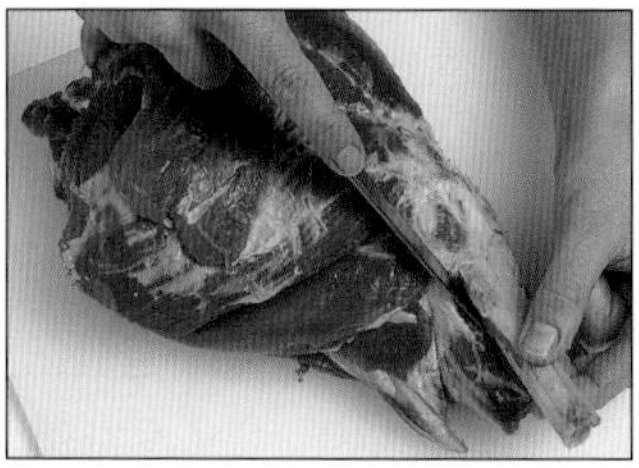

3 Carefully scrape the flesh away from the shank bone using a small, sharp knife (reserve any meat trimmings to include in stuffing), then cut through the tendons on the leg joint and pull out the shank bone.

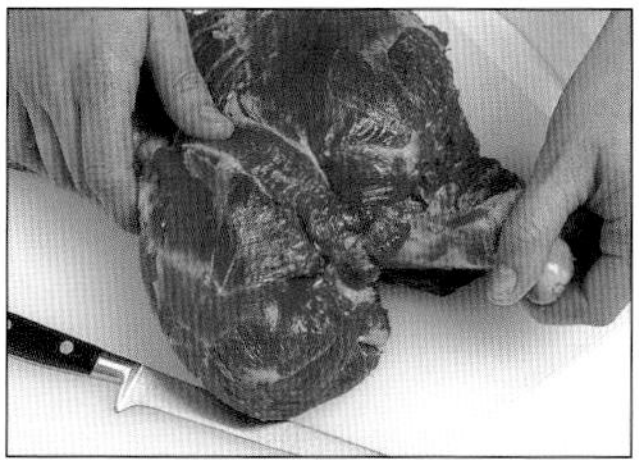

4 Cut around the leg bone, then twist and remove it.

Preparing a butterfly leg

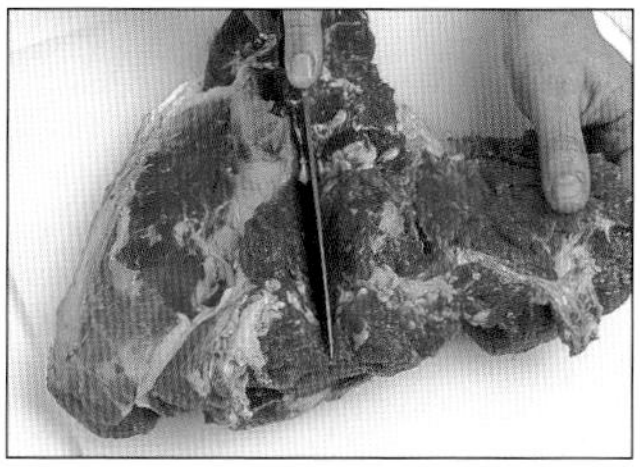

When the bones have been removed from the leg, cut the meat lengthways and open out the joint. When boning a leg for a butterfly finish, the meat can be cut down its length to remove the bones; this is easier than twisting them out. Open out the meat flat. The meat can be stuffed and rolled, or metal skewers can be inserted widthways to keep it flat, which is useful when grilling the whole leg on a barbecue.

Preparing rack of lamb

The best end of neck, or rack of lamb, is taken from one side of the rib cage. There are usually 6–9 cutlets in a rack.

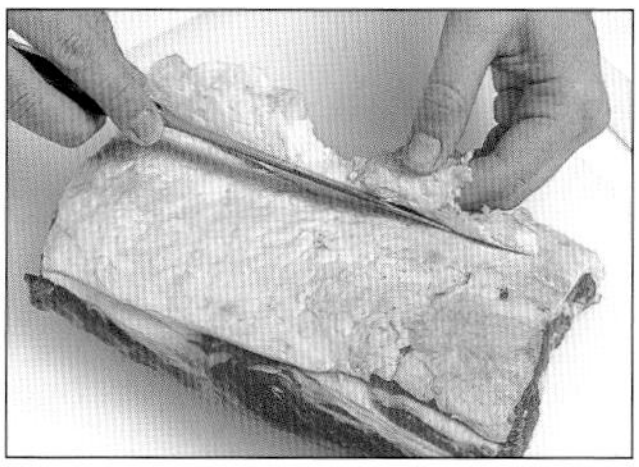

1 Cut off the skin and most of the fat.

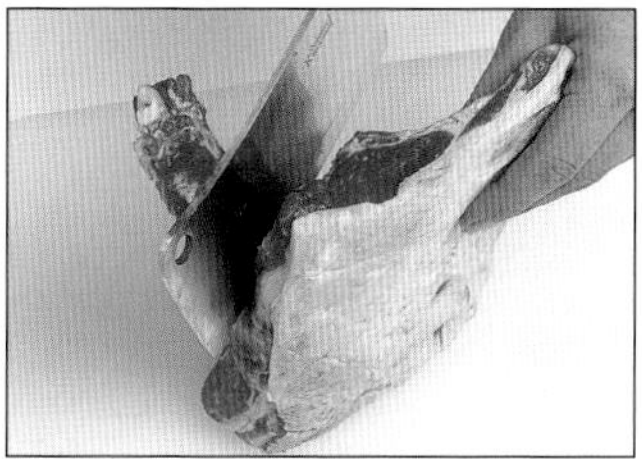

2 If the rack isn't "chined", place the rack on its side and cut off the chine bone (the back bone).

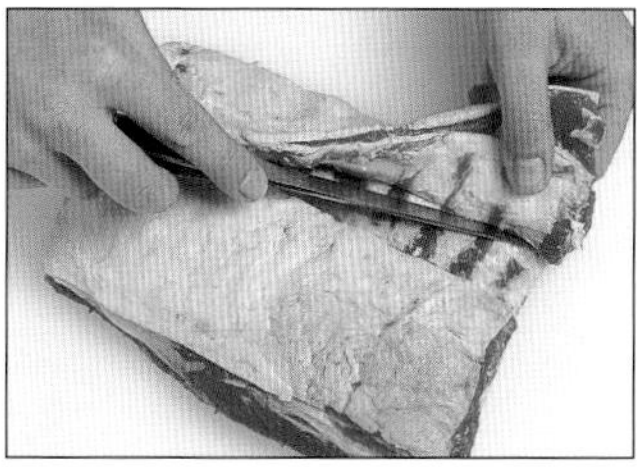

3 Cut the fat off the ribs down the top 5cm/2in from the bone ends. Turn the joint over and score between the bones.

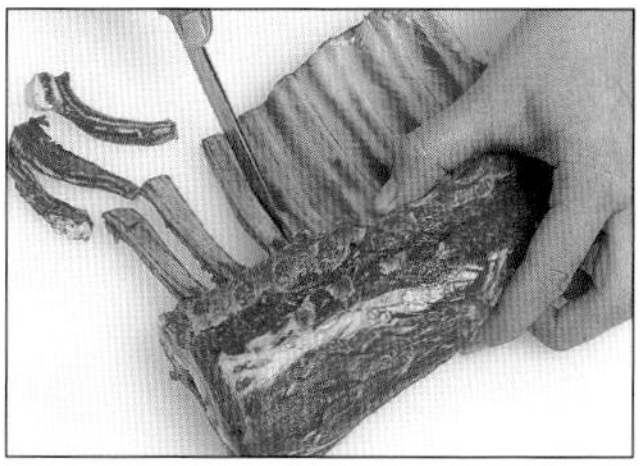

4 Cut and scrape away the meat and connective tissue between the bones.

Flavouring rack of lamb

A rack of lamb can be flavoured before roasting. First, sear the fat on the joint. Heat a little oil in a large frying pan and press the joint, fat side down, in the hot oil until browned, then remove from the pan and leave to cool. Spread the fat with 15ml/1 tbsp Dijon mustard. Press a mixture of chopped fresh herbs, ground spices and dried breadcrumbs into the mustard with your fingers.

Preparing crown roast

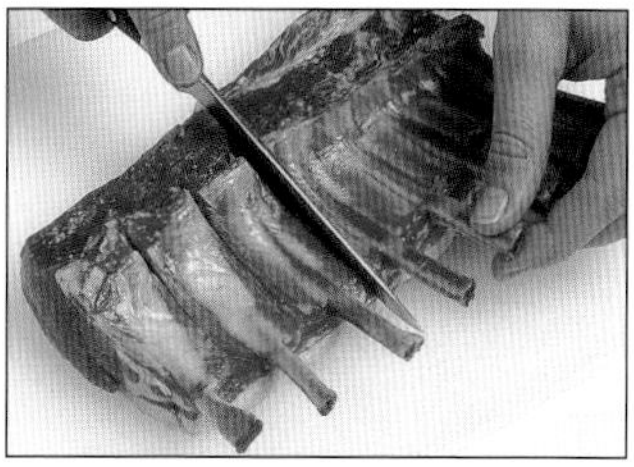

1 Prepare two racks of lamb as described left, then carefully cut the tissue between each rib so that the rack can be bent into position.

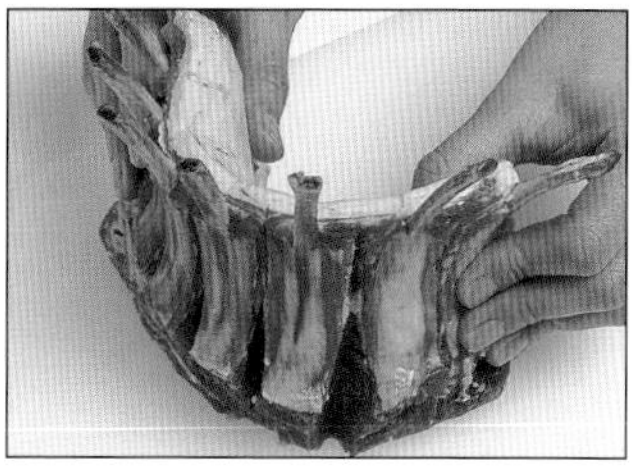

2 Stand the rack and carefully bend it into a semicircle, with the meat outside, to form the shape of one side of the crown. Push the ribs outwards at the top so that the crown will sit up straight.

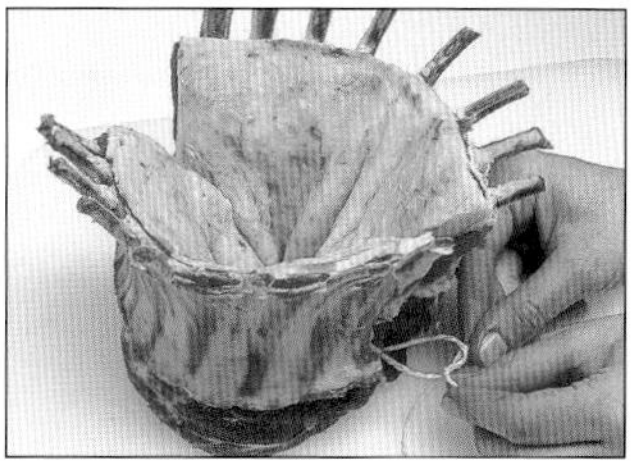

3 Bend the second rack into shape and then tie string around the crown at 2.5cm/1in intervals to hold the racks together and in shape.

4 The crown of lamb is now ready for roasting. However, if you prefer, the central cavity of the crown of lamb can be stuffed (see the garlic and herb stuffing recipe, left) before roasting.

Preparing guard of honour

This consists of a pair of racks of lamb interlocked like soldiers' swords in a military guard of honour.

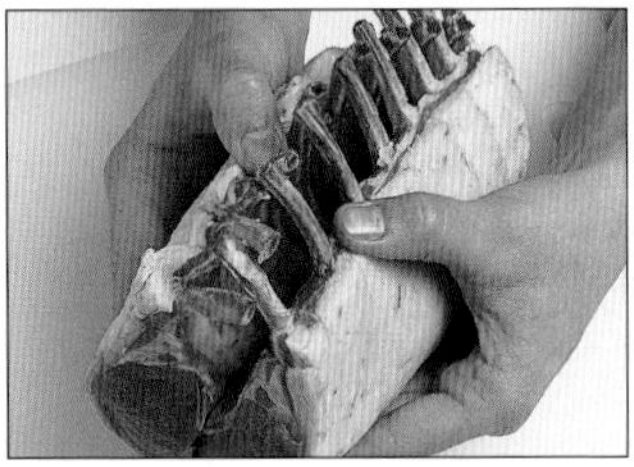

Prepare two racks of lamb. Hold one rack in each hand and push the racks together, interlocking the bones. Tie the racks at regular intervals to secure.

Cutting noisettes

Noisettes are thick slices of the boned and rolled loin. They can be pan-fried, chargrilled or griddled.

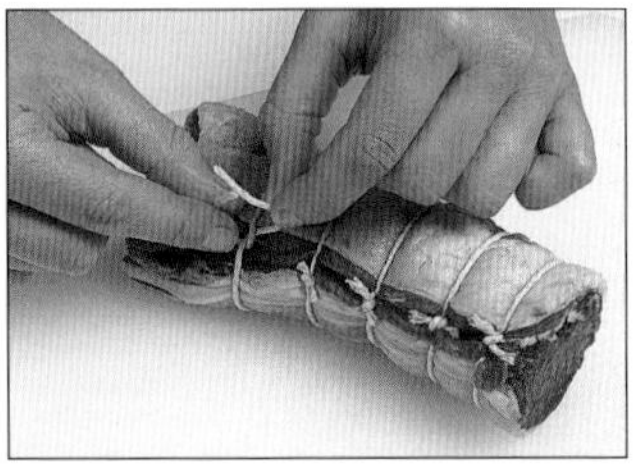

1 Trim off the thin fatty edge of the flap along the side of the boned loin, then tie the meat into a cylinder shape at 3.5cm/1¼in intervals.

2 Cut the loin into thick slices between the string. Flatten each noisette slightly.

Trimming and cutting fillet

The fillet is cut from the middle of the neck of lamb. It is a lean and tender cut that is well marbled with internal fat and it can be cut into medallions or cubes.

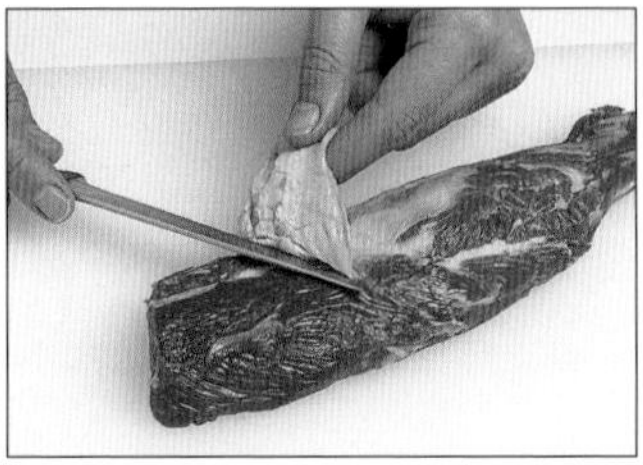

1 Trim off the thin membrane and any large areas of fat on the fillet.

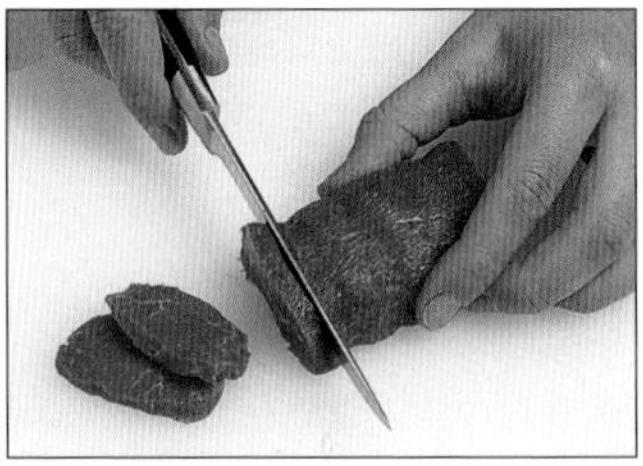

2 To make medallions of lamb, cut the fillet into thin slices of an even width. Medallions can be either pan-fried or braised, then served in a sauce (see pan-frying, right).

3 To cut the fillet into cubes, first cut the meat lengthways into thick strips using a sharp knife, then cut the strips across into cubes. These tender cubes of lamb are ideal for marinating and making into kebabs (see making kebabs, right).

Marinating

This adds flavour and helps to keep the meat moist during cooking. Marinating overnight is best as this allows time for the flavours to develop fully and penetrate the meat. When time is short, marinating for 1–2 hours will still make all the difference to the taste.

1 Mix together the ingredients for the marinade in a dish that is large enough to hold the meat in a single layer. Do not use uncoated metal as this reacts with acids such as vinegar, or plastic containers, which pick up the flavour of strong ingredients such as garlic. A glass dish or bowl is ideal.

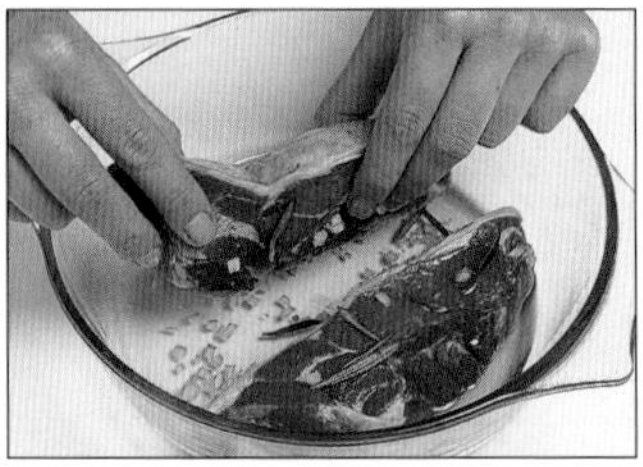

2 Add the meat to the marinade in the dish and turn it in the marinade to thoroughly coat both sides.

3 Cover the dish with clear film and then leave the meat to marinate in a cool place or the fridge for several hours, turning the meat once or twice.

COOK'S TIP

Before cooking lamb, always remove it from the fridge about an hour before cooking and let it warm to room temperature. This improves the flavour of the meat and makes it more tender.

COOKING LAMB

Pan-frying

This is the traditional method for cooking lamb steaks, cutlets or chops. It is also a useful method for medallions.

Preheat the pan thoroughly, then grease it lightly with a little oil before adding the meat. Medallions are tender and cook quickly, so as soon as they are browned (2–3 minutes), turn and cook the second sides. When the medallions are cooked, transfer them to warmed plates and stir double cream into the cooking juices with a sprinkling of fresh thyme leaves, salt and pepper. Heat until boiling to make a delicious, rich sauce. Spoon over the cooked lamb, serve at once.

Griddling noisettes

Noisettes cook evenly and quickly, and many people prefer them to meat on the bone. The cooking time depends on the thickness of the noisettes: ensure they are all evenly thick so that they cook in the same length of time.

Heat a ridged griddle until hot, then add a little oil or butter. When the oil is hot or the butter foaming, add the noisettes and cook for 4–5 minutes on each side.

Grilling

This is a quick, easy and healthy way of cooking lamb cutlets or chops, allowing the fat to drip away during cooking. The high heat seals the meat quickly to lock in the juices and give a succulent result. Sprigs of rosemary can be inserted into the meat before cooking to add a delicious flavour to the cutlets or chops.

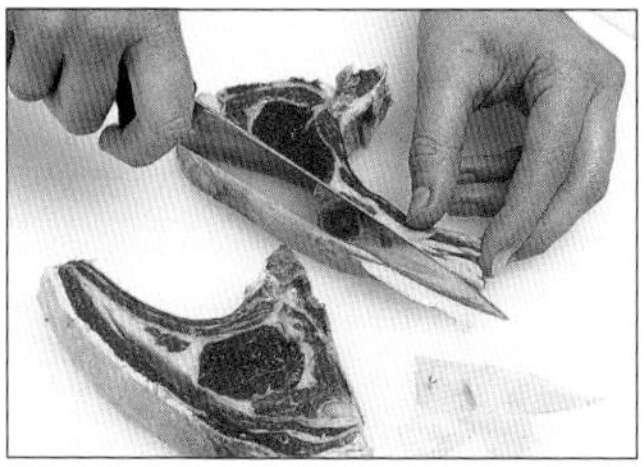

1 Trim off any excess fat around the cutlets with a sharp cook's knife. Season well with salt and black pepper.

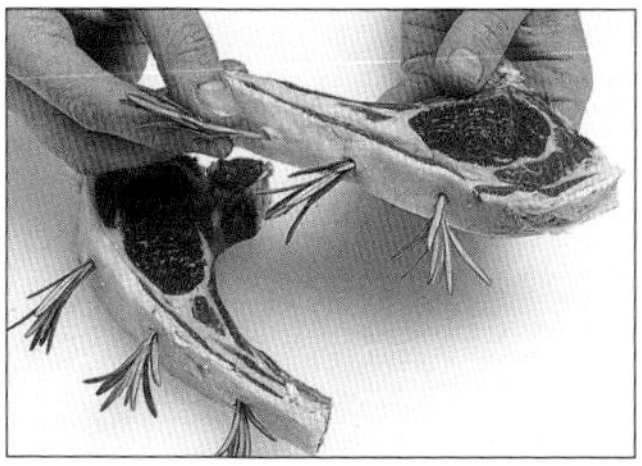

2 Make a slit through the fat into the flesh and insert a sprig of rosemary. Preheat the grill to high.

3 Place the cutlets on a lightly oiled rack over a grill pan and cook under a hot grill. Allow 4–6 minutes on each side; turning halfway through cooking.

Making kebabs

Use metal skewers or soak bamboo skewers in water for 30 minutes before threading the meat on them. Soaking wooden skewers helps to prevent them from burning during cooking.

1 Cut boneless leg, shoulder or neck fillet into 3.5cm/1¼in cubes.

2 Marinate the lamb, then drain the lamb and thread on to oiled skewers, alternating with vegetables. Leave a little space between each piece to ensure they cook evenly. Place the kebabs on an oiled rack over a preheated barbecue or under a very hot grill and cook, turning them frequently, for 6–8 minutes.

All about kebabs

The word kebab comes from the Arabic and means "on a skewer". Lamb makes excellent kebabs because it is lean and tender, and cooks very quickly.

Shish kebab, which means "meat on a skewer", was first eaten by Turkish soldiers who cooked chunks of lamb on their swords over open fires. Chunks of lamb are skewered with vegetables and grilled over charcoal.

Doner kebab consists of a whole leg of lamb, boned, marinated and roasted on a rotating vertical spit. It is often made with lamb that has been ground and then compressed into the shape of a leg of lamb. Slices are cut off and served with salad in pitta bread.

Barbecuing

Heat the barbecue about 30 minutes in advance, until the coals are ashen and very hot. Chops, leg steaks, cutlets and noisettes are all suitable for barbecuing.

Brush the meat with a little oil before placing on the barbecue. Cook for about 3 minutes on each side.

Stewing

Scrag end and middle neck are suitable cuts for stewing. Lamb on the bone can be layered in a casserole with sliced onions, bay leaves and other herbs or aromatics, then water, stock or wine can be poured in to cover the meat. Season, then cook from a cold start for 2–3 hours at a low temperature, for a succulent, well-flavoured result.

Alternatively, the meat can be browned first. This is the best method for stews made with cubed lamb; it is also good for cooking lamb on the bone.

1 Brown the meat in a frying pan, then transfer to a flameproof casserole. Fry a chopped onion in the fat remaining in the pan, add stock, water or wine and bring to the boil, scraping all the residue off the pan. Pour this liquid over the lamb in the casserole. Add any chopped herbs or bay leaves.

2 Cover, then simmer gently for about 2½ hours or until very tender.

Braising

Leg steaks are an excellent choice for braising on a bed of root vegetables. Prepare the vegetables, such as carrots, swede, parsnips and onions, cutting them into chunks, then place them in a flameproof casserole.

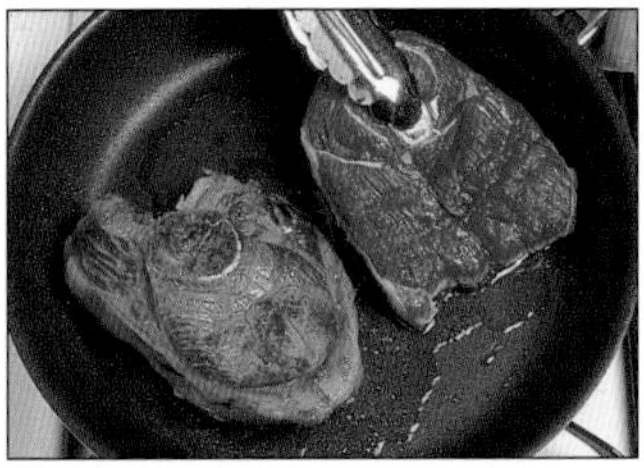

1 Heat a little oil in a frying pan; brown the lamb steaks quickly on both sides.

2 Lay the lamb steaks on top of the vegetables. Add stock to the frying pan used for browning the meat and bring to the boil, stirring to mix in all the sediment. Pour the stock over the steaks – it should cover the vegetables and part-cover the meat. Cover and simmer gently for 45–60 minutes.

Pot-roasting lamb shanks

Lamb shanks are tender and delicious when pot-roasted in the oven or on the hob, on a bed of chopped aromatic vegetables moistened with a little red wine or well-flavoured stock, in a covered casserole.

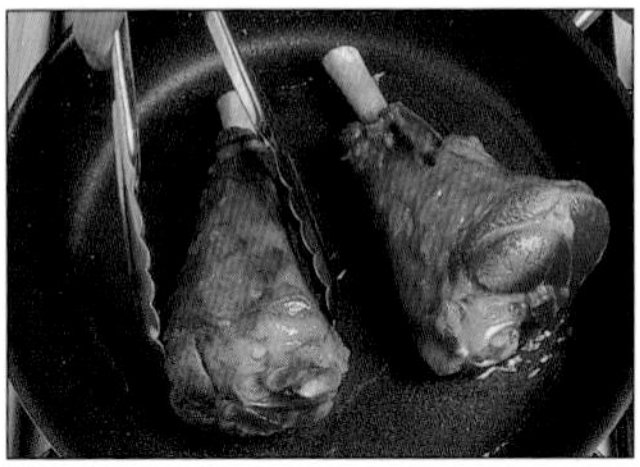

1 Heat a large, heavy-based frying pan and add a little sunflower or olive oil. When the oil is hot, add the lamb shanks, in batches if necessary, and fry them over a high heat, turning them occasionally using tongs, until they are well browned on all sides.

2 Meanwhile, prepare a bed of thickly sliced or roughly diced vegetables, such as carrots, swede, leeks and onions, layered with sprigs of fresh thyme, bay leaves, rosemary, marjoram, or other aromatic herbs in a large, deep, flameproof casserole.

3 Place the lamb shanks on top of the vegetables and pour in enough robust red wine or stock to just partially cover the vegetables. Cover the casserole with a tight-fitting lid or foil and cook in a preheated oven at 180°C/350°F/Gas 4 for 1–1½ hours, until the lamb is very tender. Check halfway through cooking and add more liquid if necessary.

Roasting

Lamb is often served rare or medium rare. A meat thermometer is useful for checking the internal temperature of the meat. Insert it into the middle of the thickest part of the joint.

Roasting times for lamb

For rare lamb
Weigh the joint, then roast in a oven preheated to 230°C/450°F/Gas 8 for 10 minutes. Reduce the oven temperature to 180°C/350°F/Gas 4, and cook the lamb for the remaining time, allowing 18 minutes per 450g/1lb. The internal temperature of the joint should be 60°C/140°F.

For a medium result
Roast at 230°C/450°F/Gas 8 for 10 minutes, then at 180°C/350°F/Gas 4 for a further 25 minutes per 450g/1lb, plus 25 minutes. The internal temperature should be 70°C/158°F.

For well-cooked lamb
Roast at 230°C/450°F/Gas 8 for 10 minutes, then at 180°C/350°F/Gas 4 for a further 30 minutes per 450g/1lb, plus 30 minutes. The internal temperature should be 80°C/176°F.

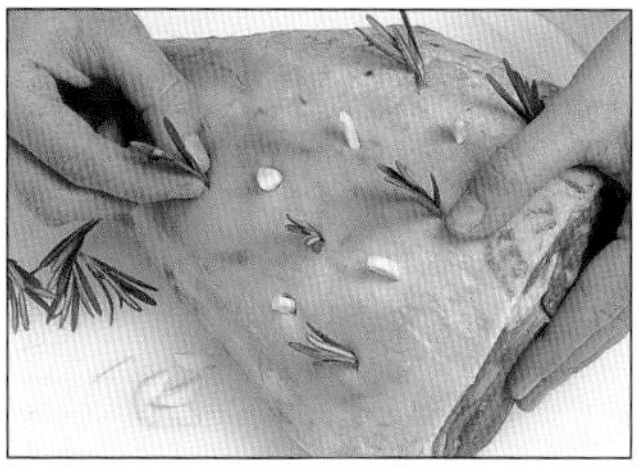

1 Weigh the joint. Cut small, deep, slits all over the meat using the point of a small, sharp knife. Insert thin slivers of peeled garlic and small fresh rosemary or thyme sprigs into the slits.

2 Lay the leg of lamb in a roasting tin, fat-side up, and sprinkle with salt. Roast for the times given above.

3 Cover the cooked meat loosely with foil and leave to stand in a warm place for 10 minutes before carving. This standing time allows the meat to relax and the internal temperature to even out, making the meat easier to carve.

Carving leg of lamb

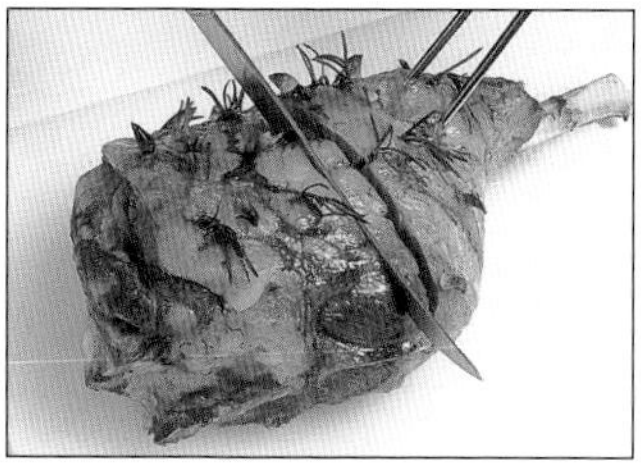

1 Start by cutting a wedge of meat from the top of the leg, near the thin end of the leg, but not right at the end. Cut down through the thick part of the meat as far as the bone.

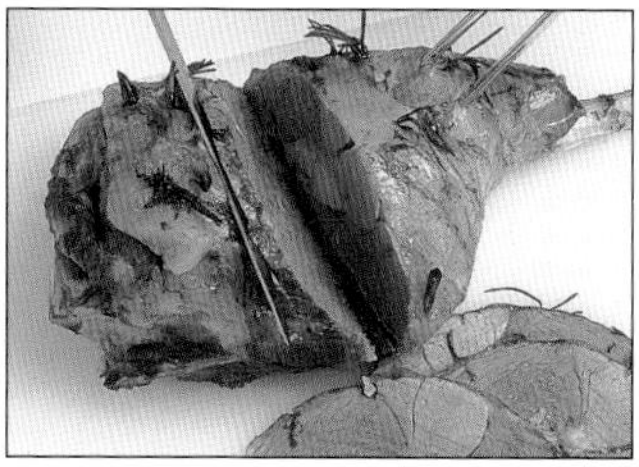

2 Holding the joint firmly at the leg end, carve slices following the first cut made by the wedge; these are the prime slices of meat.

3 Turn the joint over and cut small slices down across the grain to remove the remaining meat.

Carving rack of lamb

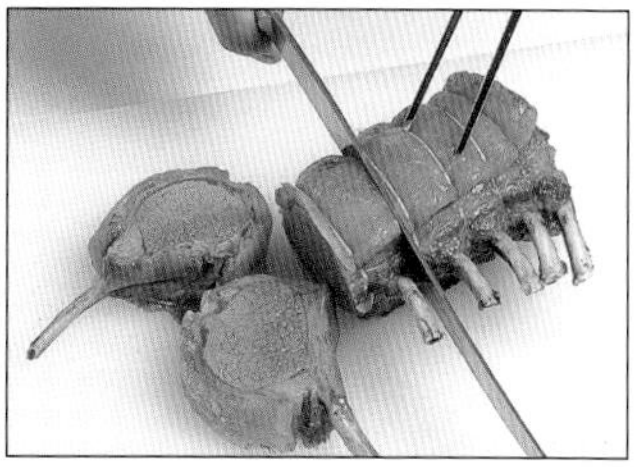

Cut between the rib bones and serve the roast rack as cutlets. This method is also used for crown roast and guard of honour; scoop out any stuffing with a spoon before cutting between the cutlets. Remove string from a crown roast before carving.

Wines to serve with lamb

Smooth, medium-bodied red wines best complement lamb. A good Margaux or St Emilion from Bordeaux goes down very well with roast lamb. As a less expensive alternative, try a Minervois, Fitou or Côtes du Roussillon from the south of France.

New Zealand is famous for its lamb and a Cabernet Sauvignon or Merlot from Hawkes Bay will complement most lamb dishes.

The Middle East is also sheep country and some of the better red wines from the Lebanon go down very well with lamb. Most of the country's vineyards are on the sides of the Bekaa Valley and they yield excellent fruity red wine from Cabernet Sauvignon, Carignan, Syrah and Grenache grapes.

It is also worth sampling some of the softer Napa Valley reds from California, or a medium-bodied Chianti from Italy with lamb chops. Unoaked Chilean Merlot goes well with moussaka and a fruity Australian Shiraz will make the most of lamb with mint sauce. Pour a lightly oaked Spanish Rioja to turn shepherd's pie into a real treat.

PORK, BACON, GAMMON AND HAM

You can use more or less every part of a pig for cooking. It is comparatively inexpensive, very versatile, generally tender and has an excellent flavour. However, pork, bacon, gammon and ham are not universally acceptable and Jews and Muslims do not eat it. There are many theories as to why the meat of the pig is considered to be unclean, apart from the religious origins of the ban. Perhaps it is literally because of the mucky circumstances in which pigs are often reared; their close proximity to man in some countries and the dangers of shared infection from eating the meat less than well-cooked; or the fact that pork does not keep well in a hot climate.

PORK

The pig has long been an important source of food in other communities throughout Europe, Asia and South and Central America. Pigs are inexpensive and easy to look after. They will eat anything and, unlike sheep and cattle, do not need a large area of land to graze. Until less than 50 years ago, pigs were reared in suburban backyards, fattened on kitchen leftovers and killed by the local butcher.

From ears to trotters, virtually every part can be eaten, including the skin (but excluding a few internals organs, such as the spleen). Whole roasted suckling pig, highly seasoned brawns and meat pastes, stuffed and roasted joints, crisp-fried sweet-and-sour pork, and rich pork simmered in milk are a few examples to highlight the vast range of methods of cooking and serving pork. As for other meats, there are prime roasts and cuts that grill well; unlike other meats, the carcass does not yield very tough cuts. With careful trimming to remove sinews and excess fat, the majority of the meat is tender.

Pork is widely used in Chinese and Asian dishes, so much so that in Chinese cooking it is referred to as "meat" rather than by type. In both Chinese and Western cooking, the crisp, roasted skin is a delicacy. In Eastern European cooking, pork is excellent combined with cabbage or sauerkraut and fruits; it is also popular with dried beans and pulses in European and American dishes. Fresh pork was traditionally a food for late autumn, when pigs were fattened through the summer and killed in the cooler weather, ready for winter. Meat that could not be used fresh was cured for long keeping, providing bacon and ham.

The farmed pig is a descendant of wild boars that once roamed the woods and forests of Europe and Asia. There are two basic breeds, the long-backed Chinese pig and the heavier European or Danish pig. Pigs farmed today are well removed from the shorter, fatter and rounder animals that yielded fatty meat – they are longer, leaner and their carcasses contain a larger proportion of lean, prime cuts. They are reared primarily for curing and to supply the bacon market.

This process of selective breeding started in 1760 when Robert Bakewell, a Leicestershire farmer, crossed a Chinese pig with a European pig for the first time. The cosmetic Chinese features were bred out quite quickly, but the plumpness and the sweetness stayed behind. Traditionally, the pig's diet was adapted according to the ultimate use for which its meat was required, ensuring that the texture and flavour of the meat was the best, for example for certain cured hams. Specialist farmers still rear to these standards and old-fashioned breeds are again of great interest. Apart from specialist suppliers and high-quality pork products, some supermarkets also stock sausages labelled with the breed of pig from which the meat they contain was taken.

> **Free-range pork**
> While cattle and sheep spend most of their lives outside, eating grass and moving freely around fields, some pigs are housed in buildings where light and temperature are strictly controlled. With increasing consumer awareness and demand for food with flavour, farmers are now reverting to more traditional and often organic methods of rearing pigs. Free-range pork and its products might cost more, but they have a far superior taste and come from pigs reared under humane conditions.

Above: The meat of pigs is considered unclean by some religions – this could relate to the pigs' living conditions.

Buying

Look for firm, pale-pink flesh, which is moist but not damp or oily. The fat should be white, and the bones should be tinged with red. The skin should be dry and silky, not slimy or damp. Most pigs are slaughtered at around six months, when they yield meat with a fine texture. Coarse flesh and hard, white bones indicate that the animal is older and the meat less tender.

Storing

To avoid cross-contamination by meat juices, which may drip on to food that is to be eaten uncooked, store pork on a low shelf in the fridge, well away from and below cooked food and food that is eaten raw. Ideally, the meat should be placed on a rack in a dish and covered with a lid so that moisture can be retained while air can circulate freely. Pre-packed meat is best kept in its packaging as long as this is sealed and undamaged.

Always check and observe the use-by dates on packaged meats. As a guide when buying loose meat, minced pork will keep in the fridge for one to two days; pork cuts and joints for three to four days. Pork can be frozen for four to six months.

Nutrition

Pork was once thought of as a very fatty meat, however, modern breeding, rearing and butchering has resulted in pork becoming one of the lowest-fat meats available. The fat it does contain is also less saturated than the fat in other meats. Pork is a high-quality protein food, a good source of iron, zinc and B vitamins. It also provides many other trace elements, including copper, manganese and selenium.

BACON, GAMMON AND HAM

Originally, bacon was meat taken only from the back, or side, of a pig. Today it means cured meat taken usually, but not exclusively, from the back and sides of the pig. Gammon, which is the same joint as ham but milder in flavour, comes from the hind leg and is left attached to the side during bacon curing, and cut from it afterwards. Bacon is available as joints and chops as well as different types of rashers.

Below: More and more pigs are being bred outdoors in rearing units like this one in Norfolk, England.

In Anglo-Saxon English, ham was the term for the part of the leg at the back of the knee (hence hamstring). It later came to refer to the thigh in general and in the 17th century began to mean the thigh of an animal that had been dried, salted and usually smoked. It was, typically, a pig's thigh, but mutton hams, venison hams and even bear hams were enjoyed in the 18th and 19th centuries.

In Britain and America, ham now refers to cured pig meat. It is most widely used for the cooked or ready-to-eat product or for dry-cured hams that can be eaten raw as well as cooked. Gammon steaks and cured and pressed pork shoulder are sometimes incorrectly referred to as ham.

Curing methods

There are three curing methods for bacon and gammon, using dry coarse salt, brine or a mixture of salt, sugar, seasonings and preservatives. After salting, the meat is sometimes smoked.

Every region and country has its own traditional method and recipe for curing ham, first in dry salt or brine and then sometimes smoked over a hardwood fire. The brine can be varied by the addition of sugar or molasses, herbs, spices or berries. Finally, the ham is left to dry and mature. The temperature and humidity during the drying, or smoking and drying, can be varied to produce different results. The geographical differences are still evident in the names of the hams that are available today: Parma ham from Tuscany in Italy; Virginia ham from the southern states of America; and York ham, Cumberland ham, Wiltshire ham and Suffolk ham from different regions of England.

Some dry-cured, smoked hams are eaten raw. Italian prosciutto is probably the most famous of these. In France, Bayonne ham is the equivalent, and German Westphalian ham is eaten uncooked. These are all sliced very finely before serving. They are also cooked for use in some dishes.

The hind legs and the loin make the best cured pork and ham.

Buying

Good-quality bacon has clear, pink, moist, but not wet, meat with an even layer of creamy-white fat.

When buying uncooked ham, such as Parma ham, look for deep-pink flesh and creamy-white fat. The ham should be moist, but not damp and should lay flat, not dry and curled at the edges. Unless pre-packed, the ham should be freshly sliced for you when you buy it. Look for a supplier who is competent at cutting large, paper-thin slices. The rind and some of the fat should be trimmed off before the ham is sliced. Reject broken slices and those that have been reduced to shreds, or slices that are too thick to be palatable when served raw.

Storing

Observe the use-by date on pre-packed bacon. Leave the bacon in its pack, then, when it is opened, store any leftovers wrapped in clear film. Follow the storage instructions on the packet. If you buy good-quality loose bacon, wrap it in waxed paper or greaseproof paper and a polythene bag. It will keep fresh for up to three weeks in the fridge. Keep the bacon in the coolest part of the fridge.

Store ham in the fridge. Leave pre-packed meat in its wrapping and use by the recommended date. Wrap slices of loose ham in waxed paper or greaseproof paper and clear film.

Bacon and ham do not freeze well as the salt used in curing promotes rancidity once they are frozen. Vacuum-packed bacon and ham have a slightly improved freezer life. The storage time depends on the curing process. As a general rule, it is not worth freezing high-quality bacon and ham cured by traditional methods as they keep for only two to three weeks and tend to be inferior when thawed. However, meat cured by modern methods will keep for one month or in some cases manufacturers suggest a freezer life of up to three months. This short freezing time also applies to dishes containing bacon – they will keep for up to four weeks. The bacon becomes rancid on longer storage and taints the dish.

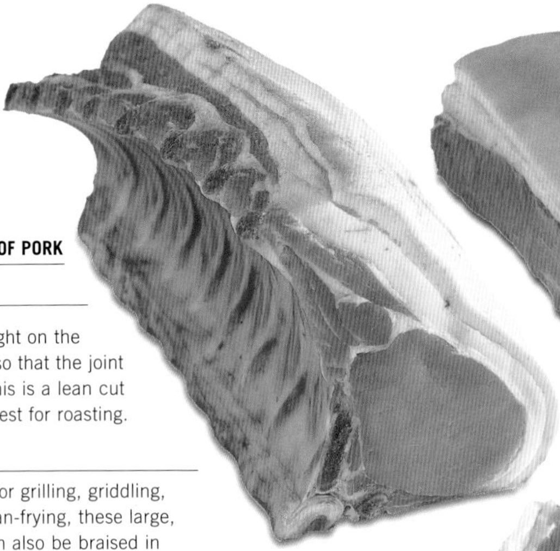

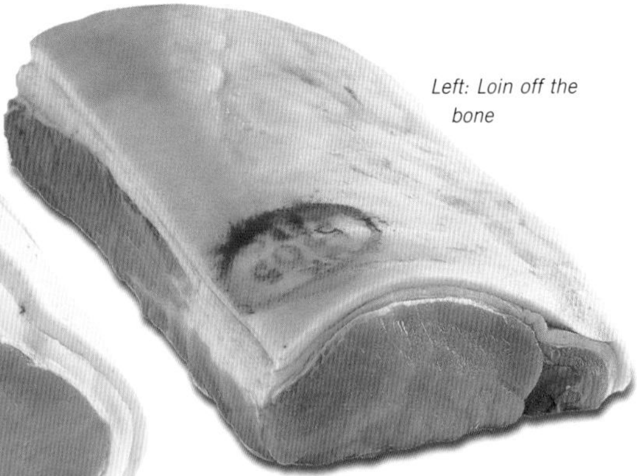

Left: Loin off the bone

THE BASIC CUTS OF PORK

Loin

This can be bought on the bone or boned, so that the joint can be rolled. This is a lean cut and one of the best for roasting.

Loin chops

A prime choice for grilling, griddling, barbecuing or pan-frying, these large, tender chops can also be braised in delicious casseroles.

Above: Loin on the bone

Below: Loin chops

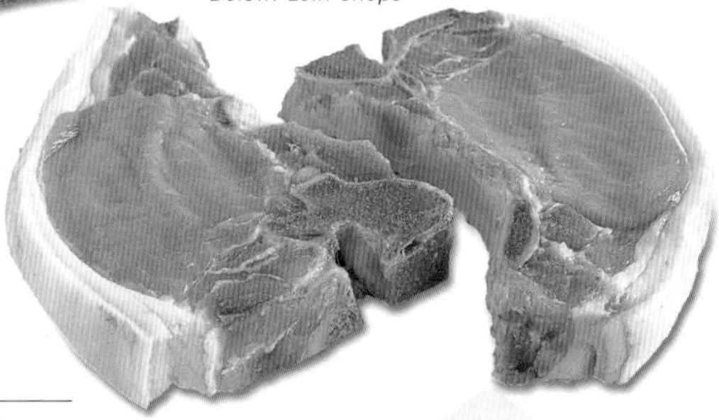

Tenderloin or fillet

This is a boneless eye of very lean meat and is the equivalent of fillet of beef. Tenderloin is taken from under the ribs and backbone. It is a lean, fine-textured cut of pork and is good for both grilling and pan-frying. If roasted, it cooks very quickly and should be basted frequently to prevent it from drying out.

Chump or hind loin

A lean cut from the hindquarters sold on or off the bone. Whole joints are ideal for roasting.

Below: Chump or hind loin

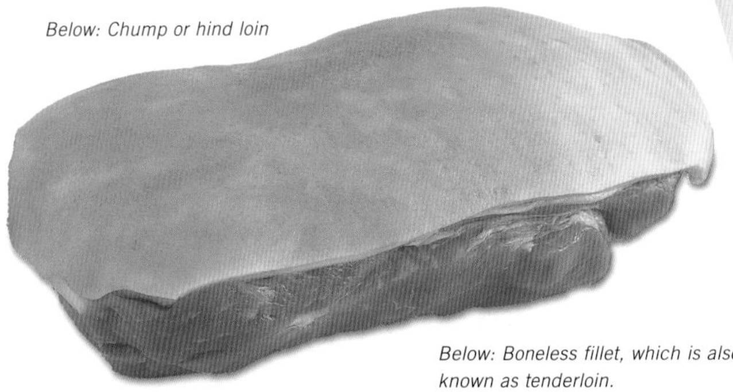

Chump chops

Large and bony, chump chops can be grilled, griddled, barbecued, roasted, fried, stewed or braised.

Leg

The hind leg is sold whole or split into two joints. A whole leg makes a marvellous roast for a large number of people. It is sold on the bone or boned and rolled. Leg steaks, cut across the top of the leg, can be grilled, griddled, barbecued, fried, stewed or braised. Thin slices of leg are sometimes prepared as escalopes.

Below: Chump chop

Below: Boneless fillet, which is also known as tenderloin.

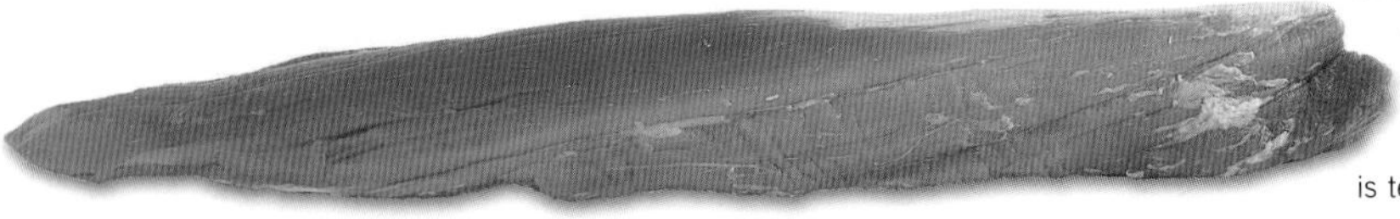

Leg fillet

Also known as fillet of the leg. This is cut across the top of the leg, including the bone in the middle. It is tender and good for roasting.

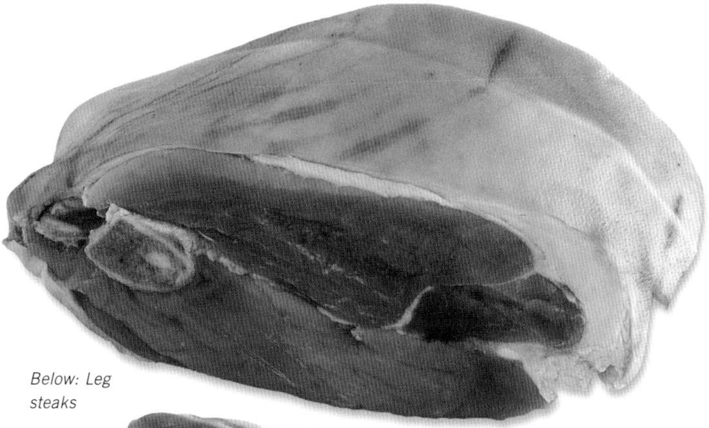

Above: The top end of a leg of pork on the bone is a large joint that makes an excellent roast.

Below: Leg steaks

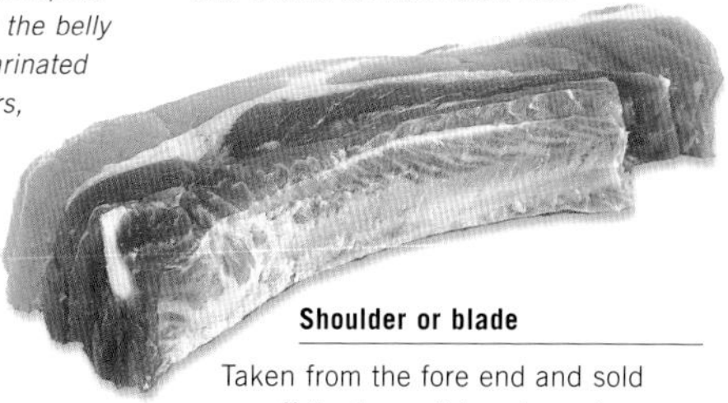

Right: Chinese-style spare ribs are cut from the belly and are best marinated for several hours, then grilled or barbecued.

Left: Shoulder steaks are sold both with and without the bone, but either way they are delicious and succulent, and good cooked in a wide range of methods from grilling to braising.

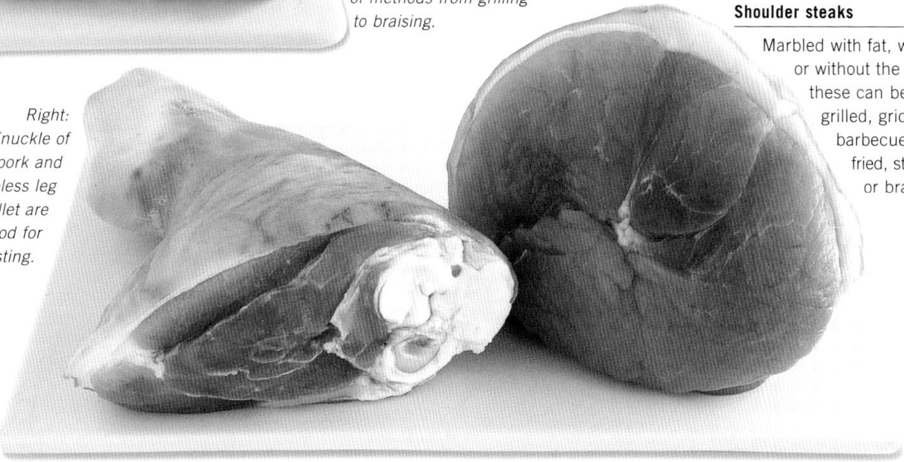

Right: Knuckle of pork and boneless leg fillet are good for roasting.

Knuckle (or shank)

This joint is cut from the lower part of the leg and provides succulent meat when roasted slowly; it also has plenty of crackling.

Spare rib and spare rib chops

Taken from the fore end of the animal and sold either whole as a spare rib joint or cut up into spare rib chops. Suitable for slow roasting, braising and casseroling, grilling or griddling.

Spare ribs

Chinese-style spare ribs are cut from the belly rather than from the neck end of the carcass, the area from which spare rib chops and joints are cut. They are best either grilled or barbecued, and should be marinated first.

Shoulder or blade

Taken from the fore end and sold on or off the bone, this cut can be roasted or pot-roasted (if whole) but is mostly boned, trimmed of sinews and membranes, then cut into cubes for making stews, casseroles or kebabs.

Shoulder steaks

Marbled with fat, with or without the bone, these can be grilled, griddled, barbecued, fried, stewed or braised.

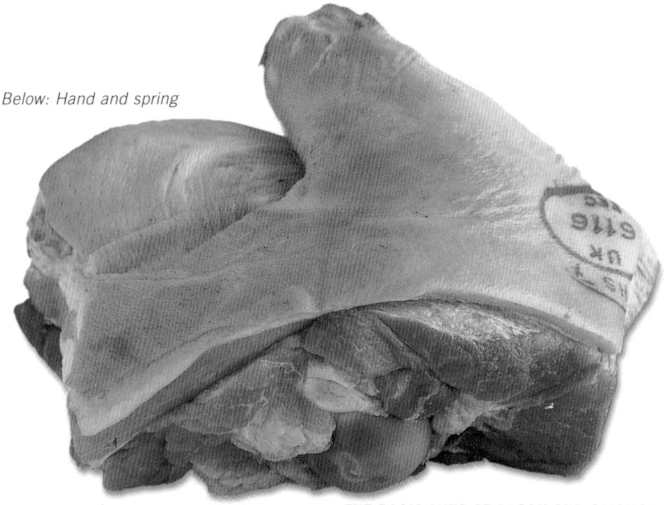

Below: Hand and spring

Hand and spring

From the fore end of the animal, this has quite a lot of sinew and connective membranes, but, when trimmed, the meat is tender and has an excellent flavour. Suitable for slow roasting or braising as a joint as well as trimming and using in cubes.

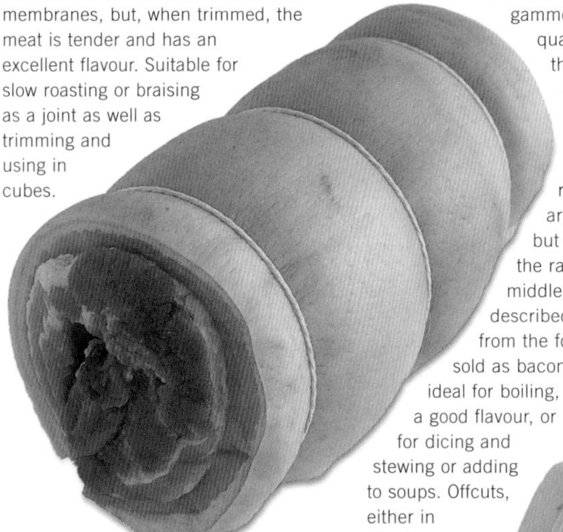

Above: Rolled belly of pork is a fatty joint that is good either slow roasted or pot-roasted.

Belly

Traditionally a fatty cut, but less so on the modern pork carcass, this meat can be rolled and tied to make a neat joint. It is also used for mincing or making sausages. Belly of pork can be slow roasted, pot-roasted, grilled, griddled, barbecued or stewed. It is a traditional cut for pâtés and terrines.

THE BASIC CUTS OF BACON AND GAMMON

Bacon and bacon joints are cut from the fore quarter; ham and gammon from the hind quarter. Collar from the front of the carcass is sold as joints, for boiling, or as wide, fairly lean rashers. These are economical, but not as tender as the rashers from the middle of the carcass, described below. Joints from the fore quarter are sold as bacon joints and are ideal for boiling, giving a good flavour, or for dicing and stewing or adding to soups. Offcuts, either in chunks or diced, are trimmings from both bacon and gammon. They are inexpensive and ideal for flavouring dishes.

Middle gammon

Gammon is the cured leg and may be cooked on the bone or boned and rolled. Middle gammon is a prime cut taken from the wide part of the leg. It can be boiled or baked, or cooked by a combination of both methods.

Gammon slipper

A small joint, which is very lean, but not considered as good as middle gammon.

Gammon hock

This is a large joint, almost the whole gammon, but without the bony knuckle.

Gammon knuckle

The end of the gammon, this includes the bone, when it is often used as a flavouring for soups or making stock, or it can be boned and rolled. This is a small joint for boiling or baking. It can also be cut into cubes for casseroles.

Gammon steaks

These are thick slices cut from the gammon joint.

Middle or through-cut bacon

This is the back and streaky bacon in one piece, which curves from the top of the carcass around under the belly (the streaky end).

Right: Gammon leg joints may be sold on the bone or boned.

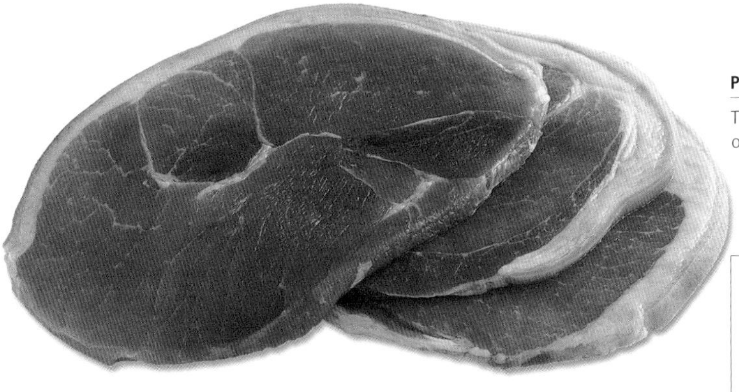

Above: Gammon steaks are cut from the boneless gammon joint.

Above: Lean rashers of back bacon

Below: Middle bacon includes both streaky and back in one piece.

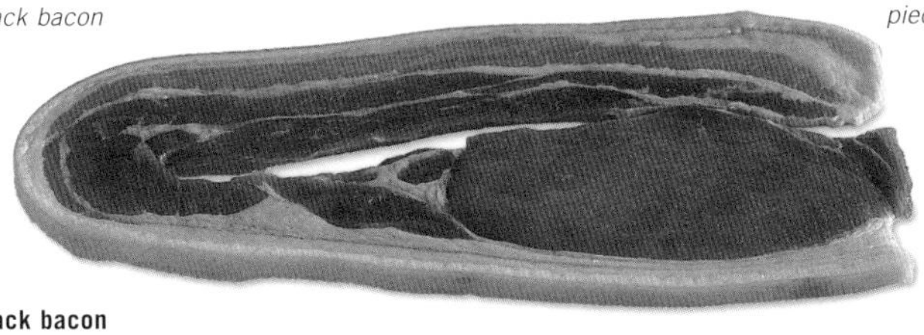

Back bacon

This lean cut comes from the back, along the top of the carcass. The width of the rashers vary according to the position along the carcass and the size of the carcass. Bacon chops are thick slices of cured back – they can be grilled, griddled, baked, barbecued, pan-fried or prepared in the same ways as pork chops.

Streaky bacon

Traditionally very fatty, but less so now as modern breeding and rearing have produced pigs with a smaller amount of fat. This is the belly end of the middle or through-cut. It is best grilled, but can also be used for barding the breasts of poultry and game birds before roasting.

Pancetta

This fatty bacon is the Italian equivalent of streaky bacon and can be bought in strips or round slices cut from a roll. It is cured by traditional methods, and may be unsmoked or smoked.

Wines to serve with pork, gammon, ham and bacon

At its best, Beaujolais is deliciously light, heady and fruity. Examples include the smooth wines of Brouilly, Fleurie, Moulin-à-Vent and Saint Amour. These go well with pork, as do some of the reds from the south of France such as Minervois, Fitou and Côtes du Roussillon.

While most people tend to drink soft, fruity reds with pork, others prefer light, rounded white wines, such as the buttery Chardonnays from the Hunter Valley in Australia. These go well with grilled pork chops, or gammon, bacon or ham. If you want to be a little more adventurous, try a medium sweet Kabinett from Germany. These wines are not particularly fashionable, but they can be very enjoyable with pork dishes, particularly those cooked in cream sauces. And, of course, cider goes extremely well with all pork and apple dishes.

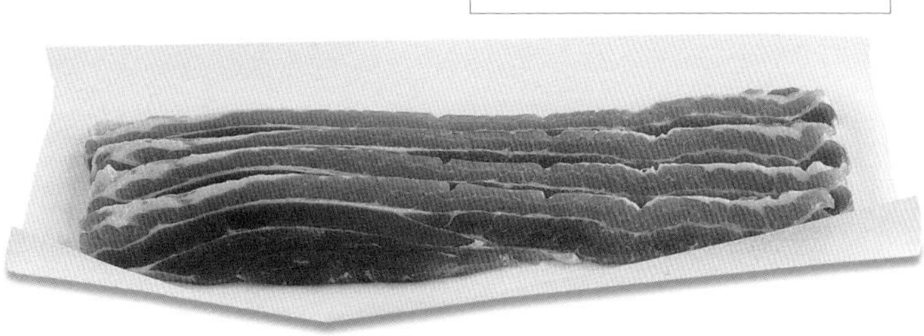

Above: Streaky bacon

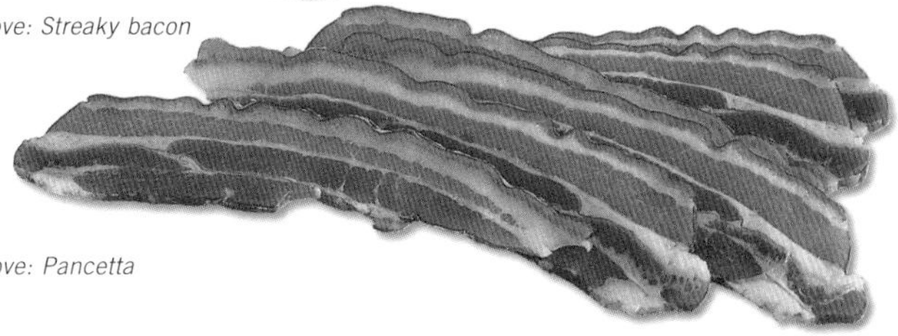

Above: Pancetta

THE BASIC TYPES OF HAM

There are many different types of ham. Some, like the famous Parma ham from Tuscany, are intended to be eaten in their raw, cured state in paper-thin slices, others require further cooking, and many are sold pre-cooked. Factors that influence the flavour of hams include the breed of pig and its diet, and the curing process: whether the meat has been dry-salted and brined, the length of time that it has been cured and whether it has been air-dried or smoked (and if so whether over applewood, beechwood, hickory or oak). A wide variety of flavouring ingredients, such as treacle and beer, may be added during the curing process.

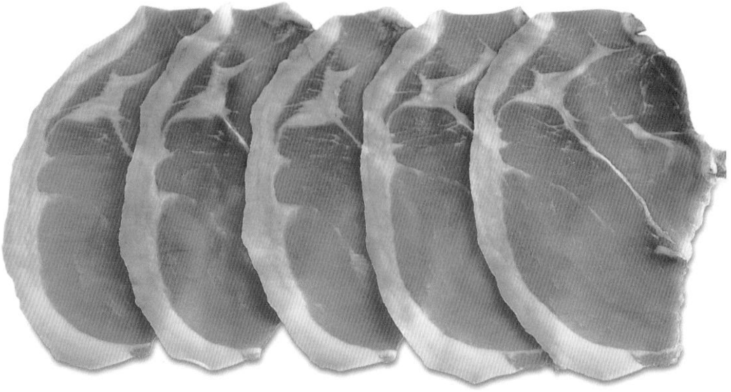

Above: Jambon d'Ardennes is a pale-pink, raw ham from Belgium.

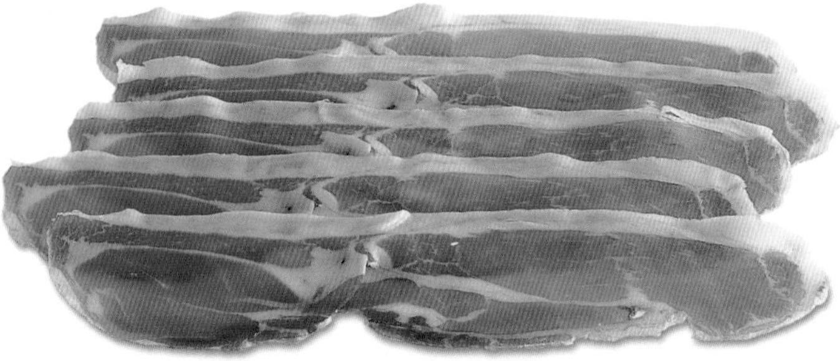

Above: Bayonne ham

Above: Iberico ham

Above: Serrano ham

Hams for Eating Raw

Bayonne ham Golden-coloured, French cured, smoked ham.
Iberico ham This exceptional raw, cured ham is made in south and west Spain. The hams come only from Iberian pigs.
Jambon d'Ardennes This is a pale-pink, raw, cured ham from Belgium. It can be very thinly sliced and eaten as is or sliced more thickly and then pan-fried.
Landrauch A dry, strongly flavoured, smoked ham from Germany.
Lachsschinken This pink, moist ham from Germany is made from smoked foreloin and is wrapped in a thin layer of creamy-white pork fat. The small, round slices are eaten raw.
Prosciutto crudo This is the Italian term for raw, cured ham; **Parma ham** or **prosciutto di Parma** is probably the most famous type. The ham comes from pigs fed on parsnips, and whey left over from making Parmesan cheese. It is dry-cured with salt, sugar and spices for at least nine months and sometimes up to two years. For part of this time it is weighted, which gives the ham its classic, flattened shape.
Serrano ham *Jamón serrano*, or "mountain ham", is a Spanish dry-salted, raw ham. The name was formerly used for all Spanish raw hams, but now refers to hams from white pigs reared in two regions of southern Spain.
Westphalian This is a German raw, cured and smoked ham. The pigs are fed on acorns and the ham is smoked over beech and juniper.

Above: Lachsschinken, a German raw ham often eaten with horseradish.

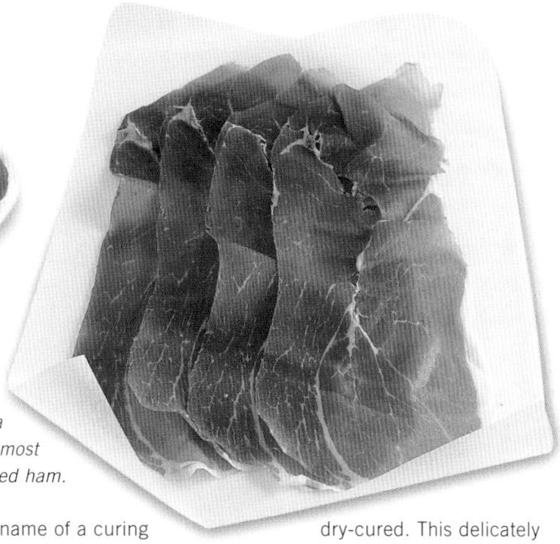

Right: Parma ham is perhaps the most famous type of cured ham.

Cooked Hams

Bradenham ham This smoked, black-skinned ham from Chippenham in England has been made since 1781. The ham, which has a sweet flavour, is first dry-cured, then placed in a mixture of spices, brown sugar and molasses.
Brunswick ham This is a mild-flavoured ham from Germany.
Jambon de Paris/jambon blanc/jambon glacé These lightly salted, unsmoked French hams are usually bought cooked and sliced, and are eaten cold.
Kentucky ham An American dry-salted ham with a delicate flavour, which is smoked over corn cobs, and hickory and apple or sassafras wood. The pigs are fattened on acorns, beans, clover and grains, and the hams are left to mature for up to a year after salting.
Virginia ham A group of lean, smoked hams from the United States, of which **Smithfield ham** is considered the best. This ham comes from razor-back pigs raised outdoors in Virginia and North Carolina, where they feed on acorns, beechnuts and hickory nuts, before being fattened on peanuts and corn. The ham is cured by dry-salting with salt and pepper and is then smoked over hickory, apple and oak, and aged for a year. It can be served raw, but is usually boiled or baked, and can be eaten hot or cold.

York ham This is the name of a curing method rather than a type of ham, and the hams are now made in countries other than England. The ham is dry-salted and smoked, then matured for several months. **Green York ham** is also dry-cured. This delicately flavoured ham can be bought raw and needs to be cooked, either by boiling or baking (or both), or it can be bought ready cooked and sliced. It is eaten either hot or cold.

Right: Bradenham ham is a rich-tasting English ham flavoured with spices.

Above: York ham was originally only produced in England, but it is now made in countries all over the world.

PREPARING PORK

Trimming fillet

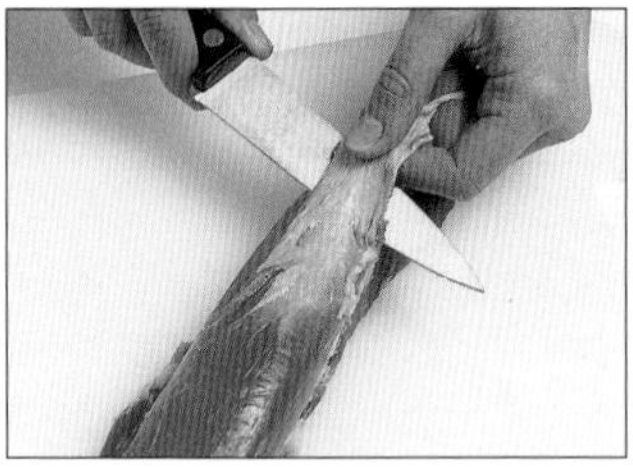

Lift the edge of the fatty membrane and carefully peel it away from the fillet. You can do this easily with your fingers, but it helps if you run the blade of a sharp knife down the underside of the membrane close to the meat to help separate it from the meat.

Cutting strips of fillet

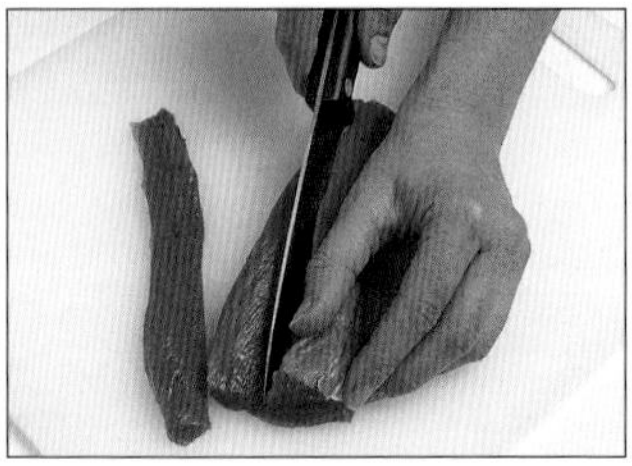

Lay the trimmed fillet on a chopping board, with one of the narrow ends facing you. Use a long, sharp knife, to cut the meat lengthways into several 1–2cm/½–¾in wide strips.

Cutting cubes of fillet

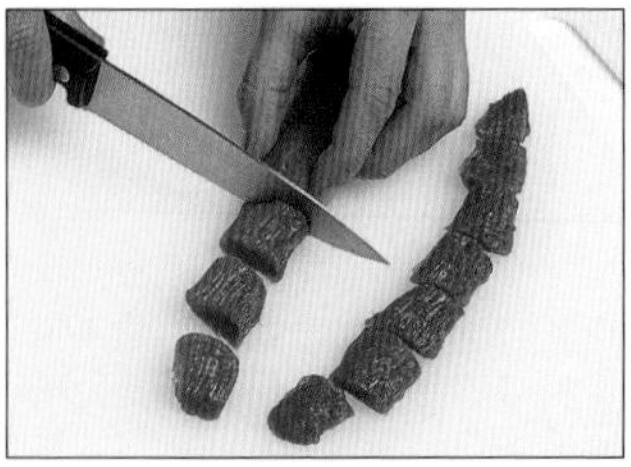

Cut across the strips of trimmed fillet to make even-size cubes. These are ideal for kebabs.

Flattening fillet

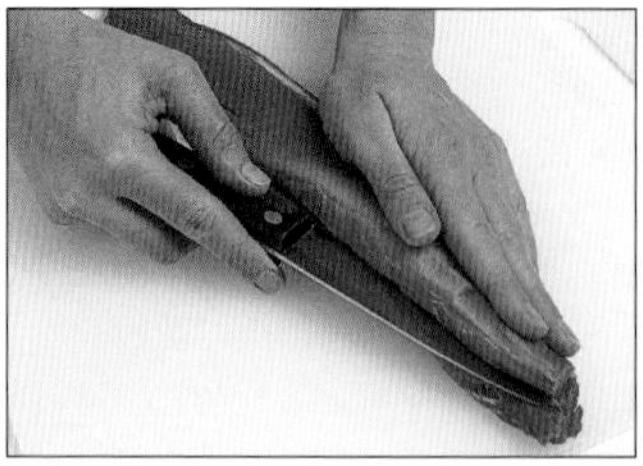

1 Trim off all fat and remove the fatty membrane from the fillet. Hold the top of the fillet and use a long, sharp knife to slice about 4cm/1½in into the meat, this should be about halfway into the fillet.

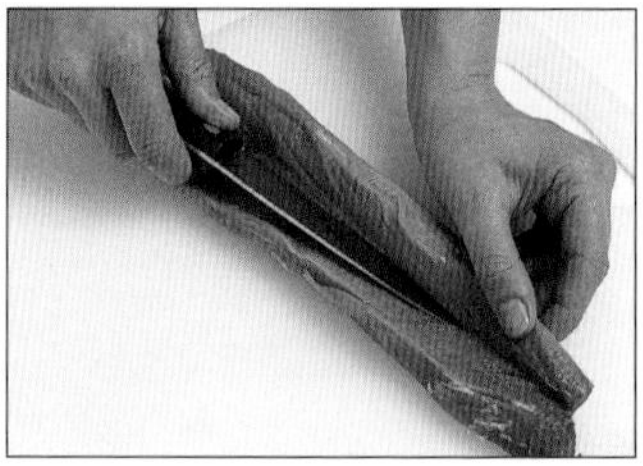

2 Lift the top slice and fold it back, as you carefully cut to within 1cm/½in of the opposite edge.

3 Lay the prepared fillet out on a sheet of clear film or greaseproof paper and fold back the top slice to open the meat to double its original width. Cover the fillet with a second sheet of clear film or greaseproof paper.

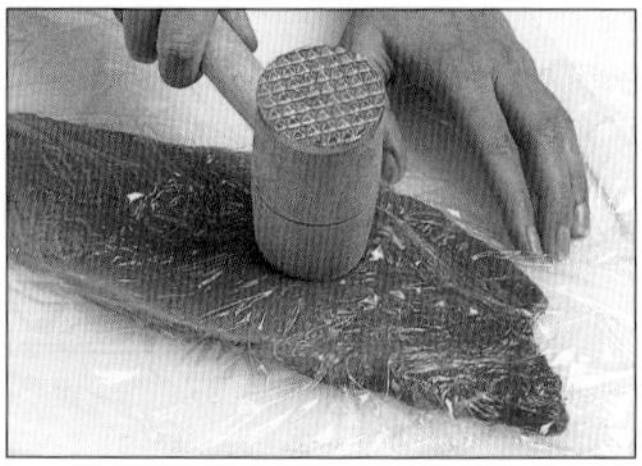

4 Use the flat side of a wooden mallet or a wooden rolling pin to carefully and evenly beat out the fillet to the required thickness for cooking.

Cutting medallions

1 Trim any fat and the thin membrane from the pork fillet, then, working from the thick end, cut off thick slices at a slight angle to make neat, round medallions of equal thickness.

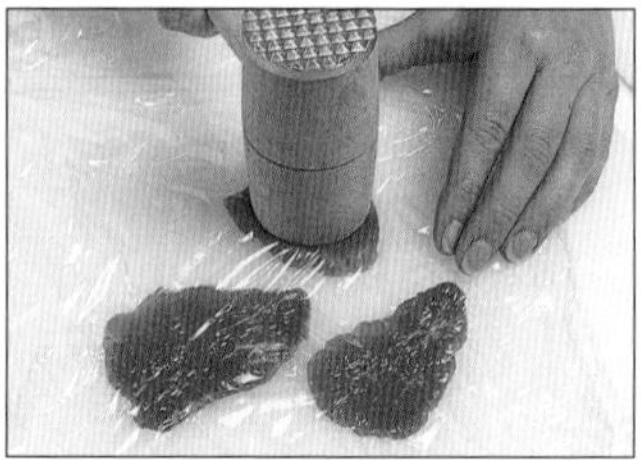

2 Place the slices between sheets of clear film and gently beat flat using the flat side of a wooden mallet or a rolling pin. Beat to the required size and thickness for cooking.

Stuffing pork chops

Pork chops cut from the loin can be boned and stuffed before they are cooked, to add extra flavour. The chops can simply be slashed horizontally from the round, meat side, but they are especially good when trimmed and boned as shown below.

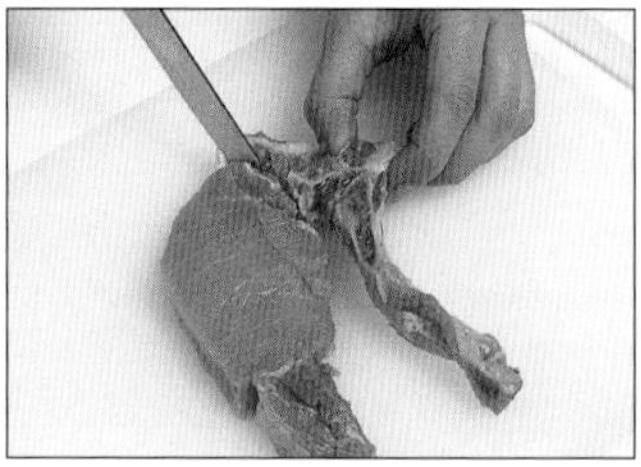

1 First trim off the fat from the chops. Use a sharp knife and work from the narrow end of the chop, carefully cutting away the rind with the band of fat. Next remove the bone from the chop. Cut the flesh along the line of the bone, keeping the knife as near as possible to it. Pull the bone away from the meat as you cut and twist the point of the knife to free the meat from the the corner of the bone.

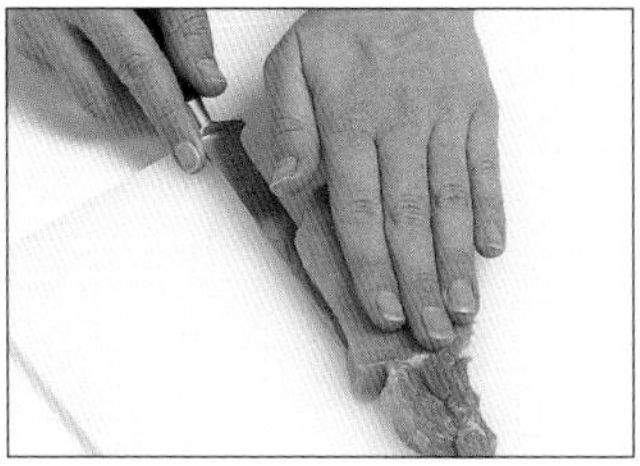

2 Cut a shallow slit about 4cm/1½in long into the rounded side of the chop, halfway up its depth. Carefully press the knife blade deeper into the chop, but not right through to the other side, and cut backwards and forwards using the point of the knife blade to hollow out a deep, wide pocket almost to the edges of the meat.

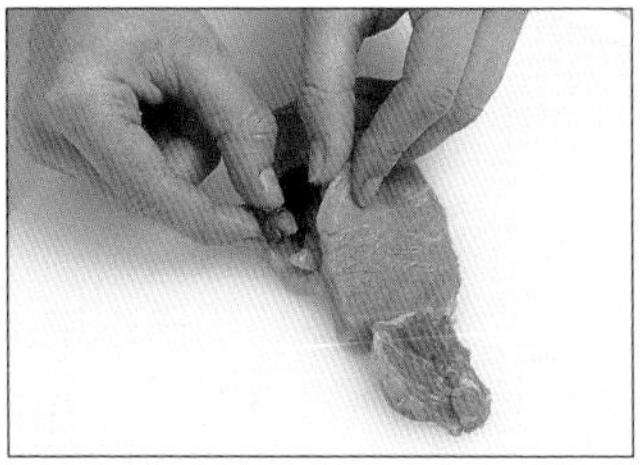

3 Open up the pocket in the chop, and push in the stuffing using your fingers or a teaspoon. Press the stuffing and meat firmly to distribute the stuffing evenly throughout the cavity.

Stuffings for pork chops
Mix the ingredients and use these stuffings as they are for a light result. Combine the stuffing ingredients with fresh white breadcrumbs for a firmer mixture.
- Shredded rocket with cored and diced eating apple. Peel the apple first, if you prefer.
- Chopped dried apricots, finely shredded spinach, chopped ham and chopped fresh parsley.
- Peeled and chopped roasted peppers with crushed garlic and finely chopped eating apples.

Boning and stuffing loin

This has two advantages: you can flavour the loin of pork with a tasty stuffing (see right for some suggested combinations) and the cooked meat is also far easier to carve.

1 Remove the skin and excess fat by cutting it off close to the meat using a large, sharp knife. Firmly pull and fold back the fat and skin as you remove them from the joint.

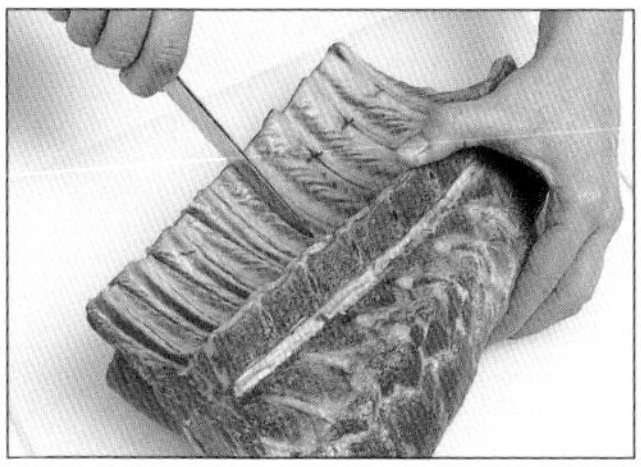

2 Hold the loin firmly in position on the board and cut between the ribs, taking care not to cut any further down into the meat than the thickness of the ribs.

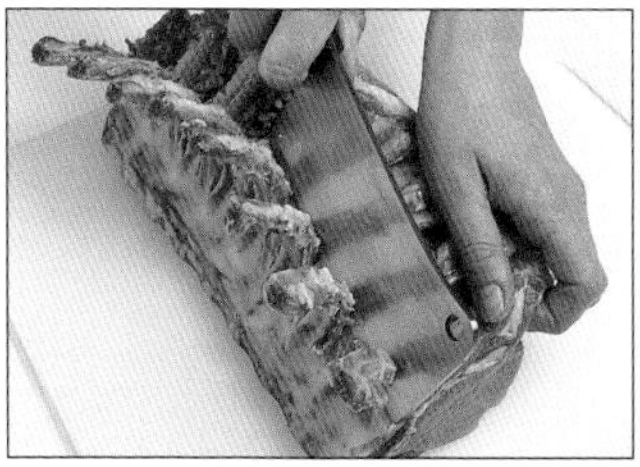

3 Using a meat cleaver or large chef's knife, carefully cut down behind the ribs, keeping the blade as near to the bones as possible.

Stuffings for loin of pork
- Diced eating apple, chopped onion, fresh white breadcrumbs and a little white wine vinegar.
- Chopped bacon, raisins, fresh white breadcrumbs and parsley.

4 Work the blade down and around the chine bone, lifting the bones away from the meat as they are cut free.

5 Open out the loin and lay it flat, then cut two slits lengthways into the meat, taking care not to cut right through. Push the stuffing into the slits that have been cut along the joint.

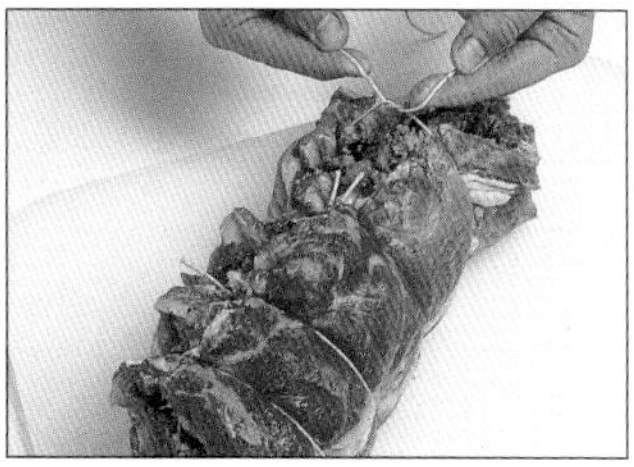

6 Roll up the loin from one long side and tie securely with fine string in several places along its length.

COOKING PORK, BACON AND GAMMON

These are tender meats and most cuts can be roasted or baked, or cooked using other dry cooking methods. Hocks and trotters are the exceptions; they should be boiled to soften the connective tissue and release the small amount of well-flavoured meat they yield. Once boiled, hocks can be trimmed, stuffed and roasted. Some cuts such as hand and spring have more sinews and benefit from slow roasting but, unlike beef, pork has no areas of tough muscle that need to be simmered for hours to become tender.

Pan-frying

This is a traditional method for cooking pork chops, steaks and escalopes. Use a heavy frying pan, preferably non-stick.

1 Dab a little sunflower oil on kitchen paper and use to grease the pan. Heat the pan until it is very hot (almost smoking). Add the meat and cook for about 3 minutes on each side.

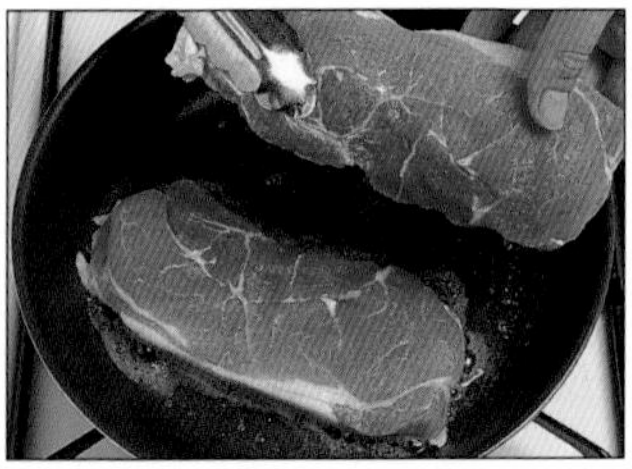

2 Alternatively pan-fry lean cuts in a mixture of butter and oil. Heat the oil in the pan before adding the butter. On its own, butter burns easily (unless it is clarified). Make sure the oil and butter are sizzling before adding the meat.

Stir-frying

This is a quick cooking method for thin, even strips or fine slices of pork. The majority of pork is suitable as long as all the sinew, membrane and fat are trimmed; prime cuts, such as fillet or escalopes cut from the leg are ideal. Most supermarkets sell pork ready cut into fine strips for stir-frying. Use a wok or a large, heavy frying pan.

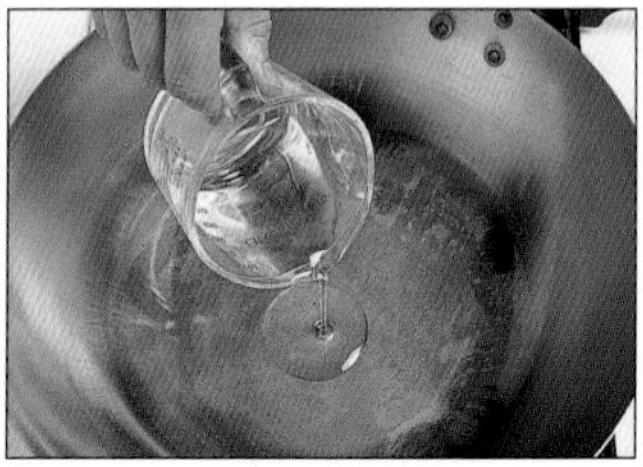

1 Heat a little oil in the wok or pan until it is smoking hot.

2 Add the pork in batches and stir-fry over a high heat. Remove the cooked meat before adding a fresh batch. If you add too many strips at once, the temperature will drop and the meat will not cook quickly enough.

Griddling

This is another method of frying, in a ridged pan. A pan with a non-stick coating is best. The fat drains off the meat into the deep ridges and the meat is seared with a lined pattern.

1 Preheat the griddle until it is almost smoking. Brush the meat very lightly with a little oil. (Sunflower oil is very mild and does not change the flavour of the meat.)

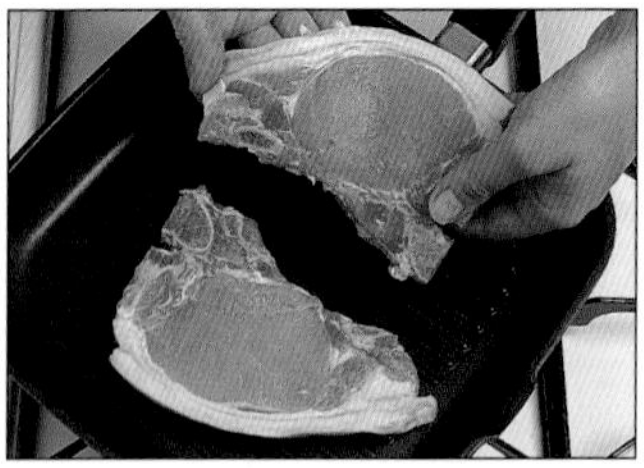

2 Add the meat to the hot griddle. Don't overfill the pan.

3 Cook for 3 minutes on each side (a pair of tongs is useful for turning chops). At the end of cooking, if the fat is not well browned, use the tongs to hold the chops with the rim of fat on the griddle. Turn the fat to brown it along its length.

Grilling

This is a quick, easy and healthy way of cooking pork chops as it allows the fat to drip away during cooking. The intense heat of the grill seals the meat quickly, keeping the juices in and giving succulent results.

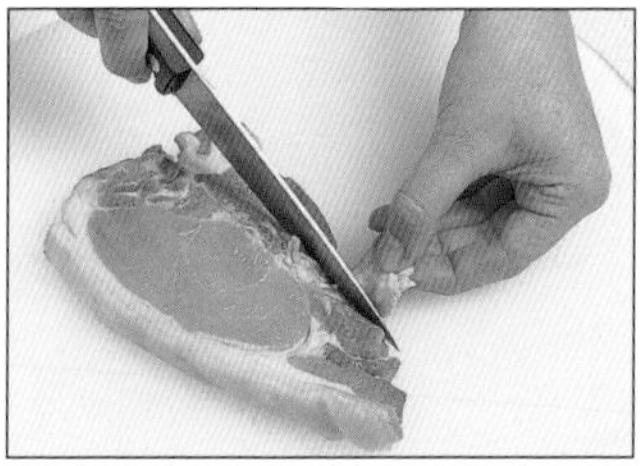

1 Preheat the grill until very hot. Using a sharp cook's knife, carefully trim off any excess fat and gristle from around the chops.

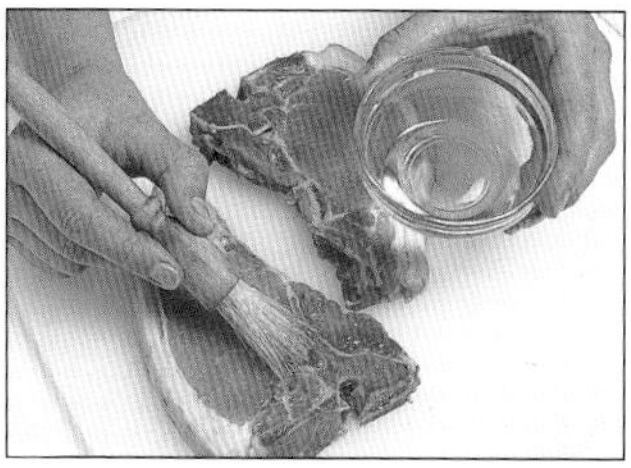

2 Brush the chops with a little sunflower oil, then place the chops on an oiled rack under the grill.

3 Cook the chops for 3 minutes on each side, or until they are well browned and cooked through.

Apple sauce
This tart sauce is the traditional accompaniment for roast pork. Cooking apples give the sauce a delicious sweet-sour flavour, which cuts the richness of roast pork.

1 Peel, core and thickly slice 450g/1lb tart cooking apples. Place the apples in a small, heavy-based saucepan and add 75g/3oz/6 tbsp demerara sugar.

2 Heat gently, stirring occasionally, until the juice runs from the apples and the sugar dissolves. Continue to cook, stirring, until the apples are soft and pulpy.

3 Beat well, then spoon into a serving dish. Cover the surface of the sauce with clear film and leave to cool before serving.

Barbecuing

The coals must be lit 30 minutes in advance and be ashen in appearance, which is when they are extremely hot but not flaming. Distribute the coals evenly before starting to cook. The cooking rack must not be too near to the coals: the heat will be too fierce and the meat will dry out and become tough. If the rack is too far from the coals, the meat will not cook properly.

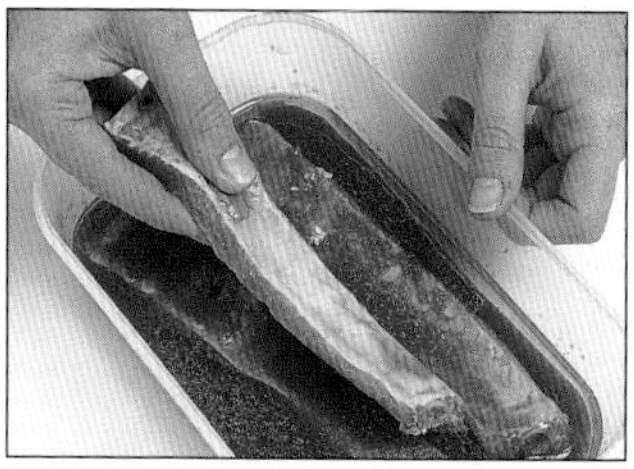

Marinating pork in a full-flavoured mixture for several hours or overnight gives the best results when barbecuing, especially with spare ribs or other cuts that are not from prime areas of the carcass. Often, spare ribs are cooked in stock until tender, then drained, cooled and marinated before being finished on the barbecue – this is practical when cooking for a crowd when there may not be as much time to attend to the cooking, making sure the ribs are turned frequently and cooked evenly.

Roasting

1 Use a meat thermometer to check the internal temperature. Insert it into the thickest part of the meat, ensuring that it does not touch any bone. Pork is done when the internal temperature of the joint reaches 80°C/176°F.

2 Cover the joint with foil and set aside for 10 minutes. This allows the meat to settle and relax, so it is easier to carve.

Roasting times for pork
For well-cooked pork allow 10 minutes at 230°C/450°F/Gas 8, then a further 30 minutes per 450g/1lb, plus an extra 30 minutes at 180°C/350°F/Gas 4.
For joints on the bone allow 35 minutes per 450g/1lb, plus an extra 35 minutes for boned and rolled joints. Weigh stuffed joints after they have been stuffed.

Pot-roasting

Since most pork is tender, this method is used for cuts that tend to have more sinew, such as knuckle. Trotters can be pot-roasted or braised.

1 First heat a little sunflower oil in a flameproof casserole until very hot.

2 Add the meat and cook over a high heat, turning frequently, until browned on all sides. Add root vegetables and a little liquid, such as stock, wine or beer. Cover and cook on the hob or in the oven until the meat is tender.

Stewing, braising and casseroling

These are all long, slow, moist methods of cooking, which can be done in the oven or on the hob. The meat is simmered gently in a flavourful liquid such as wine, water, beer or stock.

1 Trim off any excess fat and cut the meat into even-size cubes (about 2.5cm/1in).

2 The meat may be tossed in seasoned flour before cooking if a flour-thickened sauce is required. This gives a dark, rich result. Shake off any excess flour before browning the meat.

3 Heat 30ml/2 tbsp sunflower oil in a flameproof casserole. Add the meat in batches, a handful at a time, and cook over a high heat, turning frequently, until the meat is browned on all sides.

4 Use a draining spoon to remove each batch of meat from the casserole, and allow the casserole to reheat before adding the next batch. Add a little more oil if necessary before adding the meat.

5 Add any flavouring vegetables such as leeks, onions and carrots to the casserole and cook in the remaining fat and juices, stirring occasionally until softened and beginning to brown.

6 Return all the meat to the casserole and pour in the liquid. Bring to the boil on the hob, then simmer gently on the hob or transfer to a preheated oven and cook until the meat is tender. The casserole may be covered for the entire length of the cooking time or it may be uncovered towards the end of the time to allow some of the cooking liquid to evaporate to thicken the sauce.

COOKING BACON OR GAMMON

If the gammon is cured by a traditional method it may be very salty and should be soaked in cold water to cover for 12 hours. However, the majority of meat cured by modern methods is not too salty and it will be lacking in flavour if soaked. Check the information on the label or ask the butcher for details. As a guide, meats cured by traditional methods are generally available from specialist shops, high-quality butchers' or by mail order.

Boiling

Weigh the joint and calculate the cooking time at 20 minutes per 450g/1lb, plus 20 minutes.

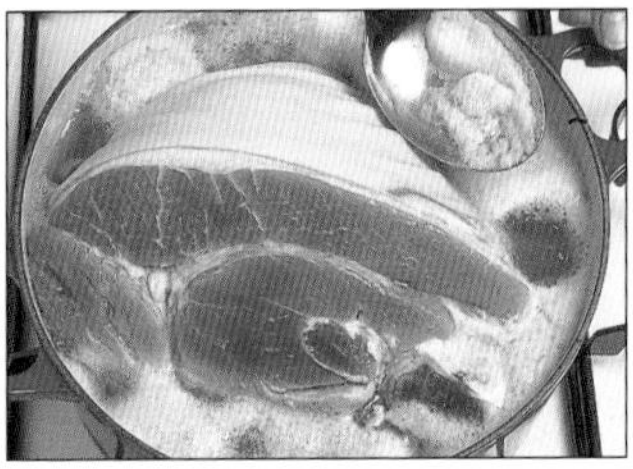

1 Put the meat in a large casserole or pan with enough fresh cold water to cover. Bring the water to the boil and skim off the scum that rises to the surface. Simmer for 30 minutes. Drain the ham and discard the water.

2 Return the drained ham to the pan and cover with fresh cold water. Start cooking again, this time adding some flavouring ingredients, such as chopped apple or onion, cider, wine or cloves depending on how you are going to serve the ham, once it is cooked.

3 Cover the casserole and simmer the ham gently for the calculated time, beginning the timing at this stage.

Removing the rind, baking and glazing

While the ham is still hot the rind will come off easily, leaving a smooth surface on the fat.

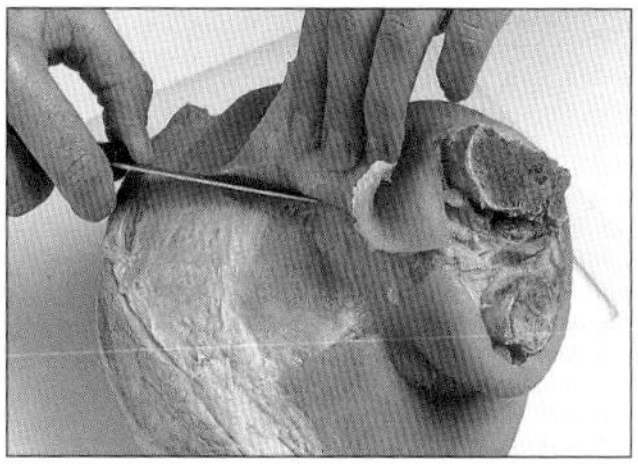

1 Leave the ham to cool slightly in its cooking stock, then drain while still hot. Use a sharp knife to loosen the rind, then fold it back as you peel it off, cutting between it and the fat. This leaves an even layer of fat on the joint.

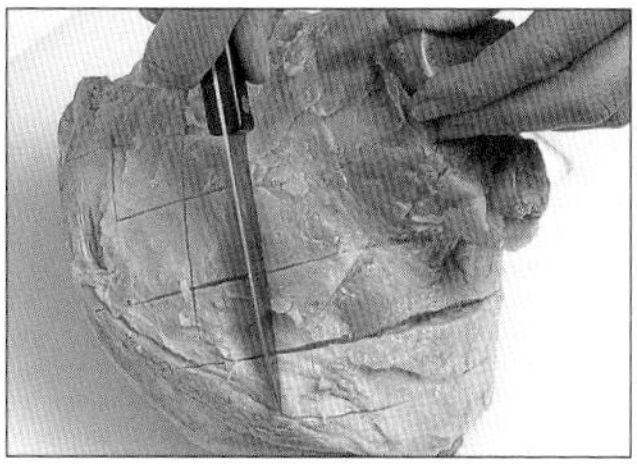

2 The fat can be finished with dried breadcrumbs or scored and studded with cloves if it is to be baked. Score deep lines across the fat, then score the fat in the opposite direction to mark out equal diamond shapes.

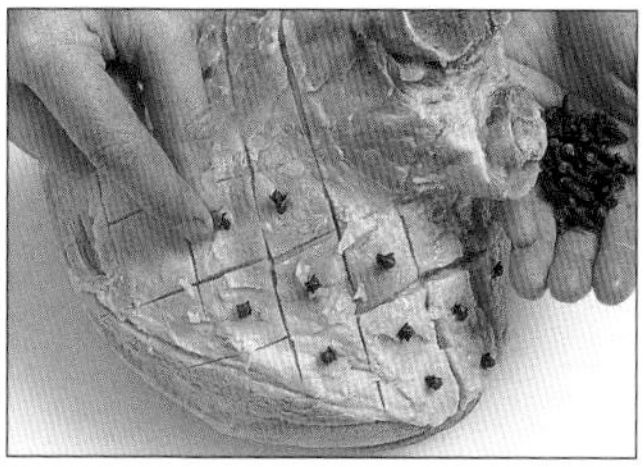

3 Stud the surface of the ham with whole cloves, placing one in the centre of each diamond of fat.

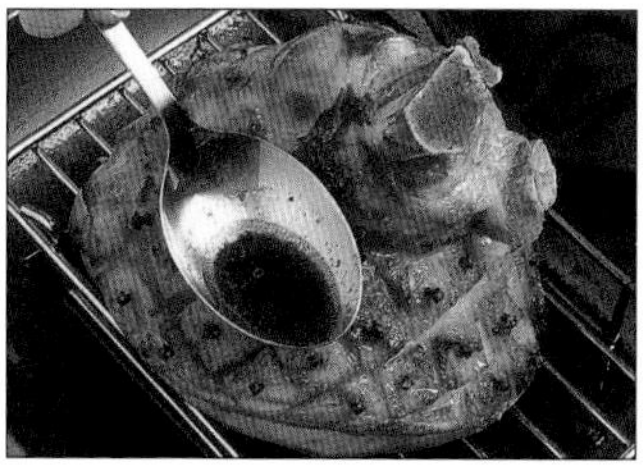

4 Sprinkle the ham generously with demerara sugar, pressing it lightly on to the fat. Bake the ham in a preheated oven at 200ºC/400ºF/Gas 6 for about 20 minutes, basting regularly, until the sugar melts and browns, giving the fat an attractive sticky glaze. The ham can be thickly sliced and served hot, or left to cool completely before slicing and serving cold.

Alternative glazing mixtures
The following ingredients all work well as glazes for baked ham as an alternative to a coating of demerara sugar: try apple juice combined with clear honey; maple syrup; soy sauce mixed with light soft brown sugar and a little medium or dry sherry; or a tangy, orange marmalade mixed with a little clear honey to sweeten it.
To ensure that the glaze gives a shiny, attractive appearance to the baked ham, baste the ham regularly during cooking with a little extra fresh glaze.

COOKING BACON

Bacon rashers can be grilled, griddled or fried. They are used in a wide variety of ways in cooking, wrapped around ingredients to flavour them and prevent them from drying out during cooking or cut up and cooked with other foods as a flavouring ingredient. When cooking whole rashers, trim off the rind first, then snip the fat at regular intervals to prevent the rashers from curling up and cooking unevenly.

Frying

This is the traditional way of cooking bacon. Grease a frying pan with a little oil on a pad of kitchen paper – there is no need to add more oil as the bacon will yield plenty of fat during cooking.

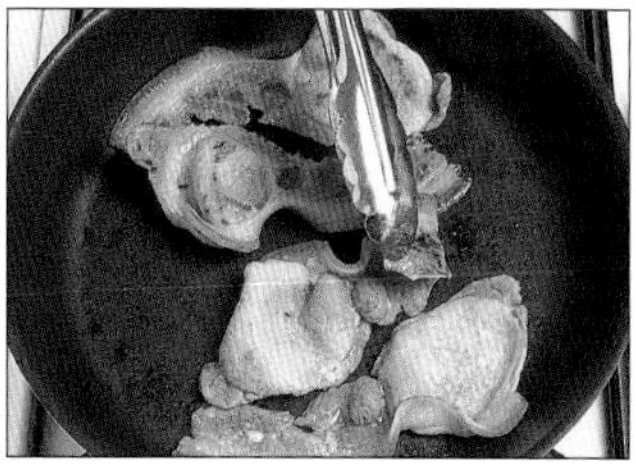

Heat the pan until hot. Lay the bacon rashers in the frying pan and fry over a medium-high heat for 4–8 minutes, turning once.

Grilling

For a crispier result, bacon is best grilled. Preheat the grill. Lay the rashers on a rack and grill for 4–8 minutes, turning once. The fat drips away from the bacon as it cooks, so this is the better method when the minimum of fat is required with the meat.

SAUSAGES AND CURED MEATS

Fresh and cured sausages are meat mixtures, usually enclosed in casings. Originally sausages were made from all the offcuts from the carcass – offal, fatty or tough scraps or irregular bits of meat. Mixed with herbs, spices, flavouring ingredients, salt and saltpetre for preservation, the meat was packed into lengths of intestine or other suitable organs, tied firmly and hung to dry and cure. These were not neat, uniformly cylindrical products even though they were, in effect, one of the earliest forms of convenience food. The casings often created sausages of different lengths, widths and shapes – haggis, the famous Scottish sausage of lamb offal packed in a sheep's stomach, is a good example.

Although casings were used for hanging and curing sausages intended for long-term storage, they were not essential. The mixture was sometimes pressed into shape, then coated with fat, flour or breadcrumbs. Faggots and French *crépinette* are both types of sausage, shaped into small balls, then wrapped in caul, the thin lacy covering of fat and membrane surrounding internal organs.

Sausages may have originated as a means of using up the remnants of the carcass after killing a pig and an essential way of preserving fresh meat, but they have moved on a long way since their humble origins.

Curing is an ancient method of preserving meat and meat products by salting and/or drying to prevent decay. Curing has long been used to preserve buffalo meat and beef. For example, *pemmican* is a dried meat mixture, prepared by Native Americans. Dried buffalo, bison or venison is pounded with fat, seasonings and dried fruit, then packed into intestines or skins made from buffalo hide. In Mexico, sun-dried strips of buffalo meat were originally known as *charqui*, which later became jerk beef or jerky.

Below: Haggis

Above: Some of the huge variety of British sausages, clockwise from top left: Beef and Guinness; pork; apple and pork chipolatas; venison; pork and beef; and Cumberland.

The three types of sausages

There are three kinds of sausage: fresh sausages; cured or dried sausages; and cooked sausages. Fresh sausages are raw and ready to cook – the British pork sausage is a good example. Cured or dried sausages are preserved sausages; salami is probably the best known of these. Cooked sausages include products for slicing, such as garlic sausage; or for spreading, such as liver sausage; plus other sausages that may be reheated or cooked again, for example Frankfurters.

Nutrition

The nutritional value of sausages varies widely, not only according to the type of sausage, but also within the different groups, because every sausage contains different ingredients or varying proportions of the same ingredients. As a rule, sausages have a high fat content compared to lean meat, poultry or offal. Cured meats have a similar nutritional value to fresh meats.

FRESH SAUSAGES

The range of fresh sausages available varies according to food fashions and their popularity. There is an incredible choice, from coarse or fine meat sausages made according to traditional recipes, to quite bizarre combinations of seasonings, fruit, nuts, vegetables and cheese added to basic meat mixtures. The selection changes according to the whim of the producer.

Classic ingredients

Fat in modest amounts is an important ingredient in traditional sausage fillings, bringing flavour and keeping the mixture moist. Fatty, flavourful cuts of pork, such as belly, are ideal for making sausages. Beef and veal are also used alone or combined with pork. Fresh bread is a traditional ingredient for binding the mixture; dried breadcrumbs and other cereals are inferior mainly because they are often added in large quantities when they absorb too much excess fat instead of allowing it to baste and flavour the meat before draining away. Inexpensive fillers are also used to make economical sausages, often with a large amount of flavouring ingredients and colouring agents added to compensate for the poor quality of the basic recipe.

Fresh or dried herbs are typical traditional seasonings, often combined with spices such as mace, nutmeg, paprika and pepper. Garlic is another important flavouring ingredient for sausages, along with onions and leeks.

Casings and coatings

Intestines (also known as chitterlings) are the traditional casings for fresh sausages, but synthetic alternatives are widely used. Skinless sausages are also available and some firmer mixtures can be coated in flour or beaten egg and fresh or dried breadcrumbs.

Buying fresh sausages

When purchasing pre-packed products, always check the information on the ingredients they contain. Check the dates by which the pack should be sold and used. Whether packed or loose, look for sausages made with a large proportion of high-quality meat (at least 70 per cent) and natural seasonings or flavouring ingredients. Look at the texture, colour and plumpness of the sausage. Avoid products that are a strange, artificial colour compared to the ingredients they contain.

Fresh sausages should look plump and well filled, but not so full that they look fit to burst. They should look moist and fresh. Reject sausages with dried patches or ends, discoloured areas or those that are wet, slimy or weeping.

Right: Italian sausages, clockwise from left: salsiccie casalinga, the large cotechino, luganeghe and salmelle.

Smell is, of course, a good indicator of freshness and it is unwise to buy from a shop or counter that smells unpleasant.

Storing fresh sausages

Leave pre-packed sausages in their wrapper and store in the coldest area of the fridge. Use within the date given on the packet. Transfer loose sausages to a suitable dish and cover with clear film or a lid, then use within two days. Be sure to keep highly aromatic sausages sealed under clear film otherwise they are likely to taint foods, such as milk, stored in the fridge.

Many types of fresh sausage freeze well, but this depends entirely on the ingredients they contain. Sausages highly flavoured with garlic should be at least double wrapped, otherwise they will taint other foods in the freezer.

TYPES OF FRESH SAUSAGE

Britain is famous for its fresh sausages: pork and beef are the main types, but chicken, venison and game sausages are all available. Italy, France and Germany all have their own specialities, but these countries are particularly known for their cured sausages. The following is an overview of the wide variety of international fresh sausages.

Left: German sausages include, clockwise from top right, Frankfurters, Bratwurst, Bockwurst and Knoblauchwurst.

Andouillette and the larger andouille These are made with pork, chitterlings, pepper, wine and onions and are sometimes smoked.

Bockwurst A smoked, German sausage that looks like a large frankfurter.

Bordeaux sausage This is a fairly small sausage that is highly seasoned.

Bratwurst A pale, fine-textured German sausage for frying. Made with pork or veal and seasoned with a combination of salt, pepper and mace.

Chipolatas Slim, fine-textured British pork sausage, traditionally high quality and a breakfast favourite. Various skinless versions are produced, which do not compare well to the traditional chipolata. A long length of chipolatas is known as a string of sausages.

Cotechino A coarse pork sausage flavoured with white wine and spices.

Cumberland sausage A coarse-textured British pork sausage seasoned with pepper. It is traditionally very long and is usually curled and cooked in a round.

Lincolnshire sausage British pork sausage flavoured with sage and thyme.

Luganeghe A thin pork sausage popular in northern Italy.

Merguez Spicy Algerian sausage made of beef and mutton and flavoured with red pepper.

Above: Toulouse sausages are flavoured with herbs and garlic.

Oxford sausage British sausage made from pork and veal.
Salchichas Small Spanish fresh sausage made with pork.
Salsiccie These Italian fresh sausages are bought ready for cooking. They are made according to local recipes, of which there are many types.
Salsiccie casalinga Meaning "home-made sausage", this is a rustic Italian sausage usually made with pure pork.
Saveloy English smoked sausage made from pork and beef; it also contains lights and a little saltpetre, which gives it a reddish hue.
Thick link sausages The standard British sausage, sometimes referred to as "links". There are traditional regional recipes made with pork or beef or a mixture of the two as well as a huge range of contemporary flavours.
Toulouse sausage This is a chubby, coarse pork sausage, which is herby, highly seasoned and flavoured with garlic.

Left: Spanish chorizo and long, thin salchichas

CURED AND SMOKED SAUSAGES

There are literally thousands of cured and smoked sausages and, between the supermarkets and independent delicatessens in larger towns and cities, the choice can be quite overwhelming.

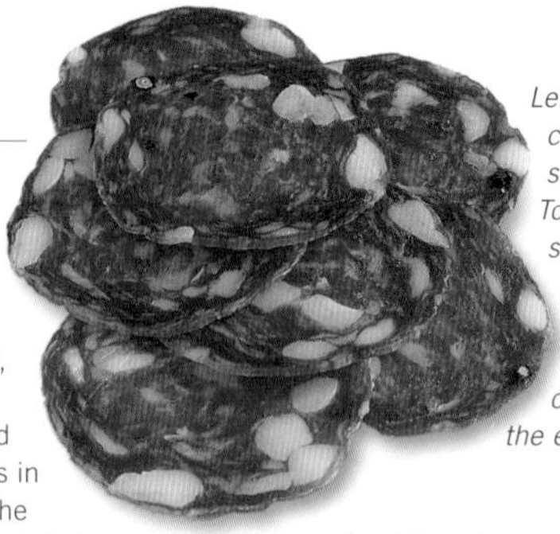

Left: Try to buy cured sausages, such as this Toscana, freshly sliced. Avoid ready-sliced sausages that look off-colour or dry around the edges.

Preserving methods

There are many different methods of curing or smoking, many still based largely on traditional principles of preservation. Salt and saltpetre (potassium nitrate) are used to preserve the meat, while spices and herbs are used for flavouring. A wide variety of other ingredients can be added for flavour, including vegetables, wine and spirits. Sugar or other sweetening may be added, particularly when the salt is used in the form of a brine rather than as a dry cure.

Above: Fuet is a thin, firm-textured Spanish cured sausage that is bought whole to slice at home.

For cured or dried sausages, the mixture is packed into the casing and then hung in an airy environment (usually cool, but sometimes hot) until dried. The middle of the sausage mixture dries more slowly than the outside and it ferments slightly. This is all part of the curing process, giving many salamis and cured sausages their slightly tangy flavour.

Smoking is an additional, traditional method of drying and imparting flavour to the cured sausages or meat. This process is carefully controlled, with specific types of wood, such as hickory, beech, juniper or oak, being used to give the sausages or cured meats their individual flavours. Sausages and meats may be lightly or heavily smoked.

Left: Felinetti is a delicately flavoured Italian salami.

Below: Milanese salami

Buying cured sausages and meats

There is such a wide range that it is difficult to make general comments. Cured sausages, and cured and cooked meats must be fresh. Avoid products that are dull or dried-out and off-colour. The cured or cooked meats or sausages should be freshly sliced for you; many supermarkets and delicatessens slice popular products in advance to save time, but check that the slices have been cut fairly recently. Meats that have been sliced for many hours will look dry, especially around the edges: reject these. Pre-packed products vary greatly in quality and it is usually easy to assess them by appearance and also by price.

Below: Kuelbasa, a strongly flavoured Polish, smooth garlic sausage

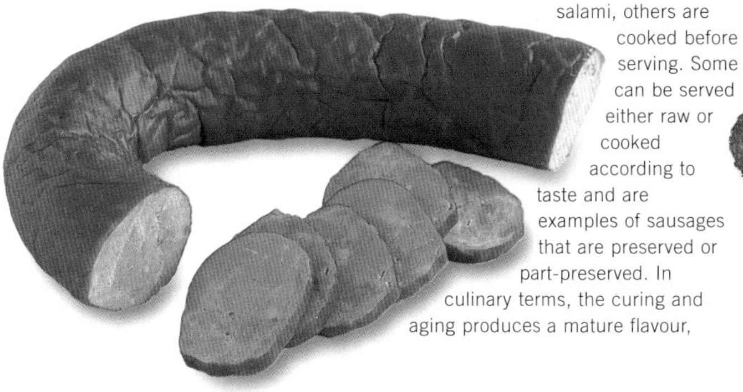

Storing cured sausages and meats

The old-fashioned larder is the ideal place for hanging whole cured meats or sausages. The fridge is the practical option for modest amounts and today's household. Leave pre-packed products in their sealed wrapping. Transfer loose, sliced meats to a plate and cover with clear film or wrap them closely in waxed paper, folding the edges together firmly to seal them, then place this in a greaseproof paper bag.

Cooked meats and sausages should be used within five days of purchase; cured sausages can be stored for longer, depending on whether they are whole or sliced and on the type. As a guide, sliced products should be used within a week.

Store all cooked and cured meats in the fridge, away from uncooked foods that may contaminate them by dripping or by direct contact.

TYPES OF CURED SAUSAGE

Some cured sausages are served finely sliced, raw, in the same way as Italian salami, others are cooked before serving. Some can be served either raw or cooked according to taste and are examples of sausages that are preserved or part-preserved. In culinary terms, the curing and aging produces a mature flavour, which is the main characteristic now that modern refrigeration and freezing are the more practical methods for long-term preservation of meat.

Left: Napoli salami

Birnenformige This is a pear-shaped German salami.

Chorizo Dry sausage made of air-cured pork (or pork and beef) and pimientos. From Andalucia, this cured sausage can be eaten raw or cooked. (Longaniza is a Portugese version of chorizo.)

Coppa di Palma Also known as coppa crudo, this is cured pork collar, which is wrapped and sliced like salami.

Above: Coppa di Palma

Danish salami Danish salamis are made from pork and veal. The popular varieties are fine and fairly soft in texture, and light rather than well matured, but are usually well seasoned with spices.

Above: Products like this sliced herb salami should be wrapped well and stored in the fridge. Eat within four or five days.

Above: Spanish lomo is made from meaty, cured pork loin.

Above: Pepperoni is a spicy Italian sausage that is often used as a topping for pizza.

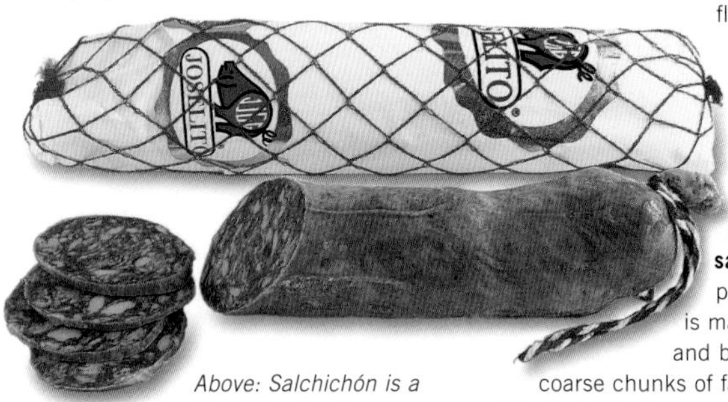

Above: Salchichón is a Spanish salami.

Below: This popular French salami is made from a finely ground mixture of pork and beef and is coated with very coarsely crushed black pepper.

Felinetti
From Parma, these are delicate small salami flavoured with white wine, peppercorns and garlic.

Fiorentino This is one of the many types of flavourful salami from Tuscany in Italy. It is made with pork and other lean meats combined with fat.

French herb salami Cured meat highly flavoured with garlic, which is dried and smoked, then finished with a thick coating of herbs.

French pepper salami This popular salami is made from pork and beef, mixed with coarse chunks of fat and seasoned with whole black peppercorns.

Fuet Spanish cured sausage, long and thin in shape, and firm in texture.

Italian salami There are dozens of different regional specialities in Italy, as almost every village and town has its favourite preparation.

Kabanos There are various types of this Polish sausage, some that are suitable for cooking and others for serving cold. They are highly spiced and smoked.

Katenrauchwurst A firm, dark German sausage, made with coarsely cut, smoked pork.

Knoblauchwurst This German garlic sausage can be either poached or grilled.

Kuelbasa Made with ground pork and beef, this Polish sausage is well flavoured with garlic and seasoning.

Lomo Cured Spanish sausage made from pork loin.

Milanese salami Made with lean pork and beef, and pork fat, this is a mild Italian salami, flavoured with white wine, pepper and garlic.

Napoli Very hot Italian salami made with pork and beef seasoned with black and red pepper.

Pepperoni Made from coarsely chopped pork and beef, this Italian cured sausage is highly seasoned with ground red pepper and other spices.

Salchichón A cured sausage or salami from Spain.

Toscana A fairly coarse Italian salami seasoned with peppercorns.

TYPES OF COOKED SAUSAGE

These are ready to eat cold, sliced or spread, or they may be reheated or cooked before serving. In some cases, the first cooking is considered to be a process of blanching or light poaching and the sausage would never be served without further cooking: black pudding is a good example. Ham sausage, liver sausage and garlic sausage are examples of popular types of cooked sausages that are ready to serve and there are many international versions of these.

Above: Bierschinken

Bierschinken A pork and ham sausage with pistachio nuts.

Bierwurst Pork and beef sausage, which is usually quite spicy and well flavoured with garlic.

Black pudding This is a British blood sausage that is usually highly spiced

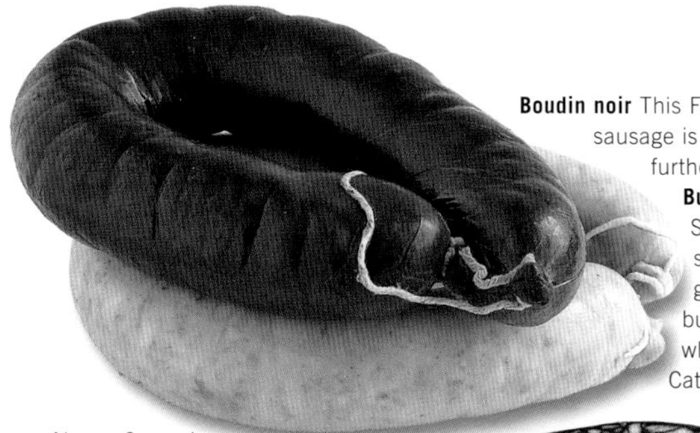

Above: Several countries make black and white puddings; these are butifarra negra and bianca from Spain.

and dotted with fat. There are many variations. This is not strictly a fresh sausage, as it is bought poached, but it is sliced and cooked before serving.

Bockwurst A delicate white sausage made with pork and veal, chives, parsley, milk and eggs.

Boudin blanc French white pudding, made from chicken, veal, rabbit and/or pork, enriched with cream and white wine according to the particular recipe.

Above: Kalbfleischwurst

Above: Mortadella is studded with chunks of fat and pistachio nuts.

Boudin noir This French blood sausage is poached ready for further cooking.

Butifarra bianca Spanish poached sausage. Although grouped with butifarra negra, this white sausage from Catalan is made from pork.

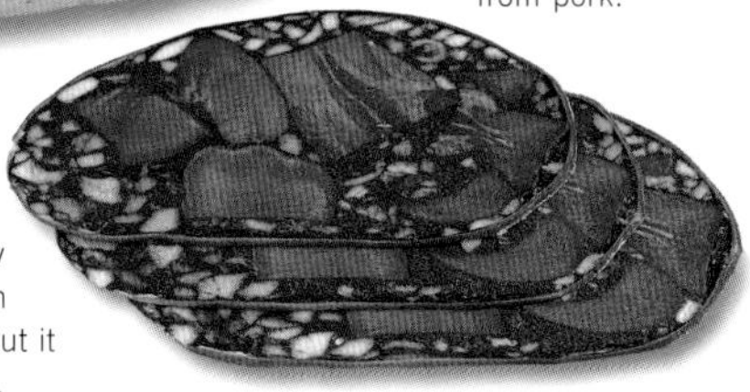

Above: Zungenwurst

Butifarra negra Spanish blood sausage, which is similar to morcilla.

Crépinette This French offal mixture is shaped into small sausages or balls and wrapped in caul fat. They are similar to British faggots. Sold cooked ready for reheating or further cooking.

Extrawurst Large, pale pink, smooth pork and beef sausage which slices easily.

Faggots A British speciality, made from offal and highly seasoned. Traditionally wrapped in caul fat and sold cooked, ready for frying or poaching.

Frankfurter Originally this was a cold smoked sausage made with pork and salted bacon fat, but the name has since been adopted, particularly in north America, for any cooked sausage with a smoky flavour that is suitable for making hot dogs.

Haggis A Scottish sausage of lamb and lamb's offal, highly spiced and bound together with oatmeal or other cereal, is traditionally packed into a cleaned and blanched sheep's stomach ready for lengthy boiling. Nowadays haggis is generally sold cooked, ready for further cooking or reheating.

Kalbfleischwurst Pale pink, very fine, large veal sausage.

Knoblauchwurst A sausage made from pork, peppers and spices, strongly flavoured with garlic.

Mettwurst Pork and beef sausage, which can be firm enough to slice or soft enough to spread and may be either coarse or smooth.

Morcilla A blood sausage, which is usually highly seasoned and spicy.

Mortadella A large, smooth, cooked sausage made with pork and flavoured with garlic. Studded with pistachio nuts and pieces of fat.

Pfeffer plockwurst A square sausage coated with black pepper.

Presskopf Sausage made with pork, veal and beef.

Schinken jagdwurst Made from minced pork with diced pork fat and ham.

Schinken kalbfleischwurst Made from minced pork, beef and veal, with pieces of ham and a little garlic.

Zungenwurst Tongue sausage, often spicy and coarse-textured.

Chinese sausages and cured meats

Wind-dried Chinese sausages are shrunken, hard and wrinkled. They are made with pork and/or offal, flavoured with spices and are slightly sweet. Most large Chinese supermarkets offer a selection, some strung and hanging loose, others in shrink-wrapped packs. The sausages vary in colour from pink-red to dark brown-red and the latter tend to be made with a high percentage of offal. Check the ingredients list or go by colour, selecting the paler sausages for a light, meaty flavour or the dark colour for a distinct offal taste. The sausages are steamed for 30–45 minutes, until they are plump and tender, then sliced at a slant and served as part of a selection of cooked wind-dried foods or used in a variety of dishes. They may be stir-fried or added to braised dishes.

As well as sausages, meats and poultry are cured and dried, including pork and the rather spectacular-looking ducks, that are opened out and flattened.

TYPES OF CURED MEAT

Pork is a main ingredient for cured meat products, and is also used to make raw and cooked hams (see section on basic types of ham in previous chapter). However, there are other cured meats made using pork and meats, such as beef, venison and buffalo. The following is a small selection of the international types that are available.

Biltong Traditional African air-dried and smoked strips of beef, buffalo, antelope, venison or ostrich.

Bresaola Italian beef tenderloin, aged for a couple of months until it is a deep, rich, red colour. Good served sliced, with extra virgin olive oil, lemon juice and chopped parsley.

Bündnerfleisch Also called Bindenfleisch, this is the Swiss equivalent to bresaola. It is traditionally made only in the winter and is flavoured with white wine and treated with salt, herbs and onion before being air-dried.

Corned beef Originally derived from the word corns, the grains of salt that are used in brine prepared for salting beef, this is the north American term for salt beef or pickled beef. In Britain, the term is used exclusively for canned salt beef, which is compressed pieces of cured, cooked meat. Corned beef is generally thinly sliced and served in sandwiches or salads, but it can also be chopped and pan-fried with chunks of cooked potato to make corned beef hash.

Ox tongue Sold cooked and pressed as a cold meat. This is available smoked, corned or pickled.

Above: Corned beef

Above: Pastrami is a deep red, dry-cured and smoked beef.

Pastrami This is a spiced, smoked beef, which is eaten either hot or cold. Although the name originates from the Romanian *pastrama* (from the verb *pastra*, which means to preserve), the word is Yiddish. It is famously eaten as pastrami on rye – that is, as a sandwich made with rye bread, particularly in the many Jewish delicatessens and sandwich bars of New York.

Salt beef Beef, usually brisket or silverside, which is soaked in brine with seasonings and spices. This is available uncooked for boiling and serving hot, or sold cooked with other cold meats on deli counters. Salt beef sandwiches made with rye bread or bagels and dill pickles are a staple part of Jewish-American delicatessen cuisine.

Smoked pork loin This is a small, round nugget of lean pork, which resembles a neat sausage.

Below: Bresaola is served sliced, with olive oil and lemon juice.

Above: Salt beef

Above: Biltong

MAKING SAUSAGES

The advantage of making sausages is that you can select high-quality meat, control the quantity of fat added and include the most wonderful mix of flavouring ingredients and seasonings (see below). Special sausage-filling equipment and machines are available, but there is no need for special utensils. Casings can be natural or synthetic and they are available from good butchers. Natural casings come salted and have to be soaked to remove excess salt and become soft.

The important point to remember when making sausages is not to overfill the casings. If there is too much mixture in the casing, the sausage cannot be twisted and separated to make individual sausages. Remember that overfilled casings will burst as the content expands during cooking.

Remember to allow enough empty casing for tying into a knot (or securing with string) before squeezing in the filling, and leave a similar length of empty casing at the end.

To make a good sausage, use good-quality ingredients. Minced pork is the traditional meat, but you can use beef, lamb or venison, as well as chicken, turkey and duck. Flavour with aromatic fresh or dried herbs and spices.

1 Soak the sausage casings in cold water for 1–2 hours. Drain and rinse the casings several times, then place in cold water until required.

2 Fit a piping bag with a large, plain nozzle and fill with the mixture. Thread the casing on to the nozzle, pushing it as far up as possible.

3 When you cannot push any more of the casing up on to the nozzle, cut and twist or knot the end. Holding the casing on to the nozzle, squeeze the filling from the bag, allowing the casing to slide off the nozzle as it is filled.

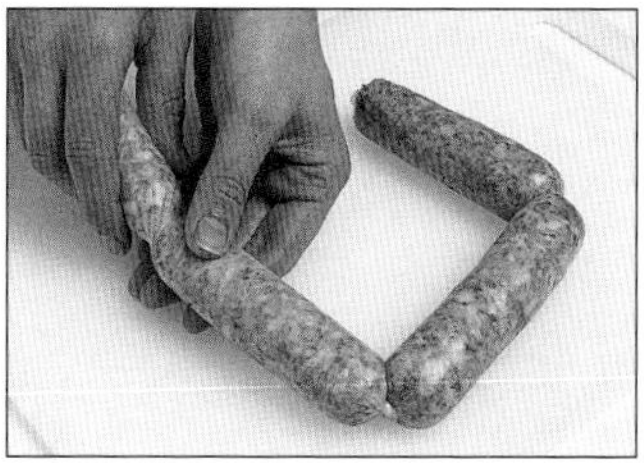

4 When the sausage casing is full, tie the end securely to prevent the filling from escaping, then knot the other end of the casing and twist the sausage into even-size links.

COOKING SAUSAGES

The golden rule when cooking sausages is to cook them gently and thoroughly, allowing plenty of time for them to cook right through and become crisp and golden outside. Cook sausages too fiercely and the skins will split or burst, or they will overcook outside before the middle is done.

Sausages that are made with natural casings do not need to be pricked before cooking as the casings allow fat and juices to escape. Sausages made with synthetic casings should be lightly pricked before cooking, otherwise they may burst. Most sausages can be grilled, barbecued or fried, while others, such as the Frankfurter and Bockwurst are poached. Sausages can also be added to stews or casseroles, or braised.

Grilling

Place the sausages on a rack in a grill pan and cook well away from the heat source under a preheated grill. Cook thick sausages for about 10 minutes, turning frequently, until evenly browned.

Frying

Pour a little oil into a frying pan, then add the sausages and cook over a low to moderate heat. Allow plenty of time for the sausages to cook through and brown evenly, turning them occasionally.

Poaching

French andouille and German sausages such as Bockwurst and Frankfurters are cooked by poaching in water.

Add the sausages to a pan of hot water. Cover and simmer for about 5 minutes, depending on the size and type.

OFFAL

This is the term for the offcuts from the carcass, including the edible internal organs, tail, feet and head parts. In everyday use, the term usually refers to the internal organs, such as liver, kidneys, tripe, heart and sweetbreads. Unlike meat, which has to be hung and matured before use, offal does not keep well and it has to be cooked or processed quickly. Before modern refrigeration and freezing, when an animal was slaughtered the entire carcass had to be processed promptly. The offal had to be removed, cleaned and cooked or preserved in some way. Intestines – specifically chitterlings (the small intestine) – from a pig were used not only as a casing for sausages, but also as part of the filling. Salting or curing and drying were methods used to preserve the chitterlings on their own, as well as filled sausages and meat.

Pâtés and terrines were also a means of short-term preservation: the highly seasoned offal mixture was cooked in a closed dish and air was excluded by covering the surface of the mixture with a layer of fat. Fat was an important ingredient for preserving cooked meat products, acting as a seal or barrier to prevent contamination.

Below: Fine-textured calf's liver (top) has a more delicate flavour than the more economical lamb's liver.

Humble or prized offerings

In Western supermarkets, where food has been sanitized and segregated from any grubby or unpleasant origins, internal organs that look unattractive are rarely displayed. Many people dislike the idea of eating organs such as head, ears, eyes or testicles, and prefer to avoid any other than neatly sliced or diced offal. In other parts of the world, not only is offal an essential food in less affluent societies, but the smaller parts can also be prized – eyes and testicles are the classic examples that are anathema to some, but considered delicacies by others. The eyes from a sheep's head are savoured in the Middle East, and by tradition are offered to the guest of honour at a meal.

In fact, the majority of offal is rich and highly flavoured, and valued in dishes, such as steak and kidney pie or pâté. Liver and kidney are the most widely used; sweetbreads, brains and heart are prepared by many traditional methods; and tripe is cooked in simple or spiced dishes loved by those who appreciate its texture and flavour. The distinctive flavour and texture of offal are often due to the high blood content of the organs or the functions they perform in the living animals, and whereas to some offal is a gourmet treat, to others it is completely unappetizing.

Nutrition

The nutritive value depends on the specific type of offal, but it is generally a good source of animal protein, while being lean and lower in fat than meat. Liver and kidney are rich sources of iron, vitamin A and some of the B complex vitamins, including folic acid.

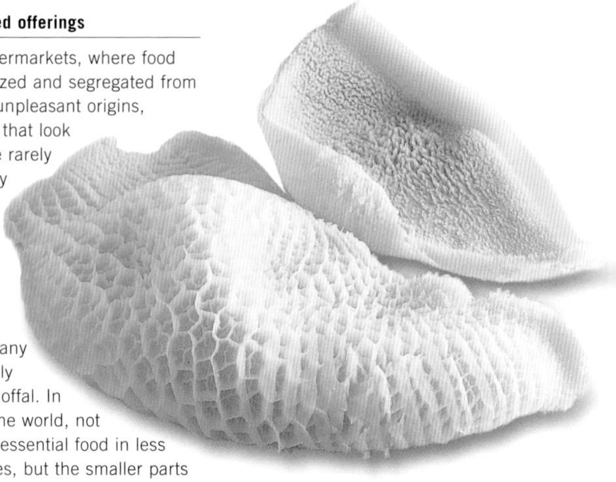

Above: The unusual honeycomb texture of tripe means that, like other types of offal, it is an acquired taste.

Buying

Offal should always be fresh. Check sell-by dates on pre-packed offal and buy from a supermarket where the offal is neatly displayed in uncluttered fridges that are not overfilled. When buying offal loose from a butcher, it should always look fresh, moist and clean, with an even colour and texture. Whole organs or cuts should not be damaged or tatty and they should not be sitting in puddles of blood. Offal should always smell fresh – never buy offal that has a pronounced, stale odour. Buy only from a butcher who clearly stores, prepares and displays offal in hygienic, cold conditions. The seller should have a speedy turnover.

Foie gras

In France, where foie gras is a speciality, varieties of goose are bred especially for this purpose. Fattened goose liver is pale and creamy in texture. It tastes wonderful and is considered a great delicacy by many gourmets. However, the way it is produced makes it a controversial ingredient in some parts of the world.

Storing

Always leave sealed, pre-packed offal in its container and use it by the date given on the packet. Transfer offal bought loose to a deep dish and cover it tightly with clear film or a close-fitting lid. Use loose offal within 24 hours of purchase. Store the offal in the fridge, in the coldest part (a low shelf in a larder fridge) and where any drips which may escape will not contaminate other foods.

Above: Ox (top) and veal kidneys

THE DIFFERENT TYPES OF OFFAL

Liver

The fine, close texture and pronounced, fairly "dry" flavour of liver makes it probably the most popular and versatile of offal. Calf's liver has the finest texture and lightest flavour. It is comparatively expensive and regarded as a prime cut in Western cooking. Lamb's liver also has a fairly mild flavour. It is cheap, readily available and widely used as a main ingredient in its own right as well as for pâtés. Pig's and ox liver are strong in flavour and they have a coarser texture. Pig's liver is a particularly good ingredient for rich pâtés. Chicken, turkey and duck livers are similar in size, flavour and texture. They are significantly lighter in flavour, fine-textured and rich, and are more versatile than the other types of liver. Goose liver is larger and paler in colour (see box on *foie gras*, left).

*Above, clockwise from top left: chicken, goose (*foie gras*), turkey and duck livers*

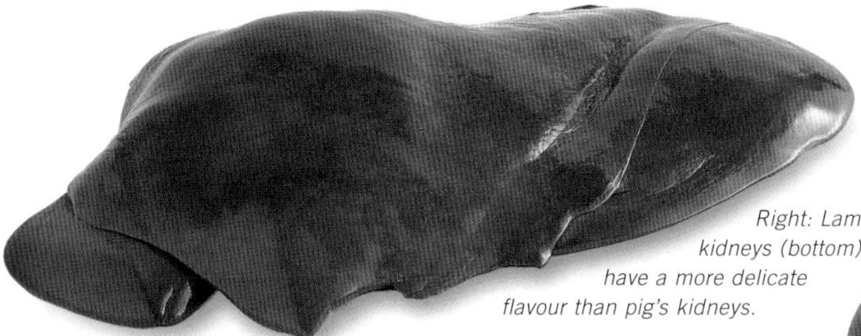

Above: Ox liver

Right: Lamb's kidneys (bottom) have a more delicate flavour than pig's kidneys.

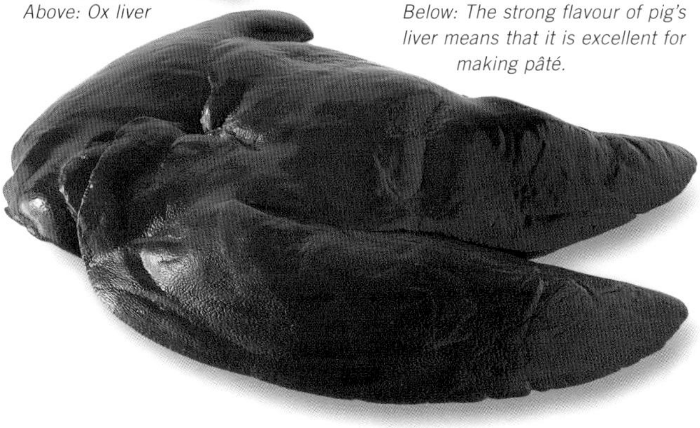

Below: The strong flavour of pig's liver means that it is excellent for making pâté.

Kidney

This type of offal has a distinctive taste that varies according to type. Lamb's kidneys are small, tender and comparatively delicate in flavour. They are often cooked halved or whole. Veal kidneys are very tender. Ox kidney is strongly flavoured and firm. It is the classic ingredient for steak and kidney pie (although lamb's kidneys are often used for a lighter flavour). Pig's kidney, which has a strong, robust flavour, is used in terrines and French *charcuterie*.

Above: Oxtail is generally sold cut into thick pieces ready for braising or stewing.

Tail

Oxtail has a fairly large amount of creamy-white fat covering a modest amount of dark red meat, with about an equal proportion of meat to bone. It requires long, moist cooking. Oxtail has a rich flavour.

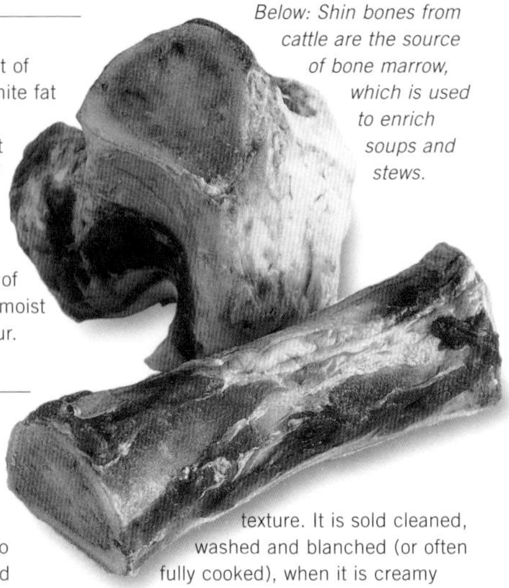

Below: Shin bones from cattle are the source of bone marrow, which is used to enrich soups and stews.

Tongue

Ox tongue is sold fresh or cured in brine; veal tongue is popular in France. A large tongue (usually ox) is part-boiled so that the thick layer of skin can be removed, then the remaining, trimmed, meat requires lengthy cooking until tender. It can be used in hot dishes or pressed and served as a cold meat (a particular British speciality). Small lamb's tongues can be casseroled.

Below, from top: Ox, veal and lamb tongues

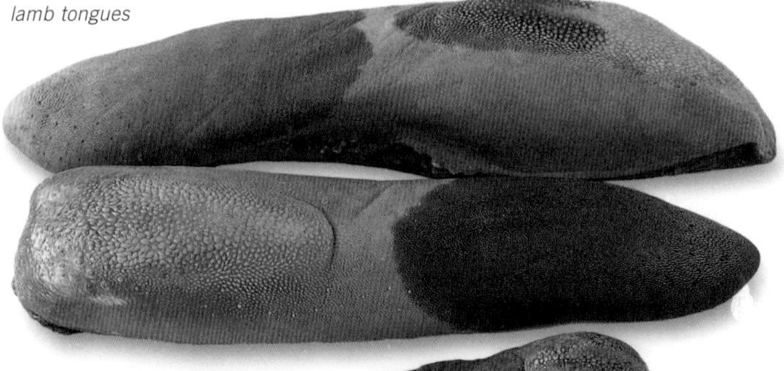

Bone marrow

Found in hollow bones, particularly shin bones, from cow or calf carcasses, this pale, fatty substance has a full flavour. When poached, marrow can be scooped out and used to enrich soups, stews, sauces and risottos. It is also served hot as a spread or as a topping for canapés. Bone marrow is a prized part of the Italian veal casserole *osso bucco,* in which slices of veal are cooked on the bone.

Below: Pressed ox tongue

Tripe

This comes from the cow's stomach. Tripe from the first stomach (the rumen) is plain in texture, but that from the second stomach (the reticulum) has the typical honeycomb texture. It is sold cleaned, washed and blanched (or often fully cooked), when it is creamy white in colour. It is easily digestible and very nutritious. Tripe has a distinctive flavour – not strong in the same way as liver or kidney, but pronounced and determined to dominate even spicy sauces. It is usually stewed, either with onions in milk to make a pale *blanquette* or in a spicy tomato sauce with onions and dried mushrooms in Polish style.

Head

Brains and tongue are treated as separate types of offal from the head. Sheep's head is a traditional ingredient for making broth or soup all over Europe. Calf's and pig's heads are traditionally used for making brawn. The heads are boiled until the meat is falling off the bone. The stock is then strained, the meat picked over, chopped, then set in the broth.

A pig's head can be ordered and the butcher will chop it into chunks that are not too ghastly for the squeamish to handle. The meat from pig's head makes delicious brawn or if potted to a firmer pâté, a dish known as pork cheese. The cheek when cured as a ham is known as a bath chap: a small ham covered with fat and coated with breadcrumbs; these are available from some traditional butchers.

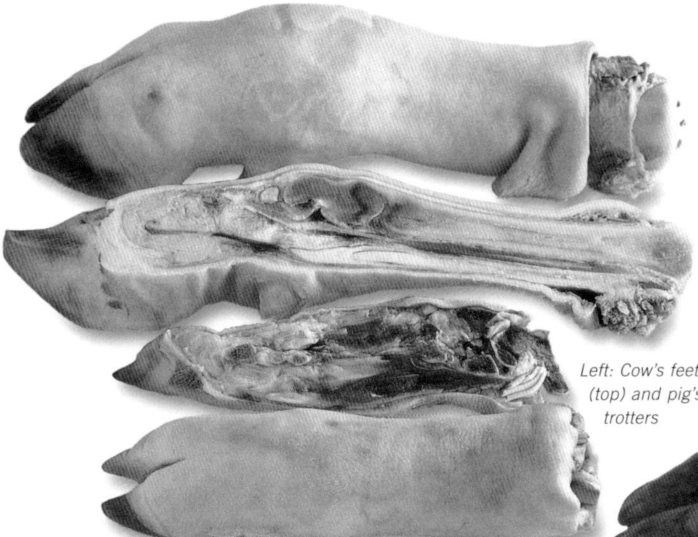

Left: Cow's feet (top) and pig's trotters

Sweetbreads

The thymus glands taken from the neck and heart of young animals, such as calves and lambs. Pink and delicate with a tender, meaty texture when cooked by braising or boiling, they are often pressed and fried after blanching.

Brains

Lamb and veal brains are pale pink and delicate. Once rinsed, soaked and blanched they can be fried or braised.

Trotters and feet

Pig's trotters and calf's feet can be bought whole or split in half. They are boiled to make stocks that set firmly when cold. They can also be used to enrich stews or soups; cooked and jellied, then served cold; or grilled and served with a sauce.

Right: Lights are popular in many countries, but in Britain and America they are used to make pet food.

Above: Calf's and lamb's sweetbreads

Above: Tiny chicken hearts

Chitterlings

These are pig's intestines used as sausage casings or chopped up as part of the filling. They can also be blanched and grilled or fried. Chitterlings are particularly popular in France, Greece and North America.

Right, clockwise from top: Ox, pig and lamb hearts are extremely nutritious, but need long, slow cooking.

Lights

These are lungs of an animal. In Britain and America they are usually sold for pet food, but they are used in traditional dishes in some countries. Lamb or pork lights may be served with a piquant sauce, added to stews or used for making pork *pâté de foie*.

Heart

This is nutritious and with very little waste. Lamb heart is the most tender and lightest in flavour. Pork or pig's heart is larger and slightly coarser; beef or ox heart is big but not very tender, while chicken heart is very small and usually sold as part of the giblets with a cleaned bird. All need long, slow cooking and careful trimming.

PREPARING AND COOKING OFFAL

Offal is generally easy to prepare and cook. The majority of types are sold trimmed and ready to prepare and cook, and some, such as tripe, are sold blanched or completely cooked.

Offal can be cooked in a variety of ways: poaching suits many cuts, especially tongue and brains, robust cuts such as heart can be braised, while liver, kidneys and sweetbreads are good pan-fried in butter.

Trimming liver

The majority of liver is sold trimmed and ready to cook, but it is still a good idea to check for any stray tubes or areas of skin before cooking.

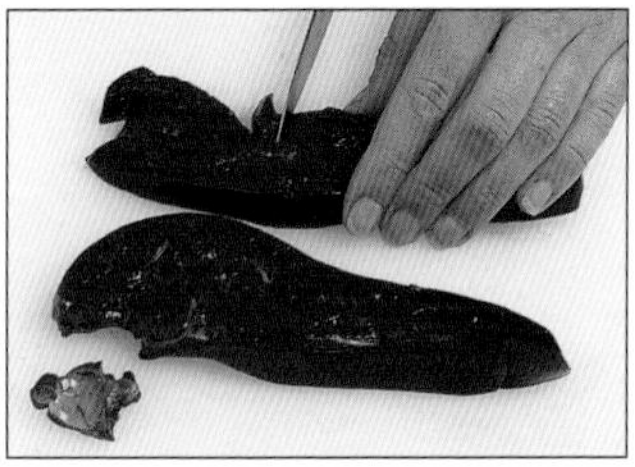

1 Trim off any patches of pale gristle or small pieces of tube that may still be attached. Use a small, pointed knife to cut out the trimmings.

2 A fine skin or membrane sometimes remains on the surface of the liver, often in patches where it has not been thoroughly trimmed. Rub your fingertips over the liver to feel the skin, then gently pull any excess away. For pan-frying, cut the liver into neat, even slices, about 1 cm/½in thick. Cut slightly thicker slices for grilling.

Frying liver

Liver should be cooked through but it should be still slightly pink (not rare) in the middle, when it will still be tender. If the liver is cooked over a medium heat for too long, it will become tough and dry out before it browns.

Melt a little butter in a heavy frying pan and add the liver when the butter is foaming and hot. Cook briefly over a fairly high heat until it is browned underneath, then, using tongs, turn the liver over and cook the slices on the second side. If you prefer to grill liver, brush it with a little melted butter or vegetable oil and cook under a hot grill for 3–4 minutes on each side.

Trimming kidneys

Kidneys are surrounded by a pad of firm, creamy fat, which is usually removed before they are sold. (The fat around ox kidneys is used for suet.)

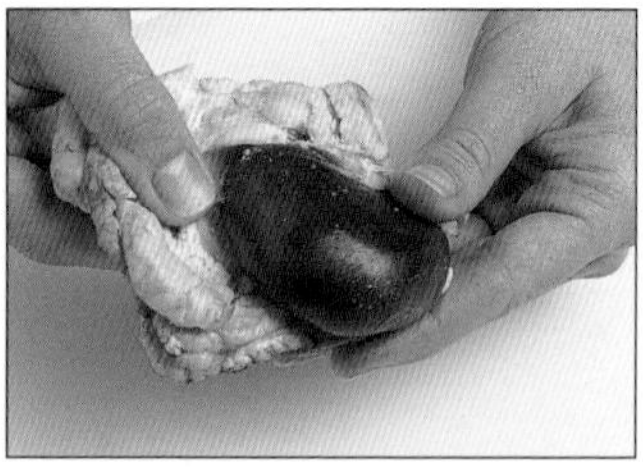

1 If the fat is still in place, snip or cut it, then slide and pull it away from around the kidney. Carefully peel off the thin membrane covering the kidney. A white core of membrane and tubes lies in the middle of the kidney (it looks like a solid fatty lump) and this should be removed before cooking.

2 Cut the kidney in half using a sharp knife – here a lamb's kidney is being split lengthways.

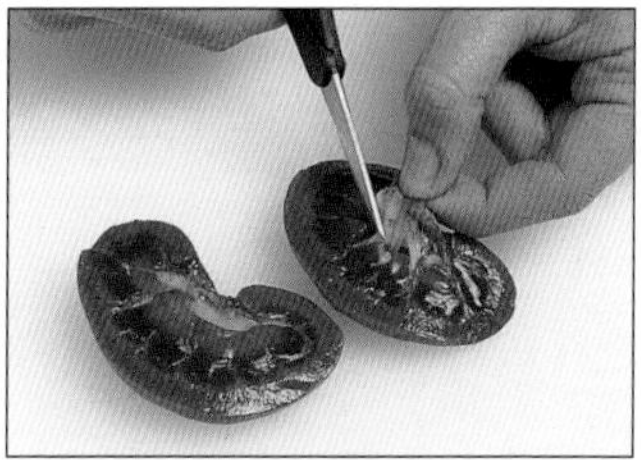

3 Use sharp kitchen scissors to snip out the tubes and pale core. If they are not removed, these are unpleasant and tough in the cooked kidney.

Cooking kidneys

Lamb's kidneys are tender and they cook quickly. Griddling is a good alternative to pan-frying or grilling. Heat the griddle until very hot, then add a little butter or oil and heat it again for a few seconds.

Lay the halved kidneys on the griddle, cut-sides down and cook until browned and firm underneath. Turn and cook the second side until browned. The kidneys feel just firm when cooked.

Cooking tongue

Ox tongue is sold cleaned and ready to cook, usually with the root trimmed off the end.

1 Place the tongue in a large saucepan with cold water to cover. Add flavouring ingredients such as carrot, celery, onion and a bouquet garni of powerful, aromatic herbs such as sage, thyme, bay leaves and rosemary.

2 Bring slowly to the boil, skim off any surface scum, then reduce the heat so that the water simmers steadily. At this stage, spices, such as peppercorns, cloves, coriander seeds and juniper berries can be added. Cover and simmer for 3–4 hours, or until the meat is tender. Leave the tongue to cool in its cooking liquid until it is just cool enough to handle.

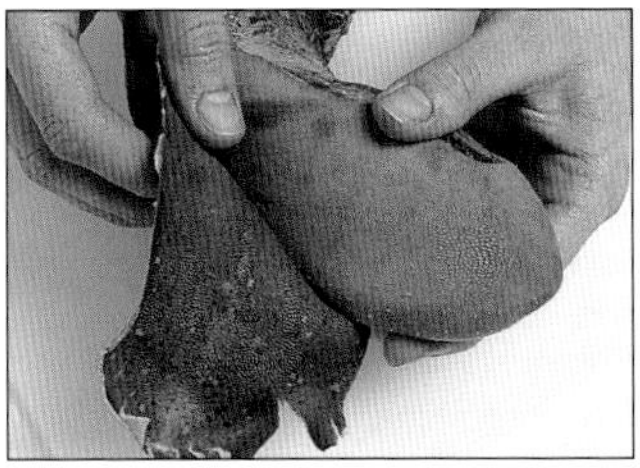

3 Drain the tongue and discard the cooking liquid. Cut away any tough, white gristle at the wide end of the toungue, if necessary (this root may already have been removed). Then peel off the thick skin. The tongue is then ready for cutting up and reheating in a sauce or it can be curled into a small round dish or tin and weighted, then allowed to cool completely.

4 Pressed tongue should be unmoulded and sliced thinly, then it can be served in the same way as cooked ham. It is excellent with mustard or pickles.

Pot-roasting trotters

Trotters are sold cleaned and ready for cooking. Rinse and dry them, then singe off any hairs by going over the surface of the skin with a lighted taper or match. Heat a little oil in a large, flameproof casserole and brown the trotters on all sides. Remove them from the casserole and set aside. Add thickly sliced onions, carrots, peeled garlic cloves and herbs, such as bay leaves, sage and thyme, to the casserole, then replace the trotters on the bed of vegetables and herbs. Pour in enough water, stock or wine (or a mixture) to cover the vegetables. Cover and cook in the oven at 180°C/350°F/Gas 4 for about 2 hours, turning the trotters occasionally, or until they are golden brown and tender.

Extracting marrow from bones

Ask the butcher to saw the marrow-bones into pieces about 7.5cm/3in long. To serve the bone marrow as a starter or a spread for toast, brush the bones with oil and roast at 200°C/400°F/Gas 6 for 45 minutes, or until well browned. The bones may also be roasted at the same time as a joint of meat.

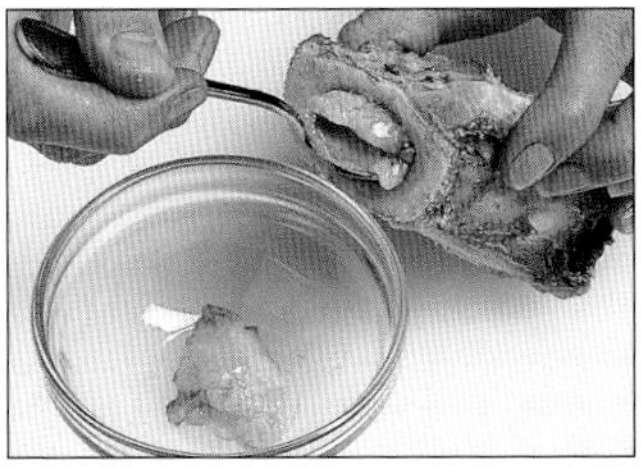

Alternatively, poach the bones in a large pan of salted boiling water for about 3 minutes to soften the marrow, then drain well and use a teaspoon to scoop out the marrow. Poached bone marrow can be used to enrich stock, sauce or risotto, or it can be seasoned and served as a spread.

Preparing sweetbreads

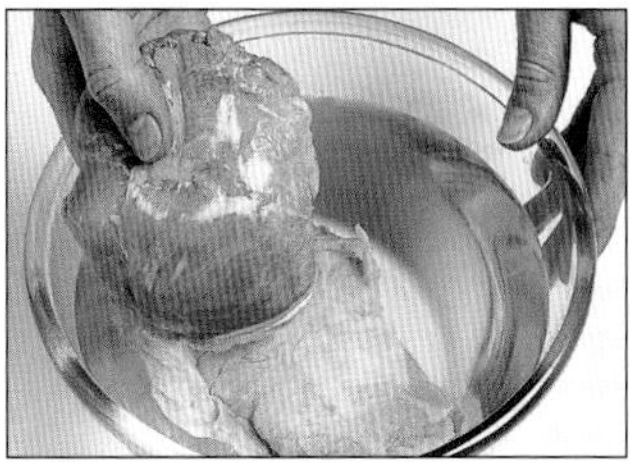

1 Soak the sweetbreads in cold water for 2 hours, changing the water several times. Rinse the sweetbreads well: they are ready for cooking when all signs of blood have been soaked or rinsed away. Drain, then place in a saucepan and pour in cold water to cover. Bring to the boil, then immediately reduce the heat and simmer for 5 minutes, or until the sweetbreads are firm and white.

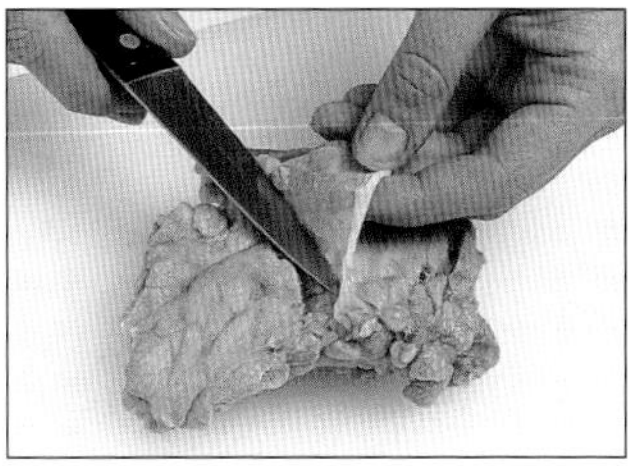

2 Drain the sweetbreads and peel off the membrane, then remove any pieces of gristle or fat and ducts. Cool and chill until firm. When firm, the sweetbreads can be sliced or cut into pieces, coated in a little flour and pan-fried or sautéed in butter, then simmered in a sauce. Sweetbreads are also good coated in egg and breadcrumbs, shallow fried and served with lemon wedges.

Preparing brains

These are prepared in the same way as sweetbreads, by thorough rinsing, soaking and blanching, then trimming. They are then either poached in a sauce until tender or lightly pressed under weights until cold, when they can be sliced and coated with breadcrumbs and pan-fried. Brains have a creamy texture when cooked.

NEW MEATS

Beef, lamb, pork, chicken, turkey, duck and goose are long established as international meats, but there is also a wide selection of other types that have, until comparatively recently, rarely been sampled away from their countries of origin. Modern farming, rearing, butchering, food transportation, communications and marketing have fuelled interest in different culinary cultures. Unlike exotic fruit and vegetables, which tend to look and smell appetizing, many of the animal food sources have less visual appeal and they rarely sound exciting. These meats may not have the same impact as aromatic fruit or brightly coloured vegetables, but they are steadily gaining acceptance and arousing the interest of enthusiastic cooks.

Above: Alligator steaks have a flaky texture.

Buying and storing

When they are available from the supermarket, the majority of these meats are neatly prepared ready for cooking, and displayed in sealed packs. Labelling information includes a date by which the product should be used and, often, instructions or ideas for basic cooking methods. Always treat them as you would other fresh meat, by storing the sealed pack in a dish in the coldest area of the fridge. Specialist butchers offer a wider selection of cuts, and they will also be able to offer expert advice on which cuts to buy and on cooking methods, too. Some new meats have been frozen and are sold thawed. Do not re-freeze previously frozen meats.

TYPES OF NEW MEAT

Alligator

There is a long tradition of cooking alligator in the southern states of America, particularly Louisiana. Fears of extinction meant that alligators in the wild were protected and so farmed alligator were introduced. Alligators are farmed (and found in the wild) right across the southern states of America, from Texas to the Carolinas, but the Mississippi Delta is the heartland. The meat from young alligators is eaten. It is white, flaky and tender, almost a cross between fish and chicken, with a hint of the texture of pork, and it can be cooked by the same methods as chicken and other light meats.

Below: Crocodile can be cut into fillets or steaks.

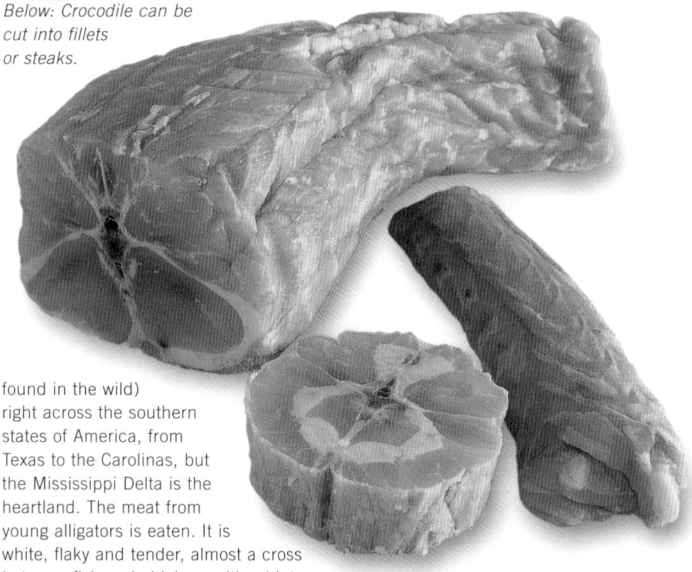

Crocodile

Larger than alligators, crocodiles are found in the northern part of the Nile Delta, the swamps of Florida and Asia, from Australia and the Philippines right across to southern India. The meat is popular in the Northern Territory of Australia where both freshwater and marine species are farmed. Like alligator, crocodile is a tender meat with a delicate flavour, similar to chicken or pork, but it has a slightly flaky texture. Crocodile is available as steaks or fillets, and is cooked as for chicken.

Below: Dark ostrich mince is very lean.

Ostrich

This bird is native to Africa, where it has been eaten since prehistoric times. It is now farmed in North America and Western Europe. Ostrich meat is dark in colour and finer in texture than beef. It is a lean meat with a full flavour, stronger than beef but not quite as pronounced as game, and is sold as prepared cuts, including slices, steaks, fillet and mince. Prepare and cook as for beef steaks: by grilling, pan-frying, stir-frying, roasting or braising. Minced ostrich can be used instead of beef for burgers, meatloaves and sauces.

Emu

Indigenous to Australia, where it is farmed as well as being found in the wild. Emu meat is dark and lean. It is darker than beef but has a softer texture. Emu should be cooked in the same way as tender beef. It is also smoked and sold as a cured meat; and used for making sausages. Cuts include fillet, steaks, cubed meat and mince. Emu can be grilled, roasted, pan-fried or braised.

Below: Emu steak

Above: Ostrich fillet and steak have a rich, gamey flavour.

Kangaroo

This is a generic name applied to different Australian species, including large red and small grey kangaroos, wallaroos and wallabies. Kangaroo has long been a traditional part of the Aborigine diet and is now internationally available. It is a dark, fine-textured meat with a strong flavour, more pronounced than beef; it has been compared to hare, but depending on the cooking method, kangaroo meat is not necessarily that rich. Sold as prepared cuts, including steaks and slices, kangaroo is also available as a smoked meat. In terms of cooking, it is best treated as beef. Forerib, sirloin or fillet cuts are sold for roasting; while rump, sirloin or fillet are suitable for frying or grilling. Kangaroo is a good ingredient for slow-cooked casseroles and stews.

Above: Large cuts of kangaroo can be roasted like beef, while steaks can be grilled or pan-fried.

Llama

In South America, the llama has long provided transport, clothing and a source of milk and meat, particularly among the Peruvians. To modern tastes, younger llamas are more tender and appetizing than older beasts (the meat of which is more usually dried and turned into *charqui* or jerky). Roast a joint or leg of llama; pan-fry, griddle or barbecue cutlets or loin chops.

Below: Buffalo is similar to beef and has corresponding cuts, like this rolled and tied joint, which can be roasted.

Buffalo

The Cape buffalo is hunted and eaten in Africa, and air-dried and smoked to make biltong. In Asia two main types of water buffalo, the river buffalo and the swamp buffalo, are found in huge numbers. In North America there is the bison. Buffalo meat is similar to beef, with cuts that can be roasted, grilled, fried, stewed or braised.

COOKING NEW MEATS

Smaller cuts can all be cooked quickly by dry methods such as grilling, pan-frying and griddling. Larger joints can be roasted following timings for beef.

Pan-frying buffalo

Buffalo steak should be treated in the same way as beef steak. Trim off excess fat, and beat out the meat with a meat mallet to ensure that it is evenly thick.

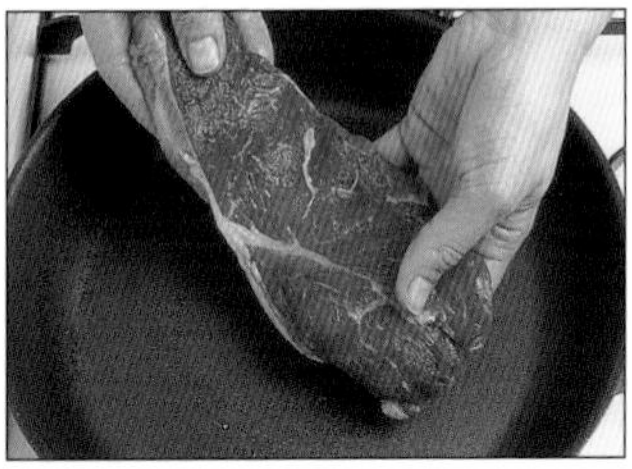

Grease a frying pan very lightly with oil and heat it well. Add the steak to the pan and cook over a high heat until it is browned on both sides. For a well-cooked steak, reduce the heat slightly and continue cooking until the meat is cooked through to your liking.

Pan-frying kangaroo

Tender steaks from the fillet, rump or sirloin can be pan-fried as for beef.

Grease a frying pan with a little oil and heat it until hot before adding the meat. Cook over a high heat until browned on one side, then turn and cook the second side. Kangaroo steaks can be served rare, medium or well cooked. For a well-cooked steak, reduce the heat slightly once the meat is browned and cook until cooked right through.

Pan-frying emu

Tender emu steak should be cut evenly, 2–5cm/¾–2in thick.

Heat a little oil in a frying pan, then add the meat when the oil is very hot. Cook for 1–2 minutes on each side, until well browned and just cooked through. Do not overcook the steak. Add salt and pepper to taste and serve at once.

Preparing ostrich stir-fry

1 Lay the ostrich steak between two sheets of greaseproof paper and beat it out evenly with a meat mallet. Cut the thinned steak into fine strips.

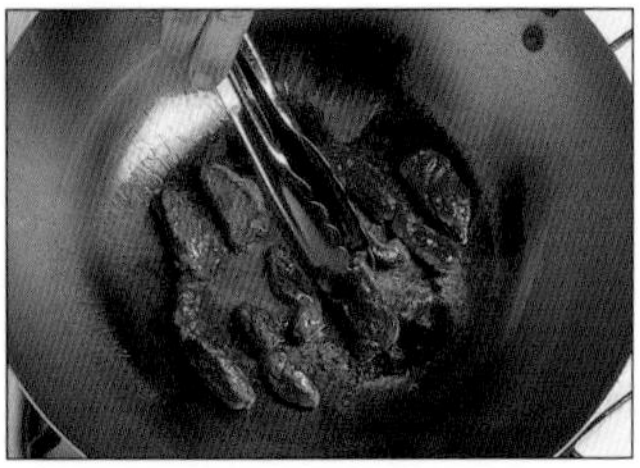

2 Heat a wok, then add a little oil. When very hot, add the ostrich strips and cook over a high heat for 30–60 seconds, stirring or turning frequently until the strips are evenly browned.

3 Use a draining spoon to remove the meat from the pan and set it aside. Cook the vegetables for the stir-fry and replace the meat for 1–2 minutes before adding a sauce and serving.

Preparing and sealing diced ostrich

Ostrich (and emu) are good casseroled or braised.

1 Cut the ostrich steak into strips, then across into even-size cubes.

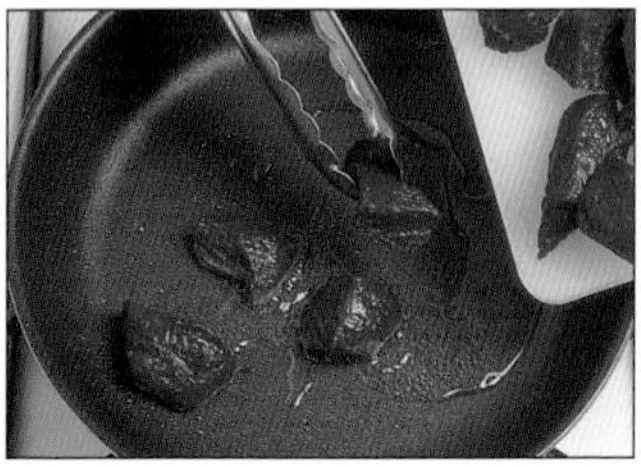

2 Heat a little oil in a frying pan. Add the cubed meat and cook, turning occasionally, until browned on all sides. Use a draining spoon to remove the meat from the pan, then continue preparing the casserole and sauce. Return the ostrich to the pan for a final 5–10 minutes of gentle reheating, but do not overcook it.

Griddling ostrich

This is an excellent method for ostrich meat, which is best served still rare or medium in the middle.

Heat the griddle until very hot, then add a little vegetable oil and heat again. Lay the ostrich steaks on the griddle and cook for 1–2 minutes on each side. Serve at once.

Grilling ostrich

Similar, speedy cooking is essential when grilling ostrich steaks.

Thoroughly preheat the grill. Lay the meat on a grill rack and brush lightly with oil, then season with freshly ground black pepper. Cook for no more than 2 minutes on each side, until well browned outside but moist in the middle. Top with a knob of herb and lemon butter and serve at once.

Grilling crocodile steaks

1 Preheat the grill to high. Select evenly thick crocodile steaks and lay them on a grill rack. Brush them with a little oil or a basting sauce.

2 Place at a medium distance from the grill and cook until well browned. Turn and brush with more oil or sauce.

3 Cook until well browned on the other side. Test the centre of the steak with the point of a knife to check that the meat is cooked through: it should be firm and flake easily. If the meat is soft and uncooked, reduce the heat slightly and continue grilling the steak.

Cooking alligator or crocodile in a rich cream sauce

1 Melt a knob of butter in a little oil in a frying pan. When foaming, add small portions of alligator or crocodile fillet.

2 Cook over a high heat until browned on one side, then turn and brown the second side until the pieces are firm and just cooked through.

3 Grate a little lime rind over the meat and season well with salt and ground black pepper.

4 Add a splash of dry white wine, then pour in some double cream and cook gently until the cream is just below simmering point. Stir occasionally to move the pieces of meat around in the sauce. Taste for seasoning and sprinkle with chopped parsley. Serve at once.

Baking crocodile fillet en papillote

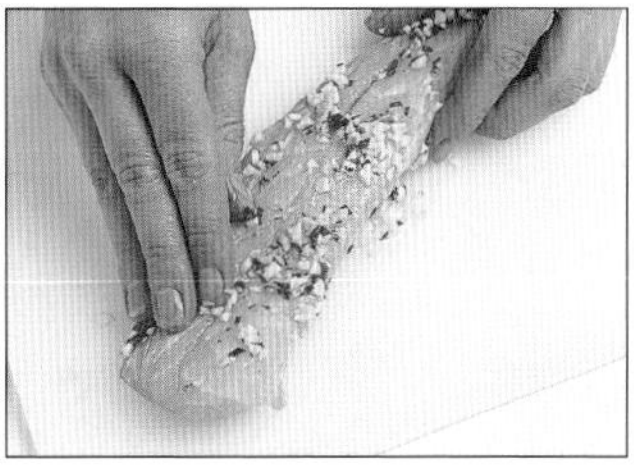

1 Season the fillet well and rub it all over with the chosen flavouring ingredients. Here finely chopped garlic and chillies are used. Cut the fillet into neat, even-size portions.

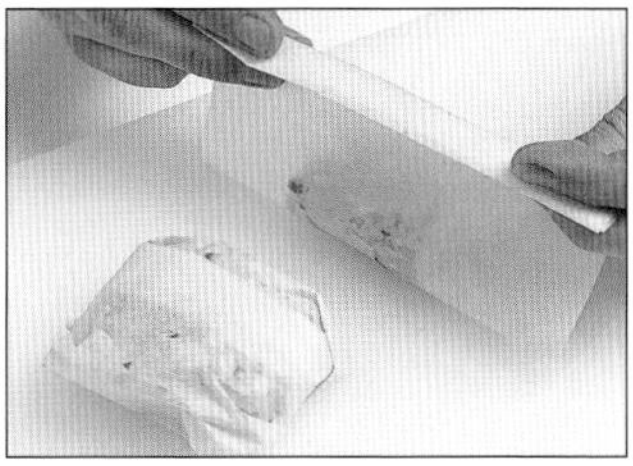

2 Wrap each portion of meat in a piece of non-stick baking paper (or greased greaseproof paper). Fold the edges of the paper together and tuck the ends under to seal. Place in a roasting tin and cook in the oven at 200°C/400°F/ Gas 6 for about 20 minutes.

POULTRY AND GAME

Poultry describes domesticated birds – chicken, duck, guinea fowl and turkey – and game refers to wild birds and animals hunted for food. The varieties of domesticated or farmed birds that are reared are fairly limited, but the type of game varies widely. Many game birds and animals are now bred in large numbers, so the dividing line between them and domesticated creatures is becoming less distinct.

Chicken and Other Small Poultry

Being small and easy to keep, chickens have been domesticated for thousands of years. As was the practice with other animals, early chickens were reared not only for food, but they also played their part in Roman sacred rites. Originating from Malaysian jungle birds, the chickens we eat today are directly descended from the fowl that were first domesticated in the Indus valley more than 4,000 years ago. Chicken farming is not a modern industry – even before the Romans turned their attentions to hatching methods, the Egyptians had already done so.

Although the European idea of hens pecking about the farmyard conjures an idyllic image, in many early, poor farms that was not always the case. Chickens were kept in backyards or small gardens as well as on farms. Many birds were sadly undernourished and forced to scavenge in every unhygienic nook and cranny. Their ends were often as undignified as their lives: neck wrung or topped with a blunt chopper, which resulted in them running around in headless circles. So the country cock that made it to the peasant's table was likely to be a sad culinary offering, with little meat and the necessity for hours of boiling, rendering minimal flavour to all but the soup.

In the 20th century, when small traditional farms were dotted all over the countryside, chickens were kept for their eggs and killed only when they were past their laying best. Eventually, old cocks were also sent to the pot – for a thorough boiling or stewing. With neat hen houses, spacious pens and often having access to the orchard, the hen's worst nightmare was the fox, and a good farmer (or his wife) would guard against that ransacking intruder.

Before the advent of intensive rearing, chicken became a luxury food and a roast bird was an occasional treat. Intensive rearing brought chicken to every table, not only as an occasional treat, but also as an everyday food; however, quantity superseded quality, and flavour and texture diminished. As the conditions in which battery hens are kept have been exposed and the resulting hygiene and health problems realized, so public outcry has forced a reversal towards traditional methods. Rules and regulations vary and terms are many and confusing.

Ultimately, the better the conditions under which poultry are reared, the better the product they yield. Whether the end concern is the welfare of the poultry or the quality of the meat, the means to both are the same. If you want good-quality chicken, buy those that have been well-reared.

Above: Cockerels aren't often eaten, although castrated birds, known as capons are available in some countries.

Nutrition

Chicken is rich in high-quality protein, providing all the essential amino acids required by the body for growth and repair. Chicken provides B-group vitamins, especially niacin. It also provides iron (more in the leg meat than the breast meat) as well as the minerals copper and selenium. The white meat is low in fat (the fat is found in and under the skin) and contains a lower proportion of saturated fat than meat.

Choice of bird

Apart from the standard intensively reared chicken, there is a choice of birds raised by different farming methods. These are available as whole birds or in portions.

Free-range birds are not reared in battery conditions. The laws vary according to the country of origin.

Corn-fed chickens are easily recognized by their bright yellow skin, which loses its colour during cooking and yields golden fat, that also diminishes in colour during cooking. The colour is probably due to the colour in the corn feed.

Organic birds are raised in humane conditions, fed on a natural and (usually) traditional-style diet. They do not have lurid-coloured skin. Standards and conditions relating to the particular scheme or terms by which the birds are classed as organic are usually outlined on the packaging. Organic organizations and authorities readily provide information on their standards.

Below from left: corn-fed, free-range and organic chickens

Below: Boiling chicken

Buying

Poultry can be bought fresh, chilled or frozen. Look for birds with a clear, soft skin (there should be no blemishes or bruises). A soft, thin skin shows that the bird is young; the tougher the skin, the older the bird. The bigger the bird, the better its value because the proportion of meat to bone will be higher. As well as whole birds, chicken is available in a choice of portions such as quarters, legs, wings, thighs, breasts and drumsticks. The portions may be on the bone or boneless, with or without skin. Sliced, diced and minced chicken breast is also available. Stir-fry strips, marinated cuts and stuffed portions are all sold fresh or frozen.

Storing

Place poultry that has been purchased loose in a deep dish and cover it closely. Check pre-packed poultry to make sure that the packs are sealed before placing them in the fridge. Store in the coldest part of the fridge.

Use pre-packed poultry by the date suggested or loose poultry within about two days of purchase.

Raw, fresh poultry can be frozen successfully. Remove the giblets from a whole bird, if necessary. Wrap portions individually in clear film or freezer film. Pack the poultry or portions in a freezer bag and seal tightly.

The best way to thaw frozen poultry is in the fridge. Place in a suitable container, cover closely and leave in the fridge overnight. Remove the giblets from a whole bird as soon as possible.

Handling

Poultry is particularly susceptible to bacterial growth, which can cause food poisoning if it is allowed to contaminate uncooked foods that are eaten raw (such as salads) or if the poultry is eaten without being thoroughly cooked.

Always keep poultry chilled, as bacteria thrive in warmth. Select poultry towards the end of a shopping session and avoid leaving it to warm up in the car before going home. Unpack and chill it promptly. Leave the poultry in the fridge until you are ready to cook it.

Before preparing raw poultry, assemble all the utensils and dishes you will need. Weigh out all the other ingredients you are using, then unpack and cut, coat or prepare the poultry. When making an entire meal in one session, including dishes that are to be served uncooked or ready-cooked ingredients, such as cooked fish or meat in a starter, salads, or desserts, it is a good idea to prepare these foods first before handling the raw poultry to avoid cross-contamination.

Thoroughly wash utensils, surfaces and hands after handling and cooking poultry. Remember to wash utensils used to lift or stir part-cooked poultry before using them with cooked poultry.

Left: Organic chickens are raised in humane, free-range, conditions.

Below: A capon is a large bird with a high proportion of white meat.

Stewing or boiling chicken

Also known as a boiling hen or fowl, this is an older bird. It requires long, slow simmering as the flesh is tough, but its flavour is excellent. As a guide to age, the older the chicken, the harder and more rigid the breastbone. Boiling fowl are not readily available these days as demand is low, so they have to be sourced from a specialist butcher. Stewing chickens are used for pies, fricassées, ballottines and galantines and, most often of all, in soups, stews and casseroles.

Capon

This is a young cockerel that has been castrated and then fattened on a special diet to make it plump and flavourful. The practice is prohibited in many countries, including Britain. Capons are large birds and can weigh between 2.7–4.5kg/6–10lb. In the past they were often cooked for celebration meals at Christmas and Thanksgiving in place of turkey. They have a fairly large proportion of white meat to dark.

Cook well, eat well

Poultry should be cooked through, without any sign of raw flesh or juices. This is the way to ensure all the bacteria are destroyed. To check if poultry is cooked, pierce the thickest area of the meat with a thin metal skewer. If there is any sign of pink in either the flesh or the juices, then the meat is not cooked and it must be returned to the heat or the oven for further cooking.

TYPES OF SMALL POULTRY

Roasting chicken

Sometimes called a roaster, this is a young cockerel or hen about 12 weeks old. Roasting chickens usually weigh about 1.3kg/3lb, but they may be as big as 3kg/6–7lb. Older birds (up to 20 weeks old) and up to 4.5kg/10lb in weight are available from specialist butchers' shops.

Above: Poussin

Left: Double poussin

Left: Roasting chicken

Poussin

This is the French name for a young chicken, four to six weeks old and weighing 350–675g/12oz–1½lb. Each bird provides an individual portion. Poussins, which are also sometimes called spring chickens, have a tender, delicate flavour. They can be roasted, when they benefit from a moist stuffing, and they can also be spatchcocked and grilled, pan-fried or barbecued.

Double poussin

A larger, older poussin that weighs about 900g/2lb and is about six weeks old. Double poussins are big enough to serve two people. Like poussins, they are tender, but they lack flavour.

Above: Chicken portions include the leg quarter, drumsticks and thighs.

Above: Boneless chicken breast (top) and a chicken supreme which includes part of the wingbone.

Rock Cornish hen

This small North American cross-breed, was developed from White Rock and Cornish chickens and is sometimes called a Rock Cornish game hen. These small birds are four to six weeks old and can weigh up to 1.2kg/2½lb. The flesh is white and flavourful, though the ratio of bone to meat is high, so each hen will usually serve only one person.

Below: An oven-ready guinea fowl, which has a slightly gamier flavour than chicken.

Guinea fowl

These are domestic fowl, which have been raised in Europe for centuries, but originally came from the coast of Guinea in West Africa. They are tender with slightly dry flesh that resembles pheasant. The flesh is not distinctly game-like in flavour, but it leans more in that direction than towards chicken. Guinea fowl are generally cooked as for chicken or pheasant, but at a high temperature – for example the birds should be barded and roasted in an oven preheated to 230°C/450°F/Gas 8 for 25–30 minutes. Alternatively, the birds can be braised or casseroled.

Cuts of chicken

A wide range of different portions are available, both on and off the bone. **Quarters** include either the leg or the wing joint, the latter having a large portion of breast meat. The leg joint includes the thigh and drumstick.
Other portions include **thighs**, which are small, neat joints, **drumsticks**, which take a surprisingly long time to cook as the meat is quite compact, and **wings**, which have very little meat.
Breast portions are sold on or off the bone, skinned or unskinned; these portions include only the white meat.
Boneless breasts may be sold as fillets.
Supremes include the wingbone.
Part-boned breasts still have the short piece of bone leading into the wing and the fine strip of breastbone.

PREPARING SMALL POULTRY

These techniques are suitable for chicken as well as other poultry, such as guinea fowl and poussin, and game birds, such as pheasant.

Jointing a bird

Many recipes specify particular joints of poultry or game and, although you can buy them ready-prepared, with the right equipment it is actually quite straightforward to joint a bird at home.

There are various joints into which the bird can be cut, depending on the recipe. For example, it can be cut into four or eight pieces. Use a large, sharp knife and poultry shears for cutting through meat and bone. The following gives four small portions from each side of the bird, eight pieces in total – two wings, two breasts, two drumsticks and two thighs.

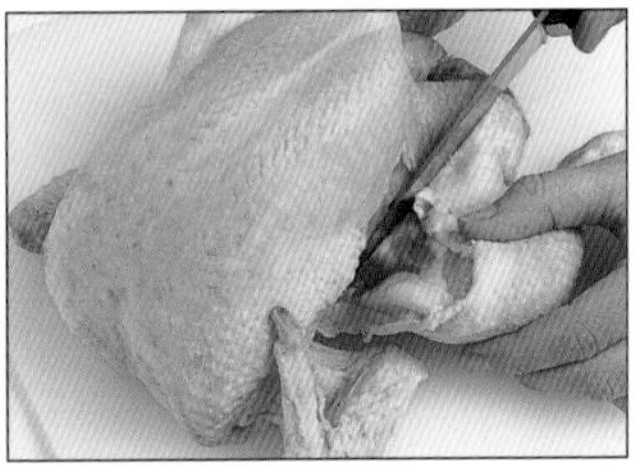

1 Put the bird breast-side up on a chopping board. Use a sharp knife to remove the leg by cutting through the skin and then through the thigh joint. Repeat with the leg on the other side.

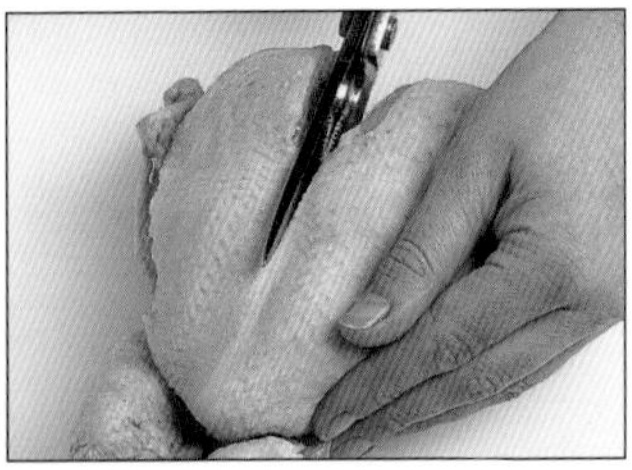

2 Following the line of the breastbone and using poultry shears, cut the breast in half, making the cut as clean as possible.

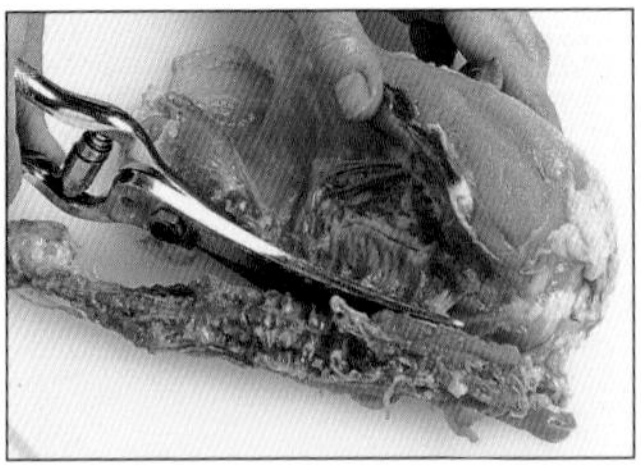

3 Turn the bird over and cut out the backbone. Leave the wings attached.

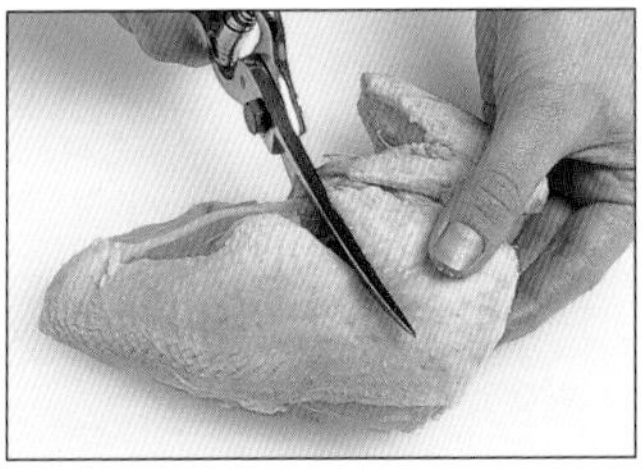

4 Cut each breast in half, leaving a portion of the breast attached to the wing.

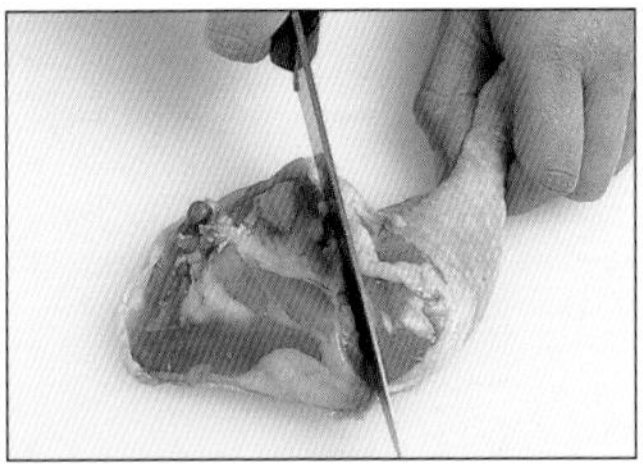

5 Cut each leg through the knee joint to separate the thigh and drumstick.

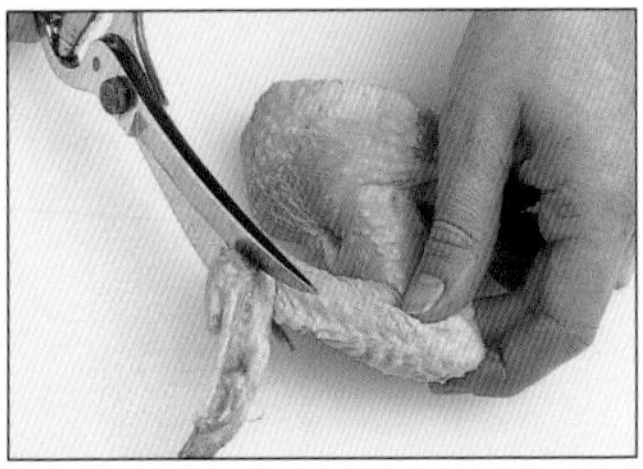

6 Using poultry shears, cut off the wing tip at the first joint.

Preparing a bird for roasting

Very little preparation is needed to roast a bird, but the following techniques make life easier.

Removing the wishbone

The wishbone is the arched bone at the neck end of the bird. It does not have to be removed, but the breast can be carved more easily without it.

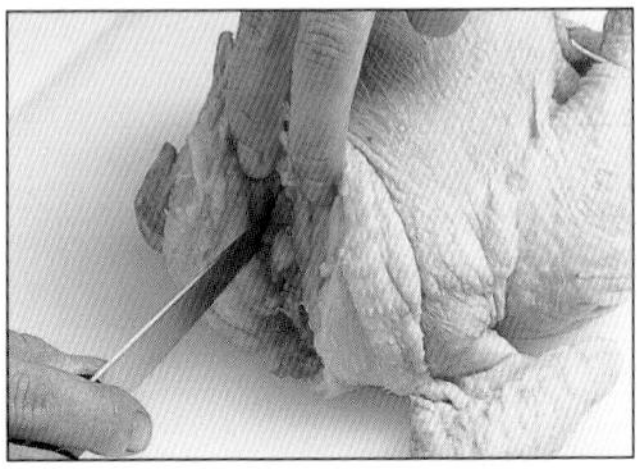

1 Using a small, sharp knife pull back the skin from the neck cavity and carefully cut around the wishbone.

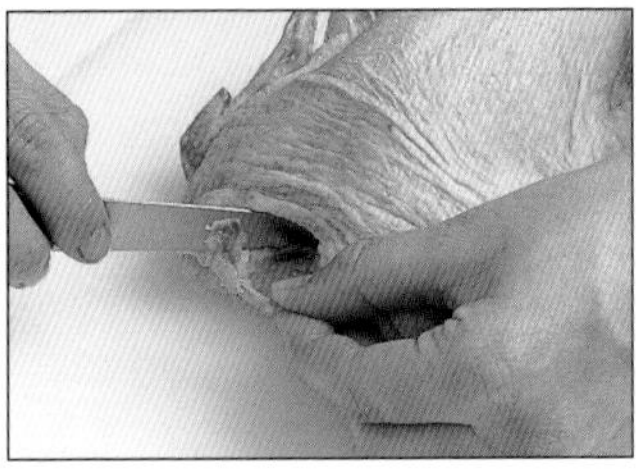

2 Scrape away the meat from the wishbone, then cut it away at the base and pull it out.

Make a lucky wish

When the roast bird is served, it is traditional for two people to pull the wishbone until it snaps. Each person is allowed to use only the little finger to hold the end of one side of the bone. On the signal to pull, the person who ends up with the larger arched top of the bone is entitled to make a wish. So, remove the wishbone and someone will be deprived of a lucky wish!

Trussing with skewers

This is a quick and useful method for a larger bird that has a greater quantity of meat and is therefore more rigid, so firmer in shape.

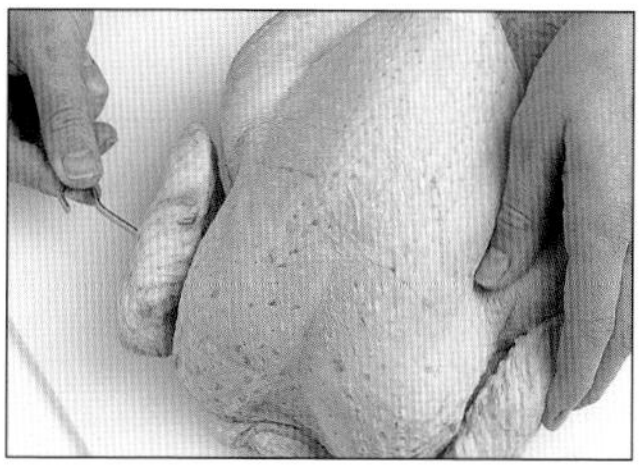

1 Push one metal skewer through both sections of the wing, into the skin of the neck and straight out through the wing on the other side.

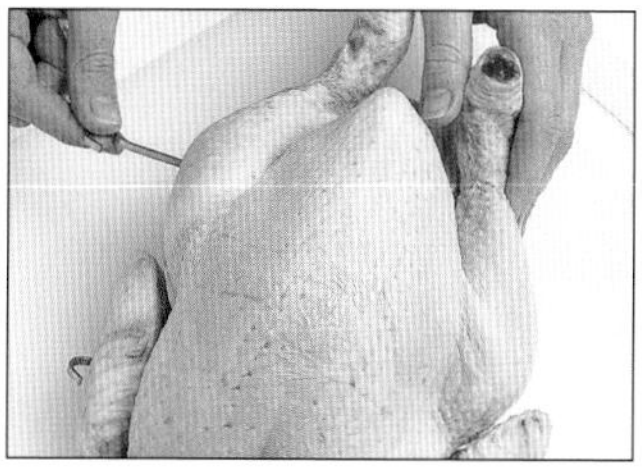

2 Push in the second metal skewer firmly, pressing it straight through the thighs and the tail cavity.

Trussing with string

Tying a bird with string keeps it in a neat, compact shape during roasting and helps it to cook more evenly.

1 Season the bird and tuck the wing tips and neck flap underneath.

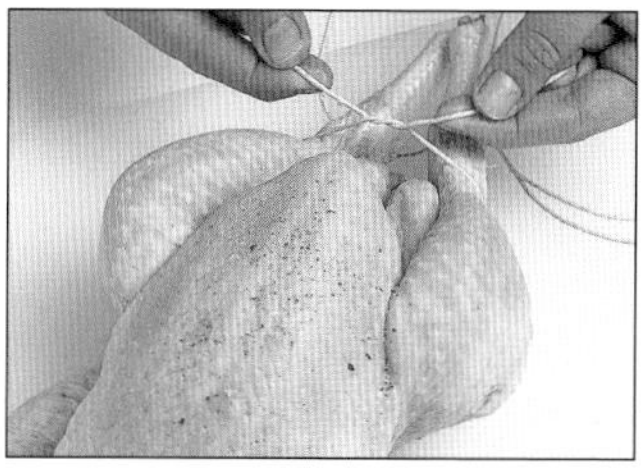

2 Tie a piece of string around the legs and under the flap of skin.

3 Bring the string towards the neck end, passing it between the legs.

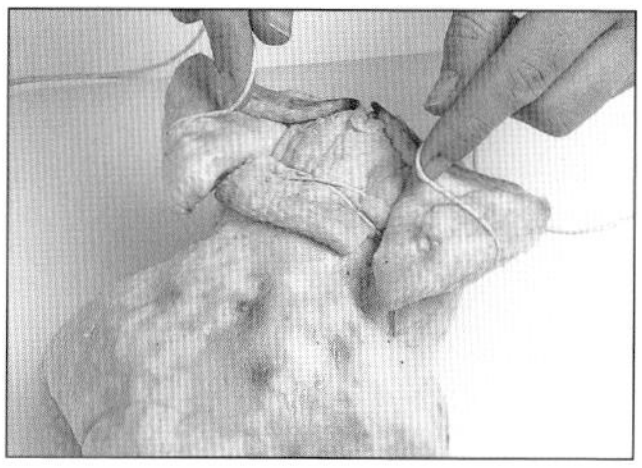

4 Turn the bird over and wrap the string around the wings to keep them flat.

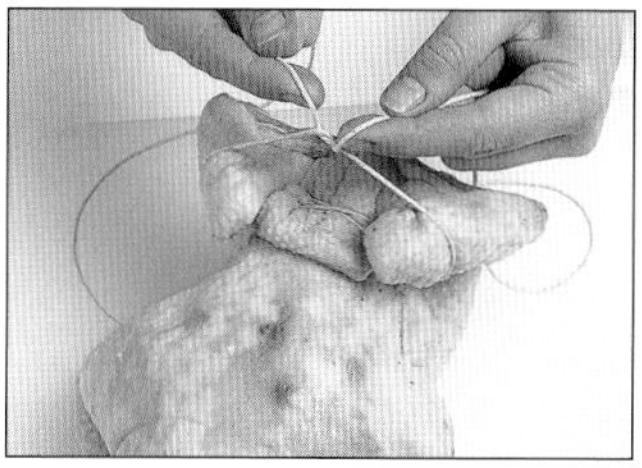

5 Pull the string tight to bring the wings together, and tie neatly.

Spatchcocking a bird

This is a method of splitting and then flattening a whole bird so that it can be grilled or roasted quickly.

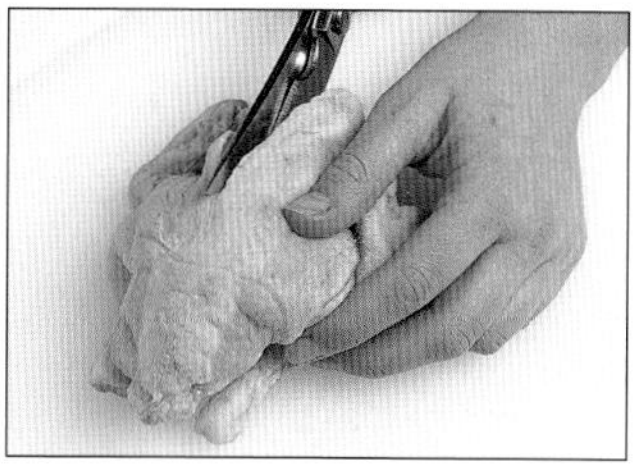

1 Tuck the wings under the bird and remove the wishbone. Turn the bird over and use a pair of poultry shears to split it along each side of the backbone. Remove the backbone.

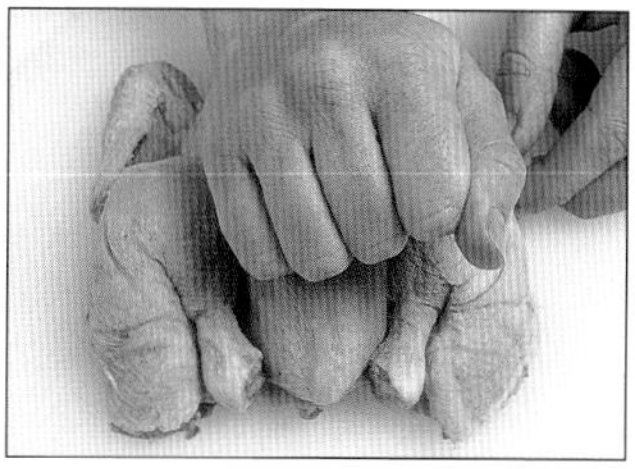

2 Turn the bird over, and place on a chopping board breast-side uppermost. Then press down firmly with the heel of one hand on the middle of the breast to flatten the bird against the board.

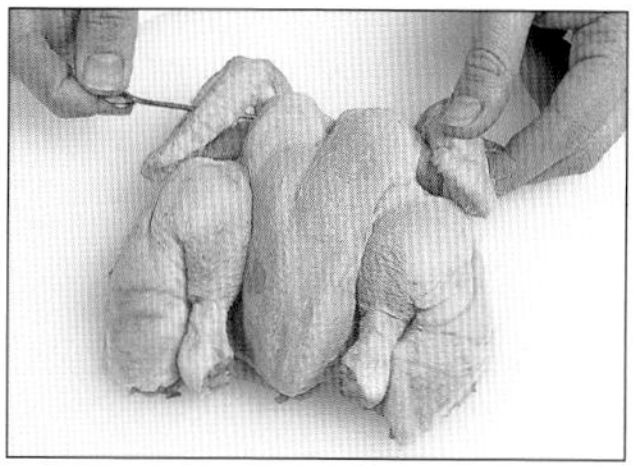

3 To keep the bird flat, push a metal skewer through the wings and breast. Then push a second metal skewer parallel to the first, through the thighs and the tip of the breast.

Tunnel boning a bird

This is a method of part-boning a bird from the breast to the joints. The skin is left in one piece and the bird is ready to stuff. This is easy with a larger bird, but can be fiddly and difficult to manage with small birds.

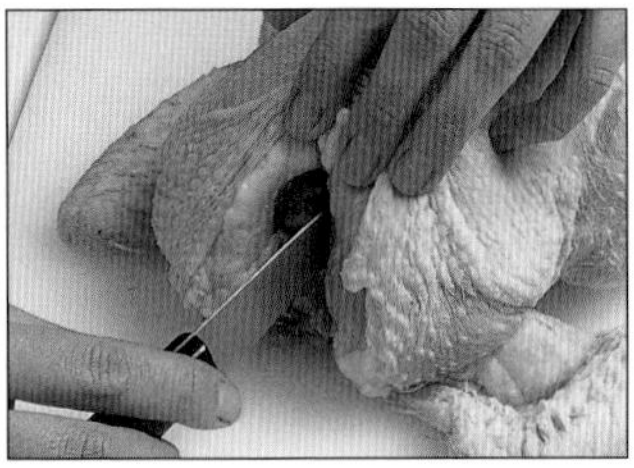

1 Pull back the skin around the neck of the bird, then carefully cut out and remove the wishbone.

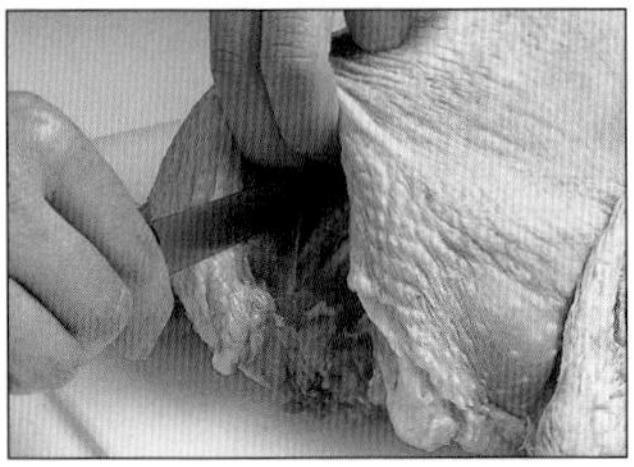

2 Feel inside the cavity for the wing joint, then use a small, sharp knife to cut the bones free as you separate the breastbone from the meat and skin from one side of the bird.

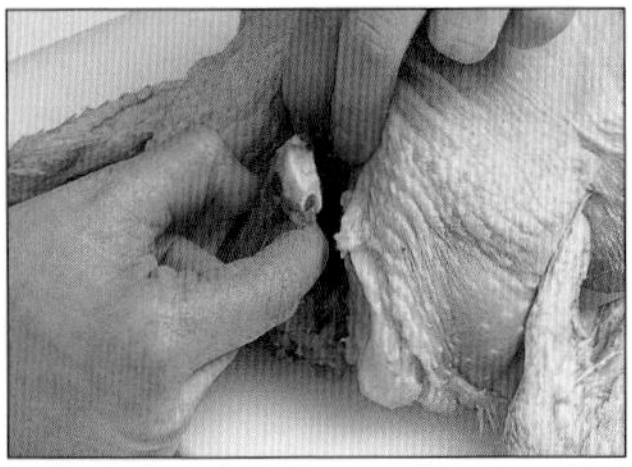

3 Find the curved bone and carefully pull it out. Continue cutting away the meat from the bone until you reach the wing joint.

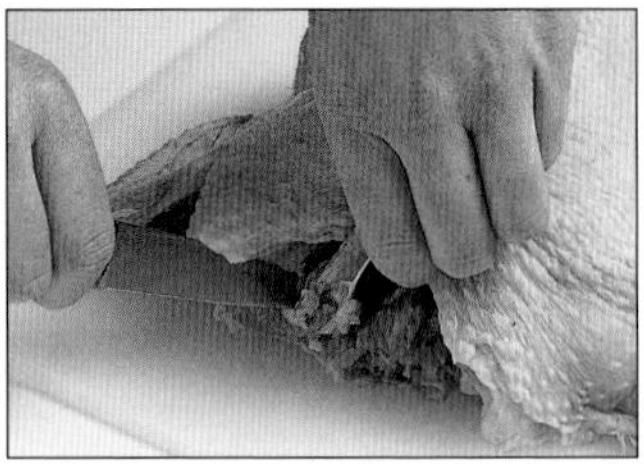

4 Cut through the wing joint firmly using the tip of the knife, then repeat on the other side of the bird. Pull the meat back from the carcass and continue cutting the flesh from the bone, keeping the knife as near to the bone as possible. Turn the carcass from one side to another, and work towards the tail end of the bird. Sever the leg joints when you reach them, leaving the bones attached to the leg meat.

5 Carefully cut and ease the skin away from the breastbone, then turn the bird outside in so that the skin is on the outside. The finished bird retains the joints, but the central part of the body is completely boneless.

Preparing boneless breast fillets

The advantage of preparing fillets yourself is that the rest of the carcass can be jointed and used to make a well-flavoured stock.

1 Joint the bird into portions, but keep the breasts whole.

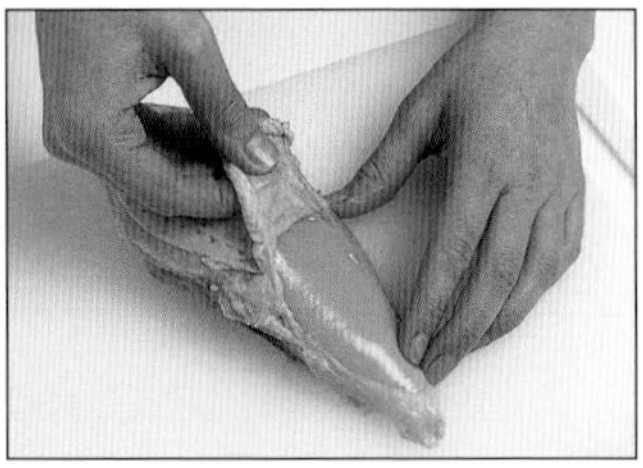

2 Use your fingers to carefully pull the skin and thin membrane away from the breast. Use a small, sharp knife to cut the meat off the rib bone and any remaining breastbone.

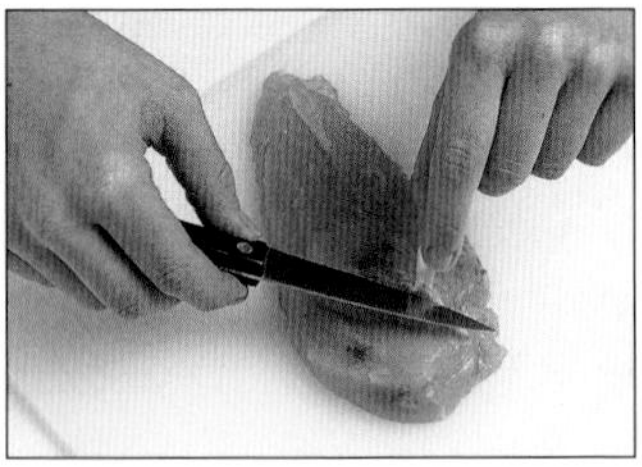

3 Remove the thin, white central tendons from the breast, using a small, sharp knife.

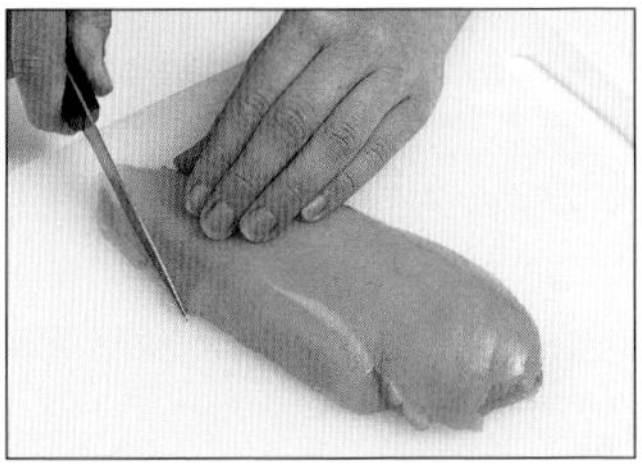

4 Trim away any pieces of fat and untidy edges from the breast.

Preparing escalopes

A chicken breast yields two escalopes. A similar technique can be used with other poultry – a duck breast will yield about three escalopes and turkey breast can be sliced into several escalopes, depending on the size of the breast.

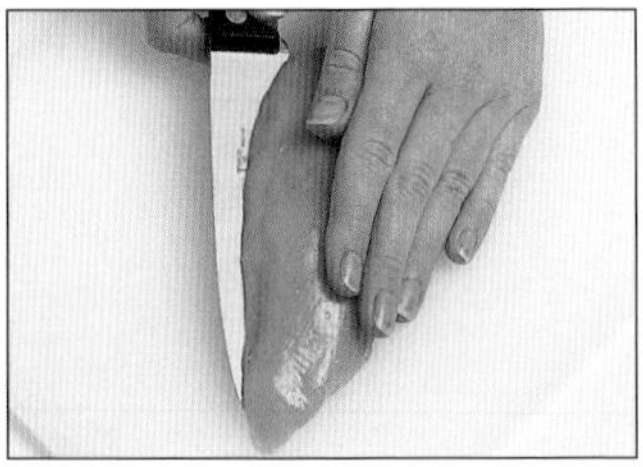

1 Place the skinless, boneless breast flat on a chopping board and, using a large, sharp knife, carefully slice the breast in half horizontally. To cut a thin, even slice, hold your hand flat on top of the chicken breast as you cut, to prevent it from moving.

2 Lay each slice of chicken between sheets of greaseproof paper or non-stick baking paper in turn and beat out gently and evenly until thin and flat, using a meat mallet or rolling pin.

Cutting strips for stir-frying

Tender poultry is ideal for stir-frying. Use a flattened escalope for stir-fry strips (see above).

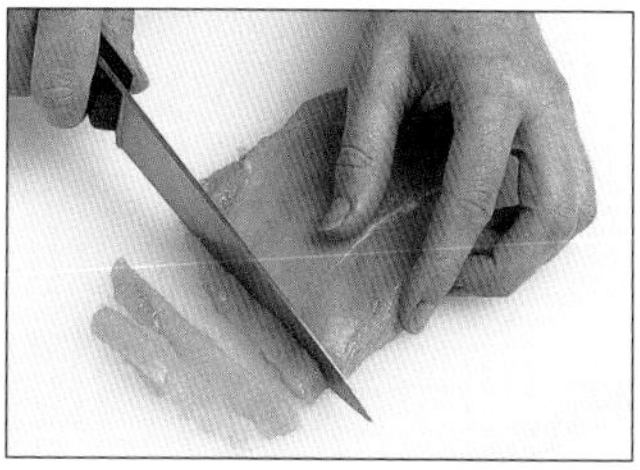

Lay the thin escalope on a board and cut it across into fine strips. When cut across the grain in this way, the meat cooks extremely quickly.

Skinning and boning chicken thighs

When boned, chicken thighs yield a neat nugget of well-flavoured meat.

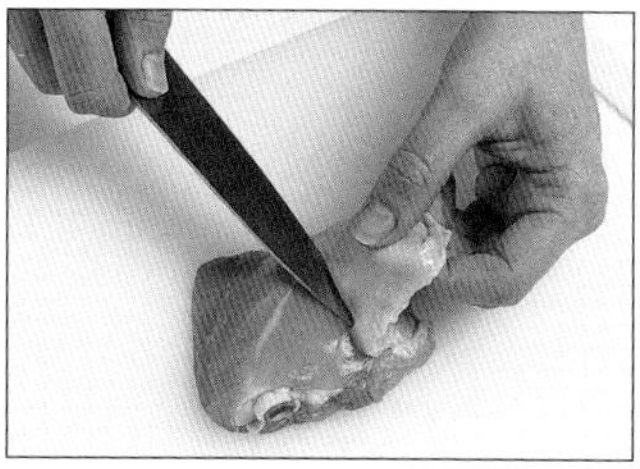

1 Use a sharp knife to loosen the skin, then pull it away from the meat.

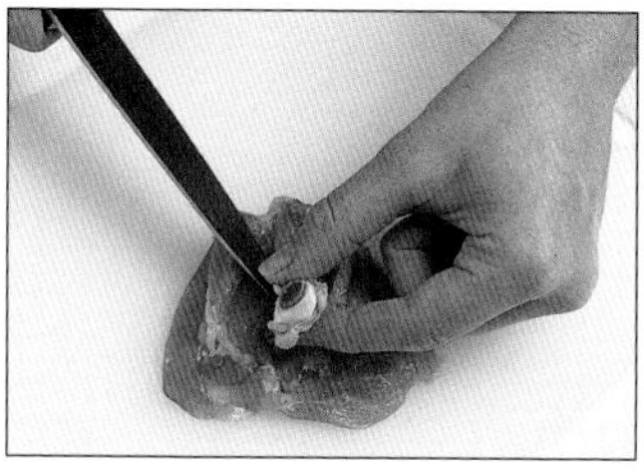

2 Carefully cut the flesh lengthways along the main thigh bone, then cut the bone out, trimming the meat close to the bone, and then lift the bone away. Continue cutting out the bones, leaving the meat open and flat.

Making kebabs

The thigh meat is ideal for kebabs. First skin and bone the thigh (as above).

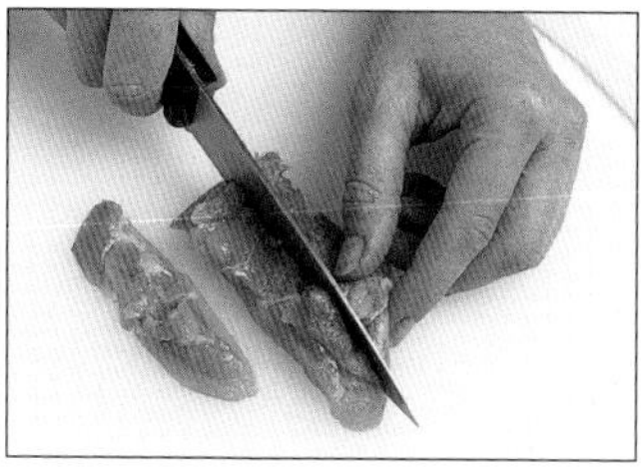

1 Cut the thigh meat across the grain into about four pieces, using a small, sharp knife.

2 Fold slightly elongated pieces of meat in half and thread them on to skewers. Add pieces of vegetable between the meat – try button mushrooms and chunks of red and green pepper – they complement chicken and will cook in the same time as the chicken.

Chicken Kiev

Deep-fried chicken breast filled with garlic butter is a modern Russian invention that is popular the world over.

SERVES FOUR

INGREDIENTS

- 115g/4oz/½ cup butter, softened
- 2 garlic cloves, crushed
- finely grated rind of 1 lemon
- 30ml/2 tbsp chopped fresh tarragon
- 4 skinless chicken supremes (with wing bone attached)
- 1 egg, lightly beaten
- 115g/4oz/2 cups fresh breadcrumbs
- oil, for deep frying
- salt and ground black pepper

1 Beat together the butter, garlic, lemon rind and tarragon with salt and pepper and shape into a 5cm/2in long rectangular block. Wrap in clear film. Chill for 1 hour.

2 Beat out the chicken supremes gently until fairly thin. Cut the butter lengthways into four pieces and put one in the centre of each chicken supreme. Fold the edges over the butter and secure with cocktail sticks.

3 Place the beaten egg and breadcrumbs in separate shallow dishes. Dip the chicken pieces first in beaten egg and then in breadcrumbs to coat evenly. Dip them a second time in the egg and breadcrumbs. Chill for at least 1 hour.

4 Heat the oil in a large pan to 180°C/350°F. Deep fry the chicken for 6–8 minutes, or until the chicken is cooked and the coating golden. Drain on kitchen paper. Remove the cocktail sticks from the chicken and serve hot.

COOKING SMALL POULTRY

Tender birds can be poached, roasted, grilled, barbecued, griddled or fried in a shallow pan or, once coated in breadcumbs or batter, in deep oil. Since older, tough birds are rarely available nowadays, tender poultry are also used in slow-cooked casseroles and stews. If you do have an older bird, it should be cooked by long, gentle and moist methods, such as braising or stewing.

Roasting

Small poultry birds, such as chickens, poussins and guinea fowl, are easy to roast and require the minimum of attention. When cooking a slightly larger bird, requiring longer cooking, you may need to cover the top of the breast loosely with foil when it is a light golden brown. Remove the foil for the final 15 minutes cooking time to complete the browning.

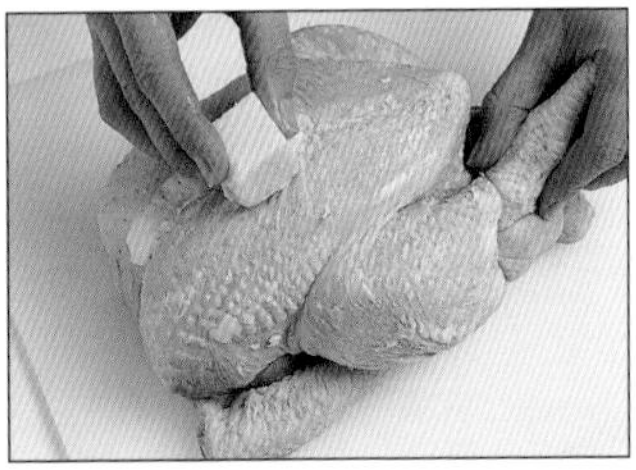

1 Rub the breast and the top of the bird generously with butter. If you are stuffing the bird, stuff it at the neck end only before trussing and then tuck the neck skin under.

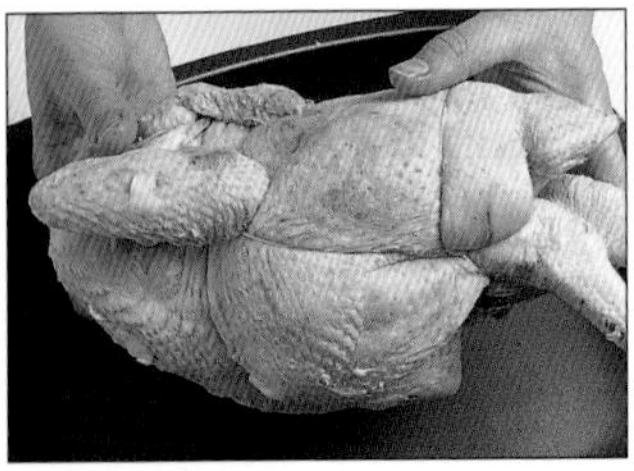

2 Place the bird breast-side down in the roasting tin for the first 30 minutes of the cooking time.

3 Turn and baste the bird, then continue cooking for the calculated time, removing the roasting tin from the oven and basting the bird every 15 minutes.

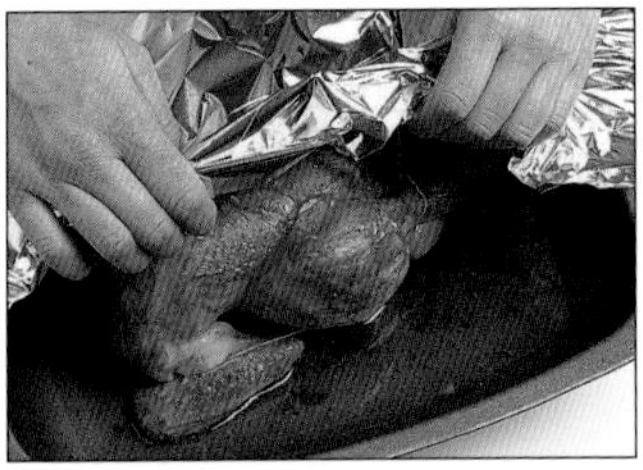

4 When the bird is completely cooked (see checking cooking progess, opposite), remove the roasting tin from the oven and then cover the cooked bird tightly with foil. Leave it to rest in a warm place for 10–15 minutes before carving and serving. Either do this in the roasting tin or, if you wish to make gravy or a sauce with the pan juices and fat, then transfer the bird to a warmed serving platter or carving dish.

Roasting times for small poultry
Preheat the oven to 200°C/400°F/Gas 6, or 230°C/450°F/Gas 8 for guinea fowl. Calculate the cooking time according to the weight of the bird. Weigh the bird when it has been trimmed and with any stuffing added.
Chicken allow 20 minutes per 450g/1lb, plus an extra 20 minutes.
Poussin allow 50–60 minutes total roasting time.
Guinea fowl allow 15 minutes per 450g/1lb, plus 15 minutes.

Grilling

This is a quick cooking method for smaller birds and portions. For even, thorough cooking, split a whole bird in half or spatchcock it. The birds can be flavoured with garlic, herbs or lemon rind. Rub flavouring ingredients into the bird 1–2 hours in advance to allow the flavours to infuse.

1 Preheat the grill on the hottest setting. Brush the bird or birds with oil and season well.

2 Place skin-side up on a rack in a grill pan and cook well below the heat source so the meat has time to cook through before the skin overbrowns.

3 Allow about 40 minutes cooking for poussin, turning them frequently and brushing with oil to keep them moist.

Griddling boneless breast fillets

This is a healthy way of cooking, allowing fat to drain away between the ridges of the pan and preventing the meat from becoming greasy.

1 Brush the breast fillets with a little vegetable oil.

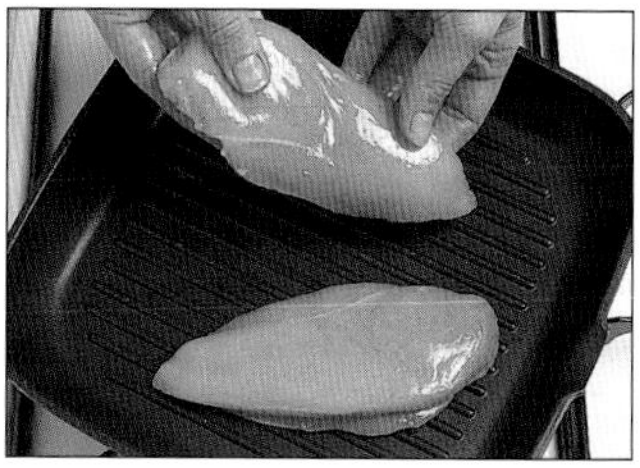

2 Preheat the griddle until it is almost smoking, then lay the breast fillets on it – don't overload the pan, or the meat will begin to steam rather than brown.

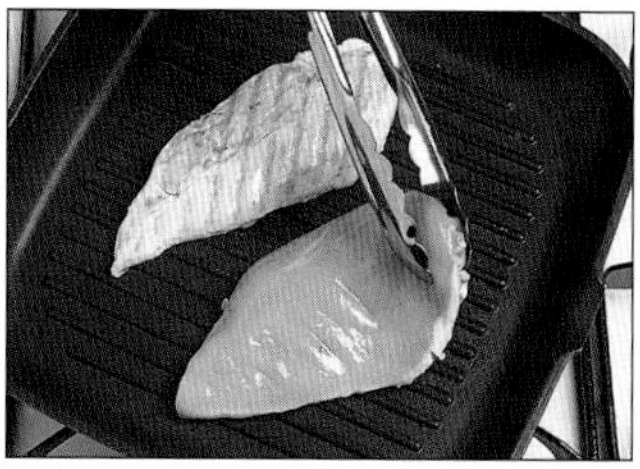

3 Cook until the meat is well browned underneath, and firm and white inside. Turn the fillets over using a pair of tongs or a spatula.

4 Continue cooking the chicken until the second side is well browned and the meat is firm and white throughout.

Barbecuing portions

Poultry must be cooked through, so it is important to ensure that the barbecue is properly heated and fuelled with enough charcoal to burn hot enough and long enough to cook the poultry thoroughly. Position the grilling rack well away from the hot coals so that the meat has plenty of time to cook through before the skin is overcooked.

1 Cut deep slashes into thick portions that require lengthy cooking. This will ensure that they cook through as well as giving the cooked poultry a good flavour. Make two or three cuts across larger drumsticks or poultry quarters. There is no need to slash small drumsticks or tender breast meat.

2 Marinating flavours poultry before cooking and provides a good basting mixture to keep it moist during cooking. Olive oil, chopped garlic, chopped fresh herbs and chopped fresh red or green chillies bring full flavours to chicken. Mix together the ingredients in a deep, non-metal container.

3 Add the poultry to the marinade and turn the pieces to coat them thoroughly. Cover and chill for at least 30 minutes or for up to 24 hours.

4 To cook, place the portions on the grill rack, brush with marinade and cook over the hot coals. Turn the pieces frequently to ensure that they cook evenly, brushing with more of the marinade to keep the meat moist.

Careful cooking

Barbecues Large drumsticks and thick, dense chicken portions, such as whole leg quarters taste excellent when barbecued, but they do require attention to ensure that they are cooked through. One solution is to poach the portions gently in just enough stock to cover until they are only just cooked – this will take about 20–30 minutes. Leave to cool in the stock, then transfer to the marinade and chill overnight. Slash the meat and barbecue as above, until thoroughly reheated and well browned – the result is succulent and delicious meat.

Checking cooking progress When you are barbecuing or cooking by another method, it is important to test that chicken and other poultry is well cooked before serving. Pierce the thickest area of meat with the point of a small, sharp knife. Check the juices – if there is any sign of pink the meat is not cooked. Then check the meat at the base of the cut, when cooked it will be firm and look white, if it is pink and soft, the bird is not cooked. Use this test on portions and whole birds. On a whole bird, the area behind the thigh takes longest to cook.

Pan-frying

The important point to remember when frying poultry is that it must be cooked through. Escalopes and boneless breasts cook quickly, so they are ideal for speedy pan-frying over a high heat. Breast meat on the bone takes longer and requires closer attention to ensure it is evenly cooked through. Uneven, thicker portions, particularly denser thigh and leg meat on the bone, require careful cooking and turning. With larger pieces, you will have to reduce the heat to low once the chicken is browned and cook it very slowly to prevent the outside from over-browning.

1 Heat a little olive oil in a large, non-stick frying pan.

2 Add the joints or pieces to the hot oil in the frying pan and cook until they are lightly browned underneath.

3 Turn the joints and cook until they are lightly browned on the second side. Reduce the heat to prevent the joints from becoming too brown before they are cooked through, and continue cooking gently until the meat is cooked. Boneless thighs take about 15–20 minutes. Drumsticks take 30 minutes or longer, depending on their size.

Stir-frying

Fine strips of poultry cook quickly and they are tender. Being very lean, light and tender, chicken and turkey can also be cut into other shapes for stir-frying. Try diced or thinly sliced pieces.

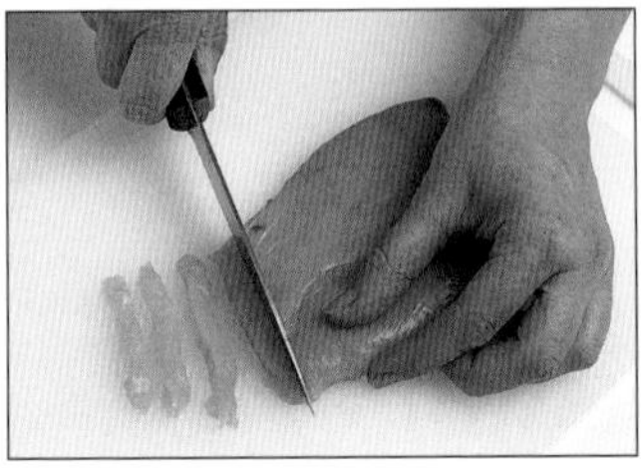

1 Cut lean pieces of breast crossways into thin, even-size strips using a large sharp knife.

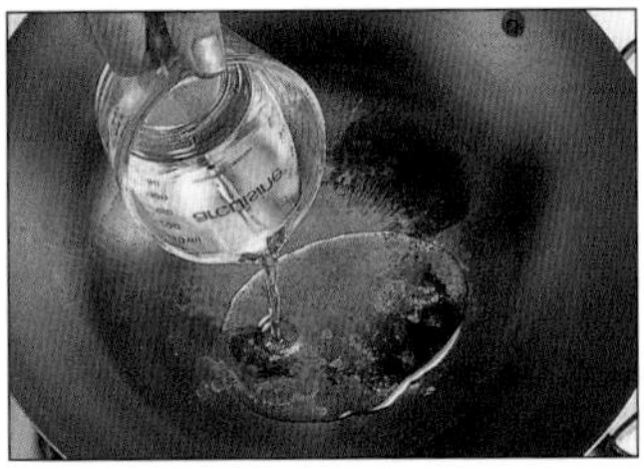

2 Heat the empty wok or a large, heavy-based frying pan until hot before adding a little oil to the pan. Heat the oil until it is very hot.

3 Add the strips of poultry (you may need to do this in batches) and stir-fry using a wooden spatula over a high heat for 3–5 minutes, until browned. The cooking time depends on the quantities, the oil and the type of pan.

Casseroling

Moist cooking methods bring out the flavour of the poultry and offer the opportunity for allowing herbs, spices and aromatics to infuse the light meat thoroughly. Whole birds and joints can be casseroled.

1 Brown the poultry pieces or bird all over first. Remove from the pan before softening chopped onion, carrot, celery and other flavouring ingredients in the fat remaining in the pan.

2 Replace the poultry before adding the chosen liquid – stock, wine, canned tomatoes or even water. Season the casserole well, then bring it just to simmering point. Cover it closely and allow it to simmer very gently on the hob. Alternatively, cook in the oven at 180°C/350°F/Gas 4.

Cooking times for casseroling
For a whole bird, allow 20 minutes per 450g/1lb, plus 20 minutes.
Large portions 45–60 minutes.
Boneless breasts take about 30 minutes.
Chunks or diced poultry 20–40 minutes, depending on their size.

Flavouring and serving poached small poultry

Water is the essential base, providing a good stock. Dry white wine or cider may be used as part of the liquid – about half and half with water. Dry sherry or vermouth can be added in small quantities to intensify the flavour.

Herbs, such as tarragon or thyme are a good choice, in combination with bay leaves and parsley. Use them in the cooking liquid and add them, freshly chopped, to a plain cream sauce for serving with poached poultry.

As well as lemon, lime or orange go well with poultry. Add the pared rind to the cooking liquid or the grated rind to a plain cream sauce for serving with hot poultry. Flavour mayonnaise or créme fraîche with citrus rind and herbs to complement cold poultry.

Carrots and onions are essential flavouring ingredients; leeks, fennel, and turnips can also be added. For a simple, traditional meal, keep the poached bird hot under tented foil in a warm place, while simmering neat chunks of potato and celeriac in the cooking liquid for 15 minutes, until just tender. Add broccoli florets and green beans about 5 minutes before the end of cooking. Serve the vegetables and seasoned broth with the poultry.

Poaching whole poultry

This is a gentle method for emphasizing the delicate flavour of a bird. The cooked bird can be served hot with a light cream sauce, or allowed to cool in its cooking liquid. The bird can then be jointed, or the meat can be carved from the bones.The meat from poached chicken is moist and succulent, and ideal for using in salads or other cold dishes. To cook a whole bird you will need a large pan or flameproof casserole to hold the bird, flavouring ingredients and plenty of cooking liquid.

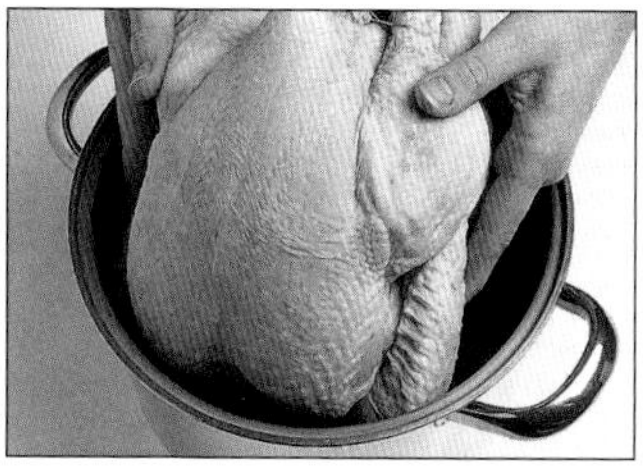

1 Truss the bird neatly and tightly with string and then place it in a large, heavy-based saucepan, stockpot or flameproof casserole.

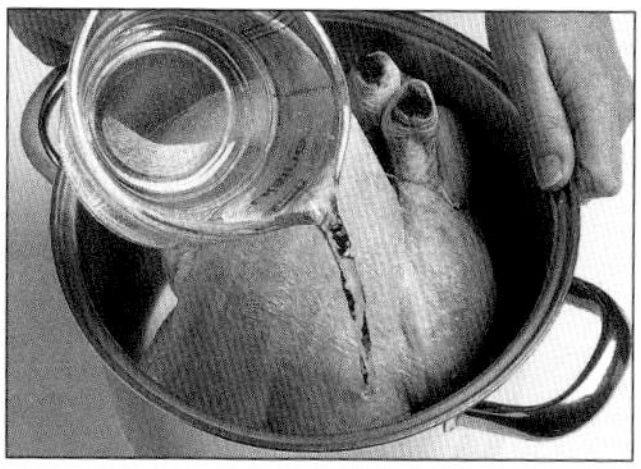

2 Pour in enough liquid (see flavouring and serving poached small poultry, left) to come just to the top of the bird. Heat gently until the liquid is just starting to simmer. Using a large spoon, carefully skim off any scum that rises to the surface of the liquid during the first few minutes of cooking, before adding any flavouring ingredients, spices or herbs.

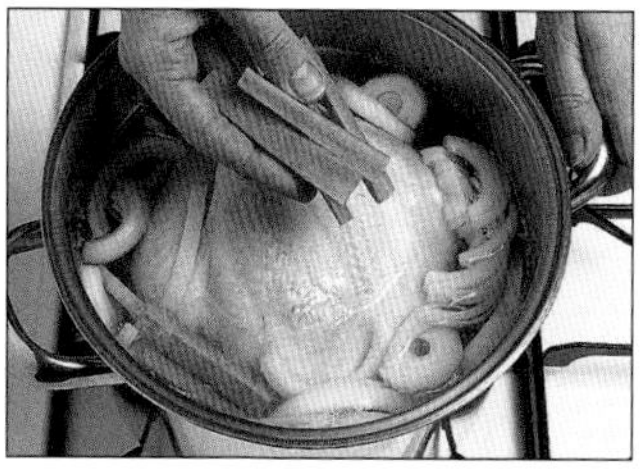

3 Add the chosen flavouring ingredients to the pan or casserole. A selection of any of the following work well: sliced onions, thick sticks of carrot, a bouquet garni, a strip of pared lemon rind, about 6 black peppercorns and a good sprinkling of salt.

4 Bring the liquid back to simmering point, reduce the heat if necessary and then cover the pan tightly. Cook gently for the calculated time.

5 Use a large draining spoon to lift the bird from the cooking liquid. Transfer the bird to a large dish and use poultry shears and a sharp knife to cut it into serving portions or use as required.

Wines to serve with small poultry

Young red Burgundies and Beaujolais or, if you prefer white, the distinctively dry steely acidity of Chablis, go well with light poultry dishes like chicken, poussin and guinea fowl. Vouvray from the Loire Valley or a crisp Pinot Gris from Alsace also complement chicken dishes, particularly light, zesty salads.

Straightforward roast guinea fowl will take a medium red – a good red Burgundy – but if the bird has been cooked in a casserole, especially with red wine, go for something fruitier with a more intense flavour, such as a Spanish Rioja or a Shiraz from California, New Zealand or Australia.

When cooking, remember the golden rule: never cook with a wine that you would not be happy to drink. It is a false economy to cook with really cheap wine as it will only spoil good-quality poultry (or meat). And, don't put it all in the pot; it makes sense to serve the same wine to drink that you used for cooking the bird.

TURKEY

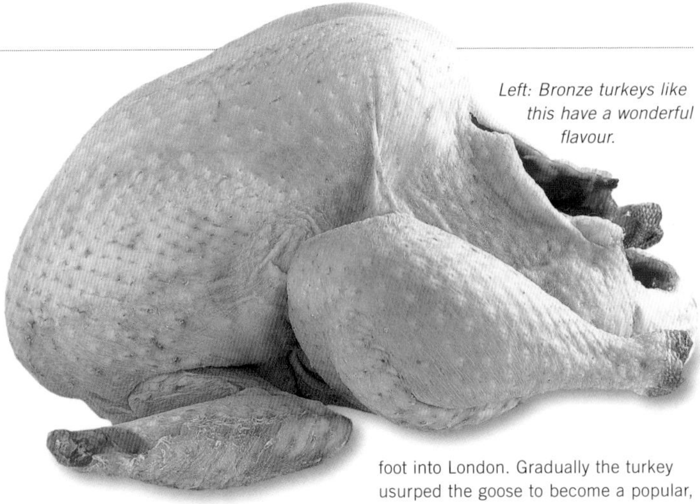

Left: Bronze turkeys like this have a wonderful flavour.

The turkey originates from America and was first domesticated by the Aztecs in Mexico. Turkeys were introduced to Europe by the Spanish, and they soon became a popular choice in France, Italy and Britain too.

When early settlers from Britain, France and Holland crossed the Atlantic to North America, the vast flocks of turkey that roamed wild provided them with sustenance. As the first crops failed in land that had not been properly cleared for cultivation, the majority of these first settlers succumbed to starvation and disease.

The plight of the early colonists was not warning enough for the Pilgrim Fathers who landed at Cape Cod in Massachusetts in 1620, after a 66-day voyage from Plymouth, England on the *Mayflower*. Being neither farmers nor trappers, they did not recognize the difficulties they faced. The Pilgrims made it through the winter with the help of the native population who already understood some English from earlier encounters with adventurers. The Native Americans shared their stores of berries, nuts and maize to supplement the settlers' diet of turkey.

In November 1621, on the first anniversary of their arrival, the Pilgrims entertained the Native Americans to a feast to show their appreciation; the celebration was said to have lasted for three days. This was how the turkey came to be established as the traditional bird for Thanksgiving celebrations and other festive occasions.

Well before turkey became popular in Europe, the bustard and peacock were served, as well as the goose and smaller fowl. Unlike unfamiliar vegetables that were brought from the Americas to Europe and treated with suspicion and caution, Europeans recognized the notion of cooking and eating large birds, so turkey soon became part of affluent feasts. In England, the birds were raised in Norfolk and Suffolk, then herded on foot into London. Gradually the turkey usurped the goose to become a popular, if expensive, Christmas treat.

Inevitably, its popularity led to the bird being farmed more intensively. Contemporary breeding and rearing have created birds with a larger proportion of breast meat, but much of the meat available is lacking in flavour. The status of the turkey as a bird for feasts has fallen and it is now an everyday choice.

Nutrition

Turkey is a lean source of high-quality protein. It provides B-group vitamins, particularly niacin, and is a good source of zinc, phosphorous, potassium and magnesium. It is also a source of iron.

Buying

Turkeys are available fresh, chilled or frozen. When buying a whole bird, look for a plump, well-rounded breast and legs, and clear, soft and evenly coloured skin. Avoid birds that are bruised, with blemishes or torn skin. Although there are likely to be small cavities left from plucking (particularly on dark-feathered birds), there should not be any patches of feathers. The bird should smell fresh. Turkeys vary enormously in weight, from about 2.75kg/6lb to over 11.25kg/25lb. They can grow up to vast sizes, such as 18kg/40lb, but the average weights available are 4.5–6.3kg/10–14lb.

Left: The best turkeys are free-range, organic birds from a known farm.

Above: A Norfolk Black, which has a very plump breast and a full flavour.

Storing

Place the turkey in a large, deep dish and cover it completely with clear film. Keep it in the coolest part of the fridge, making sure that it (or any drip from the bird) does not come into contact with other foods.

TYPES OF TURKEY

Bronze birds

These are dark-feathered birds and the skin may be spotted with slightly dark stubble remaining after plucking. Norfolk Bronze is a popular breed and Norfolk Black is a very plump-breasted bird. American Bronze is another traditional breed of turkey. Cambridge turkeys are also traditional in Britain and they have been crossed with American Bronze to breed the Cambridge Bronze.

White birds

In north America the White Holland is a popular breed of turkey. The majority of British turkeys are white, and traditional breeds include the Norfolk turkey. However, the superior-flavoured bronze and dark-feathered birds are becoming more popular, and more widely available.

Above: The majority of turkeys are white-feathered birds like this Norfolk turkey.

Free-range and/or organic birds

Both free-range and organic birds are available, and information on the rearing conditions are often provided. Birds that are labelled free-range should be checked carefully before buying, as this is not necessarily an indication of high quality. For the best turkey, seek out a source of organic birds from a known farm.

Cuts of turkey

As well as whole birds, there are a variety of prepared cuts of turkey available.

Part-boned breast This is a large roasting joint consisting of the whole breast, meat and bone, with skin on. Usually taken from large birds, these can weigh as much as a small turkey and provide a large number of portions. The joint can be stuffed under the skin. As well as a joint made up from the breast bone with meat on both sides, a breast fillet from one side, including the first part of the wing, can be removed from a whole turkey.

Boneless breast This is usually taken from one side of the breast, and neatly rolled or shaped with the skin around the outside. Quality varies – take care to distinguish between a boneless breast and a joint of "re-formed" meat, made up of scraps and off-cuts moulded into a joint under skin or a layer of fat.

Breast fillets These are skinless, boneless slices off the breast.

Turkey drumstick The leg of the bird is usually enough to provide a meal for four people with the right preparation. Turkey drumsticks have plenty of sinew running through the brown meat as well as fine bones. They can be roasted, but are better browned, then braised until the meat is succulent and tender, when they make full-flavoured casseroles.

Diced turkey Used mainly for pies and casseroles, this is often darker meat from the thigh or leg.

Stir-fry turkey These are long, thin strips of white breast meat.

Minced turkey This is good for pies, meat sauces and burgers or other recipes in which minced pork or beef would be used.

PREPARING TURKEY

Birds are usually sold cleaned and ready for stuffing or cooking. Methods of preparing small poultry apply to turkey, for example, trussing and tunnel boning are both relevant. The same rules also apply to hygiene when handling turkey. In addition, there are a few points to check before stuffing or roasting a large bird.

Singeing

Machine-plucking is not as thorough as old-fashioned hand-plucking, so birds tend to have more remnants of feathers. There are also areas of fine hair on the skin. Use tweezers to remove any remaining feathers. Then use a long lighted match to singe off any tiny feathers or hairs, allowing the smoke to burn away before drawing the flame across the surface of the skin. (Birds with dark plumage have dark "stubble", which may look slightly unpleasant, but these small pits from which the feathers have been removed will melt away during the roasting process. However, if there is a vast quantity all over the skin the bird should be rejected before purchase.

Removing fat

Check inside the neck end of the bird for any lumps of excess fat and pull or cut them away.

Stuffing

Never stuff turkey in advance. The stuffing can be made in advance, but the turkey should not be stuffed until just before it is placed in the oven. Weigh the stuffing and add this to the weight of the bird for calculating the cooking time. Truss the bird, then cook for the calculated time; never shorten the cooking time because the meat appears cooked – time must be allowed for cooking the stuffing.

Introducing aromatics

The popular method and technique generally recommended, is to place aromatics in the body cavity and pack the stuffing under the skin covering the breast. Cut a large onion in half and stud each half with 4–6 cloves. Place this in the body cavity of the bird. Cut 1 orange and 1 lemon into quarters and add these with 3–4 bay leaves, 4–6 sage sprigs and 2–3 thyme sprigs. Add 1 cinnamon stick or 1 blade of mace for a festive hint of warm spice.

Stuffing the breast

This is the most popular method. Loosen the skin over the breast meat and insert stuffing underneath it. It is a good idea to introduce some stuffing here, even when stuffing the cavity, as this protects the delicate breast meat during long cooking.

Making stuffing

Stuffings, fillings and forcemeats are highly flavoured mixtures of ingredients. They are added to plain foods (fish, poultry, meat or vegetables) to introduce complex flavours. They can take any number of forms, but bound mixtures are popular. Minced meat, particularly veal, pork or sausagemeat, is a traditional main ingredient. Mixtures are also often based on breadcrumbs. Rice is also a popular base for stuffings. In contemporary recipes, the stuffing may not be bound into a mixture that can be sliced or spooned out easily, but consist of loose combinations of chopped fruits or vegetables.

Flavourings

The essence of a stuffing is the flavouring it brings to the bird, from herbs, spices and citrus fruit to strongly flavoured vegetables. The flavourings must complement, not compete with, the poultry or meat. The binding ingredients are, essentially, the carriers that bring a balance to the mixture and make it delicious to eat.

Making stuffing balls

Any stuffing that is not used to stuff the bird can be rolled into small balls about the size of walnuts. Place these in a separate baking tin or add them to the roasting tin, arranging them around the bird, for the final 15 minutes cooking time, and then serve with the carved meat and vegetables.

Stuffing the body cavity

The stuffing can be prepared in advance and chilled separately from the bird but it should not be placed in the bird until just before roasting. Weigh both bird and stuffing, then add the weights together to calculate the cooking time. Thoroughly rinse the body cavity under cold running water, then drain it well. (Remember to thoroughly wash the sink afterwards.)

1 Wipe the turkey, inside and out, with kitchen paper.

2 Insert the sausagemeat stuffing, using your hands or a large spoon, but do not pack it in too tightly.

Stuffing the neck end

It is traditional to use two stuffings for turkey. Here sage and onion stuffing is used to fill the neck end of the bird. Before the stuffing is added, it is a good idea to remove the wishbone to make carving the breast easier.

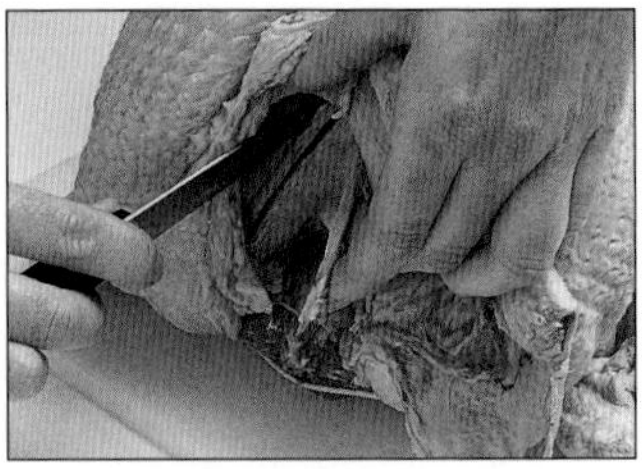

1 Fold back the flap of skin at the neck end and then use a small, sharp knife to cut out the wishbone, working right round the bone and cutting the meat as close to the bone as possible. Cut the bone free at the base on both sides.

2 Press the stuffing inside the shallow neck cavity.

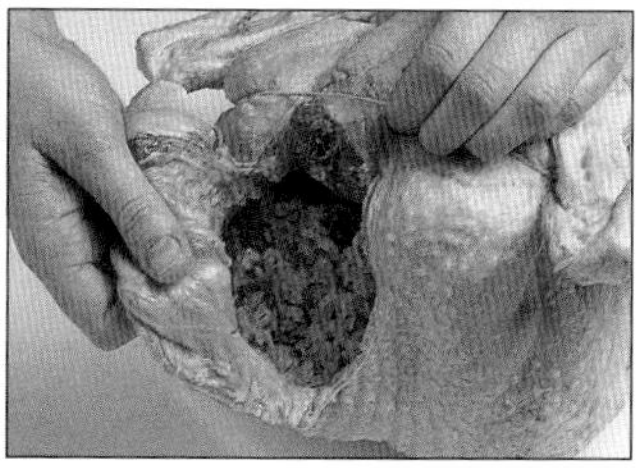

3 Turn the bird over on to its breast and pull the neck skin over the stuffing.

4 Truss the bird to secure the flap of skin in place. If necessary, use a metal skewer to keep the skin in place while trussing the bird with string.

Herbs for sausagemeat and chestnut stuffing

The stuffing is often left plain, especially when used in combination with sage and onion stuffing, but complementary herbs can be added. Try the following simple combinations:

Parsley and thyme Add 15ml/1 tbsp chopped fresh thyme and 45ml/3 tbsp chopped fresh parsley.

Tarragon and parsley Add 30ml/2 tbsp chopped fresh tarragon and 30ml/2 tbsp chopped fresh parsley.

Marjoram and orange Add 15ml/1 tbsp dried marjoram and the grated rind of 1 orange.

Sage and parsley Add 45ml/3 tbsp chopped fresh sage and 45ml/3 tbsp chopped fresh parsley.

Stuffings for turkey

Sausagemeat and chestnut These are favourite ingredients for stuffing turkey. Buy sausagemeat with a high proportion of meat, for the best stuffing. Use fresh chestnuts in season, or look for ready-prepared, vacuum-packed chestnuts.

1 Peel 900g/2lb fresh chestnuts, by slitting the peel and pulling it off. Remove the brown skin inside the shell. Cook the chestnuts in boiling water for 10–15 minutes. Drain well, then crumble the chestnuts into a large bowl.

2 Melt 25g/1oz butter in a large frying pan and add 2 finely chopped onions. Cook for 10 minutes, stirring occasionally until the onions are soft, but not browned.

3 Add the cooked onions to the chestnuts and mix well. Return the empty frying pan to the heat and then crumble in about 450g/1lb pork sausagemeat.

4 Cook the mixture over a low to medium heat, stirring frequently, until the sausagemeat is crumbly and well browned.

5 Add the sausagemeat to the chestnut mixture with 115g/4oz fresh white breadcrumbs. Season and add chopped fresh herbs if required (see below left). Beat 1 egg and mix it into the stuffing to bind the ingredients.

Sage and onion This is a classic stuffing, which is suitable for all types of poultry.

1 Melt 25g/1oz butter in a frying pan. Add 4 finely chopped onions and cook for 10–15 minutes, until soft but not browned. Set aside to cool.

2 Add the onions to 115g/4oz fresh white breadcrumbs and 60ml/4 tbsp chopped fresh sage. Season, then add 1 beaten egg and about 125ml/4fl oz stock to bind the stuffing.

COOKING TURKEY

Roasting

Turkeys are easy to roast, but require a little more attention than smaller birds. Check that the oven shelves are in the correct position before heating the oven.

1 Put the prepared, stuffed bird on a rack in a large roasting tin.

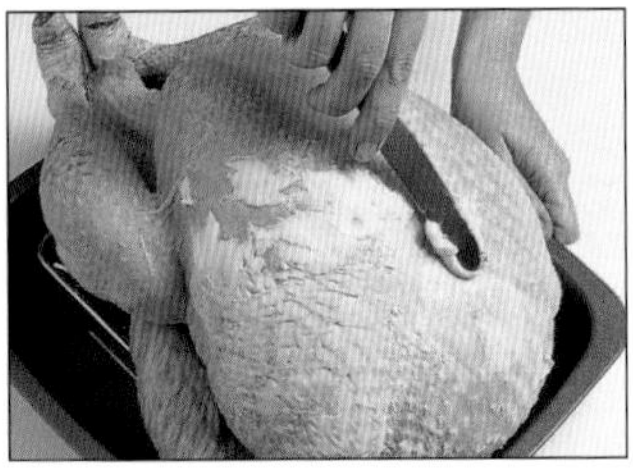

2 Smear the breast generously with butter (this helps to keep the meat moist). Season well with salt and freshly ground black pepper and place in the oven.

Thawing frozen turkey
Frozen turkey must be thawed completely before cooking. Unwrap the turkey and place it on a rack in a deep dish, so that the liquid that drips from the bird as it thaws runs below the rack and into the dish. Cover with clear film and place in the fridge.
Thawing times
Allow 2–3 days in the fridge for a 4.5kg/10lb bird.
Allow 3–4 days in the fridge for a 6.8kg/15lb bird.

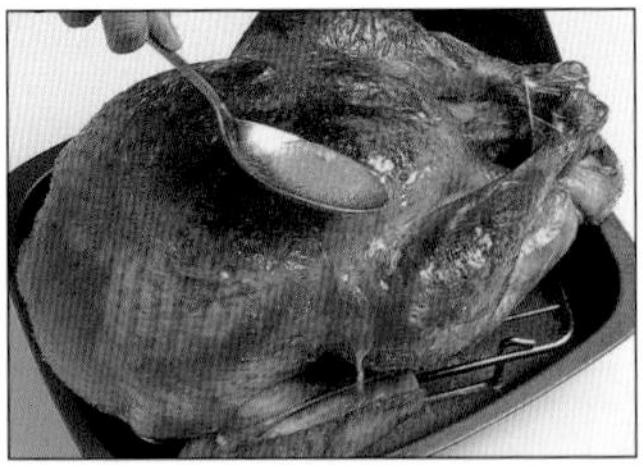

3 Baste the turkey frequently during the cooking time. When the breast has browned, cover the bird with foil and continue cooking and basting.

4 To check if the meat is cooked, insert a metal skewer into the thickest part of the thigh. If the juices run clear and the meat is white, it is cooked. If the juices run pink and the meat is soft and pink, the turkey is not ready, return it to the oven and check again after 20 minutes. Remove the foil for the final 20 minutes of cooking to finish browning the skin and give it a crisp texture.

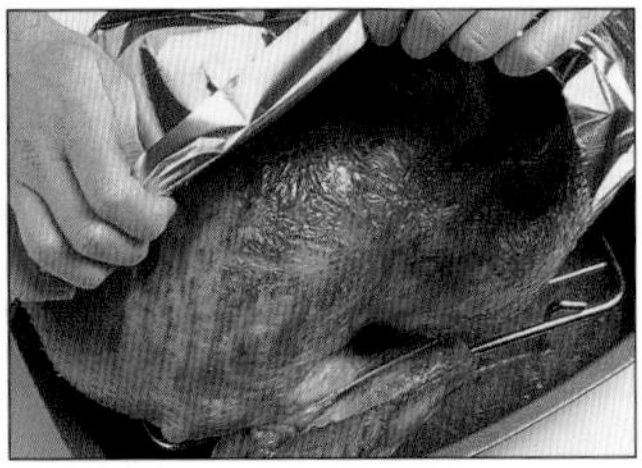

5 When the turkey is cooked, remove it from the oven and cover it closely with foil. Leave it to rest in a warm place for 15 minutes before carving. If you are going to make gravy, then transfer the turkey to a dish or carving tray.

Roasting times for turkey
Preheat the oven to 180°C/350°F/Gas 4. Calculate the cooking time, according to the weight of the bird (remember to weigh the bird and stuffing separately and add the two together, for total weight). Use the following as a guide to time, checking and basting regularly during cooking. It is difficult to estimate the exact cooking time when roasting large birds, as the shape and proportion of breast meat and the exact quantity and position of stuffing all influence the finished result.
For birds up to 4.5kg/10lb, allow 20 minutes per 450g/1lb plus an extra 20 minutes.
For birds over 4.5kg/10lb, allow 18 minutes per 450g/1lb, plus an extra 20 minutes.
For birds over 6.8kg/15lb, allow 15 minutes per 450g/1lb, plus an extra 20 minutes.

Carving turkey

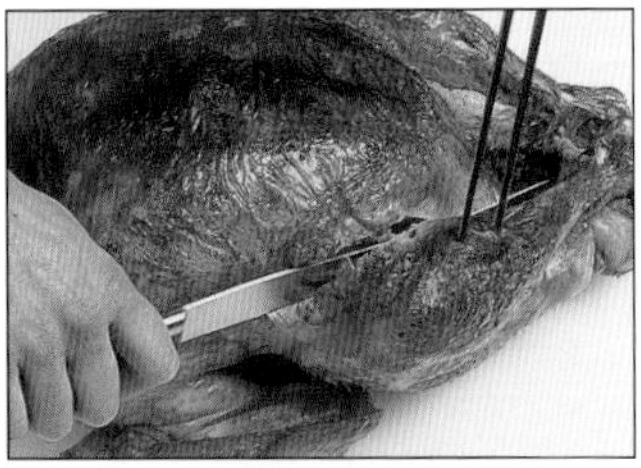

1 First remove the trussing string. Hold the bird steady in position with a carving fork. Cut off the legs from both sides of the bird, then cut these in half, or carve the meat from the bones.

2 Make a horizontal cut across the breast just above the wing.

3 Carve neat and even, vertical slices off the breast, then repeat on the other side. Arrange the slices of turkey on a warmed serving platter. Add the leg joints or meat to the platter or set them aside for serving separately.

Stir-frying turkey

Fillets of turkey breast are ideal for stir-frying. Thigh and leg meat can be slightly tough because it contains more sinew. Use turkey with Oriental-style ingredients or stir-fry the strips of meat with onions, mushrooms and a dash of sherry for a simple, lightly sauced dish. Flavour a "Western-style" stir-fry with chopped fresh herbs, such as tarragon, chives and parsley.

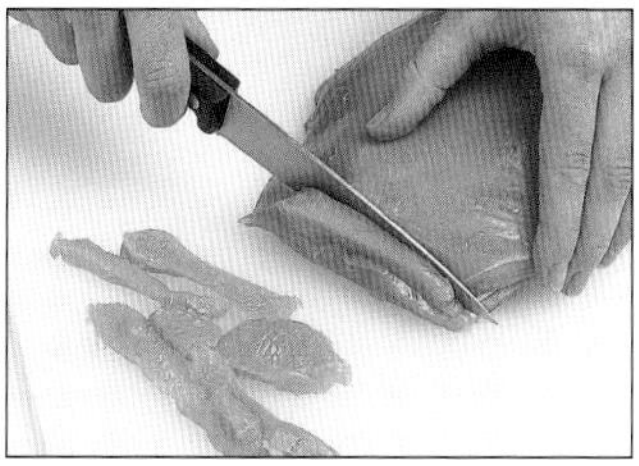

1 Cut the breast meat across the grain into thin, even strips. To save this preparation step, you can look out for ready-prepared packs of stir-fry turkey strips in the supermarket.

2 Heat a little oil in a wok or large, heavy frying pan. Sunflower, corn or groundnut oils are useful for stir-frying as they can be heated to a high temperature without smoking. Olive oil gives a good flavour, but it burns easily.

3 Stir-fry the turkey until golden brown. Cook the turkey in batches if necessary and remove the strips from the pan, continue until all the pieces are browned. Stir-fry the vegetables in the same pan, then return the turkey to the pan to finish cooking for a few minutes before serving.

Pan-frying turkey

This is a useful method for cooking fillets of turkey breast or fine escalopes. It is also the first stage for braising or casseroling poultry, particularly turkey. Small, neat portions of turkey thigh are ideal for casseroles.

1 Heat a little olive oil in a frying pan. Add the turkey pieces and cook, turning occasionally, for about 15 minutes, or until the meat is golden on all sides.

2 Once the turkey has turned golden brown, season it well and reduce the heat, then cover the pan and continue cooking gently for 15–20 minutes, or until the meat is cooked through and succulent. Serve at once.

Stewing and braising

Prepared diced turkey or portions cut from the thigh are a good choice of turkey cuts for stewing or braising. Whole drumsticks can also be cooked by this method, which renders them succulent and flavoursome.

1 First brown the pieces of turkey as for pan-frying. Instead of using a frying pan, a flameproof casserole can be used for browning and simmering or oven cooking.

2 When the turkey pieces are browned, use a draining spoon to remove them from the pan and set them aside.

3 Cook a selection of thickly sliced or coarsely chopped vegetables in the fat remaining in the casserole. As a simple base, try 1 coarsely chopped onion and 2 sliced carrots. Add other ingredients to taste: 1 sliced fennel bulb, 2 sliced celery sticks, 2 sliced garlic cloves, 1–2 bay leaves and sprigs of parsley, sage or thyme.

4 Replace the browned turkey portions and pour in enough stock just to cover them. Bring to simmering point, then reduce the heat and cover the pan. Simmer on the hob for about 1 hour or place in the oven at 180°C/350°F/Gas 4 for 1–1½ hours.

Wines to serve with turkey

The traditional wine-drinking rule that red wines are only served with red meat and white wine is reserved for poultry (and fish and shellfish) is being broken and the truth is that, nowadays, you can drink either red or white wine with turkey. It is simply a matter of personal preference.

Turkey is similar to chicken and you can drink some of the same wines with the bigger bird as you can with chicken and poussin. But turkey does have a slightly stronger flavour and it can take a fuller, fruitier wine, either red or white. Try a bright fruity red from the Côtes du Rhône or a big lightly oaked white Burgundy.

DUCK AND GOOSE

DUCK

In China, where ducks were probably first domesticated, some very prolific layers have long been appreciated for their eggs. The European types have descended from the mallard, as have North American varieties. The Peking duck, a type of mallard, is thought to have been one of the original breeds from which the American Long Island ducks are descended. The barbary, or muscovy, duck is another ancient breed from which today's birds have evolved.

American Long Island and British Aylesbury ducks have a deep, rich flavour and a significant proportion of fat. The barbary duck and the Nantes duck (popular in France) have slightly less fat. The barbary is a big bird providing a good portion of firm breast meat. The Nantes is smaller, more tender and with a delicate flavour.

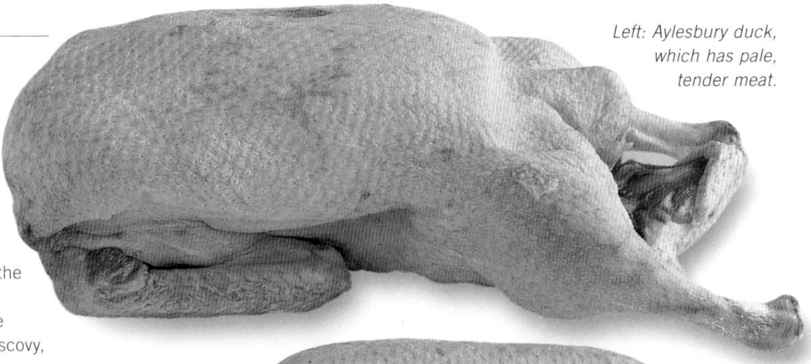

Left: Aylesbury duck, which has pale, tender meat.

Above: Barbary duck has less fat than other breeds.

Below: Geese have defied all attempts to rear them intensively, and so these birds are one of the few remaining truly seasonal foods.

The Rouen duck is more like game than duck in both taste and texture. This is due to the method by which they are slaughtered and the traditional method of cooking the bird. They are killed by being smothered to avoid loss of blood, then plucked while still warm, encouraging the blood to rush to the breast meat, making it particularly dark. The breasts are removed and lightly cooked while the remainder of the carcass is grilled, then pressed to remove any juices that it contains. These juices are the base for a rich sauce which is served on the rare breast meat.

Modern breeding and feeding methods have brought leaner ducks to the supermarket, with a good proportion of breast meat and only a fine layer of fat under the skin. The majority are ducklings, less than two months old. As well as whole birds, portions and breast fillets are readily available.

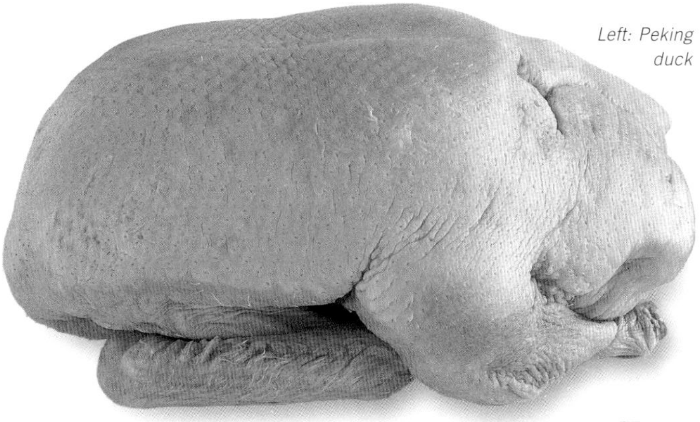

Left: Peking duck

GOOSE – A SEASONAL BIRD

Unlike other domesticated poultry and animals, the goose has defied the instigators of intensive rearing methods. Geese are not prolific layers and they are one of the few remaining sources of seasonal food. This large, fatty bird traditionally survived by pecking about and foraging for any available food. Found on poor farms because it was economical to keep and a good source of meat or fat, a special bird would be fattened for Christmas. It is the traditional celebration bird and has always been seen as a treat; a bird for both the poor and the rich.

In Britain, green goose was the young goose, so named because it had been fed off grass, rather than the stubble left in the fields after harvesting.

Above: Duck breast and a leg portion

Green goose was traditional for Michaelmas in September – country people thought that eating goose on Michaelmas day brought good luck for the rest of the year. The second season for goose was, of course, Christmas, when fattened, older birds were served.

Goose fat had all manner of uses; it was used by country people for rubbing into the chest to ward off colds and other household uses as well as for cooking. Preserved goose, the French *confit d'oie*, is the thoroughly stewed and rendered goose preserved in its own fat. Across central and Eastern Europe as well as Scandinavia, goose and goose fat are traditional in cooking.

The most popular variety of bird is the Canada goose which, at 2.75kg/6lb, serves six people. The smaller greylag and even smaller pinkfoot are both well-flavoured birds. The smallest goose is the whitefront, which weighs about 2.5kg/5½lb in feather.

Nutrition

Duck and goose are high-protein foods. They also contain B-group vitamins and some minerals. Being high in fat, duck and goose should not feature frequently in the healthy diet, but they are excellent for special meals.

Buying

Look for light-skinned, plump birds. They should be soft and moist with no blemishes, bruises or feathers. The bird should smell fresh. Goose is seasonal and is also available frozen.

Storing

Cover the bird loosely with greaseproof paper and keep on a deep tray in the bottom of a fridge so that the juices don't spill on to and contaminate other foods (especially cooked meats). The best and safest way to thaw a frozen duck or goose is slowly, in the fridge.

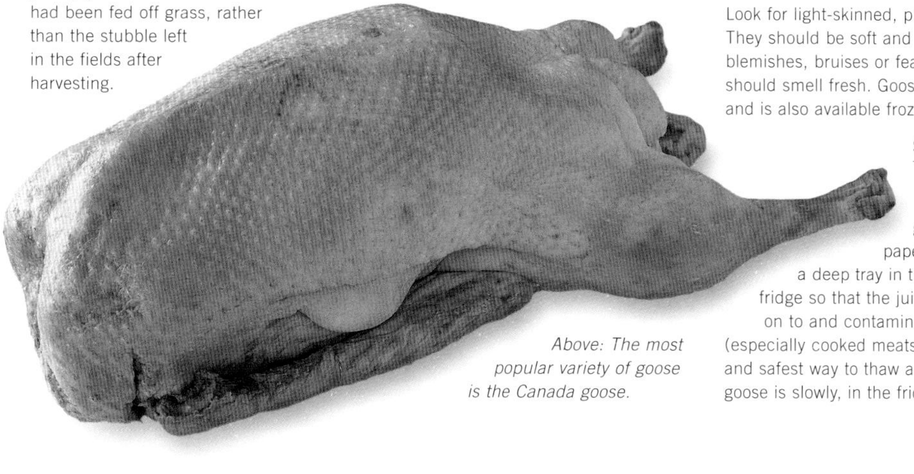

Above: The most popular variety of goose is the Canada goose.

PREPARING DUCK AND GOOSE

Duck and goose are sold prepared and ready for the oven. When buying a whole bird, remember that most are sold complete with giblets, packed in a small plastic pouch and placed in the body cavity – remember to remove these before roasting the bird (they can be used to make a rich gravy; turn to the section on gravies for instructions).

Jointing a duck

Ducks have a higher proportion of bone to meat than chicken. Therefore, rather than follow the contours of the joints, as when preparing chicken portions, it is best to cut the bird into four equal-size pieces, allocating a good amount of meat to bone on each piece. Poultry shears and good, sharp knives are essential equipment for jointing birds.

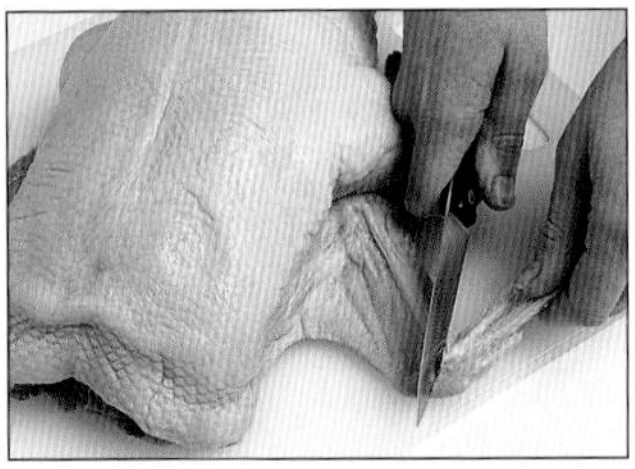

1 Use a small, sharp knife or poultry shears to trim the wing tips.

2 Carefully fold back the skin at the neck end and, using a small knife, cut out the wishbone.

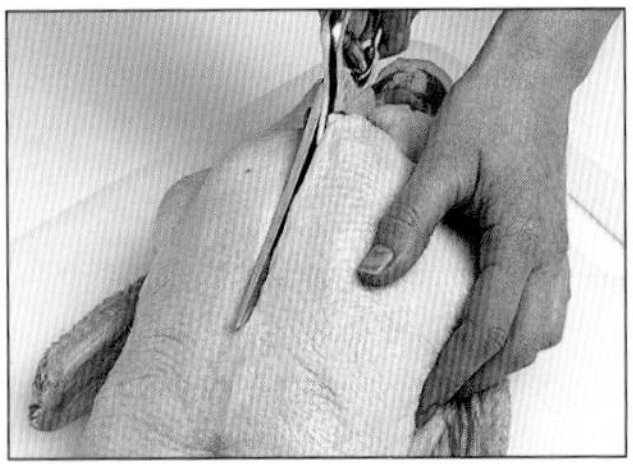

3 Use poultry shears to cut the breast in half from the tail to the neck. Split the breastbone with the shears as neatly as possible.

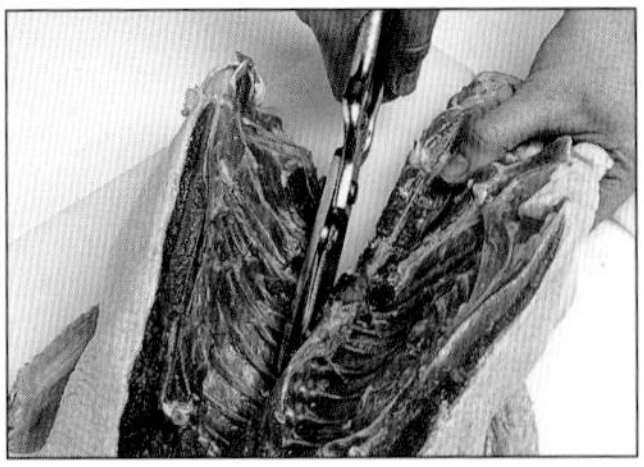

4 Separate the bird in half by cutting along each side of the backbone, then remove the backbone.

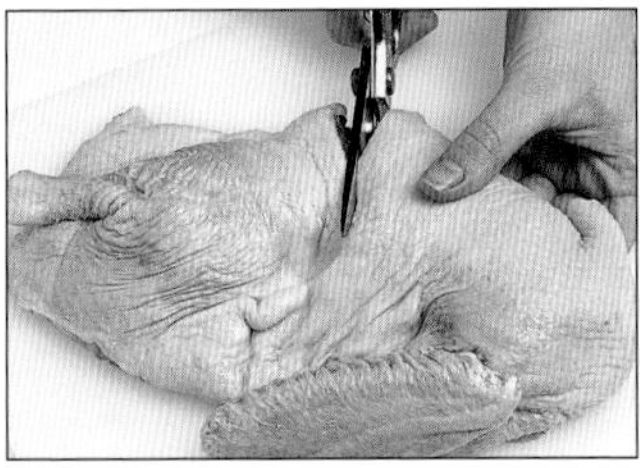

5 Cut each portion in half again. Cut diagonally to share the portion of meat equally between the 4 portions. This can be awkward – it's easier to cut through the flesh first, then the bone.

Boning duck breasts

Sometimes known as *margrets*, from the French name for them, boneless duck breasts have a much stronger flavour than chicken breasts and the meat is richer and darker. Duck breasts are a good choice if you enjoy the rich flavour of the meat, but want to have as little as possible.

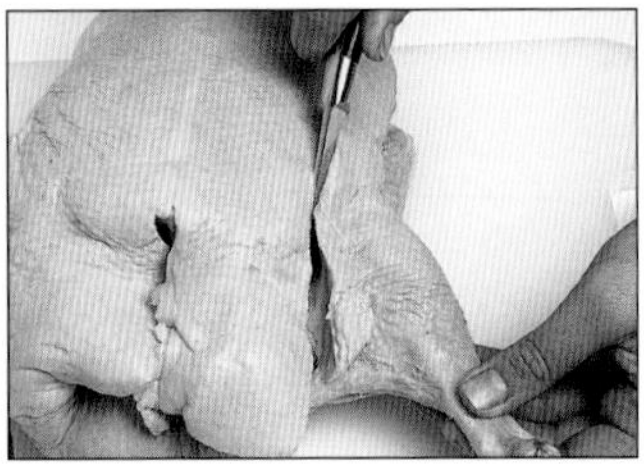

1 Use a sharp knife to cut the legs and thighs off the duck.

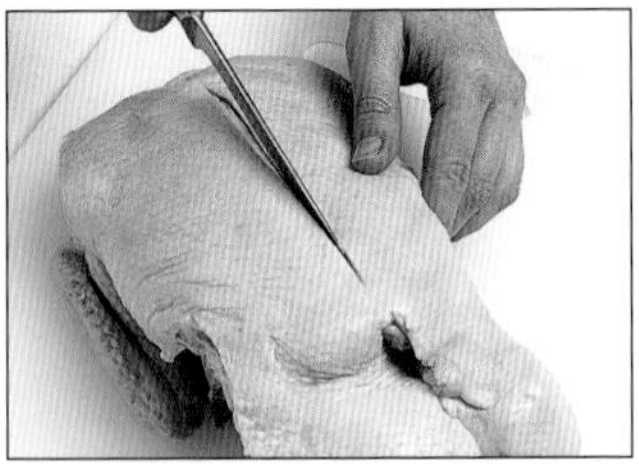

2 Place the duck on a chopping board. Cut along the breastbone on one side, working down the middle of the duck.

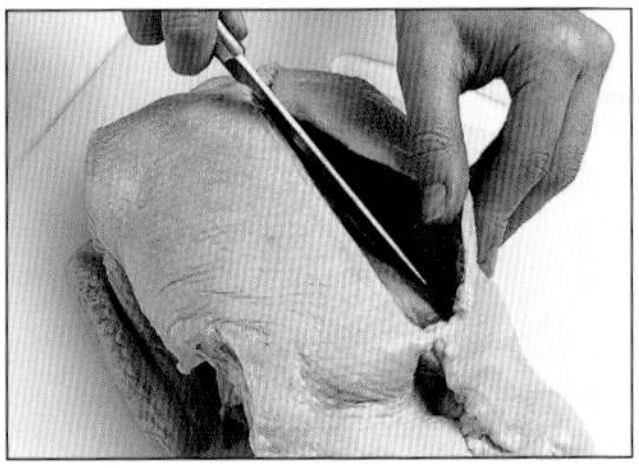

3 Gradually cut the breast meat off the bone on one side of the carcass.

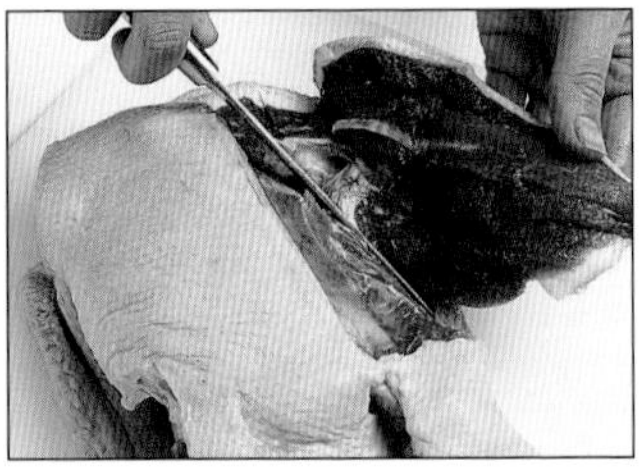

4 Lift the breast meat away as you cut it free from the carcass. Repeat on the opposite side of the carcass.

5 Turn the breast skin-side down on the board and cut out any sinews that run along the meat.

6 One way of finishing the breast before cooking is to lightly score the skin and fat in a diamond pattern, using a sharp knife. This allows the fat to escape and gives the cooked duck breast an attractive appearance as well as crisp skin and well-flavoured flesh.

Rendering duck or goose fat

Duck and goose fat are excellent for frying because they can be heated to a high temperature without burning. Potatoes fried or roasted in a little duck or goose fat become crisp and golden, as well as full-flavoured.

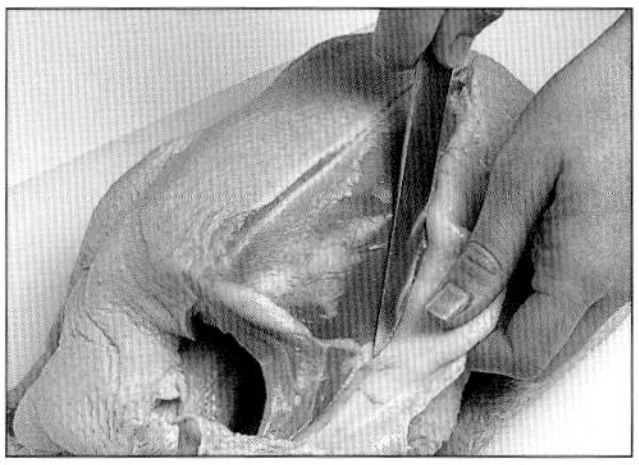

1 Cut the skin off the duck and trim all the excess fat from the bird.

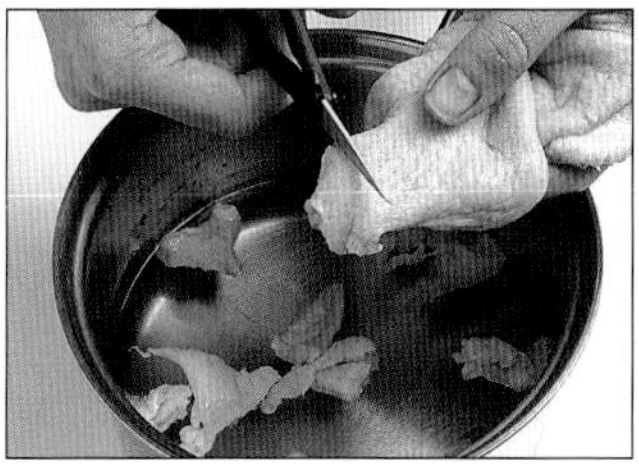

2 Cut the skin and fat into small pieces and put in a pan with 200ml/7fl oz/ scant 1 cup cold water.

3 Heat until simmering, then reduce the heat to very low and cook, uncovered, for 1½ hours or until the fat has all melted down. Strain the fat through a fine sieve and leave to cool. Then store the fat in a covered container in the fridge and use for frying.

COOKING DUCK AND GOOSE

These are fatty birds, with dark meat that has plenty of flavour. The fat helps to keep the meat moist during cooking. Goose is almost always roasted, though the legs may be added to casseroles. Ducks are generally roasted whole, or cut up for frying or casseroling.

Roasting duck and goose

When roasting duck, remember that an average duck will not yield a high proportion of breast meat when carved, so unless the bird is to be jointed into sections when cooked, it is usual to roast two small ducks to serve four people. Goose does not yield a high proportion of meat and a 4.5kg/10lb goose will serve eight to ten people.

1 Stuff the bird if required, then truss it. Sage and onion stuffing is a classic choice for both duck and goose.

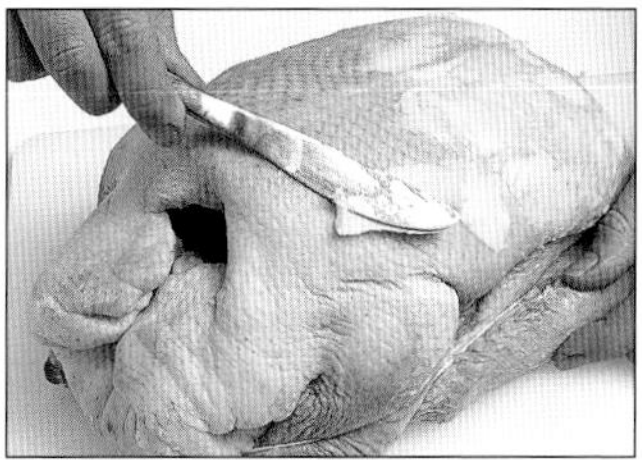

2 Season well and smear a little butter over the bird. This enriches the flesh and helps give the bird a golden colour.

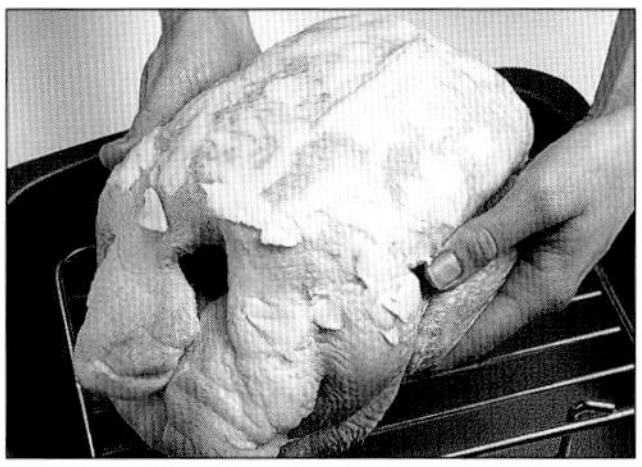

3 Put the bird on a rack in a roasting tin (the excess fat will drip into the tin). Roast the duck for the calculated time. Turn and baste the bird frequently to keep the skin and flesh moist.

Roasting times for duck and goose
Preheat the oven to 180°C/350°F/ Gas 4. Weigh the bird and calculate the cooking time, allowing about 30 minutes per 450g/1lb for duck and 15–20 minutes per 450g/1lb for goose. To crisp the skin, raise the temperature to 200°C/400°F/ Gas 6 for the last 30 minutes.

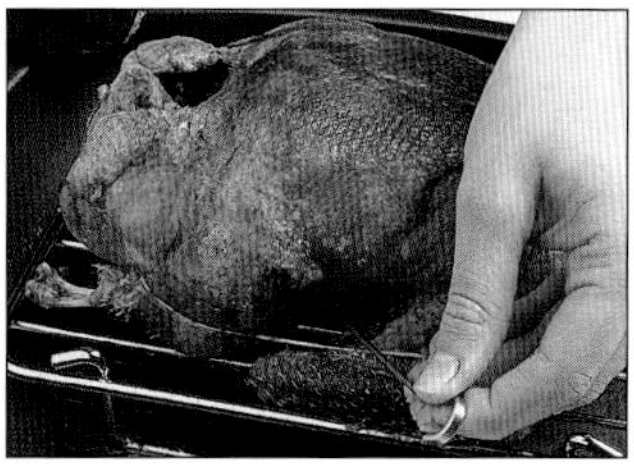

4 To check if the bird is cooked, insert a skewer into the thickest part of the thigh. If the juices run clear, the duck is cooked. If the juices are pink, the bird is not cooked.

5 Cover the roast bird tightly with foil and leave it to rest in a warm place, where it will not continue cooking. A warm grill compartment is suitable (without the heat on). Allow 10–15 minutes resting for the temperature to become even throughout the meat.

Wines to serve with duck or goose
Try a soft, medium fruity red with roast duck – for example a Chilean Merlot. A young claret or a good Beaujolais also goes well with duck, especially roast or casseroled duck served in a fruit sauce. Vouvray, a medium white wine from the Loire, which has a wonderful crisp acidity, is a good choice for matching tart sauces, such as orange. Hearty roast goose could take a full-bodied red, such as a mature Burgundy, Côtes du Rhône, Côte-Rôtie or Chateauneuf-du-Pape.

Carving roast duck or goose

A small duck of up to 2.5kg/5½lb can be halved or quartered; the meat from a larger duck can be carved into neat slices. A goose can be carved as for a duck and the breast meat cut into slices.

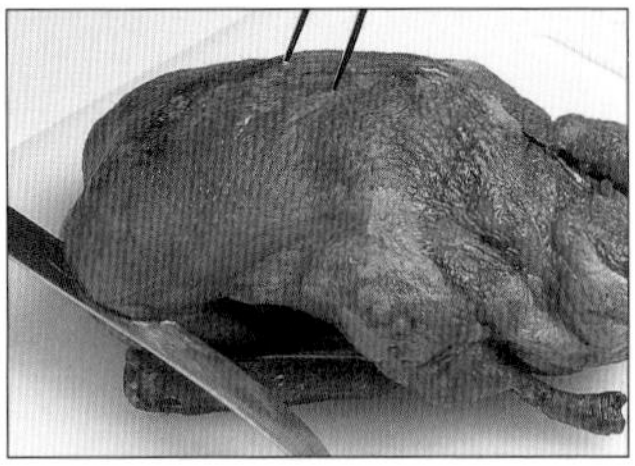

1 Cut the skin between the legs and the body, pushing the legs out with the blade of the knife to reveal the breast meat.

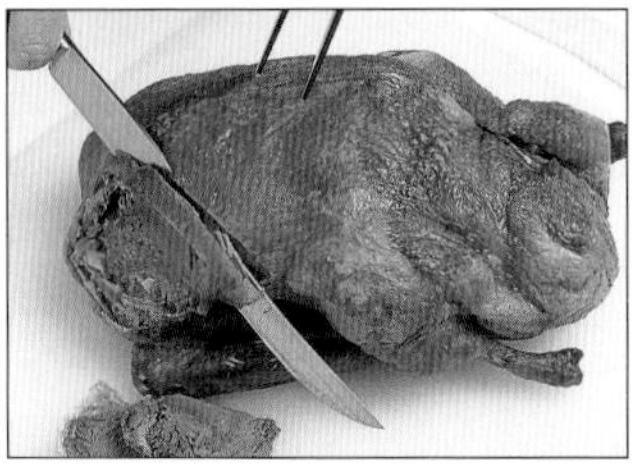

2 Make a horizontal cut just above the wing joint, through the breast meat to the bone. (If the wishbone has not yet been removed, cut it out.)

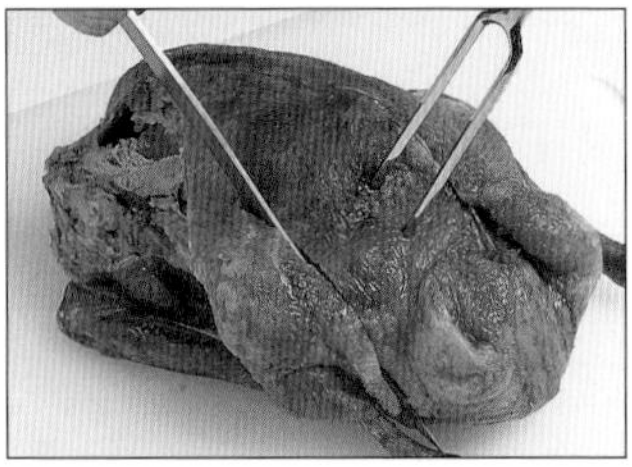

3 Carve long, neat slices off the breast, working at an angle to give diagonal slices. This provides the largest number of slices from each breast. (Alternatively cut slices the full length of the bird, parallel to the rib cage.)

4 To remove the legs, turn the bird on its side and push the fork through the thigh. Force the leg outwards to break the joint that is located under the bird. Cut the leg off. Repeat on the other side. Cut the leg portions in half through the joint.

Grilling duck

1 Preheat the grill to its hottest setting. Season the duck breasts well. If it is important to remove as much fat as possible during cooking, prick the skin all over with a fork. Leaving the skin whole tends to keep the meat as moist as possible during cooking.

2 Place the breasts skin-side up on the rack of a grill pan.

3 Cook for 4–7 minutes, turning once, until well browned on both sides.

Pan-frying duck

Duck has a high fat content and it is well suited to dry-frying, without the addition of any extra fat.

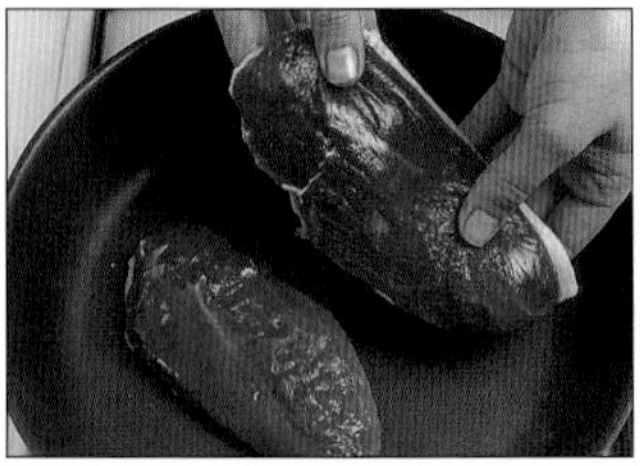

1 Heat a heavy-based frying pan or flat or ridged griddle until hot. Put the duck breasts in the dry pan, skin-side down. Don't overcrowd the pan; cook the breasts in batches if necessary.

2 Cook over a moderate heat for 3–4 minutes, pressing down using a palette knife or spatula to keep the breast flat and to force out all the fat from the skin.

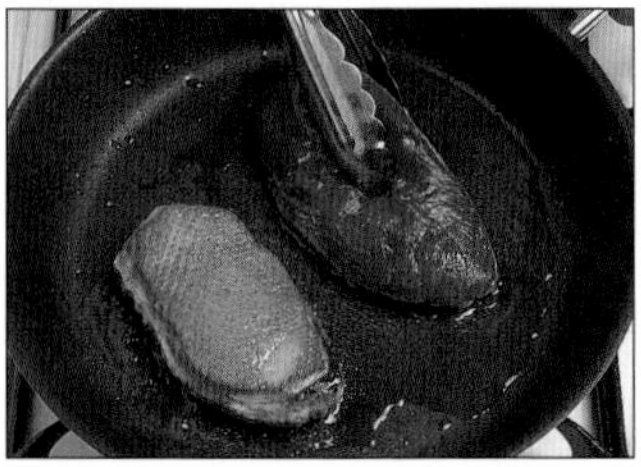

3 Turn the duck breasts over using tongs, and cook for 3–4 minutes on the second side. When cooked, the breasts should be slightly firm and still quite pink in the centre.

4 Remove from the pan and place on a plate. Cover with foil and leave to rest in a warm place for 5 minutes.

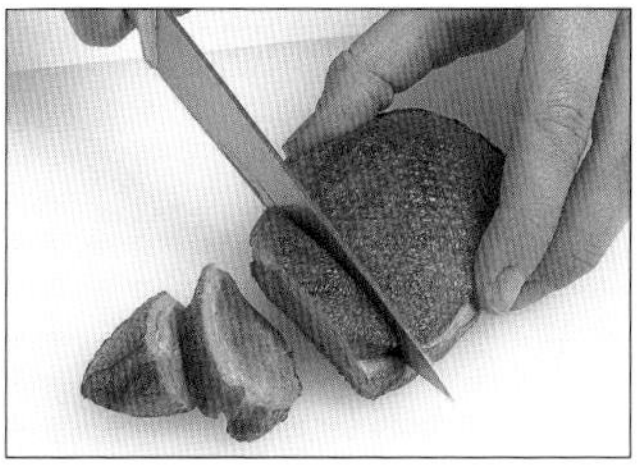

5 Use a sharp knife to cut the breasts into neat slices, working at an angle of about 45°.

Stir-frying duck

Sharp and sour flavours go well with stir-fried duck and are popular in Oriental dishes. Skinless, boneless breast meat is suitable for this method of cooking. Although duck breast meat is fairly expensive, it is a rich-tasting meat and stir-frying is a good way of making a little meat go a long way.

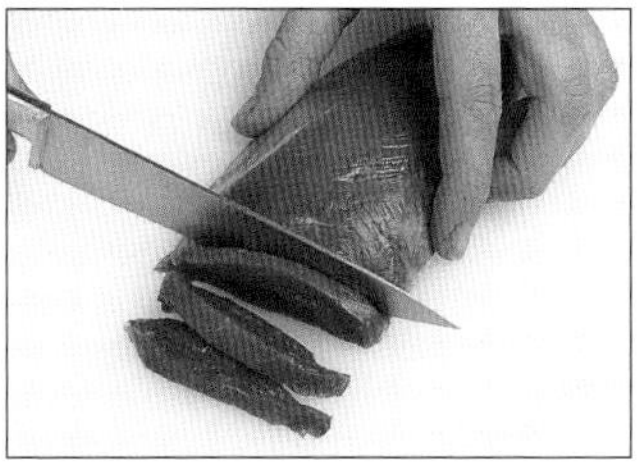

1 For quick, even cooking, the duck meat must be cut into thin strips. Use a large, sharp knife and slice the meat crossways into even-size pieces.

2 Add just a little oil to a wok or frying pan. Use groundnut, sunflower, corn or vegetable oil, which can be heated to a high temperature without burning.

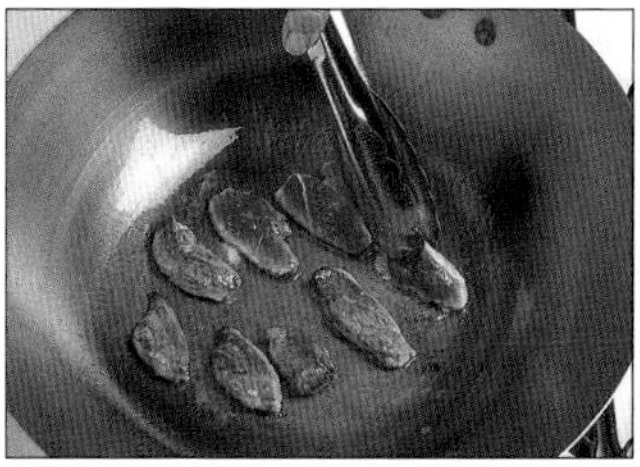

3 When the oil is very hot, add the duck and stir-fry over a medium to high heat for 2–3 minutes, or until tender.

Casseroling duck

There are many traditional recipes for duck casseroles and they were often greasy dishes. With the leaner duck available today, there is no reason to have a fatty result.

1 Brown the duck portions well first; if your casserole isn't large enough to fit the duck pieces in one layer, then do this in a heavy-based frying pan. Drain off all but a little fat before adding and softening the vegetables.

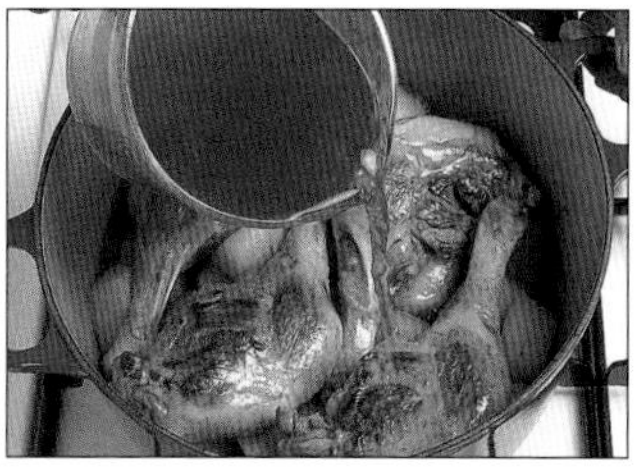

2 Transfer the vegetables and duck (or return the duck) to the casserole and pour in the liquid. This can be stock, red or white wine, or cider. Bring to the boil, then transfer the casserole to the oven and cook at 180°C/350°F/Gas 4 for about 1½ hours. Alternatively, simmer gently on the hob. Before serving, skim off any fat and adjust the seasoning.

Accompaniments to serve with duck and goose

Oranges and sharp cherries complement these rich poultry and are popular for flavouring sauces. Sharp apple sauce is also traditional. Cranberry sauce goes well with both duck and goose. Goose is traditionally stuffed with chestnuts and apples, pears and quinces. Plum or gooseberry compotes also go well with goose. Fresh herb and onion sauces and dressings are favourite accompaniments in America and Canada. Fresh peas are a classic vegetable for serving with duck. Sage, thyme, rosemary and mint are good herbs for duck.

Sharp and sweet flavours go well with fatty meats, cutting their richness. Dried fruit, such as prunes and apricots, are good examples, especially when combined with spirits, such as brandy, or fortified wine, such as port. Fresh green flavours also balance them well – watercress, chives, spring onions, rocket and tarragon are excellent ingredients for pepping up sauces or reduced roasting juices boiled with a little wine.

GAME BIRDS

Although game birds are shot for sport, historically they are a major source of food. Until recently, there seemed to be no end to the wild birds that could be acquired for the pot, but the fact that some species were in danger of becoming extinct eventually led to the introduction of conservation laws and hunting seasons in many countries. Today, game birds are protected by law.

There are "closed" seasons when game cannot be killed to allow them to grow in number again. Fresh game is only available in shops during the hunting season, but in some countries frozen game is stocked throughout the year. The seasons vary slightly from state to state in north America and from country to country in the rest of the world. In Britain, grouse, ptarmigan and snipe can only be shot between 12th August (the Glorious Twelfth), and 10th December (or 31st January in the case of snipe). The season for partridge runs from 1st September to 1st February, and for pheasant from 1st October to 1st February.

Above: Pheasants are the most plentiful of game birds and are often sold in a brace: a pair of birds that includes the smaller hen and a cock.

Left: The magnificent Capercaillie, which was hunted to extinction in Britiain in the late 18th century.

Tradition, myth and mystery surround game to such an extent that many people are swayed from sampling the birds. They are now sold prepared and ready for the oven, and are no more difficult to cook than chicken, turkey or goose. Young birds are best roasted but older birds benefit from long, slow cooking for tender results.

Nutrition

Feathered game is a high-quality protein food in the same sense as poultry. The advantage it has over most farmed meat and poultry is that it is low in fat and free from additives.

Buying

Larger supermarkets offer a good choice of game in season. Specialist butchers offer a wider choice, frozen products and extensive advice. A butcher who specializes in game will be able to tell you the age and the sex of the bird, and give you useful cooking information, too.

Below: Oven-ready cock (top) and hen pheasants.

Game birds do not look as perfect as poultry. They often look a little damaged, and they may have the odd tear in the skin, but they should not be seriously injured. Limbs should be intact, not broken. Pheasant should be even in shape with no serious shot damage (see checking for shot opposite) with a strong, but pleasant aroma. Partridge should be plump, with an obvious smell of game and soft, pale flesh. When buying grouse, look for moist, fresh skin, deep, red flesh and no serious shot damage. Fresh quail should have a good round shape and plump flesh – a bird with a high proportion of meaty flesh to bone.

Above: Red-legged (left) and grey-legged partridges are two different species – the grey-legged is generally smaller.

Storing

Birds that are sold pre-packed and sealed should be left in their packing and used by the date on the packet. Place loose birds in a deep dish and cover with a lid or clear film. Store in the coldest part of the fridge. A bird that has been hung and is ready for cooking can be kept for one to two days in a fridge or it can be frozen.

Checking for shot

Unfortunately, tiny balls of lead shot are left in game birds. Rub your fingertips over the surface of the game to try to locate any small hard balls, and then cut them out. Always warn those who are eating the dish to be aware that the bird may contain shot.

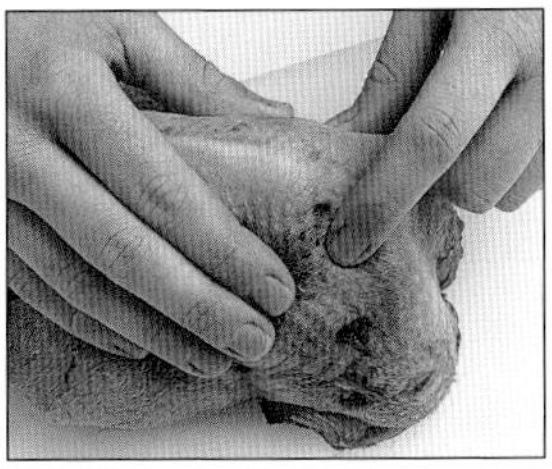

TYPES OF FEATHERED GAME

Pheasant

By far the most plentiful and popular of game birds, pheasant was originally introduced to Europe from China. Pheasant are often sold in pairs, a male and female, known as a brace. The hen is more tender and smaller than the cock and it will serve three people, while the cock will serve four.

Above: Oven-ready, red-legged and grey-legged partridges. The smaller, grey-legged bird (bottom) is considered to have a superior flavour.

Right: Mallard is the largest wild duck and should serve two or three people.

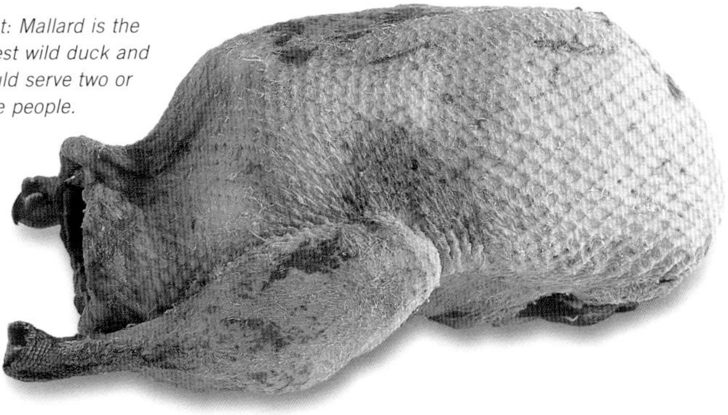

Pheasant is excellent for roasting or stewing: roast a young bird and stew an older fowl.

Grouse

Native to Scotland, where grouse is regarded as the king of feathered game, it has a wonderful, rich flavour from feeding on highland heather. One bird provides a good single portion. While young birds are usually roasted or grilled, older birds are cooked in a casserole. Complicated recipes for grouse are few and far between because this bird is best prepared and served simply.

Partridge

There are two main types of partridge, the French or red-legged partridge, which was introduced into England in 1673, and the indigenous English or grey-legged partridge. The red-legged bird is bigger but the flavour of the grey bird is often preferred. Partridge can be roasted, stewed or braised. Young birds are best roasted and served in their own cooking juices. Partridge is not very big: serve one per person.

Wild duck

This is far less fatty than domesticated duck, which is important when you come to cook it. Generally, most recipes for duck can be adapted to either bird, but it may be necessary to add a little fat when cooking the game bird. Duck taken from inland water is usually preferable to that from salty water (the latter tend to have a slightly fishy flavour). Plump **mallard** is the largest and most common of all the

Above: Wigeon

Below: Oven-ready wigeon

Below: Oven-ready teal

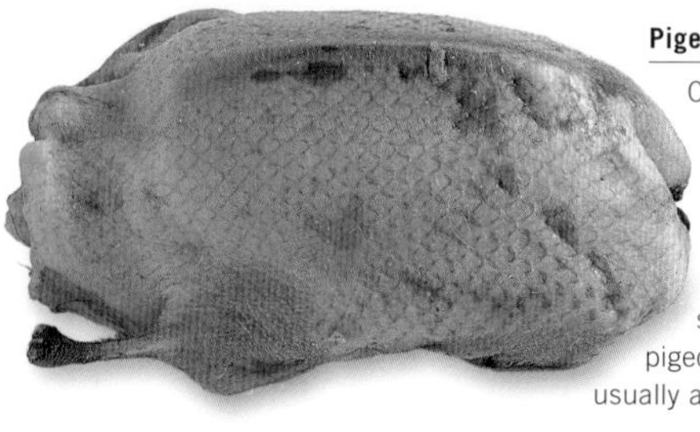

wild ducks. It is more intense in flavour than domesticated duck and is excellent for roasting. One bird serves two to three people. **Teal** is one of the smallest wild ducks and is highly prized by gourmets, and **canvasback**, **wigeon**, **gadwall**, **pintail** and **pochard** are also available. Young birds are generally tender but older ones can be quite tough and in need of long, slow cooking in a casserole.

Wild goose

The Canada goose (which averages about 4.75kg/10½lb in feather or 2.75kg/6lb dressed) is one of the plumpest and tastiest of geese and it serves six people. The smaller greylag (3.8kg/8½lb in feather) and the even smaller pinkfoot (2.7kg/6lb in feather) are also good on the plate. The smallest wild goose you are likely to come across is the whitefront (2.5kg/5½lb in feather). Roast a wild goose in the same way as a domesticated goose. As with wild duck, try to avoid those wild geese from salty water; birds that have been feeding on grass or stubble taste much better than those that have been living and eating on marshland. Also avoid birds over a year old, as these are not considered good enough to eat.

Quail

Native to the Middle East, where there are many different varieties of this small bird. Quail are available all the year round; these are very small birds, and one provides a starter or two make a main-course portion per person.

Pigeon

Cheap, plentiful and available all the year round. The pigeon is found wild all over the world, yet has never been held in particularly high esteem, but it is surprisingly tasty. Wood pigeons are meaty birds, and usually about 450g/1lb in weight.

Above: Quail

Left: Pigeon

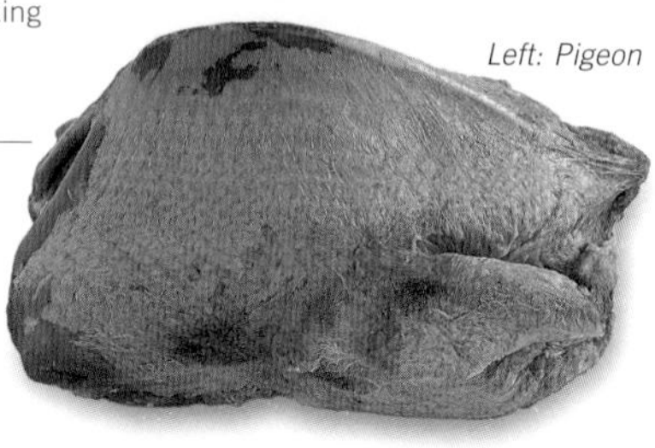

Serve one per person. Pigeons can be braised, cooked in a salmis, where the birds are first roasted, then finished in a sauce, or they can be turned into pigeon pie.

Squab

This is a young pigeon, and these small birds are now reared commercially for eating, although they are usually only available in the spring. Squabs weigh about 350g/12oz. They have meaty breasts and are more tender than older, wild pigeons, and so they can be simply larded with bacon or pork fat and then

Small birds

Coot, corncrake, moorhen and rail are marsh birds from around the world. With the exception of corncrake, they are not prized for their flavour. The corncrake (also known as a land rail) often leaves the marshes for the fields, which explains its superior flavour.

The stockdove, rock dove (ancestor of the domestic pigeon) and turtle dove have never been as popular as the wood pigeon. Lark, plover, thrush, hazel hen and mud hen are treated as game birds in some countries.

Right: Woodcock

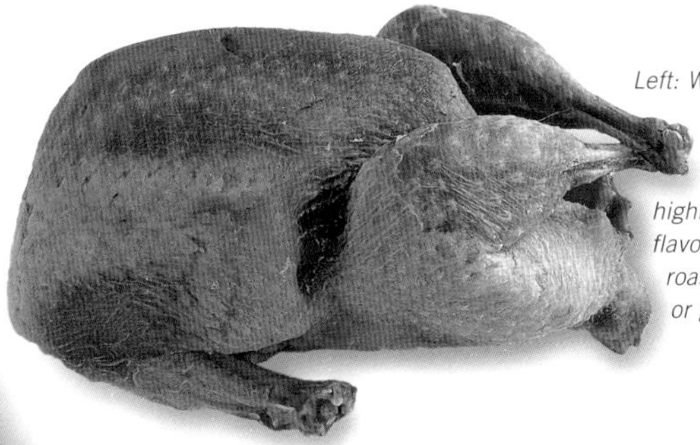

Left: Woodcock is a tiny bird with a plump, meaty breast and is highly prized for its flavour. It can be roasted, braised or grilled.

roasted at a fairly low temperature for about an hour, and served with the flesh still pink and juicy. They can also be braised, or split in half and grilled.

Woodcock

This long-beaked bird has a wonderful, rich flavour. Woodcock can be roasted, braised, grilled or broiled. It is a small bird, so one is usually served per person. When the birds are roasted it is usual to leave the innards intact as this is thought to add to the flavour. The innards or "trail" can be eaten – usually spread on toast, and served with the bird. The head is left on, but skinned and is often split after cooking as many gourmets regard the brain as quite a delicacy.

Snipe

This is a tiny, long-legged marsh bird with a very long beak. Like the woodcock, it is seldom seen for sale in butchers' or game dealers'; you are more likely to come across snipe if you, or someone you know, shoot. It is best roasted, although some are so small that they can also be grilled – split the birds in half and flatten them first. Serve one or two per person.

Capercaillie

This magnificent bird, which weighs about 4kg/9lb, resembles a very large grouse. It was hunted to extinction in Britain by the end of the 18th century. Nowadays, it is found in the mountainous regions of northern Europe and has been reintroduced to Scotland, but it is a forest forager and has an inferior flavour compared to grouse.

Above: Snipe is more likely to come your way if you or your friends shoot.

Ptarmigan

This member of the grouse family is called rock ptarmigan in North America. It is very rarely seen (or shot) because its preferred habitat is a high, stony mountainside. The flavour of the meat varies according to the wild foods that the bird has been eating, but it is somewhat similar to that of other grouse.

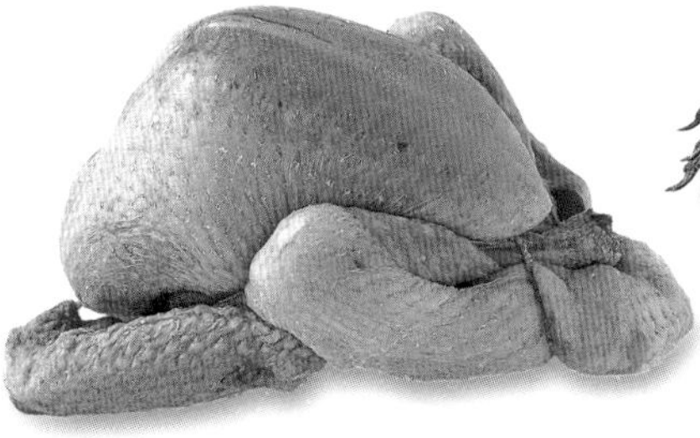

Above: Squab, which is a baby pigeon reared especially for the table, is a perfect individual portion and is best cooked and served whole.

Below: Snipe, prepared ready for cooking.

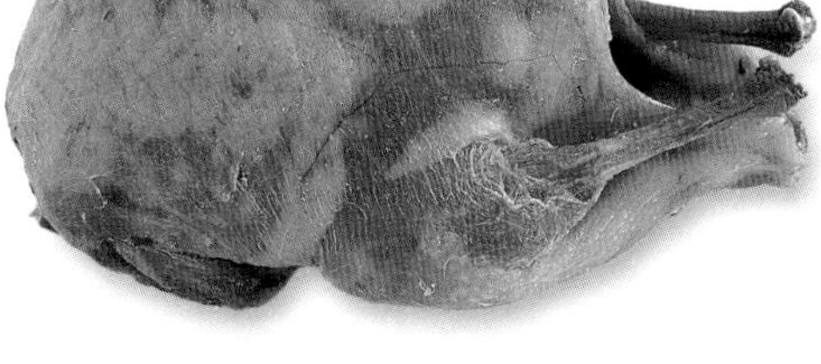

PREPARING GAME BIRDS

Game is sold hung, feathered, drawn and ready for cooking. Specialist butchers will advise on game which has been hung for a short time and is light in flavour, or they will hang game for a longer period, on request, to develop a more intense flavour. Plucking and hanging are not practical techniques for home preparation; the former is messy and can be done in an outbuilding, but, to avoid rotting game, it must be hung in suitably cool, dry and airy conditions which encourage it to mature without extensive rotting. Should you have feathered game, your local specialist butcher will probably be prepared to hang and pluck the bird for you.

Trussing a pheasant

This helps keep the bird in shape during cooking.

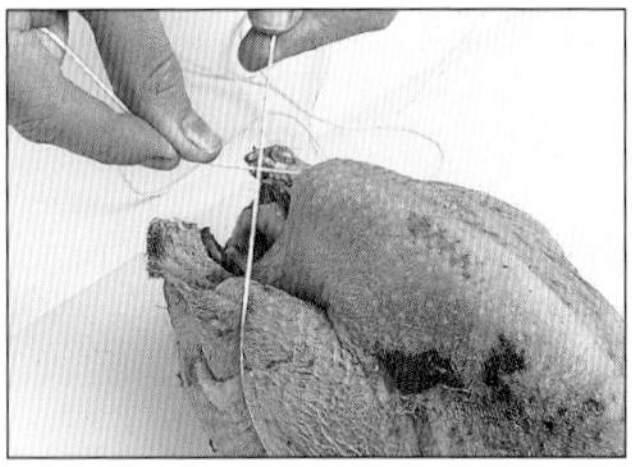

1 Season the bird well. Take a piece of string around the wing joints and bring both ends forward across the thighs. Cross the ends over.

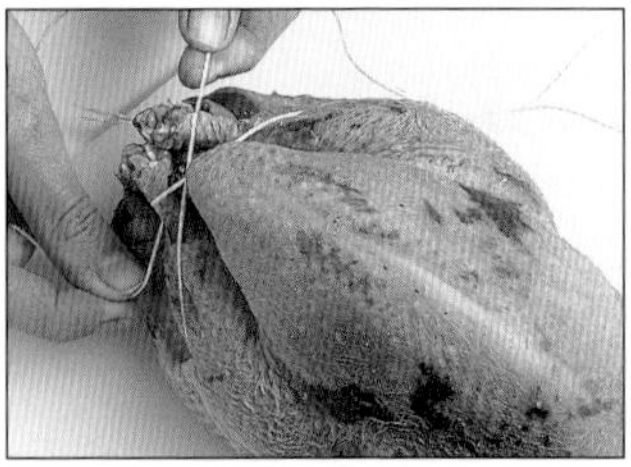

2 Wrap the string around the thighbones, then cross the ends. Pull the string under the parson's nose and tie it neatly. Tuck the ends of the thighbones neatly into the cavity.

Jointing a grouse for casseroling

When repeated on both sides, jointing produces two wings, two breasts, two thighs and two drumsticks.

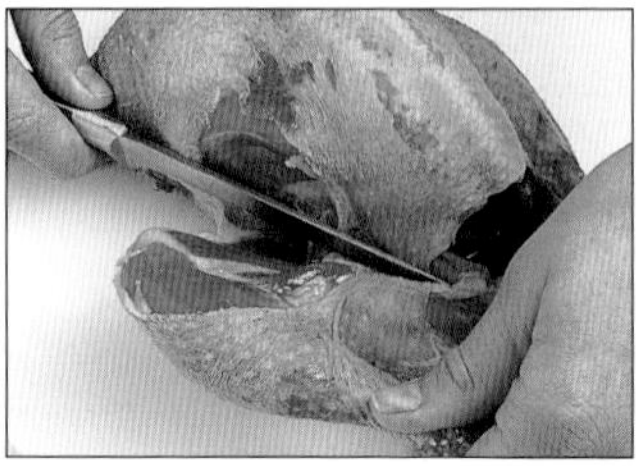

1 Using a sharp knife, remove one leg from the bird by cutting through the skin and then through the thigh joint. Repeat on the other side.

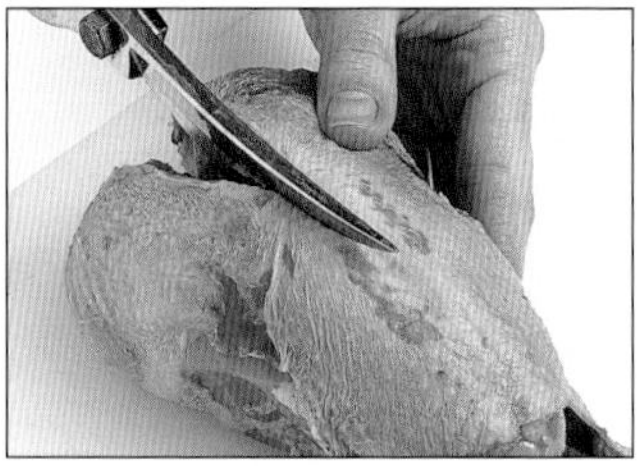

2 Using a pair of poultry shears, or sharp, kitchen scissors, cut the breast in half, splitting the breastbone.

3 Turn the bird over and then cut out the backbone using poultry shears or scissors. Leave the wings attached to the breast portions.

4 Using the poultry shears, cut each breast in half diagonally so that one piece of breast is attached to the wing.

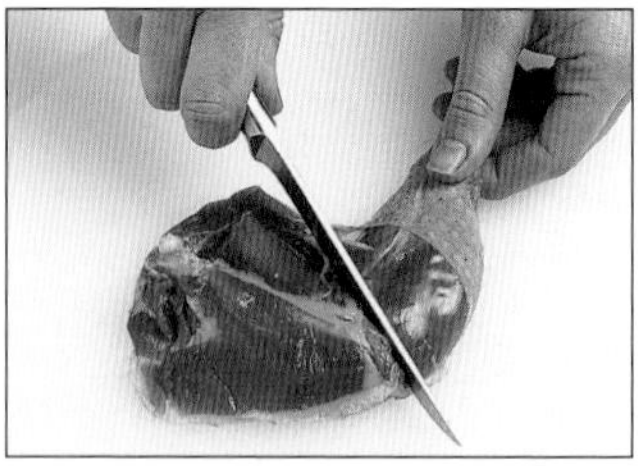

5 Using a sharp knife, cut each leg in half through the knee joint.

6 Cut off the wing tip at the first joint.

Spatchcocking a pigeon or wild duck

If you want to grill small birds it is best to spatchcock them (split and open them out flat) first to ensure that they cook evenly. The following method is essentially the same as for poultry, but it is a good idea to remember to handle smaller game birds gently to avoid damage.

1 Tuck the wings under the bird and remove the wishbone using a small, sharp knife.

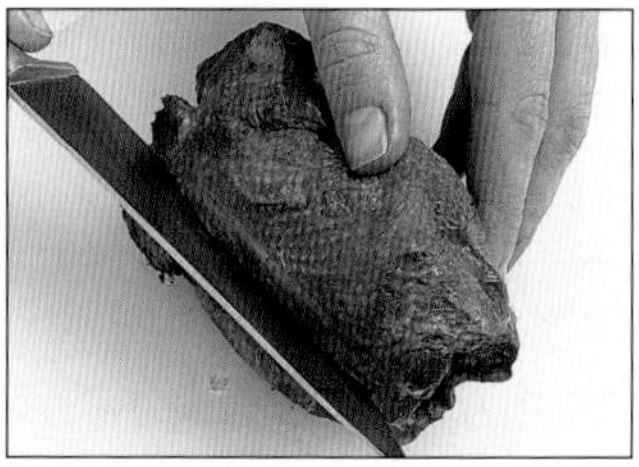

2 Turn the bird over and use poultry shears or a large sharp knife to cut along each side of the backbone.

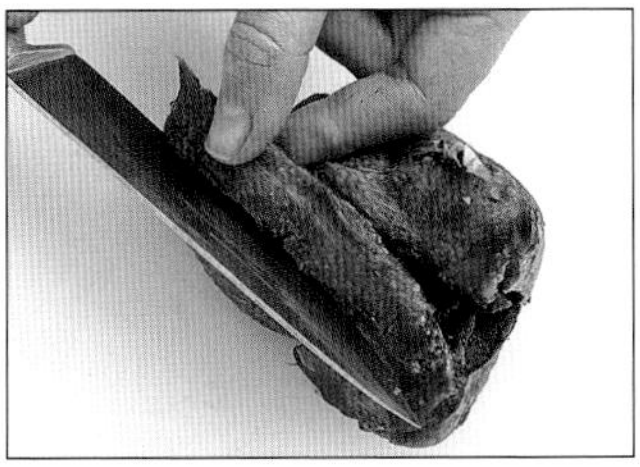

3 Remove the backbone from the bird.

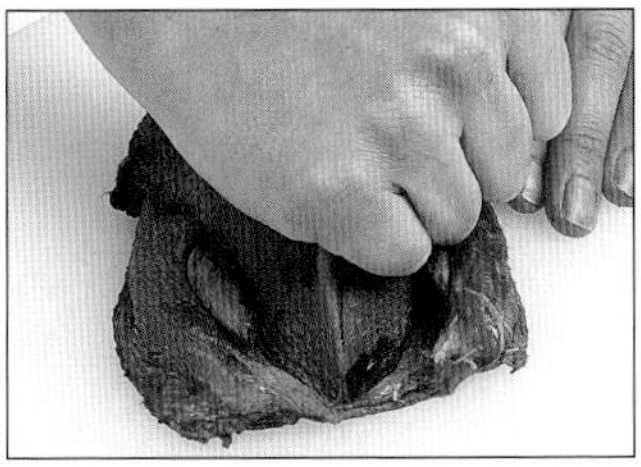

4 Put the bird on a chopping board and push down hard with your fist to break the breastbone.

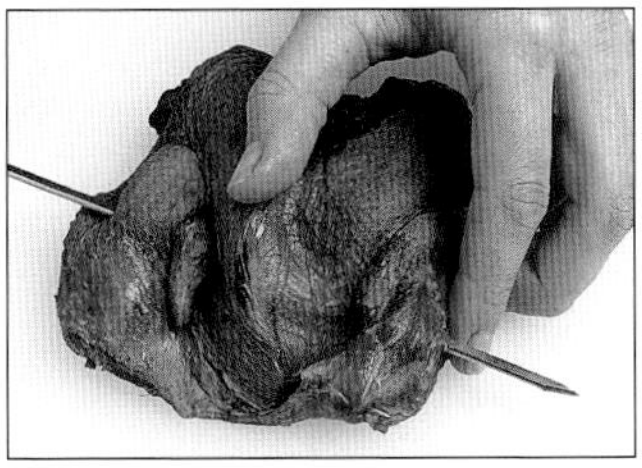

5 With the bird pressed flat, push a skewer through the wings and breast.

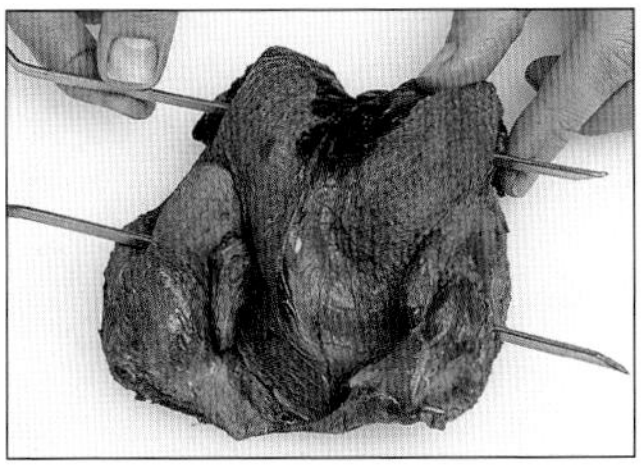

6 Push a second metal skewer through the thighs.

COOKING GAME BIRDS

Simple cooking methods are often the best for game; plain roasting for tender birds and simple casserole cooking for those that are tougher.

Roasting

With the exception of restaurant facilities, spit-roasting has been replaced by practical oven methods. Lean game birds should be basted frequently or larded with fatty bacon before roasting to keep them tender.

1 Season the bird and cover it evenly with streaky bacon.

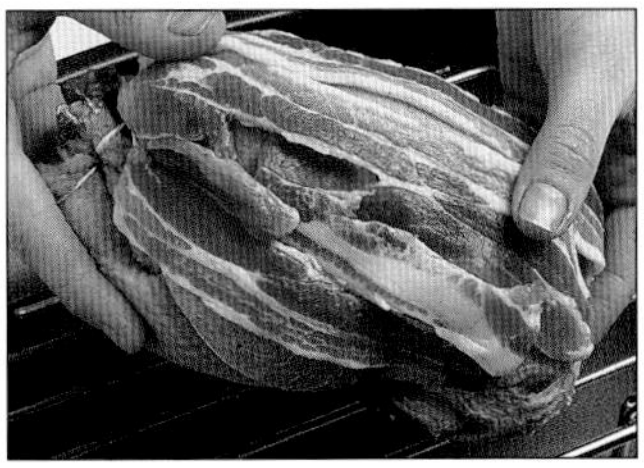

2 Put the bird on a rack in a roasting tin and place in the preheated oven.

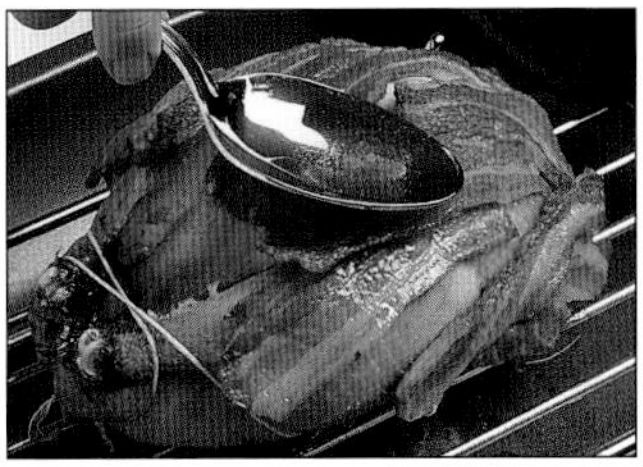

3 Baste the bird frequently to keep it moist and succulent during cooking.

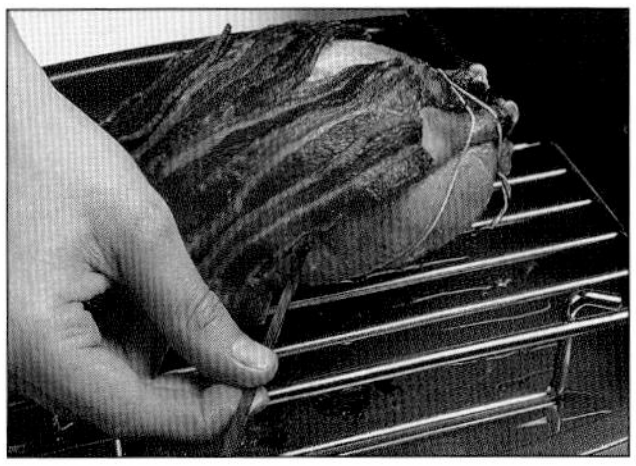

4 To check if the bird is cooked, use a metal skewer to pierce the meat at the thickest part of the thigh. If there are any signs of blood in the juices, the bird is not cooked.

5 Cover the bird closely with foil and set it aside to rest in a warm place for 5–10 minutes before carving.

Roasting times for game birds
Game birds are always roasted quickly at a high temperature. Prepare the bird or birds as described above, then weigh and calculate the cooking time. Baste frequently during cooking.

Pheasant Allow 30–45 minutes at 230°C/450°F/Gas 8.

Grouse 20–30 minutes at 230°C/450°F/Gas 8.

Partridge 15–20 minutes at 240°C/475°F/Gas 9.

Quail 18–20 minutes at 220°C/425°F/Gas 7.

Pigeon 15–20 minutes at 240°C/475°F/Gas 9.

Woodcock 15–18 minutes at 240°C/475°F/Gas 9.

Snipe 10–15 minutes at 240°C/475°F/Gas 9.

Carving game birds

Let the bird rest in a warm place for a few minutes before carving.

1 Remove the bacon used to bard the bird and cut off the trussing string.

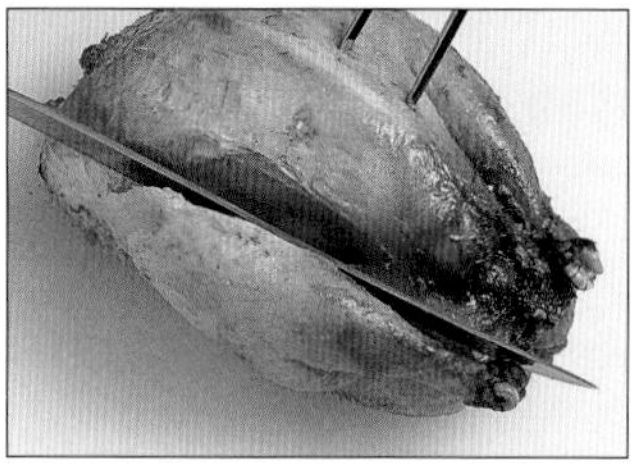

2 Cut through the skin on either side of the bird and cut off both the legs.

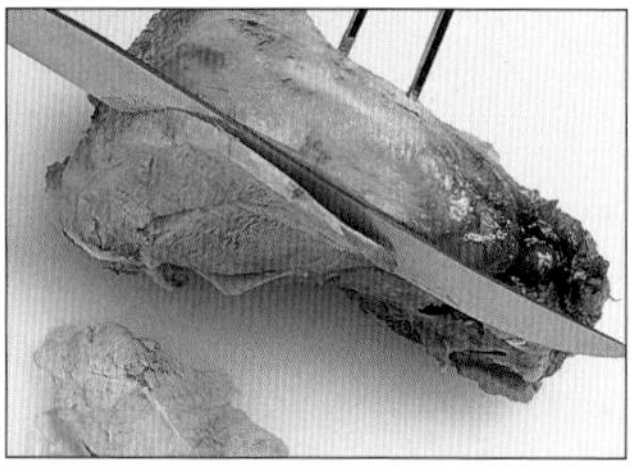

3 Carve off the breast meat in neat vertical slices. Repeat on the other side.

Accompaniments to serve with game birds

Game chips These thinly sliced, deep-fried potatoes are the classic accompaniment for game birds.

Fried breadcrumbs Fresh white breadcrumbs fried in a little butter until crisp and golden.

Roast parsnips Par-boiled parsnips, rolled in a little flour and drizzled with melted butter, then finished in a hot oven until tender and golden.

Sauces Cumberland sauce and bread sauce are traditional accompaniments.

Fruit jellies Crab apple, rowanberry, redcurrant or other fruit jellies are excellent with roast game.

Grilling

This is an ideal cooking method for smaller birds such as quail. If grilling slightly larger birds such as squab, then split them and open out flat to reduce the height and ensure they cook evenly.

1 Preheat the grill to high. Brush the birds lightly with olive oil and squeeze a little lemon juice over the top. Season with salt and plenty of freshly ground black pepper.

2 Put the birds on the rack in a grill pan. Grill under a medium to high heat for 5–6 minutes, or until well browned. Turn the birds over and cook the second side until browned.

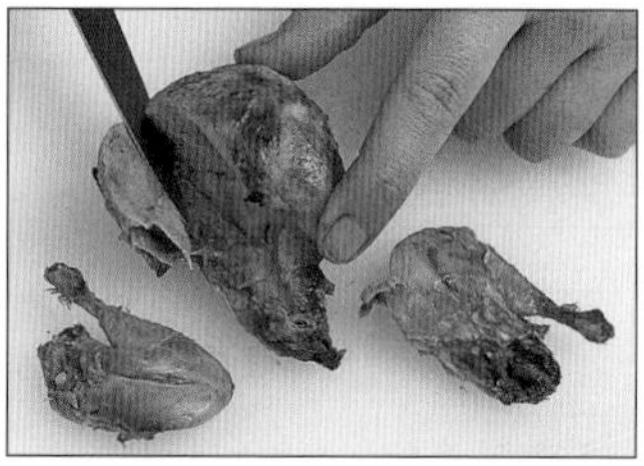

3 When cooked, the breast meat of the birds should be still slightly pink and juicy in the middle.

Pan-frying pigeon breasts

Pigeon breasts, which have been pan-fried, can be served with a sauce or salad. This is also the first stage for a sauced dish. For example, remove the browned breasts and add mushrooms and chopped spring onions. Sauté the vegetables for 2 minutes. Add 250ml/8fl oz/1 cup Madeira and bring to the boil. Boil rapidly for about 30 seconds, then replace the breasts and reduce the heat. Cook gently for 2–3 minutes, then season and serve.

1 Heat a frying pan until hot, then add a little vegetable oil and heat again.

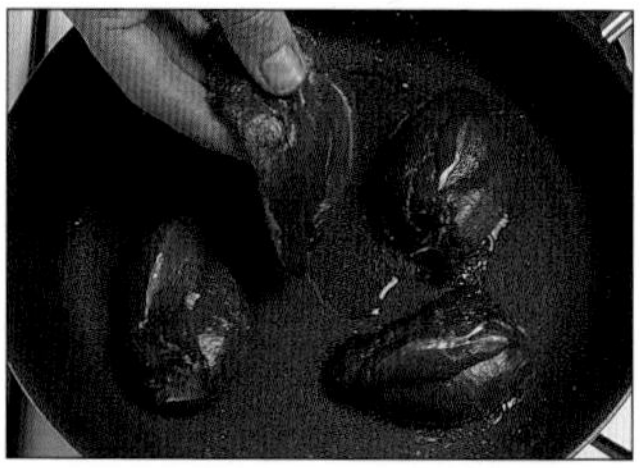

2 Add the pigeon breasts and cook until browned underneath.

3 Turn the breasts and cook until well browned on the second side.

Casseroling

Male birds and older game birds are ideal for casseroles.

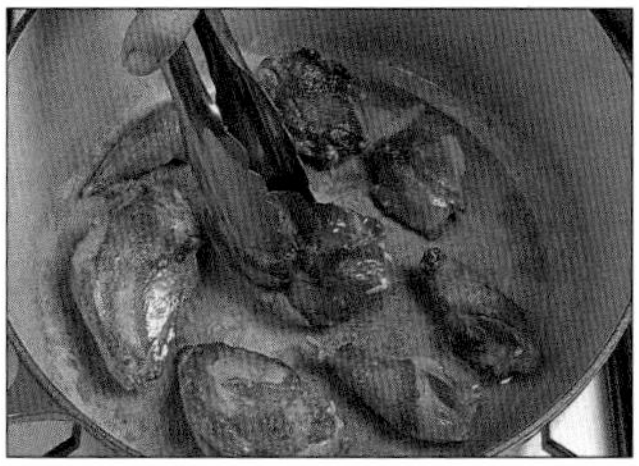

Once the pieces of game bird are browned, basic vegetables (sliced or coarsely chopped onion, carrot, celery) should be added to the casserole along with a bouquet garni, then red wine or rich stock poured in. Bring the liquid to simmering point, then transfer the casserole to a preheated oven at 180°C/350°F/Gas 4 and cook for about 1½ hours. Add sliced mushrooms and a selection of wild mushrooms and cook for a further 15 minutes. Check the seasoning before serving. The cooking juices may be thickened with beurre manié and enriched with a little double cream before serving.

Marinades for game birds
These moisten and flavour game birds, and also help to tenderize the meat and enhance its flavour. Place the whole bird or pieces in a deep, non-metallic bowl or dish, pour over the marinade and leave birds or pieces to marinate for several hours in a cool place or overnight in the fridge. Try one of the following combinations for game birds:

- Fresh orange juice, with grated lime rind and cracked peppercorns.
- Red wine with cranberry juice and juniper berries.
- White wine with allspice berries and a cinnamon stick.
- Fresh pineapple juice with grated lemon rind.

Pot-roasting

This is a good method for slightly dry game birds, such as a cock pheasant.

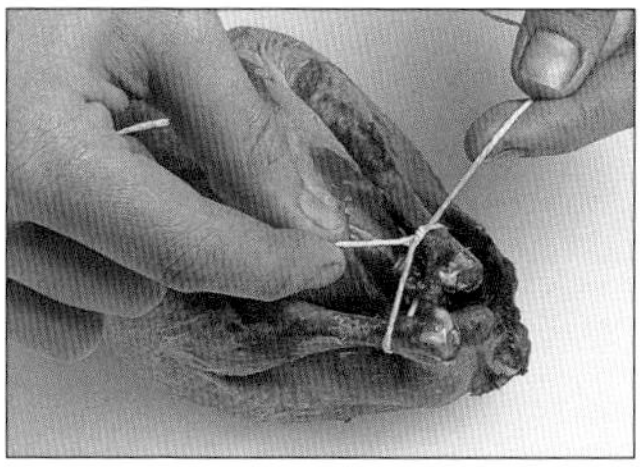

1 Tuck the neck skin and wings under the bird and then tie the legs together with string.

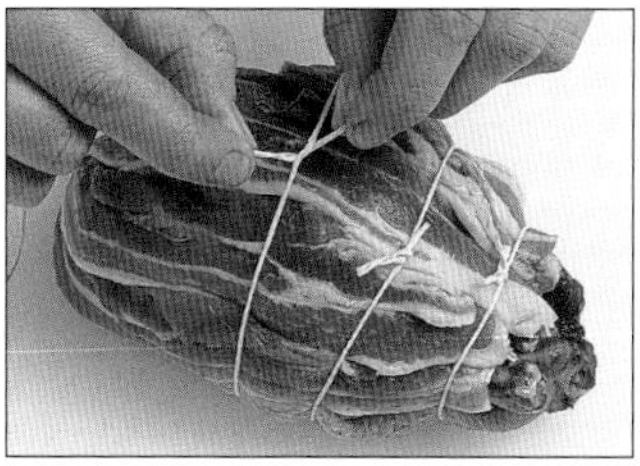

2 Season the bird well with salt and pepper. Wrap rashers of streaky bacon around the bird, and then tie them in place with string.

3 Heat about 15ml/1 tbsp oil in a large, flameproof casserole. Add the bird and brown it gently, turning occasionally.

COOK'S TIP
If you don't have a casserole that can be used on the hob, brown the birds and vegetables in a frying pan and transfer to a casserole for cooking in the oven.

Wines to serve with game birds
Full-flavoured reds go well with rich game. Try a fine claret from Bordeaux or a good bottle from the Rhône. Older, earthy Burgundies complement roast or casseroled pheasant. Soft, fruity mature reds such as Australian Grenache go well with roast partridge. Try Chianti Classico with quail. Some of the better regional French wines – Fitou, Bergerac or the better reds from the Loire Valley – complement all game birds.

4 Remove the bird from the casserole and keep warm. Add diced carrots and chopped onions with salt and pepper to taste to the casserole. Sweat the vegetables in the juices remaining in the casserole for a few minutes.

5 Return the bird to the casserole and pour over enough red wine to half-cover the bird. Bring to the boil, then reduce the heat until the liquid is just simmering. Cook gently for about 30 minutes on the hob or 1 hour in the oven at 180°C/350°F/Gas 4, or until the sauce is reduced and the bird is tender and cooked through.

Furred Game

The traditional definition of furred game was any animal killed for sport (or game) but the historical importance was as a source of food. In fact, furred game has been hunted and killed for food since prehistoric times. Long before man learned to cultivate crops and to domesticate sheep, goats, pigs and cattle, ancient man hunted small birds and animals to supplement his diet of wild fruit and root vegetables. In practically every part of the world, game – whether big game such as reindeer, elk, moose, antelope, wild boar and even bear, or small game such as rabbit, hare and squirrel – has been a vital part of the human diet for as long as man has been eating meat.

In the kitchen, game means any edible animal not raised on the farm, although, nowadays, furred game such as deer and rabbit can be farmed. The most common furred game eaten all over the world includes deer, rabbit, hare and wild boar.

Nutrition

Furred game is exceptionally nutritious meat. It is high in protein, low in cholesterol and particularly low in fat.

Buying

If you hunt or shoot, you may not need to buy furred game, but, generally, most people get game from a shop. Rabbit and some joints of venison are finding their way on to the supermarket shelf, but the best place to buy furred game is at a specialist butcher. It is here that you will get a good choice of animals and their different cuts, and also the benefit of expert advice.

Above: Moose, which is hunted in North America, is a large member of the deer family, and is similar to European elk.

Venison should have been properly hung to give the meat time to become tender. It is naturally lean, but don't be afraid of a little fat as this helps bring out the flavour of the meat and will keep it moist and juicy as it cooks.

When you buy wild boar, look for firm, pink flesh, which is moist but not damp or oily. The fat should be white, not yellow, and the bones should be tinged with red. The skin should be dry and silky, not slimy or damp.

Rabbit and hare should have an even covering of flesh, a rounded back and lean, moist pale-pink flesh

Right, clockwise from left: Prime cuts of venison include loin, haunch, best end and fillet.

Above, from left: Venison cuts that benefit from long, slow cooking include neck, shoulder and shin.

with very little visible fat. Avoid carcasses that show signs of injury or disease or which have been clumsily shot. Rabbit can be bought all the year round as it may be farmed or wild rabbit. Fresh wild hares are available in late autumn and winter; the exact dates vary from country to country. If you are preparing jugged hare and need the blood to thicken the sauce, ask your butcher to collect it for you.

Storing

Remove any packaging from the meat, wrap it in greaseproof paper and put it on a plate or small tray. Store in the bottom of the fridge, so that it can't drip on to cooked meats or other foods. Meat that is ready for cooking can be stored for one to two days in the fridge or it can be frozen.

TYPES OF FURRED GAME

Deer

The word venison was originally used to describe the meat of any furred animal killed in the chase for food, including wild boar, rabbit and hare as well as deer. Today, in Britain and Australia, the word simply means the meat from deer; although in America it is used, more broadly, to include meat from elk, moose, reindeer, caribou and antelope.

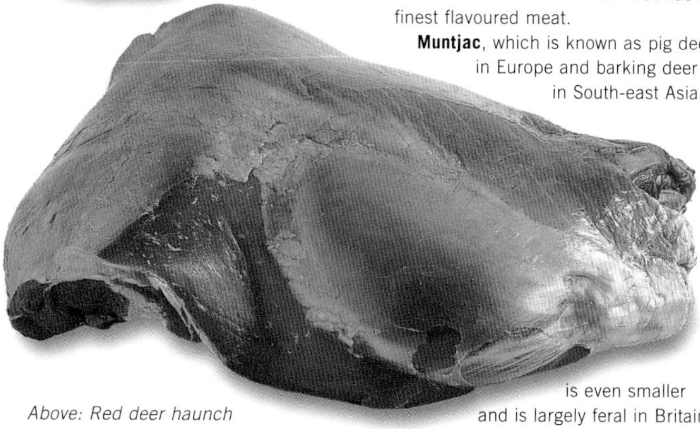

Above: Red deer haunch

Venison is a dark, close-textured meat with very little fat; what there is should be firm and white. If it is in good condition and a prime cut, such as haunch, loin, fillet or best end, it will be juicy and tender and is best served rare. Other cuts, such as neck, shoulder and shin, are often marinated and benefit from long and gentle cooking to bring out the flavour of the meat. It is not actually the type or size of the deer that matters but what the animal has been feeding on: if, for example, it has been grazing on heather and acorns, it will be full of flavour.

Red deer originally lived in the forests of northern Europe and they still live wild in the Highlands of Scotland (in areas that even now are known as deer forests although there is hardly a tree in sight). The red deer is the largest and is related to species in North Africa and Asia. **Fallow deer** are descended from those herds that lived in the deer parks on the great country estates. The **roe deer** is smaller than the red deer and the fallow deer but has the finest flavoured meat.

Muntjac, which is known as pig deer in Europe and barking deer in South-east Asia, is even smaller and is largely feral in Britain, so can be shot as vermin (when farmers report damage to crops) at any time.

The **white-tailed** or **Virginian deer** is the plentiful deer of North America and is hunted on the eastern seaboard.

Reindeer live in northern Europe and Asia, and, as well as giving Father Christmas a lift from Lapland around the world once a year, makes a popular meat dish in Finland, Sweden and Russia. Its close relation, **caribou**, has always played an important part in the diet of those living in Alaska and other frozen parts of North America.

Left: Cultivated rabbit

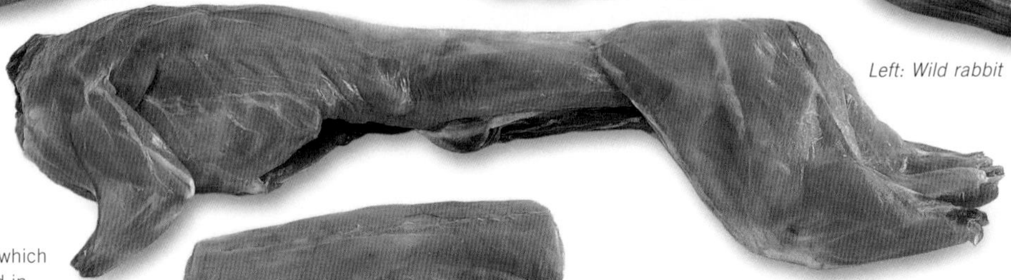

Left: Wild rabbit

Left: Rabbit: saddle (top) and leg joints

Elk, which is found in the forests and marshes of Northern Europe, is also a member of the deer family. It is a big animal, but smaller than the American elk, which is also known as wapiti. In North America **moose** is the name used for the American counterpart of the European elk.

Antelope is the collective name for a group of deer-like animals found in Africa and Asia. It includes black-buck, dik-dik, eland, hartebeest, impala, gazelle, springbok and wildebeest. All have long legs and horns and are hunted by the big cats as well as by man.

Other game animals

Animals that are hunted and eaten somewhere in the world include armadillo, bear, beaver, hedgehog, muskrat (marsh hare or marsh rabbit), opossum, porcupine, raccoon and squirrel.

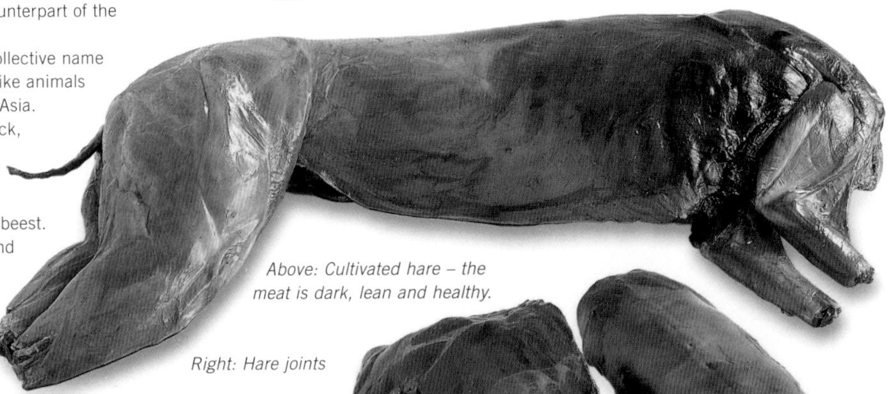

Above: Cultivated hare – the meat is dark, lean and healthy.

Right: Hare joints

Rabbit

Originally from Africa, wild rabbits are now found around the world, partly because they were easy to transport on ships but mostly because of their extraordinary propensity to breed. Even after several severe outbreaks of myxomatosis in the last 50 years the resilience of the rabbit means that they are in plentiful supply.

Rabbit and hare belong to the same family and are often confused but, nevertheless, they are different, even to the eye in the field and especially to the cook in the kitchen.

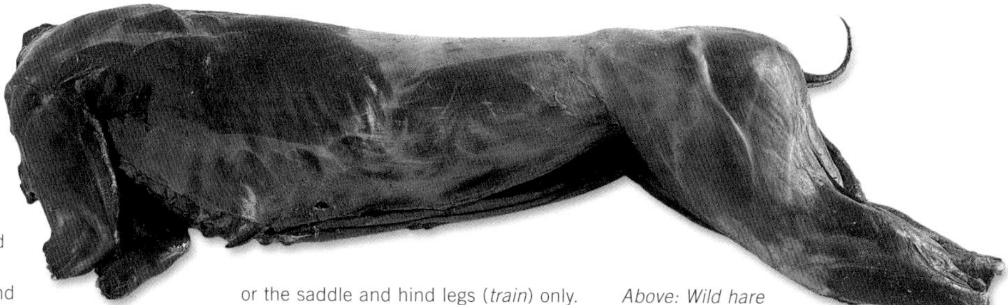

Rabbit is smaller and its flesh is pale and mild in flavour while hare is larger and its meat is dark and often very strong. Wild rabbit is usually bought whole and fresh, with or without its offal, while tame rabbit can also be bought jointed. Frozen rabbit is also available and is mainly imported from China. The meat of the doe rabbit (the female) is more tender than that of the buck (the male).

Hare

Originally from Europe, hares are also now found around the world. They are larger than rabbits with longer ears and a notched – or hare – lip and powerful hind legs. The meat is dark and lean and healthy, and (in a young animal) very tender. Its flavour is stronger than rabbit. Hare can be roasted whole or jointed and used in casseroles, stews and terrines. Older hares are usually jugged (which is when it is cooked in a jug or deep earthenware casserole, set in a pan of water, either on the hob or in the oven). The water bath tempers the heat and ensures that the meat is cooked very gently and very slowly. Many traditional French dishes call for the back or saddle (*râble*) or the saddle and hind legs (*train*) only. The classic Tuscan dish using hare is *Pappardelle al Lepre*.

Wild boar

Found across Europe, Central Asia and North Africa, wild boar has been hunted for so many years it has attained a legendary cultural status. It was hunted to extinction in Britain in the 17th century but is still found in fairly large numbers – and still hunted enthusiastically – in Europe. The meat of wild boar has a strong taste. It is dark-coloured and, because there is little fat, can be dry and tough, although its flavour is excellent. For this reason it is usually marinated. Wild boar should be cooked in the same way as pork. Joints that are to be roasted should be larded with pork fat before cooking.

Above: Wild hare – these animals are now found all over the world, although they are originally from Europe.

Wines to serve with furred game

Big reds or port are the traditional wines to serve with game. Try a Barolo with venison; a New World Cabernet Sauvignon from California, Australia or Chile; Pinotage from South Africa or a Shiraz from Australia. Pinot Noirs, particularly those from America, are very good with venison cooked in red wine.

Try a fruity, intense red such as Spanish Rioja for rabbit cooked in red wine, a dry, oaked white such as Rioja Blanco for rabbit cooked in white wine, and a medium white such as South African Chenin Blanc with rabbit cooked in cider.

Left, clockwise from left: Wild boar saddle, fillet and chops, which can be treated like free-range pork.

PREPARING FURRED GAME

Furred game is sold hung and skinned, ready for cooking. When the meat is first slaughtered it is tough and lacks flavour; hanging helps it to become tender and to develop its flavour. If you shoot furred game, your local specialist may hang and skin the animal for you.

Jointing a rabbit or hare

Rabbits can be roasted whole, but are more usually jointed and then cooked slowly in casseroles and stews.

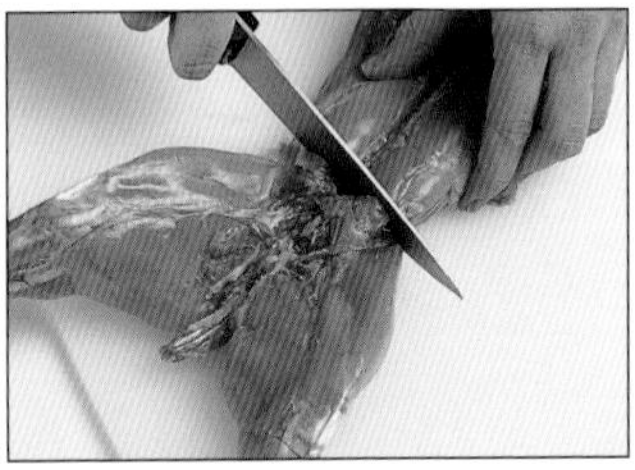

1 Cut the hind legs off the body, then cut between the hind legs.

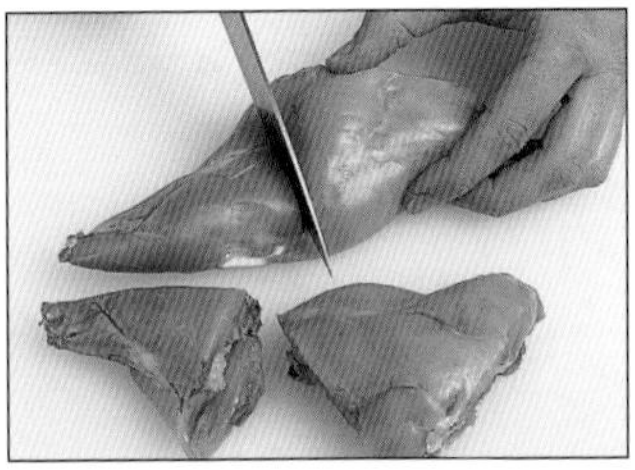

2 Cut each hind leg into two pieces.

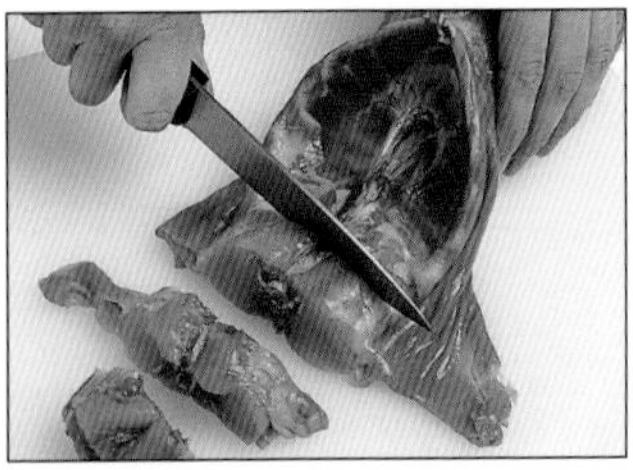

3 Cut the body into four pieces, then cut the rib section in half through the breastbone and backbone.

COOKING FURRED GAME

This is nowhere near as difficult as some people think. Approach venison in much the same way as you would a piece of beef. Wild boar is no more difficult than a piece of free-range pork. Tame rabbit can be compared with chicken, while wild rabbit simply needs patient casseroling. The secret with game is to roast young game and to braise, stew or casserole older and tougher animals. A good compromise between roasting and braising is to sauté the game, thereby using a moist rather than a dry heat to cook the meat.

Roasting venison

Prime cuts of venison, such as haunch, loin or best end, are juicy and tender when they are larded with fat, then roasted and served rare.

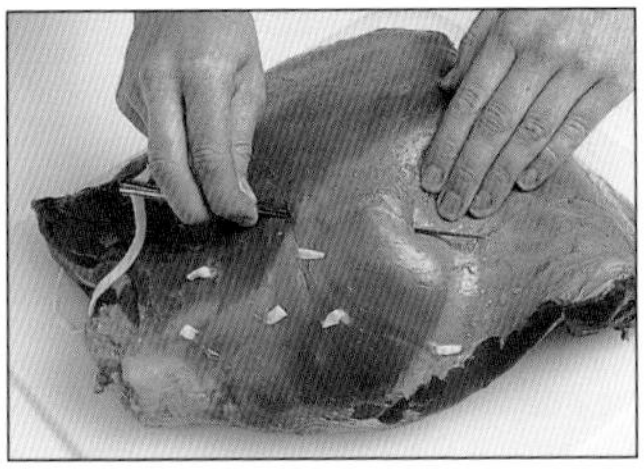

1 Venison is such a lean meat it helps to lard the joint before you roast it. Simply thread thin strips of pork fat through the outside of the meat using a larding needle.

2 Put the joint on a roasting rack, standing in a large roasting tin, and brush the joint all over with a little olive oil or melted butter to help keep it moist during cooking.

3 Place the joint in an oven preheated to 190°C/375°F/Gas 5. The cooking time depends on the thickness and the size of the joint, but, on average, venison needs 15 minutes per 450g/1lb. Baste during cooking. Once cooked, allow the joint to stand for 10 minutes to make it easier to carve.

Carving a leg of venison

1 Hold the leg firmly by the shank with one hand, rounded muscle up. Cut a couple of slices lengthways to give the meat a base to sit on.

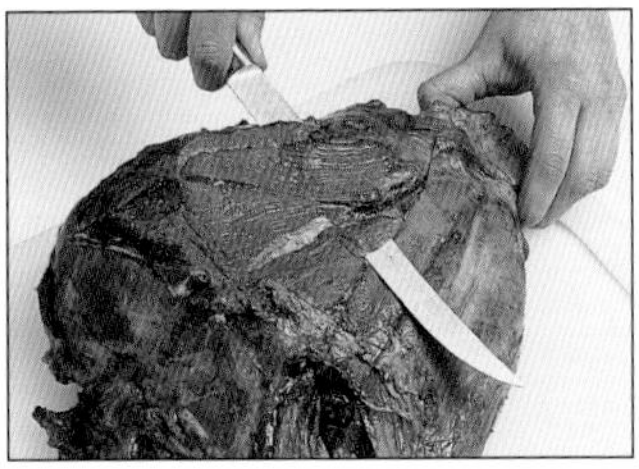

2 Turn the meat over, place it on a board and cut horizontal slices of meat until you reach the bone. Turn the meat over and cut slices from the first side.

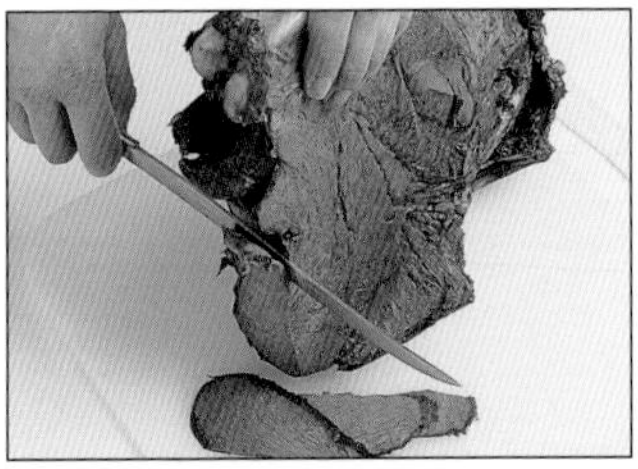

3 Cut short, thin slices from the meat remaining at the sides of the joint.

Roasting rabbit

Rabbit is generally tender enough to roast – particularly the saddle joint or saddle and hind legs.

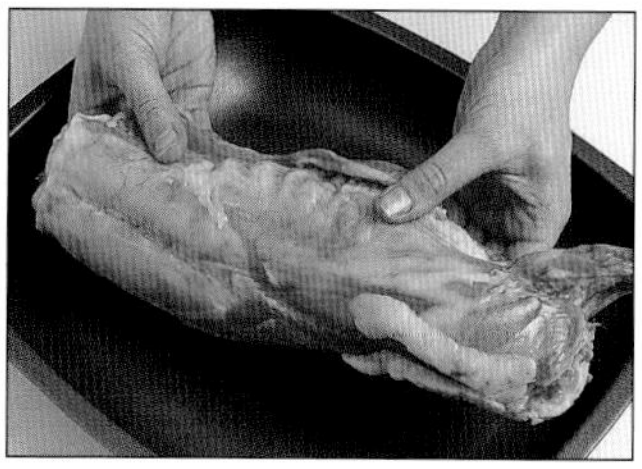

1 Ensure that your roasting tin is large enough to hold the whole joint.

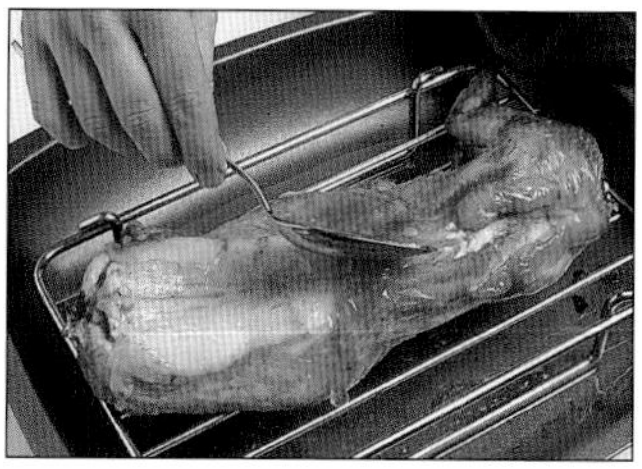

2 Place the rabbit on a rack in the roasting tin and brush the rabbit with olive oil or melted butter. Place the joint in the oven, preheated to 190°C/375°F/Gas 5 and cook for 20–30 minutes, until tender. Baste with the fat several times during cooking to keep it moist.

Marinades for furred game

Tough and dry cuts of furred game, such as venison, hare and wild boar, benefit from being marinated. Leave the game to marinate overnight in one of the following combinations.

- Red wine with 2 chopped onions, 6 peppercorns, parsley, 1 bay leaf and 3 blades of mace.
- Red wine with 30ml/2 tbsp vegetable oil, 1 chopped onion, 1 chopped garlic clove, 2 bay leaves, 2–3 juniper berries and the pared rind of a lemon.

Marinating and grilling rabbit

This is a quick and easy way of cooking well-marinated pieces of rabbit. The close contact with the intense heat seals the meat quickly, thus sealing in all the juices, so you end up with a very flavourful and succulent piece of meat.

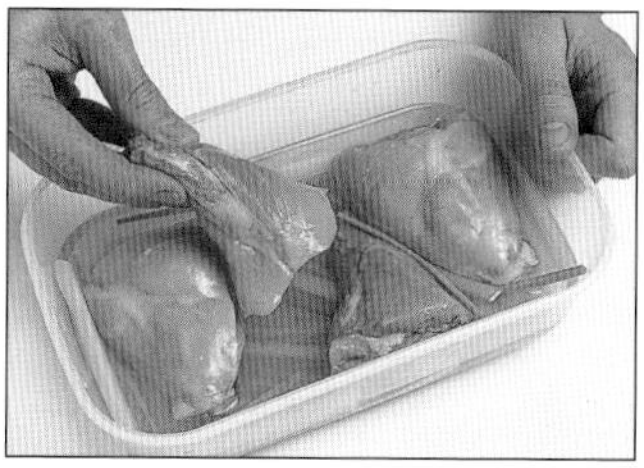

1 Put the rabbit joints in a non-metallic dish with sliced carrot and celery, 150ml/¼ pint/⅔ cup white wine and 50ml/2fl oz/¼ cup vegetable oil. Leave in the fridge to marinate overnight.

2 Place the rabbit joints on a lightly oiled grill rack.

3 Cook the rabbit portions under a very hot, preheated grill for 2–3 minutes on each side, turning once, and brushing with a little extra oil halfway through the cooking time.

Pan-frying furred game

This is a quick way of cooking fillets of rabbit, venison loin chops or escalopes of wild boar. Use a good-quality (preferably non-stick), heavy pan.

1 Dab a little sunflower oil on kitchen paper and wipe out the inside of the frying pan. Heat the frying pan until it is very hot before adding the meat.

2 Cook for 2–3 minutes on each side, turning once with tongs.

Casseroling and pot-roasting

Venison cuts such as neck, shoulder and shin are often marinated and then casseroled because they benefit from long, gentle cooking. Rabbit pieces are also excellent in casseroles.

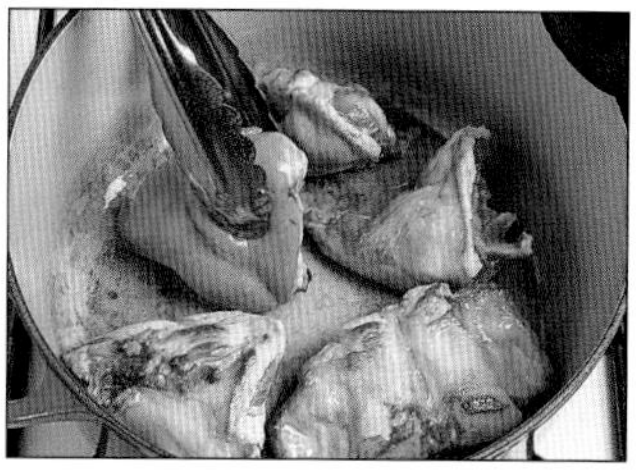

Brown the meat, then add the rest of the ingredients and simmer until tender.

Accompaniments for furred game

Game is served with the same accompaniments today as it was six or seven hundred years ago. Venison is served with redcurrant jelly, while rabbit is stewed with mushrooms and onions.

Stocks, Sauces and Gravies

A well-flavoured stock is one of the basic foundations of good cooking, and is used in a whole range of meat, game and poultry dishes, from soups and stews to pot-roasts. Sauces and gravies are an equally important part of meat cookery, and stock forms the base for many of these recipes, too.

STOCKS

We use the word stock simply because it was something most cooks kept a stock of for use in the kitchen. These days, sadly, it tends to mean something you get when you add a kettleful of boiling water to a stock cube (or a bouillon cube as it is called in the United States and France).

Traditionally, stock was the product of a pot kept simmering on the hob to which leftovers, such as pieces of meat, poultry and game as well as bones, vegetables, vegetable trimmings and herbs, were added. The cook then always had a stock of broth, packed with flavour, to use as a basis for soups, stews and sauces. These days few households have a stockpot on the go and small batches are usually made as and when required. Nevertheless, a good, home-made stock has much more flavour than a cube and it is well worth making your own.

A well-flavoured stock is the basis of good cooking – which is why young chefs are always judged by the quality of the stocks they make – and if a stock is poor then the resulting soups, casseroles, sauces and gravies coming out of the restaurant kitchen will be poor, too. That's why, although stocks are not difficult to make, professional chefs spend so long getting them right.

There are, basically, two different types of stock: a brown stock in which the bones are browned in the oven first, and a white stock in which the bones are poached rather than roasted. Brown stocks are normally made from beef and lamb and are used for making consommés, soups, and dark sauces and for cooking with dark meats. White stocks are made from veal, chicken and turkey bones and are used for making soups, white sauces and for cooking with white meats.

The reason people go wrong when making stock is that they think it's just a pot for leftovers. It was, historically, but the way to get a really good stock is to use fresh bones and vegetables. Never add salt to a stock until the end of cooking and always use whole peppercorns because ground pepper will only make the stock taste bitter.

Basic meat stock

MAKES ABOUT 1 LITRE/1¾ PINTS/4 CUPS

INGREDIENTS

- 675g/1½lb beef or veal bones
- 1 large onion, quartered
- 1 stick celery, sliced
- 1 carrot, thickly sliced
- 6 peppercorns
- bouquet garni or a selection of fresh herbs such as parsley, thyme and rosemary

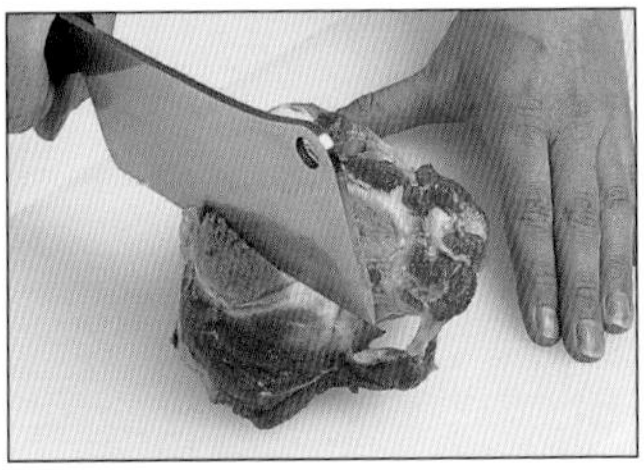

1 Use a meat cleaver to chop up larger bones so that they will fit easily into your largest pan (or get your butcher to do this). (Cutting the bones into pieces helps to extract the collagen and impart the maximum possible flavour during cooking.)

2 Transfer the bones and vegetables to the pan. Add the peppercorns, bouquet garni or herbs and 1.5–1.75 litres/ 2½–3 pints/6¼–7½ cups water to cover. Bring to the boil and, using a slotted spoon, skim off as much of the scum as possible.

3 Partially cover the pan and simmer gently (don't let it come to the boil again or the stock will become cloudy) for 2–3 hours.

4 Strain the liquid through a fine sieve into a large, heatproof bowl, then gently press the bones and vegetables to extract as much flavour as possible (but don't push so hard that the vegetables start to go into the stock).

5 Leave the liquid to cool, then chill overnight (the fat will rise to the top and can easily be removed). If you don't have time to let the stock cool, skim off as much fat as possible with a spoon and then draw absorbent kitchen paper carefully across the top of the stock to draw up any remaining surface fat.

6 Store in the fridge and boil up every day or freeze. When needed, heat the stock and taste to check its flavour. If it tastes very weak, simmer to reduce; this concentrates its flavour. Season to taste with salt and pepper.

Bouquet garni

This is a French term for a bundle of fresh or dried herbs – often parsley, thyme, chervil and chives and sometimes whole cloves and unskinned garlic. This is added to the stock pot to impart extra flavour to the stock.

White poultry stock

MAKES ABOUT 1 LITRE/1¾ PINTS/4 CUPS

INGREDIENTS
1 fresh or cooked poultry carcass
1 large onion, quartered
1 celery stick, sliced
1 carrot, thickly sliced
6 peppercorns
bouquet garni

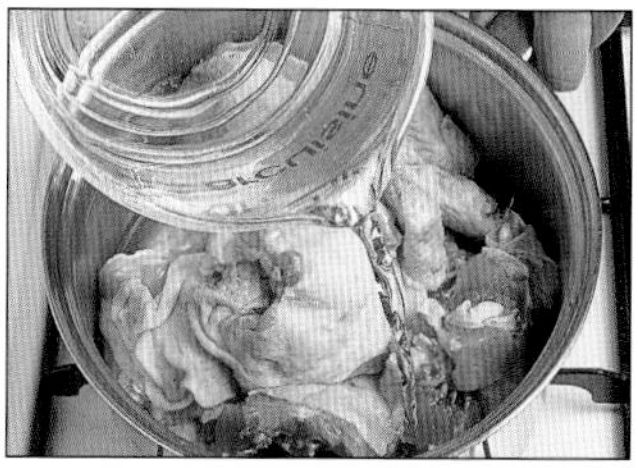

1 Using poultry shears, chop the carcass into pieces and put in a large pan. Cover with water.

2 Add the vegetables, peppercorns and bouquet garni to the pan and bring slowly to the boil.

3 Using a slotted spoon, skim well, removing as much scum as possible, and simmer gently for 2–3 hours.

4 Strain through a sieve, then gently press the bones and vegetables to extract as much flavour as possible (but don't push so hard that the vegetables start to go into the stock).

5 Leave the liquid to cool completely, then chill it overnight (the fat will rise to the top, then solidify, when it can easily be removed).

6 If you don't have time to let the stock cool, skim off as much fat as possible with a spoon and then carefully draw absorbent kitchen paper across the top of the stock to remove the surface fat. Store in the fridge and boil up every day or freeze.

COOK'S TIP
Another way of removing fat from stock is to drop a couple of ice cubes into cold stock. The fat will cling to the ice cubes and set, and both ice cubes and fat can then be discarded.

Brown meat stock

MAKES ABOUT 1 LITRE/1¾ PINTS/4 CUPS

INGREDIENTS
675g/1½lb beef or veal bones
1 large onion, quartered
1 stick celery, sliced
1 carrot, thickly sliced
6 peppercorns
bouquet garni

1 Use a cleaver to chop up the larger bones so they will fit easily into your largest pan. (Cutting the bones into pieces helps to extract the collagen and impart the maximum possible flavour during cooking.) Put the bones and vegetables in a large, heavy roasting tin.

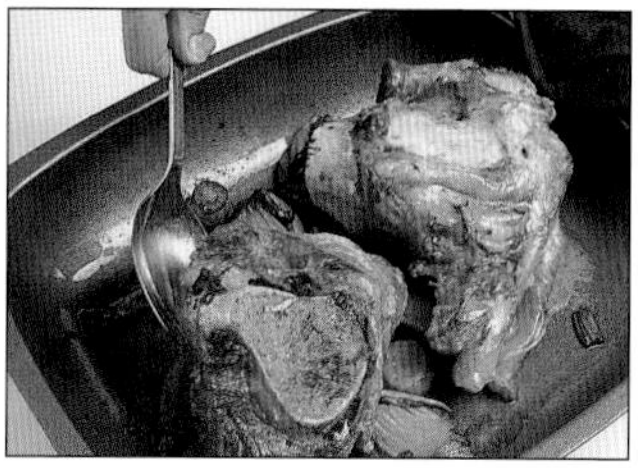

2 Cook the bones and vegetables in a preheated oven at 230°C/450°F/Gas 8, stirring frequently, until browned.

3 Transfer the bones and vegetables to a large pan. Add the peppercorns, bouquet garni and 1.5–1.75 litres/ 2½–3 pints/6¼–7½ cups water to cover. Bring to the boil, skim well to remove as much scum as possible and simmer gently (don't let it boil again or the stock will become cloudy) for 2–3 hours.

4 Strain the liquid through a sieve, then gently press the bones and vegetables to extract as much flavour as possible (but don't push so hard that the vegetables start to go into the stock). Discard the bones and vegetables.

5 Leave the liquid to cool then chill overnight (the fat will rise to the top and can then easily be removed). If you don't have time to let the stock cool, skim off as much fat as possible with a spoon and then draw kitchen paper carefully across the top of the stock to remove the surface fat. Store in the fridge and boil up every day or freeze.

Other stock bones
Beef and veal bones are the best choice for stock. It is not usual to make stock using ham bones because they are so salty. Lamb bones are not used because of their strong flavour but can be mixed with other bones. Pork bones are usually mixed with other meat bones because they make the stock very sweet.

SAUCES

The famous, classic sauces of French cuisine were invented to enhance the flavour of meat, game and poultry.

White sauce

The basic roux-based milk sauce.

MAKES ABOUT 600ML/1 PINT/2½ CUPS

INGREDIENTS
- 50g/2oz/¼ cup butter
- 30ml/2 tbsp plain flour
- 600ml/1 pint/2½ cups milk
- salt and ground white pepper

1 Melt the butter in a small saucepan.

2 Add the flour and cook for 1 minute, stirring all the time.

3 Turn off the heat and gradually stir in the milk.

4 Return the pan to the heat, bring the sauce to the boil, stirring all the time.

5 Simmer gently for 1 minute and season. This makes a coating sauce. To make a thin, pouring sauce, add another 300ml/½ pint/1¼ cups milk.

Béchamel sauce

Follow the recipe for white sauce but add 1 quartered onion, 1 sliced carrot, 1 sliced celery stick, 1 bay leaf and 6 peppercorns to the milk. Bring to the boil, infuse for 30 minutes, then strain.

Parsley sauce

This is the traditional sauce to serve with ham and bacon dishes.

Follow the recipe for white sauce and add 30ml/2 tbsp finely chopped parsley with the salt and pepper.

Mushroom sauce

This is a perfect accompaniment for griddled or pan-fried steaks.

Follow the recipe for white sauce but first, pan-fry 115g/4oz/1⅔ cups sliced mushrooms, such as shiitake, and 1 chopped garlic clove. Stir the mushroom mixture into the white sauce.

Onion sauce

This is good served with offal and grilled meats such as beef, lamb and pork. Follow the recipe for white sauce but first finely chop 1 onion and cook in the butter before adding the flour.

Horseradish cream sauce

The traditional sauce for roast beef.

MAKES ABOUT 300ML/½ PINT/1¼ CUPS

INGREDIENTS
- 300ml/½ pint/1¼ cups double cream
- 25g/1oz fresh horseradish, grated
- pinch each sugar and mustard powder
- dash of vinegar

Whip the cream to soft peaks, then fold into the horseradish. Add sugar, mustard powder and vinegar to taste.

Béarnaise sauce

This classic, hot, creamy sauce, which takes its name from Béarn in south-west France, is ideal to serve with griddled, grilled, pan-fried or roast beef. Add the butter dice by dice in the final stage or the mixture will curdle.

MAKES ABOUT 450ML/¾ PINT/2 CUPS

INGREDIENTS
- 90ml/6 tbsp white wine vinegar
- 12 black peppercorns
- 2 bay leaves
- 2 shallots, finely chopped
- 4 fresh tarragon sprigs
- 4 egg yolks
- 225g/8oz/1 cup unsalted butter, softened and cut into small dice
- 30ml/2 tbsp chopped fresh tarragon
- salt and ground white pepper

1 Put the vinegar, peppercorns, bay leaves, shallots and tarragon in a small pan and simmer until reduced to 30ml/2 tbsp. Strain through a sieve.

2 Beat the egg yolks in a heatproof bowl, set over a pan of very gently simmering water. Season. Beat in the strained vinegar mixture, then the butter, dice by dice. Add the tarragon, then serve at once.

Mint sauce

The classic accompaniment to roast lamb.

MAKES ABOUT 90ML/6 TBSP

INGREDIENTS
- bunch of mint, about 15g/½oz
- 10ml/2 tsp caster sugar
- 15ml/1 tbsp boiling water
- 30ml/2 tbsp white wine vinegar

Finely chop the mint with the sugar. Add the boiling water and mix, stirring until the sugar has dissolved. Add the vinegar 15ml/1 tbsp at a time. Leave the sauce to stand until ready to serve.

Apple sauce

This is the perfect accompaniment to serve with roast or grilled pork.

MAKES ABOUT 300ML/½ PINT/1¼ CUPS

INGREDIENTS
- 450g/1lb Bramley apples (or other tart apples)
- 30ml/2 tbsp cider or water
- 25g/1oz/2 tbsp soft brown sugar (or to taste)
- 25g/1oz/2 tbsp butter

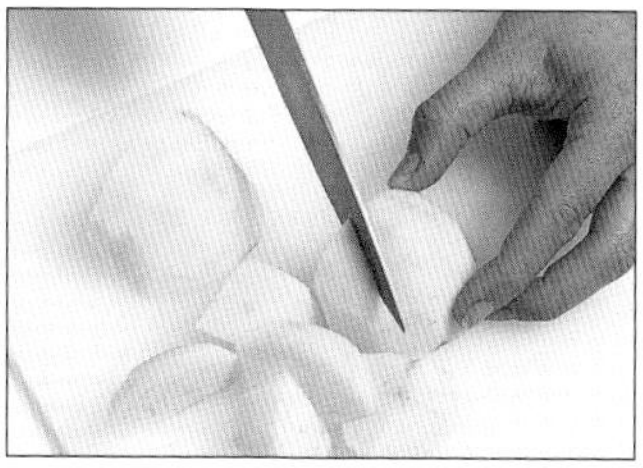

1 Peel the apples, remove the cores and chop the apples into large chunks.

2 Put the apples, cider and sugar in a pan. Cook for 5–10 minutes, until soft.

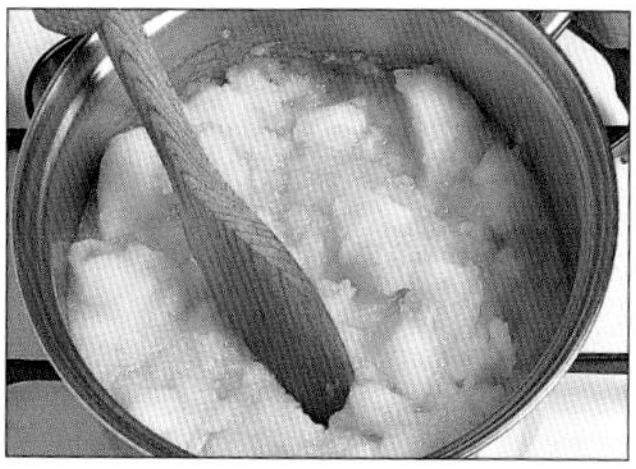

3 Beat well with a wooden spoon or blend in a food processor depending on whether you like your apple sauce chunky or smooth. Beat in the butter and reheat, if necessary.

Cranberry sauce

This is the traditional accompaniment for roast turkey and baked ham.

MAKES ABOUT 600ML/1 PINT/2½ CUPS

INGREDIENTS
- 350g/12oz/3 cups fresh or frozen cranberries
- 175g/6oz/scant 1 cup golden caster sugar
- 15ml/1 tbsp Cointreau
- 1.5ml/¼ tsp mixed spice
- ground black pepper
- grated rind 2 oranges
- 50ml/2fl oz/¼ cup orange juice

Put all the ingredients in a large heavy-based pan. Cook gently over a low heat until the sugar is completely dissolved, stirring frequently. Bring to the boil, then reduce the heat slightly and simmer, stirring occasionally, for 20–25 minutes, or until thickened.

Tomato sauce

This is delicious served with pork, lamb, sausages and alligator.

MAKES ABOUT 1.2 LITRES/2 PINTS/5 CUPS

INGREDIENTS
- 900g/2lb ripe tomatoes, quartered
- 225g/8oz onions
- 450g/1lb cooking apples, peeled and cored
- 1.2 litres/2 pints/5 cups distilled white vinegar
- 25g/1oz mustard seeds, crushed
- 1 dried chilli
- 5cm/2in piece cinnamon stick
- 3 blades mace
- 6 peppercorns
- 2.5ml/½ tsp grated nutmeg
- 50g/2oz/¼ cup sea salt
- 225g/8oz/generous 1 cup golden granulated sugar

1 Put the tomatoes in a preserving pan. Finely chop the onions and apples, and add to the pan with half the vinegar. Stir in the spices, flavourings and salt, and stir well. Bring the mixture slowly to the boil and simmer for 1–1½ hours, or until reduced by about one-third.

2 Sieve the pulp. Return the mixture to the pan with the remaining vinegar and all of the sugar and stir over a gentle heat until the sugar has dissolved. Bring to the boil and simmer for 30 minutes, or until the sauce has thickened. Pour into sterilized, warmed bottles and seal. Store in the fridge for up to 1 week.

Orange sauce

A tangy sauce for roast duck and game.

MAKES ABOUT 450ML/¾ PINT/2 CUPS

INGREDIENTS
- 25g/1oz/2 tbsp butter
- 40g/1½oz/⅓ cup plain white flour
- 300ml/½ pint/1¼ cups poultry stock
- 150ml/¼ pint/⅔ cup red wine
- 2 oranges
- 10ml/2 tsp lemon juice
- 15ml/1 tbsp orange-flavoured liqueur
- 30ml/2 tbsp redcurrant jelly
- salt and ground black pepper

1 Melt the butter in a small pan over a medium heat. Add the flour and cook for about 3 minutes, stirring all the time, until lightly browned.

2 Without heating, gradually stir in the stock and red wine. Bring to the boil, stirring, then simmer for 5 minutes.

3 Thinly peel the orange rind from one of the oranges using a swivel-bladed peeler. Put the rind in a pan, cover with cold water and bring to the boil. Cook for 5 minutes, then drain.

4 Meanwhile, squeeze the juice from both oranges into the sauce. Add the lemon juice, orange-flavoured liqueur and orange rind, with the redcurrant jelly. Stir the sauce, then reheat gently. Season to taste with salt and pepper before serving.

Bread sauce

Perfect for poultry and game birds.

MAKES ABOUT 450ML/¾ PINT/2 CUPS

INGREDIENTS
- 1 onion
- 6 cloves
- 1 bay leaf
- 300ml/½ pint/1¼ cups milk
- 150ml/¼ pint/⅔ cup single cream
- 115g/4oz/2 cups fresh white breadcrumbs
- knob of butter
- salt and ground black pepper

1 Stud the onion with the cloves. Put the onion, bay leaf and milk in a pan and bring slowly to the boil. Remove from the heat and leave to stand for at least 30 minutes to allow the flavour of the onion to infuse into the milk.

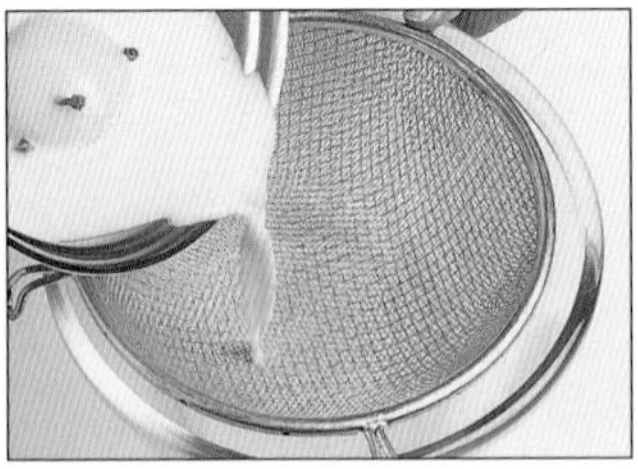

2 Strain the milk and discard the clove-studded onion and the bay leaf.

3 Pour the milk into a clean pan and add the single cream and breadcrumbs. Bring slowly to the boil, then reduce the heat and simmer gently for 5 minutes.

4 Stir in the butter and season with salt and pepper to taste just before serving.

GRAVIES

The classic gravies, served with meat dishes by Auguste Escoffier at the Savoy and the Ritz Carlton in the 1890s, are a world away from the gravy that comes by adding boiling water to stock cubes or freeze-dried gravy granules. The traditional British meat gravy – which ranges in colour from pale gold to dark brown – is made with what is left in the bottom of the tin after a joint has been roasted, deglazed with good stock and carefully seasoned. Some gravies are really quite thick, others rather thin; it is really a matter of personal preference. Many cooks add a spoonful of flour to help thicken the gravy although purists condemn the practice.

In France, *jus de viande* is a version of a thin British gravy. Red eye gravy, famous in the American south for being served with ham and other pork dishes, is made by adding a little water (or, sometimes, strong black coffee) to the roasting tin and simmering it until it bubbles and turns red. Another version adds a teaspoon of brown sugar, stirred in until it caramelizes, before the water is added.

Thickened gravy

This classic gravy is perfect to serve with all roast meats and poultry.

MAKES ABOUT 450ML/¾ PINT/2 CUPS

INGREDIENTS
- 25g/1oz/¼ cup plain flour
- 450ml/¾ pint/scant 2 cups good-quality stock
- 45ml/3 tbsp port or sherry
- salt and ground black pepper

1 Tilt the roasting tin slightly and spoon off almost all the fat, leaving the meat juices behind.

2 Sprinkle the flour into the tin and heat gently for 1 minute, stirring constantly. Gradually add the stock, stirring all the time until thickened. Add the port or sherry, season with salt and pepper and simmer gently for 1–2 minutes. Taste and adjust the seasoning, if necessary. Serve piping hot.

Onion gravy

This is the ideal gravy to serve with fried or grilled sausages and offal.

MAKES ABOUT 450ML/¾ PINT/2 CUPS

INGREDIENTS
- 30ml/2 tbsp olive oil
- 25g/1oz/2 tbsp butter
- 8 onions, sliced
- 5ml/1 tsp caster sugar
- 15ml/1 tbsp plain flour
- 300ml/½ pint/1¼ cups brown meat stock
- salt and ground black pepper

1 Heat the oil and butter in a pan until foaming, then add the onions. Mix well, so the onions are coated in the butter mixture. Cover the pan and cook gently for 30 minutes, stirring frequently. Add the caster sugar and cook for a further 5 minutes; the onions will soften, caramelize and reduce.

2 Turn off the heat and stir in the flour.

3 Gradually add the stock and return the pan to the heat. Bring the onion gravy to the boil, stirring all the time.

4 Simmer for 2–3 minutes or until thickened, then season with salt and pepper to taste.

A glaze is used to give a dish an especially smooth, shiny (and sometimes transparent) finish. A meat glaze is made by the prolonged reduction of meat stock, resulting in a syrupy liquid. Alcohol, such as Madeira, is often added to the reduction and a little butter, whisked in at the end, to give a smooth, satiny appearance.

THE RECIPES

Meat, poultry and game of every kind prove their enormous versatility in this section. The chapters are divided by type of meat, and each includes a wide range of superb recipes. There are timeless classics, such as celebration roasts, warming casseroles, robust stews and slow-cooked braised dishes, as well as exciting, contemporary ideas that are quick and easy to cook – perfect for a modern, busy lifestyle. The recipes not only include all the traditional meats, such as beef, pork and lamb, poultry and game, but also cured meats and sausages, and new exotic meats, such as kangaroo, alligator and ostrich.

BEEF AND VEAL

These succulent meats have terrific taste and texture. The wide range of cuts available means that they are also extremely versatile, suitable for every kind of meal, from quick and easy suppers to Sunday lunch. This chapter includes the time-honoured classic Roast Rib of Beef with Yorkshire puddings, as well as great traditional dishes such as Boeuf Bourguignonne, Steak Béarnaise and Osso Bucco with Risotto Milanese. But although beef and veal are great meats for robust, classic dishes, both can also be used to make light and modern meals that are quick and easy to cook, such as Italian Meatballs, Chunky Burgers with Spicy Relish, or the sensational – and spicy – Thai Beef Salad.

ROAST RIB OF BEEF

THIS JOINT LOOKS SPECTACULAR, AND SERVED IN TRADITIONAL STYLE, WITH YORKSHIRE PUDDINGS AND HORSERADISH SAUCE, IT MAKES A PERFECT CELEBRATION MEAL.

SERVES EIGHT TO TEN

INGREDIENTS

- 45ml/3 tbsp mixed peppercorns
- 15ml/1 tbsp juniper berries
- 2.75kg/6lb rolled rib of beef
- 30ml/2 tbsp Dijon mustard
- 15ml/1 tbsp olive oil

For the Yorkshire puddings

- 150ml/¼ pint/⅔ cup water
- 150ml/¼ pint/⅔ cup milk
- 115g/4oz/1 cup plain flour
- pinch of salt
- 2 eggs, beaten
- 60ml/4 tbsp lard, melted, or sunflower oil (optional)

For the caramelized shallots

- 20 shallots
- 5 garlic cloves, peeled
- 60ml/4 tbsp light olive oil
- 15ml/1 tbsp caster sugar

For the gravy

- 150ml/¼ pint/⅔ cup red wine
- 600ml/1 pint/2½ cups beef stock
- salt and ground black pepper
- flat leaf parsley, to garnish (optional)

1 Preheat the oven to 230°C/450°F/ Gas 8. Coarsely crush the peppercorns and juniper berries. Scatter half the spices over the meat, then transfer to a roasting tin and roast for 30 minutes.

COOK'S TIP

If you prefer to cook beef on the bone, buy a 3.6kg/8lb forerib. Trim off the excess fat, scatter over the spices, then follow the instructions in steps 1 and 2. Roast at the lower temperature for 2 hours for rare beef, 2½ hours for medium rare, and 3 hours for well done.

2 Reduce the oven temperature to 180°C/350°F/Gas 4. Mix the mustard and oil into the remaining crushed spices and spread the resulting paste over the meat. Roast the meat for a further 1¼ hours if you like your meat rare, 1 hour 50 minutes for a medium-rare result or 2 hours 25 minutes for a joint that is medium to well done. Baste the joint frequently during cooking.

3 Make the Yorkshire puddings as soon as the beef is in the oven. Stir the water into the milk. Sift the flour and salt into a bowl. Make a well in the middle and gradually whisk in the eggs followed by the milk and water to make a smooth batter. Cover and leave to stand for about 1 hour. (The batter can be made well in advance and chilled overnight in the fridge if convenient.)

4 An hour before the beef is due to be ready, mix the shallots and garlic cloves with the light olive oil and spoon into the roasting tin around the beef. After 30 minutes, sprinkle the caster sugar over the shallots and garlic, stir the shallots and garlic two or three times during cooking.

5 Transfer the meat to a large serving platter, cover tightly with foil and set aside in a warm place for 20–30 minutes. (This resting time makes carving easier.) Increase the oven temperature to 230°C/450°F/ Gas 8. Divide 60ml/4 tbsp dripping from the meat or the lard or oil, if using, among 10 individual Yorkshire pudding tins or 16 large patty tins, and heat in the oven for 5 minutes.

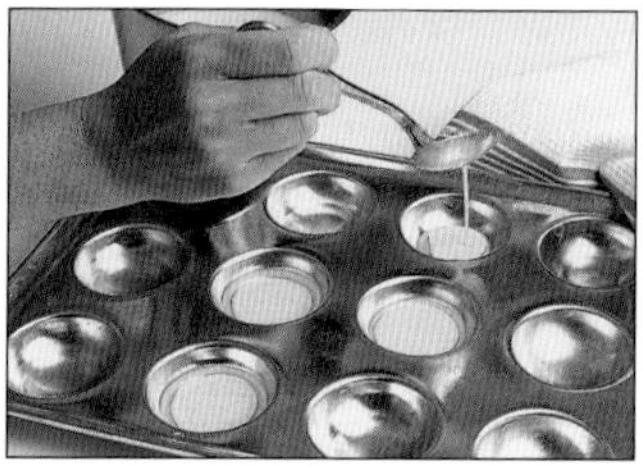

6 Spoon the Yorkshire pudding batter into the hot fat in the tins and bake for 20–30 minutes, or until risen, firm and a golden brown colour. The time depends on the size of the tins: larger Yorkshire puddings will take longer than those in patty tins.

7 Make the gravy while the Yorkshire puddings are cooking. Simmer the red wine and beef stock together in a saucepan for about 5 minutes to intensify the flavour of the gravy.

8 Skim the fat from the meat juices in the roasting tin, then pour in the wine mixture and simmer until the gravy is reduced and thickened slightly to a syrupy consistency. Stir frequently with a wooden spoon to remove all of the roasting residue from the roasting tin. Season to taste.

9 Serve the beef with the individual Yorkshire puddings, caramelized shallots and gravy. Offer roast potatoes or game chips as accompaniments along with a selection of lightly cooked, seasonal vegetables.

Boeuf Bourguignonne

The classic French dish of beef cooked in Burgundy style, with red wine, small pieces of bacon, baby onions and mushrooms, is cooked for several hours at a low temperature. Using top rump or braising steak reduces the cooking time.

SERVES SIX

INGREDIENTS

- 175g/6oz rindless streaky bacon rashers, chopped
- 900g/2lb lean braising steak, such as top rump of beef or braising steak
- 30ml/2 tbsp plain flour
- 45ml/3 tbsp sunflower oil
- 25g/1oz/2 tbsp butter
- 12 shallots
- 2 garlic cloves, crushed
- 175g/6oz/2⅓ cups mushrooms, sliced
- 450ml/¾ pint/scant 2 cups robust red wine
- 150ml/¼ pint/⅔ cup beef stock or consommé
- 1 bay leaf
- 2 sprigs each of fresh thyme, parsley and marjoram
- salt and ground black pepper

1 Preheat the oven to 160°C/325°F/Gas 3. Heat a large flameproof casserole, then add the bacon and cook, stirring occasionally, until the pieces are crisp and golden brown.

2 Meanwhile, cut the meat into 2.5cm/1in cubes. Season the flour and use to coat the meat. Use a draining spoon to remove the bacon from the casserole and set aside. Add and heat the oil, then brown the beef in batches and set aside with the bacon.

VARIATION

Use lardons, which are available from large supermarkets, instead of the bacon.

3 Add the butter to the fat remaining in the casserole. Cook the shallots and garlic until just starting to colour, then add the mushrooms and cook for a further 5 minutes. Replace the bacon and meat, and stir in the wine and stock or consommé. Tie the bay leaf, thyme, parsley and marjoram together into a bouquet garni and add to the casserole.

4 Cover and cook in the oven for 1½ hours, or until the meat is tender, stirring once or twice. Season to taste and serve the casserole with creamy mashed root vegetables, such as celeriac and potatoes.

COOK'S TIP

Boeuf Bourguignonne freezes very well. Transfer the mixture to a dish so that it cools quickly, then pour it into a rigid plastic container. Push all the cubes of meat down into the sauce or they will dry out. Freeze for up to 2 months. Thaw overnight in the fridge, then transfer to a flameproof casserole and add 150ml/¼ pint/⅔ cup water. Stir well, bring to the boil, stirring occasionally, and simmer steadily for at least 10 minutes, or until the meat is piping hot.

STEAK BÉARNAISE

BÉARNAISE, AFTER BÉARN IN SOUTH-WEST FRANCE, IS A CREAMY EGG AND BUTTER SAUCE FLAVOURED WITH FRESH TARRAGON. IT IS A CLASSIC ACCOMPANIMENT FOR GRIDDLED, GRILLED OR PAN-FRIED STEAK AND ALSO EXCELLENT WITH ROAST BEEF. ROASTED VEGETABLES MAKE A GOOD ACCOMPANIMENT.

SERVES FOUR

INGREDIENTS

- 4 sirloin steaks, each weighing about 225g/8oz, trimmed
- 15ml/1 tbsp sunflower oil (optional)
- salt and ground black pepper

For the Béarnaise sauce

- 90ml/6 tbsp white wine vinegar
- 12 black peppercorns
- 2 bay leaves
- 2 shallots, finely chopped
- 4 fresh tarragon sprigs
- 4 egg yolks
- 225g/8oz/1 cup unsalted butter, diced and warmed to room temperature
- 30ml/2 tbsp chopped fresh tarragon
- freshly ground white pepper

1 Start by making the sauce. Put the vinegar, peppercorns, bay leaves, shallots and tarragon sprigs in a small saucepan and simmer until reduced to 30ml/2 tbsp. Strain the vinegar through a fine sieve.

2 Beat the egg yolks with salt and freshly ground white pepper in a small, heatproof bowl. Stand the bowl over a saucepan of very gently simmering water, then beat the strained vinegar into the yolks.

3 Gradually beat in the butter, one piece at a time, allowing each addition to melt before adding the next. Do not allow the water to heat beyond a gentle simmer or the sauce will overheat and curdle.

4 While cooking the sauce, heat a frying pan, griddle or grill until very hot.

COOK'S TIP

If you are confident about preparing egg and butter sauces, the best method is to reduce the flavoured vinegar before cooking the steak, then finish the sauce while the steak is cooking. This way, the sauce does not have to be kept hot and there is less risk of overheating it or allowing it to become too thick.

5 Beat the chopped fresh tarragon into the sauce and remove the pan from the heat. The sauce should be smooth, thick and glossy.

6 Cover the surface of the sauce with clear film or dampened greaseproof paper (to prevent a skin forming) and leave over the pan of hot water (still off the heat) to keep hot while you cook the steak.

7 Season the steaks with salt and plenty freshly ground black pepper.

8 A pan is not usually oiled before cooking steak, but if it is essential to grease the pan, add only the minimum oil. Cook the steaks for 2–4 minutes on each side. The cooking time depends on the thickness of the steaks and the extent to which you want to cook them. As a guide, 2–4 minutes will give a medium-rare result.

9 Serve the steaks on warmed plates. Peel the clear film or dampened greaseproof paper off the sauce and stir it lightly, then spoon it over the steaks.

FILLET OF BEEF STROGANOFF

LEGEND HAS IT THAT THIS FAMOUS RUSSIAN RECIPE WAS DEVISED BY COUNT PAUL STROGANOFF'S COOK TO USE BEEF FROZEN BY THE SIBERIAN CLIMATE. THE ONLY WAY IN WHICH IT COULD BE PREPARED WAS CUT INTO VERY THIN STRIPS. THE STRIPS OF LEAN BEEF WERE SERVED IN A SOURED CREAM SAUCE FLAVOURED WITH BRANDY.

SERVES EIGHT

INGREDIENTS

- 1.2kg/2½lb fillet of beef
- 30ml/2 tbsp plain flour
- large pinch each of cayenne pepper and paprika
- 75ml/5 tbsp sunflower oil
- 1 large onion, chopped
- 3 garlic cloves, finely chopped
- 450g/1lb/6½ cups chestnut mushrooms, sliced
- 75ml/5 tbsp brandy
- 300ml/½ pint/1¼ cups beef stock or consommé
- 300ml/½ pint/1¼ cups soured cream
- 45ml/3 tbsp chopped fresh flat leaf parsley
- salt and ground black pepper

1 Thinly slice the fillet of beef across the grain, then cut it into fine strips. Season the flour with the cayenne pepper and paprika.

2 Heat half the oil in a large frying pan, add the onion and garlic, and cook gently until the onion has softened.

3 Add the mushrooms and stir-fry over a high heat. Transfer the vegetables and their juices to a dish, set aside.

4 Wipe the pan, then add and heat the remaining oil. Coat a batch of meat with flour, then stir-fry over a high heat until browned. Remove from the pan, then coat and stir-fry another batch. When the last batch of steak is cooked, replace all the meat and vegetables. Add the brandy and simmer until it has almost evaporated.

5 Stir in the stock or consommé and seasoning and cook for 10–15 minutes, stirring frequently, or until the meat is tender and the sauce is thick and glossy. Add the soured cream and sprinkle with chopped parsley. Serve at once with rice and a simple salad.

COOK'S TIP

If you do not have a very large pan, it may be easier to cook the meat and vegetables in two separate pans. A large flameproof casserole may be used.

BEEF WELLINGTON

THIS DISH, WHICH WAS POPULAR IN THE 19TH CENTURY, IS A FILLET OF BEEF BAKED IN PUFF PASTRY. DERIVED FROM THE CLASSIC FRENCH BOEUF EN CROÛTE, THE ENGLISH NAME WAS APPLIED TO THE DISH IN 1815 IN HONOUR OF THE DUKE OF WELLINGTON, FOLLOWING HIS VICTORY AT THE BATTLE OF WATERLOO. START PREPARING THE DISH WELL IN ADVANCE TO ALLOW TIME FOR THE MEAT TO COOL BEFORE IT IS WRAPPED IN PASTRY.

SERVES SIX

INGREDIENTS

- 1.5kg/3¼lb fillet of beef
- 45ml/3 tbsp sunflower oil
- 115g/4oz mushrooms, chopped
- 2 garlic cloves, crushed
- 175g/6oz smooth liver pâté
- 30ml/2 tbsp chopped fresh parsley
- 400g/14oz puff pastry, thawed if frozen
- beaten egg, to glaze
- salt and ground black pepper
- fresh flat leaf parsley, to garnish

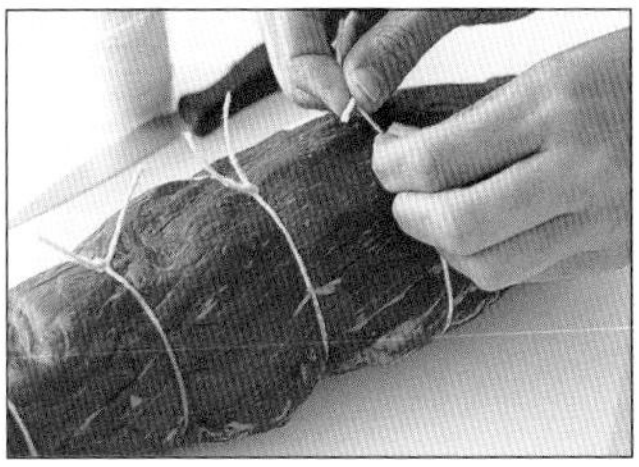

1 Preheat the oven to 220°C/425°F/ Gas 7. Tie the beef at regular intervals with string. Heat 30ml/2 tbsp of the oil in a large frying pan, and fry the beef over a high heat for about 10 minutes, or until brown on all sides. Transfer to a roasting tin, bake for 20 minutes. Cool.

2 Heat the remaining oil in a frying pan and cook the mushrooms and garlic for about 5 minutes. Beat the mushroom mixture into the pâté with the parsley, season well. Set aside to cool.

3 Roll out the pastry into a sheet large enough to enclose the beef, plus a strip to spare. Trim off the spare pastry, then trim other edges to neaten. Spread the pâté mix down the middle of the pastry. Untie the beef and lay it on the pâté.

4 Preheat the oven to 220°C/425°F/ Gas 7. Brush the edges of the pastry with beaten egg and fold the pastry over the meat to enclose it in a neat parcel. Place the parcel on a baking tray with the join in the pastry underneath. Cut leaf shapes from the reserved pastry. Brush the parcel with beaten egg, garnish with the pastry leaves and brush with egg. Chill for 10 minutes, or until the oven is hot.

5 Bake the Beef Wellington for 50–60 minutes, covering it loosely with foil after about 30 minutes to prevent the pastry from burning. Serve cut into thick slices garnished with parsley.

STEAK, MUSHROOM AND ALE PIE

THIS ANGLO-IRISH DISH IS A FIRM FAVOURITE ON MENUS AT RESTAURANTS SPECIALIZING IN TRADITIONAL FARE. PIPING HOT, CREAMY MASHED POTATOES OR PARSLEY-DRESSED BOILED POTATOES AND SLIGHTLY CRUNCHY CARROTS AND GREEN BEANS OR CABBAGE ARE PERFECT ACCOMPANIMENTS; FOR A BAR-STYLE MEAL, CHIPS OR BAKED POTATOES AND A SIDE SALAD CAN BE SERVED WITH THE PIE.

SERVES FOUR

INGREDIENTS

- 25g/1oz/2 tbsp butter
- 1 large onion, finely chopped
- 115g/4oz/1½ cups chestnut or button mushrooms, halved
- 900g/2lb lean beef in one piece, such as rump or braising steak
- 30ml/2 tbsp plain flour
- 45ml/3 tbsp sunflower oil
- 300ml/½ pint/1¼ cups stout or brown ale
- 300ml/½ pint/1¼ cups beef stock or consommé
- 500g/1¼lb puff pastry, thawed if frozen
- beaten egg, to glaze
- salt and ground black pepper

1 Melt the butter in a large, flameproof casserole, add the onion and cook gently, stirring occasionally, for about 5 minutes, or until it is softened but not coloured. Add the halved mushrooms and continue cooking for a further 5 minutes, stirring occasionally.

2 Meanwhile, trim the meat and cut it into 2.5cm/1in cubes. Season the flour and toss the meat in it.

COOK'S TIP

To make individual pies, divide the filling among four individual pie dishes. Cut the pastry into quarters and cover as above. If the dishes do not have rims, press a narrow strip of pastry around the edge of each dish to seal the lid in place. Cook as above, reducing the cooking time slightly.

3 Use a draining spoon to remove the onion mixture from the casserole and set aside. Add and heat the oil, then brown the steak in batches over a high heat to seal in the juices.

4 Replace the vegetables, then stir in the stout or ale and stock or consommé. Bring to the boil, reduce the heat and simmer for about 1 hour, stirring occasionally, or until the meat is tender. Season to taste and transfer to a 1.5 litre/2½ pint/6¼ cup pie dish. Cover and leave to cool. If possible, chill the meat filling overnight as this allows the flavour to develop. Preheat the oven to 230°C/450°F/Gas 8.

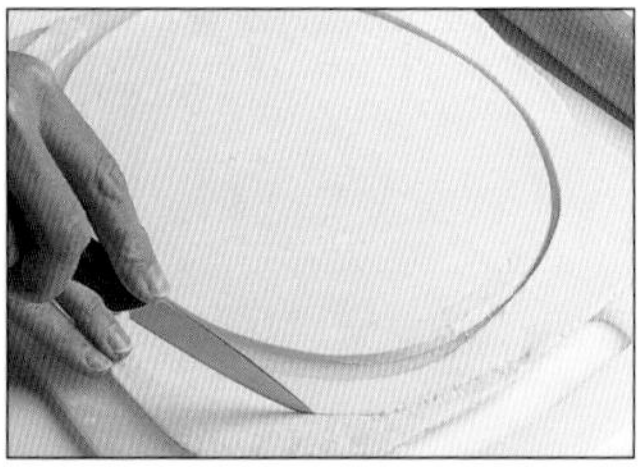

5 Roll out the pastry in the shape of the dish and about 4cm/1½in larger all around. Cut a 2.5cm/1in strip from the edge of the pastry. Brush the rim of the dish with water and press the pastry strip on it. Brush the pastry rim with beaten egg and cover the pie with the pastry lid. Press the lid firmly in place and then trim the excess from around the edge.

6 Use the blunt edge of a knife to tap the outside edge of the pastry, pressing it down with your finger as you seal in the filling. (This technique is known as knocking up.)

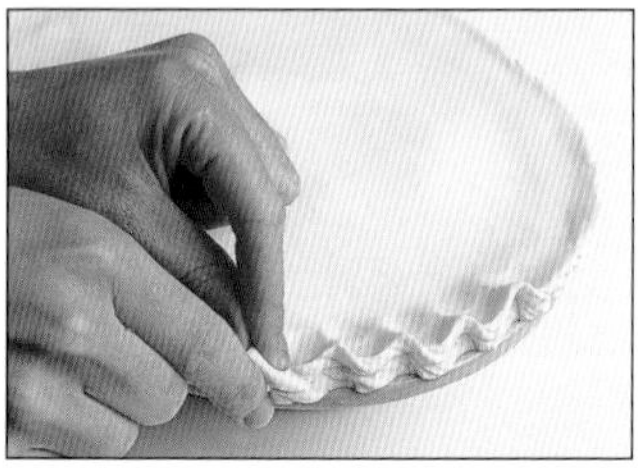

7 Pinch the pastry between your fingers to flute the edge. Roll out any remaining pastry trimmings and cut out shapes to garnish the pie, brushing the shapes with a little beaten egg before pressing them lightly in place.

8 Make a hole in the middle of the pie to allow steam to escape, brush the top carefully with beaten egg and chill for 10 minutes to rest the pastry.

9 Bake the pie for 15 minutes, then reduce the oven temperature to 200°C/400°F/Gas 6 and bake for a further 15–20 minutes, or until the pastry is risen and golden.

VEAL AND HAM PIE

POPULAR FOR OVER TWO CENTURIES, THIS CLASSIC PIE IS MOIST AND DELICIOUS. THE FLAVOURS OF THE TWO TENDER MEATS MARRY PERFECTLY IN THE DELICATE FILLING.

SERVES FOUR

INGREDIENTS

- 450g/1lb boneless shoulder of veal, diced
- 225g/8oz lean gammon, diced
- 15ml/1 tbsp plain flour
- large pinch each of dry mustard and ground black pepper
- 25g/1oz/2 tbsp butter
- 15ml/1 tbsp sunflower oil
- 1 onion, chopped
- 600ml/1 pint/2½ cups chicken or veal stock
- 2 eggs, hard-boiled and sliced
- 30ml/2 tbsp chopped fresh parsley

For the pastry

- 175g/6oz/1½ cups plain flour
- 75g/3oz/6 tbsp butter
- iced water, to mix
- beaten egg, to glaze

1 Preheat the oven to 180°C/350°F/Gas 4. Mix the veal and gammon in a bowl. Season the flour with the mustard and freshly ground black pepper, then add it to the meat and toss well. Heat the butter and oil in a large, flameproof casserole until sizzling, then cook the meat mixture in batches until golden on all sides. Use a draining spoon to remove the meat from the pan.

2 Cook the onion in the fat remaining in the casserole until softened, but not coloured. Gradually stir in the stock, then replace the meat mixture and stir until thoroughly combined. Cover and cook in the oven for 1½ hours, or until the veal is tender.

3 To make the pastry, sift the flour into a bowl and rub in the butter until the mixture resembles fine crumbs. Mix in enough iced water to bind the mixture into clumps, then press these together with your fingertips to make a dough.

4 Spoon the veal mixture into a 1.5 litre/2½ pint/6¼ cup pie dish. Arrange the slices of hard-boiled egg on top and sprinkle with the parsley.

5 Roll out the pastry on a lightly floured work surface to about 4cm/1½in larger than the top of the pie dish. Cut a strip from around the edge of the pastry, dampen the rim of the pie dish and press the pastry strip on it. Brush the pastry rim with beaten egg and cover it with the pastry lid.

6 Press the pastry around the rim to seal in the filling and cut off any excess. Use the blunt edge of a knife to tap the outside edge of the pastry, pressing it down with your finger as you seal in the filling. (This is known as knocking up.) Pinch the pastry between your fingers to flute the edge. Roll out any remaining pastry trimmings and cut out decorative shapes to garnish the top of the pie.

7 Brush the top of the pie with beaten egg and bake for 30–40 minutes, or until the pastry is well-risen and golden brown. Serve hot with slightly crunchy, steamed green cabbage and creamy mashed potato.

OSSO BUCCO WITH RISOTTO MILANESE

OSSO BUCCO, LITERALLY MEANING BONE WITH A HOLE, IS A TRADITIONAL MILANESE STEW OF VEAL, ONIONS AND LEEKS IN WHITE WINE. MANY OF TODAY'S VERSIONS ALSO INCLUDE TOMATOES. RISOTTO MILANESE IS THE ARCHETYPAL ITALIAN RISOTTO AND THE CLASSIC ACCOMPANIMENT FOR OSSO BUCCO.

SERVES FOUR

INGREDIENTS
- 50g/2oz/¼ cup butter
- 15ml/1 tbsp olive oil
- 1 large onion, chopped
- 1 leek, finely chopped
- 45ml/3 tbsp plain flour
- 4 large portions of veal shin, hind cut
- 600ml/1 pint/2½ cups dry white wine
- salt and ground black pepper

For the risotto
- 25g/1oz/2 tbsp butter
- 1 onion, finely chopped
- 350g/12oz/1⅔ cups risotto rice
- 1 litre/1¾ pints/4 cups boiling chicken stock
- 2.5ml/½ tsp saffron strands
- 60ml/4 tbsp white wine
- 50g/2oz/⅔ cup Parmesan cheese, coarsely grated

For the gremolata
- grated rind of 1 lemon
- 30ml/2 tbsp chopped fresh parsley
- 1 garlic clove, finely chopped

1 Heat the butter and oil until sizzling in a large, frying pan. Add the onion and leek, and cook gently for about 5 minutes without browning the onions. Season the flour and toss the veal in it, then add them to the pan and cook over a high heat until they brown.

COOK'S TIP
When buying veal shin, ask for the pieces to be cut thickly so that they will retain the marrow during cooking (or check that they are prepared this way if purchasing prepacked meat).

2 Gradually stir in the wine and heat until simmering. Cover the pan and simmer for 1½ hours, stirring occasionally, or until the meat is very tender. Use a draining spoon to transfer the veal to a warm serving dish, then boil the sauce rapidly until reduced and thickened to the required consistency.

3 Make the risotto about 30 minutes before the end of the cooking time for the stew. Melt the butter in a large pan and cook the onion until softened.

4 Stir in the rice to coat all the grains in butter. Add a ladleful of boiling chicken stock and mix well. Continue adding the boiling stock a ladleful at a time, allowing each portion to be absorbed before adding the next. The whole process takes about 20 minutes.

5 Pound the saffron strands in a mortar, then stir in the wine. Add the saffron-scented wine to the risotto and cook for a final 5 minutes. Remove the pan from the heat and stir in the Parmesan.

6 Mix the lemon rind, parsley and garlic for the gremolata. Spoon some risotto on to each plate, then add some veal. Sprinkle with gremolata and serve at once.

Roast Veal with Parsley Stuffing

Cooking this joint of veal, with its fragrant parsley and leek stuffing, in a roasting bag ensures that it is succulent and full flavoured when served.

SERVES SIX

INGREDIENTS
- 25g/1oz/2 tbsp butter
- 15ml/1 tbsp sunflower oil
- 1 leek, finely chopped
- 1 celery stick, finely chopped
- 50g/2oz/1 cup fresh white breadcrumbs
- 50g/2oz/½ cup chopped fresh flat leaf parsley
- 900g/2lb boned loin of veal
- salt and ground black pepper

VARIATION
Other mild herbs can be used in the stuffing instead of parsley. Try tarragon, chervil and chives, but avoid strong-flavoured herbs, such as marjoram, oregano and thyme, which tend to overpower the delicate flavour of veal.

1 Preheat the oven to 180°C/350°F/Gas 4. Heat the butter and oil in a frying pan until foaming. Cook the leek and celery until they are just starting to colour, then remove the pan from the heat and stir in the breadcrumbs, parsley and seasoning.

2 Lay the joint of veal out flat. Spread the stuffing over the meat, then roll it up carefully and tie the joint at regular intervals to secure it in a neat shape.

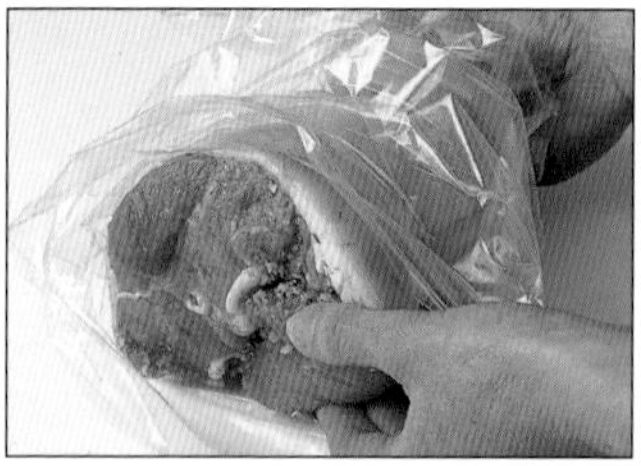

3 Place the veal in a roasting bag and close the bag with an ovenproof tie, then place it in a roasting tin. Roast the veal for 1¼ hours.

4 Pierce the joint with a metal skewer to check whether it is cooked: when cooked the meat juices will run clear. Leave the joint to stand for 10–15 minutes, then carve it into thick slices and serve with a light gravy, sautéed potatoes, asparagus and mangetouts.

Escalopes of Veal with Cream Sauce

This quick, easy dinner-party dish is delicious served with buttered tagliatelle and lightly steamed green vegetables.

SERVES FOUR

INGREDIENTS
- 15ml/1 tbsp plain flour
- 4 veal escalopes, each weighing about 75–115g/3–4oz
- 30ml/2 tbsp sunflower oil
- 1 shallot, chopped
- 150g/5oz/2 cups oyster mushrooms, sliced
- 30ml/2 tbsp Marsala or medium-dry sherry
- 200ml/7fl oz/scant 1 cup crème fraîche
- 30ml/2 tbsp chopped fresh tarragon
- salt and ground black pepper

COOK'S TIP
If the sauce seems to be too thick, add 30ml/2 tbsp water.

1 Season the flour and use to dust the veal escalopes, then set aside.

2 Heat the oil in a large frying pan and cook the shallot and mushrooms for 5 minutes. Add the escalopes and cook over a high heat for about 1½ minutes on each side. Pour in the Marsala or sherry and cook until reduced by half.

3 Use a fish slice to remove the veal escalopes from the pan. Stir the crème fraîche, tarragon and seasoning into the juices remaining in the pan and simmer gently for 3–5 minutes, or until the sauce is thick and creamy.

4 Return the escalopes to the pan and heat through for 1 minute before serving.

THAI BEEF SALAD

ALL THE INGREDIENTS FOR THIS TRADITIONAL THAI DISH – KNOWN AS YAM NUA YANG – ARE WIDELY AVAILABLE IN LARGER SUPERMARKETS.

SERVES FOUR

INGREDIENTS
- 675g/1½lb fillet or rump steak
- 30ml/2 tbsp olive oil
- 2 small mild red chillies, seeded and sliced
- 225g/8oz/3¼ cups shiitake mushrooms, sliced

For the dressing
- 3 spring onions, finely chopped
- 2 garlic cloves, finely chopped
- juice of 1 lime
- 15–30ml/1–2 tbsp fish or oyster sauce, to taste
- 5ml/1 tsp soft light brown sugar
- 30ml/2 tbsp chopped fresh coriander

To serve
- 1 cos or romaine lettuce, torn into strips
- 175g/6oz cherry tomatoes, halved
- 5cm/2in piece cucumber, peeled, halved and thinly sliced
- 45ml/3 tbsp toasted sesame seeds

1 Preheat the grill until hot, then cook the steak for 2–4 minutes on each side depending on how well done you like steak. (In Thailand, the beef is traditionally served quite rare.) Leave to cool for at least 15 minutes.

2 Use a very sharp knife to slice the meat as thinly as possible and place the slices in a bowl.

VARIATION
If you can find them, yellow chillies make a colourful addition to this dish. Substitute one for one of the red chillies.

3 Heat the olive oil in a small frying pan. Add the seeded and sliced red chillies and the sliced mushrooms and cook for 5 minutes, stirring occasionally. Turn off the heat and add the grilled steak slices to the pan, then stir well to coat the beef slices in the chilli and mushroom mixture.

4 Stir all the ingredients for the dressing together, then pour it over the meat mixture and toss gently.

5 Arrange the salad ingredients on a serving plate. Spoon the warm steak mixture in the centre and sprinkle the sesame seeds over. Serve at once.

Chilli Con Carne

Originally made with finely chopped beef, chillies and kidney beans by hungry labourers working on the Texan railroad, this famous Tex-Mex stew has become an international favourite. Serve with rice or baked potatoes to complete this hearty meal.

SERVES EIGHT

INGREDIENTS
- 1.2kg/2½lb lean braising steak
- 30ml/2 tbsp sunflower oil
- 1 large onion, chopped
- 2 garlic cloves, finely chopped
- 15ml/1 tbsp plain flour
- 300ml/½ pint/1¼ cups red wine
- 300ml/½ pint/1¼ cups beef stock
- 30ml/2 tbsp tomato purée
- fresh coriander leaves, to garnish
- salt and ground black pepper

For the beans
- 30ml/2 tbsp olive oil
- 1 onion, chopped
- 1 red chilli, seeded and chopped
- 2 x 400g/14oz cans red kidney beans, drained and rinsed
- 400g/14oz can chopped tomatoes

For the topping
- 6 tomatoes, peeled and chopped
- 1 green chilli, seeded and chopped
- 30ml/2 tbsp snipped fresh chives
- 30ml/2 tbsp chopped fresh coriander
- 150ml/¼ pint/⅔ cup soured cream

1 Cut the meat into thick strips and then cut it crossways into small cubes. Heat the oil in a large, flameproof casserole. Add the chopped onion and garlic, and cook until softened but not coloured. Meanwhile, season the flour and place it on a plate, then toss a batch of meat in it.

VARIATION
This stew is equally good served with tortillas instead of rice. Wrap the tortillas in foil and warm through in the oven.

2 Use a draining spoon to remove the onion from the pan, then add the floured beef and cook over a high heat until browned on all sides. Remove from the pan and set aside, then flour and brown another batch of meat.

3 When the last batch of meat is browned, return the first batches with the onion to the pan. Stir in the wine, stock and tomato purée. Bring to the boil, reduce the heat and simmer for 45 minutes, or until the beef is tender.

4 Meanwhile, for the beans, heat the olive oil in a frying pan and cook the onion and chilli until softened. Add the kidney beans and tomatoes and simmer gently for 20–25 minutes, or until thickened and reduced.

5 Mix the tomatoes, chilli, chives and coriander for the topping. Ladle the meat mixture on to warmed plates. Add a layer of bean mixture and tomato topping. Finish with soured cream and garnish with coriander leaves.

CHUNKY BURGERS WITH SPICY RELISH

Burgers are easy to make and these taste terrific – far better than any you can buy. Use lean minced beef so that the burgers are not fatty.

SERVES FOUR

INGREDIENTS

- 450g/1lb lean minced beef
- 1 shallot, chopped
- 30ml/2 tbsp chopped fresh flat leaf parsley
- 30ml/2 tbsp tomato ketchup
- salt and ground black pepper

For the spicy relish

- 15ml/1 tbsp olive oil
- 1 shallot, chopped
- 1 garlic clove, crushed
- 1 small green chilli, seeded and finely chopped
- 400g/14oz can ratatouille

To serve

- 4 burger buns
- 1 little gem lettuce heart, separated into leaves

1 Mix the lean minced beef, chopped shallot, chopped fresh flat leaf parsley, ketchup and seasoning in a mixing bowl until thoroughly combined. Divide the mixture into quarters and shape into four chunky burgers, pressing them firmly between the palms of your hands. Place the burgers on a plate and set aside until ready to cook.

2 To make the spicy relish, heat the olive oil in a frying pan and cook the shallot, garlic and chilli for a few minutes, stirring, until softened. Stir in the ratatouille and simmer for 5 minutes.

3 Meanwhile, preheat the grill, a griddle or frying pan. Grill or fry the burgers for about 5 minutes on each side, or until cooked through.

4 Split the burger buns and toast them, if you like. Arrange a few lettuce leaves on the bun bases, then top with the burgers and add a little of the warm spicy relish. Add the bun tops and serve at once, offering the remaining relish and any extra lettuce leaves separately. Serve with chunky chips or baked potatoes.

ITALIAN MEATBALLS

Succulent meatballs in a colourful pepper sauce are delicious with rice or pasta and they are always a hit with children as well as adults.

SERVES FOUR

INGREDIENTS

- 10ml/2 tsp sunflower oil
- 1 shallot, chopped
- 2 garlic cloves, finely chopped
- 15ml/1 tbsp fresh thyme leaves
- 675g/1½lb lean minced beef
- 1 slice white bread, crust removed, reduced to crumbs
- 1 egg
- salt and ground black pepper
- fresh thyme leaves, to garnish

For the sauce

- 3 red peppers, halved and seeded
- 1 onion, quartered
- 400g/14oz can chopped tomatoes

1 Heat the oil in a frying pan and cook the shallot and garlic for 5 minutes, or until softened. Remove the pan from the heat and add the thyme, then turn the mixture into a bowl.

2 Add the minced beef, breadcrumbs, egg and seasoning to the shallot mixture. Mix until all the ingredients are thoroughly combined. Shape the mixture into 20 small meatballs, then chill them until the sauce is ready.

3 To make the sauce, preheat the grill. Arrange the peppers on a grill rack with the pieces of onion. Grill for 12–15 minutes, turning frequently, or until the pepper skins are blackened. Remove from under the heat, cover the peppers with a dish towel and leave to cool. Peel the peppers and place them in a blender or food processor with the grilled onion and the tomatoes. Process until smooth, then add seasoning to taste.

COOK'S TIP

Both the meatballs and sauce freeze well. Freeze the meatballs after shaping. Thaw thoroughly before cooking.

4 Cook the meatballs in a large, non-stick frying pan for about 10–15 minutes, gently rolling them around to brown them evenly all over.

5 Add the puréed pepper and tomato mixture and bring to the boil, then simmer for 10 minutes. Transfer to a dish and scatter with thyme leaves to garnish, then serve at once.

Lamb

Naturally tender, succulent and full of flavour, lamb is one of the truly international meats and is cooked in almost every country – a fact reflected in this eclectic range of recipes, which includes Moussaka, a dish made in both Greece and Turkey, Spiced Lamb with Tomatoes and Peppers from India, and the North African classic, Tagine of Lamb with Couscous. There are western European and American favourites, such as Roast Leg of Lamb, and traditional recipes with an enticing, contemporary twist such as Redcurrant-glazed Lamb Chops with Celeriac and Thyme Mash, and Braised Shoulder of Lamb with Pearl Barley and Baby Vegetables.

Roast Leg of Lamb

When young lamb was seasonal to springtime, a roast leg was an Easter speciality, served with a sauce using the first sprigs of mint of the year and early new potatoes. Roast lamb is now well established as a year-round family favourite for Sunday lunch, often served with crisp roast potatoes.

SERVES SIX

INGREDIENTS
- 1.5kg/3¼lb leg of lamb
- 4 garlic cloves, sliced
- 2 fresh rosemary sprigs
- 30ml/2 tbsp light olive oil
- 300ml/½ pint/1¼ cups red wine
- 5ml/1 tsp honey
- 45ml/3 tbsp redcurrant jelly
- salt and ground black pepper

For the roast potatoes
- 45ml/3 tbsp white vegetable fat or lard
- 1.3kg/3lb potatoes, such as Desirée, cut into chunks

For the mint sauce
- about 15g/½oz fresh mint
- 10ml/2 tsp caster sugar
- 15ml/1 tbsp boiling water
- 30ml/2 tbsp white wine vinegar

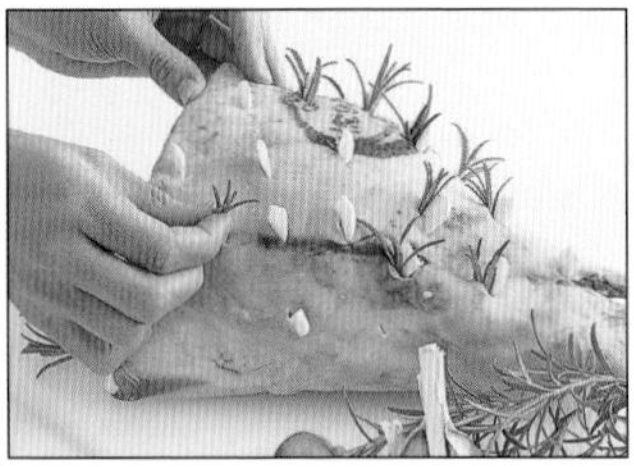

1 Preheat the oven to 220°C/425°F/Gas 7. Make small slits into the lamb all over the joint. Press a slice of garlic and a few rosemary leaves into each slit, then place the joint in a roasting tin and season well. Drizzle the oil over the lamb and roast the joint for about 1 hour.

COOK'S TIP
To make a quick and tasty gravy from the pan juices, add about 300ml/½ pint/1¼ cups red wine, stock or water and boil, stirring occasionally, until reduced and well-flavoured. Season to taste, then strain into a sauce boat to serve.

2 Meanwhile, mix the wine, honey and redcurrant jelly in a small saucepan and heat, stirring, until the jelly melts. Bring to the boil, then reduce the heat and simmer until reduced by half. Spoon this glaze over the lamb and return it to the oven for 30–45 minutes.

3 To make the potatoes, put the fat in a roasting tin on the shelf above the meat. Boil the potatoes for 5–10 minutes, then drain them and fluff up the surface of each with a fork.

4 Add the prepared potatoes to the hot fat and baste well, then roast them for 40–50 minutes, or until they are crisp.

5 Make the mint sauce while the potatoes are roasting. Place the mint on a chopping board and scatter the sugar over the top. Chop the mint finely, then transfer the mint and sugar to a bowl.

6 Add the boiling water and stir until the sugar has dissolved. Add 15ml/1 tbsp vinegar and taste the sauce before adding the remaining vinegar. (You may want to add slightly less or more than the suggested quantity.) Leave the mint sauce to stand until you are ready to serve the meal.

7 Cover the lamb with foil and set it aside in a warm place to rest for 10–15 minutes before carving. Serve with the crisp roast potatoes, mint sauce and a selection of seasonal vegetables.

HERB-CRUSTED RACK OF LAMB WITH PUY LENTILS

THIS ROAST IS QUICK AND EASY TO PREPARE, YET IMPRESSIVE WHEN SERVED: THE PERFECT CHOICE WHEN ENTERTAINING. BOILED OR STEAMED NEW POTATOES AND LIGHTLY COOKED BROCCOLI OR SUGAR SNAP PEAS ARE SUITABLE ACCOMPANIMENTS FOR THE LAMB. SERVE WITH A LIGHT RED WINE.

SERVES FOUR

INGREDIENTS

- 2 x 6-bone racks of lamb, chined
- 50g/2oz/1 cup fresh white breadcrumbs
- 2 large garlic cloves, crushed
- 90ml/6 tbsp chopped mixed fresh herbs, such as rosemary, thyme, flat leaf parsley and marjoram, plus extra sprigs to garnish
- 50g/2oz/¼ cup butter, melted
- salt and ground black pepper

For the Puy lentils

- 1 red onion, chopped
- 30ml/2 tbsp olive oil
- 400g/14oz can Puy or green lentils, rinsed and drained
- 400g/14oz can chopped tomatoes
- 30ml/2 tbsp chopped fresh parsley

1 Preheat the oven to 220°C/425°F/Gas 7. Trim any excess fat from the lamb, season well with salt and pepper.

2 Mix together the breadcrumbs, garlic, herbs and butter, and press on to the fat-sides of the lamb. Place in a roasting tin and roast for 25 minutes. Cover with foil; stand for 5 minutes before carving.

3 Cook the onion in the olive oil until softened. Add the lentils and tomatoes and cook gently for 5 minutes, or until the lentils are piping hot. Stir in the parsley and season to taste.

4 Cut each rack of lamb in half and serve with the lentils and new potatoes. Garnish with herb sprigs.

BRAISED SHOULDER OF LAMB WITH PEARL BARLEY AND BABY VEGETABLES

PEARL BARLEY ABSORBS ALL THE WONDERFUL MEAT JUICES AND STOCK TO BECOME FULL-FLAVOURED AND NUTTY IN TEXTURE WHEN COOKED.

SERVES FOUR

INGREDIENTS

- 60ml/4 tbsp olive oil
- 1 large onion, chopped
- 2 garlic cloves, chopped
- 2 celery sticks, sliced
- a little plain flour
- 675g/1½lb boned shoulder of lamb, cut into cubes
- 900ml–1 litre/1½–1¾ pints/3¾–4 cups lamb stock
- 115g/4oz pearl barley
- 225g/8oz baby carrots
- 225g/8oz baby turnips
- salt and ground black pepper
- 30ml/2 tbsp chopped fresh marjoram, to garnish

1 Heat 45ml/3 tbsp of the oil in a flameproof casserole. Cook the onion and garlic until softened, add the celery, then cook until the vegetables brown.

2 Season the flour and toss the lamb in it. Use a draining spoon to remove the vegetables from the casserole. Add and heat the remaining oil with the juices in the casserole. Brown the lamb in batches until golden.

3 When all the meat is browned, return it to the casserole with the vegetables. Stir in 900ml/1½ pints/3¾ cups of the stock and the pearl barley. Cover, then bring to the boil, reduce the heat and simmer for 1 hour, or until the pearl barley and lamb are tender.

4 Add the baby carrots and turnips to the casserole for the final 15 minutes cooking. Stir the meat occasionally during cooking and add the remaining stock, if necessary. Stir in seasoning to taste, and serve piping hot, garnished with marjoram. Warm, crusty bread would make a good accompaniment.

REDCURRANT-GLAZED LAMB CHOPS WITH CELERIAC AND THYME MASH

This is a brilliant supper dish to lift the spirits on a cold winter's evening. The redcurrant glaze helps to seal the juices into the meat and it complements the flavour of the lamb to perfection.

SERVES FOUR

INGREDIENTS
- 30ml/2 tbsp redcurrant jelly
- 30ml/2 tbsp mint jelly
- grated rind and juice of 1 orange
- 12 lamb cutlets, trimmed
- fresh rosemary, to garnish

For the celeriac mash
- 675g/1½lb celeriac, diced
- 675g/1½lb potatoes, diced
- 25g/1oz/2 tbsp butter
- 30ml/2 tbsp double cream
- 15ml/1 tbsp fresh thyme leaves
- salt and ground black pepper

VARIATION

To make a more colourful vegetable mash, use sweet potatoes or carrots in place of some or all of the celeriac. Add parsley in place of thyme, if you prefer.

1 First prepare the celeriac mash. Cook the celeriac and potatoes together in boiling salted water for 20 minutes, or until tender. Drain well, then add the butter, cream and thyme. Mash the vegetables and season to taste.

2 Heat the jellies with the orange rind and juice in a small pan, stirring occasionally until smooth. Bring to the boil and cook until reduced by half.

3 Arrange the lamb cutlets on a hot griddle pan and season them well. Drizzle half the redcurrant and mint glaze over the cutlets and then cook for 3–5 minutes. Turn the cutlets and pour the remaining glaze over them. Cook for a further 3–5 minutes.

4 Garnish the glazed cutlets with rosemary and serve at once, with the celeriac and thyme mash.

BARBECUED LAMB STEAKS WITH RED PEPPER SALSA

Vibrant red pepper salsa brings out the best in succulent lamb steaks to make a dish that looks as good as it tastes. Serve a selection of salads and crusty bread with the lamb.

SERVES SIX

INGREDIENTS
- 6 lamb steaks
- about 15g/½oz fresh rosemary leaves
- 2 garlic cloves, sliced
- 60ml/4 tbsp olive oil
- 30ml/2 tbsp maple syrup
- salt and ground black pepper

For the salsa
- 200g/7oz red peppers, roasted, peeled, seeded and chopped
- 1 plump garlic clove, finely chopped
- 15ml/1 tbsp snipped chives
- 30ml/2 tbsp extra virgin olive oil
- fresh flat leaf parsley, to garnish

1 Place the lamb steaks in a dish and season with salt and pepper. Pull the leaves off the rosemary and scatter them over the meat. Add the slices of garlic cloves, then drizzle the oil and maple syrup over the top. Cover and chill until ready to cook. The lamb can be left to marinate in the fridge for up to 24 hours.

2 Make sure the steaks are liberally coated with the marinating ingredients, then grill them over a hot barbecue for 2–5 minutes on each side. The cooking time depends on the heat of the barbecue coals and the thickness of the steaks as well as the result required – rare, medium or well cooked.

3 While the lamb steaks are cooking, mix together all the ingredients for the salsa. Serve the barbecued lamb steaks freshly cooked, and offer the salsa separately or spoon it on to the plates with the meat. Garnish with sprigs of flat leaf parsley.

MOUSSAKA

This is a traditional Eastern Mediterranean dish, popular in both Greece and Turkey. Layers of minced lamb, aubergines, tomatoes and onions are topped with a creamy yogurt and cheese sauce in this delicious, authentic recipe.

SERVES FOUR

INGREDIENTS
- 450g/1lb aubergines
- 150ml/¼ pint/⅔ cup olive oil
- 1 large onion, chopped
- 2–3 garlic cloves, finely chopped
- 675g/1½lb lean minced lamb
- 15ml/1 tbsp plain flour
- 400g/14oz can chopped tomatoes
- 30ml/2 tbsp chopped mixed fresh herbs, such as parsley, marjoram and oregano
- salt and ground black pepper

For the topping
- 300ml/½ pint/1¼ cups natural yogurt
- 2 eggs
- 25g/1oz feta cheese, crumbled
- 25g/1oz/⅓ cup freshly grated Parmesan cheese

1 Cut the aubergines into thin slices and layer them in a colander, sprinkling each layer with salt.

2 Cover the aubergines with a plate and a weight, then leave to drain for about 30 minutes. Drain and rinse well, then pat dry with kitchen paper.

3 Heat 45ml/3 tbsp of the oil in a large, heavy-based saucepan. Fry the onion and garlic until softened, but not coloured. Add the lamb and cook over a high heat, stirring often, until browned.

4 Stir in the flour until mixed, then stir in the tomatoes, herbs and seasoning. Bring to the boil, reduce the heat and simmer gently for 20 minutes.

5 Meanwhile, heat a little of the remaining oil in a large frying pan. Add as many aubergine slices as can be laid in the pan, then cook until golden on both sides. Set the cooked aubergines aside. Heat more oil and continue frying the aubergines in batches, adding oil as necessary.

COOK'S TIP

Aubergines that are available today do not taste bitter; therefore it is not usually necessary to salt them before cooking. However if they are to be fried, as in this recipe, salting and drying them reduces the amount of fat that they absorb and helps them to brown.

6 Preheat the oven to 180°C/350°F/ Gas 4. Arrange half the aubergine slices in a large, shallow ovenproof dish.

7 Top the aubergine slices with about half of the meat and tomato mixture, then add the remaining aubergine slices. Spread the remaining meat mixture over the aubergines.

8 Beat together the yogurt and eggs, then mix in the feta and Parmesan cheeses, pour the mixture over the meat and spread it evenly.

9 Transfer the moussaka to the oven and bake for 35–40 minutes, or until golden and bubbling. Serve with a simple, mixed leaf, green salad.

VARIATION

Use large courgettes in place of the aubergines, if you like, and cut them diagonally into fairly thick slices. There is no need to salt the courgettes before frying them.

SPICED LAMB WITH TOMATOES AND PEPPERS

Select lean tender lamb from the leg for this lightly spiced curry with succulent peppers and wedges of onion. Serve warm naan bread to mop up the tomato-rich juices.

SERVES SIX

INGREDIENTS
- 1.5kg/3¼lb lean boneless lamb, cubed
- 250ml/8fl oz/1 cup natural yogurt
- 30ml/2 tbsp sunflower oil
- 3 onions
- 2 red peppers, seeded and cut into chunks
- 3 garlic cloves, finely chopped
- 1 red chilli, seeded and chopped
- 2.5cm/1in piece fresh root ginger, peeled and chopped
- 30ml/2 tbsp mild curry paste
- 2 x 400g/14oz cans chopped tomatoes
- large pinch of saffron strands
- 800g/1¾lb plum tomatoes, halved, seeded and cut into chunks
- salt and ground black pepper
- chopped fresh coriander, to garnish

1 Mix the lamb with the yogurt in a bowl. Cover and chill for about 1 hour. (Marinating in yogurt helps to tenderize the meat and reduce the cooking time.)

2 Heat the oil in a karahi, wok or large saucepan. Drain the lamb and reserve the yogurt, then cook the lamb in batches until it is golden on all sides – this takes about 15 minutes in total. Remove from the pan and set aside.

3 Cut two of the onions into wedges (six from each onion) and add to the oil remaining in the pan. Fry the onion wedges over a medium heat for about 10 minutes, or until they are beginning to colour. Add the peppers and cook for a further 5 minutes. Use a draining spoon to remove the vegetables from the pan and set aside.

4 Meanwhile, chop the remaining onion. Add it to the oil remaining in the pan with the garlic, chilli and ginger, and cook, stirring often, until softened.

5 Stir in the curry paste and canned tomatoes with the reserved yogurt marinade. Replace the lamb, add seasoning to taste and stir well. Bring to the boil, reduce the heat and simmer for about 30 minutes.

6 Pound the saffron to a powder in a mortar, stir in a little boiling water to dissolve the saffron. Add this liquid to the curry. Replace the onion and pepper mixture. Stir in the fresh tomatoes and bring back to simmering point, then cook for 15 minutes. Garnish with chopped coriander to serve.

TAGINE OF LAMB WITH COUSCOUS

A TAGINE IS A CLASSIC MOROCCAN STEW AND IT IS ALSO THE NAME GIVEN TO THE EARTHENWARE POT WITH A CONICAL LID IN WHICH THE STEW IS COOKED. COUSCOUS HAS TWO MEANINGS AND REFERS TO A FINISHED DISH AS WELL AS AN INGREDIENT. FROM THE ARABIC KUSKUS, *THE TITLE IS GIVEN TO THE POPULAR NORTH AFRICAN STEW OF MEAT (OR CHICKEN) AND VEGETABLES IN A THIN, YET FULL-FLAVOURED AND SPICY, SAUCE SERVED ON COUSCOUS, THE CRACKED WHEAT PRODUCT THAT IS NOW WIDELY AVAILABLE IN INSTANT, PRE-COOKED FORM.*

SERVES SIX

INGREDIENTS

- 1kg/2¼lb lean boneless lamb, such as shoulder or neck fillet
- 25g/1oz/2 tbsp butter
- 15ml/1 tbsp sunflower oil
- 1 large onion, chopped
- 2 garlic cloves, chopped
- 2.5cm/1in piece fresh root ginger, peeled and finely chopped
- 1 red pepper, seeded and chopped
- 900ml/1½ pints/3¾ cups lamb stock or water
- 250g/9oz ready-to-eat prunes
- juice of 1 lemon
- 15ml/1 tbsp clear honey
- 1.5ml/¼ tsp saffron strands
- 1 cinnamon stick, broken in half
- 50g/2oz/½ cup flaked almonds, toasted
- salt and ground black pepper

To serve

- 450g/1lb/2½ cups couscous
- 25g/1oz/2 tbsp butter
- 30ml/2 tbsp chopped fresh coriander

1 Trim the lamb and cut it into 2.5cm/1in cubes. Heat the butter and oil in a large flameproof casserole until foaming. Add the onion, garlic and ginger and cook, stirring occasionally, until softened but not coloured.

2 Add the lamb and red pepper and mix well. (The meat is not sealed in batches over high heat for an authentic tagine.) Pour in the stock or water.

3 Add the prunes, lemon juice, honey, saffron strands and cinnamon. Season with salt and pepper and stir well. Bring to the boil, then reduce the heat and cover the casserole. Simmer for 1½–2 hours, stirring occasionally, or until the meat is melt-in-the-mouth tender.

4 Meanwhile, cook the couscous according to packet instructions, usually by placing in a large bowl and pouring in boiling water to cover the "grains" by 2.5cm/1in. Stir well, then cover and leave to stand for 5–10 minutes. The couscous absorbs the water and swells to become tender and fluffy. Stir in the butter, chopped fresh coriander and seasoning to taste.

5 Taste the stew for seasoning and add more salt and pepper if necessary. Pile the couscous into a large, warmed serving dish or on to individual warmed bowls or plates. Ladle the stew on to the couscous and scatter the toasted flaked almonds over the top.

Lamb and Ginger Stir-fry with Egg Noodles

Stir-frying is a traditional Oriental technique; it can also be one of the quickest, easiest and healthiest cooking methods. A wok is the classic pan, but a large skillet (frying pan with sides that are deeper than usual) can be used, or even a large pan is suitable – it is important to have plenty of space for tossing and turning ingredients.

SERVES FOUR

INGREDIENTS
- 45ml/3 tbsp sesame oil
- 3 spring onions, sliced
- 2 garlic cloves, crushed
- 2.5cm/1in piece fresh root ginger, peeled and finely sliced
- 1 red chilli, seeded and finely sliced
- 1 red pepper, halved, seeded and sliced
- 450g/1lb lean boneless lamb, cut into fine strips
- 115g/4oz/1½ cups fresh shiitake mushrooms, sliced
- 2 carrots, cut into matchstick strips
- 300g/11oz fresh Chinese egg noodles
- 300g/11oz pak choi, shredded
- soy sauce, to serve

1 Heat half the oil in a wok or large frying pan. Stir-fry the spring onions and garlic for about 5 minutes, or until golden. Add the ginger, chilli and red pepper and continue stir-frying for 5 minutes, until the chilli and pepper start to soften. Use a draining spoon to remove the vegetables and set aside.

2 Add the remaining oil and stir-fry the lamb in batches until golden. Add the mushrooms and carrots and stir-fry for 2–3 minutes. Remove from the wok and set aside with the red pepper mixture. Add the noodles and pak choi to the wok and stir-fry for 5 minutes.

3 Finally, replace all the cooked ingredients and stir-fry for a couple of minutes or until the mixture is heated through. Serve at once, offering soy sauce to season at the table.

COOK'S TIP

If fresh egg noodles are not available, use the dried type. Cook them according to the packet instructions, drain and rinse under cold water, then drain well.

Italian Braised Shanks with Ratatouille

For this modern Mediterranean meal, lamb shanks are braised in Italian style with ratatouille: a dish of mixed vegetables simmered in olive oil.

SERVES FOUR

INGREDIENTS
- 4 lamb shanks
- 45ml/3 tbsp olive oil
- 1 large red onion, finely chopped
- 2 large garlic cloves, finely chopped
- 1 large aubergine, diced
- 3 courgettes, diced
- 2 x 400g/14oz cans chopped tomatoes
- 300ml/½ pint/1¼ cups well-flavoured lamb stock
- 400g/14oz can flageolet beans, rinsed and drained
- 15ml/1 tbsp chopped fresh oregano
- 15ml/1 tbsp chopped fresh rosemary
- 5ml/1 tsp clear honey
- salt and ground black pepper

1 Season the lamb shanks with salt and ground black pepper. Heat the oil in a large flameproof casserole and fry the shanks until golden on all sides, then remove from the pan and set aside.

2 Add the finely chopped onion and garlic and cook gently until the onion is softened. Add the diced aubergine and courgettes and cook the vegetable mixture for a further 5 minutes.

3 Stir in the tomatoes and stock, then nestle the lamb shanks back into the vegetable mixture. Bring to the boil, reduce the heat and cover the casserole. Simmer for about 1 hour.

4 Remove the lamb. Stir the beans into the vegetables with the herbs and honey, and simmer, covered, for about 45 minutes more, topping up with stock if necessary. Replace the lamb 10 minutes from the end of cooking to heat through. Serve with mashed potatoes or couscous.

COOK'S TIP

Butchers are usually happy to supply less-popular cuts, such as lamb shanks, given a couple of days' notice, so remember to order them in advance. Alternatively, try lamb chump chops or neck of lamb in this dish.

Pork, Bacon and Ham

As the food of commoners rather than kings, pork, bacon and ham have, over the centuries, been taken for granted. That's a shame, because these are extremely tasty meats – as perfect for quick meals as for slow-cooked roasts. Traditional recipes such as Somerset Cider-glazed Ham or the French classic, Pork and Bacon Rillettes with Onion Salad will reward the time spent in the kitchen. Others such as creamy Carbonara Abruzzi or Stir-fried Pork with Mushrooms are quick to cook and ideal for midweek meals, while delicious Muffins with Bacon, Eggs and Quick Hollandaise Sauce can be served at any time of the day – or night.

STUFFED ROAST LOIN OF PORK WITH APPLE SAUCE

ROASTS MAKE GREAT SUNDAY LUNCHES BECAUSE THEY REQUIRE MINIMUM ATTENTION ONCE THEY ARE IN THE OVEN, SO THE COOK CAN RELAX WITH THE FAMILY OR FRIENDS.

SERVES SIX

INGREDIENTS

- 15ml/1 tbsp light olive oil
- 2 leeks, chopped
- 150g/5oz/⅔ cup ready-to-eat dried apricots, chopped
- 150g/5oz/1 cup dried dates, stoned and chopped
- 75g/3oz/1½ cups fresh white breadcrumbs
- 2 eggs, beaten
- 15ml/1 tbsp fresh thyme leaves
- 1.5kg/3¼lb boned loin of pork
- salt and ground black pepper

For the apple sauce

- 450g/1lb cooking apples
- 30ml/2 tbsp cider or water
- 25g/1oz/2 tbsp butter
- about 25g/1oz/2 tbsp caster sugar

1 Preheat oven to 220°C/425°F/Gas 7. Heat the oil in a large pan and cook the leeks until softened. Stir in the apricots, dates, breadcrumbs, eggs and thyme, and season with salt and pepper.

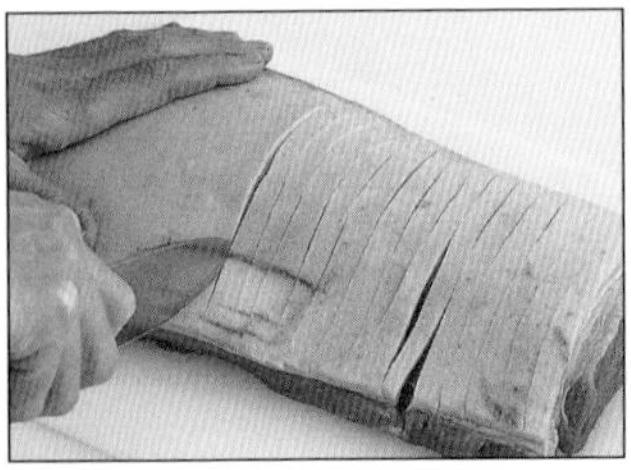

2 Lay the pork skin side up, and use a sharp knife to score the rind crossways.

3 Turn the meat over and cut down the centre of the joint to within 1cm/½in of the rind and fat, then work from the middle outwards towards one side, cutting most of the meat off the rind, keeping a 1cm/½in layer of meat on top of the rind. Cut to within 2.5cm/1in of the side of the joint. Repeat on the other side of the joint.

4 Spoon half the stuffing over the joint, then fold the meat over it.

5 Tie the joint back into its original shape, then place in a roasting tin and rub the skin liberally with salt. Roast for 40 minutes, then reduce the oven temperature to 190°C/375°F/Gas 5 and cook for a further 1½ hours, or until the meat is tender and cooked through.

6 When cooked, cover the meat closely with foil and leave to stand in a warm place for 10 minutes before carving.

COOK'S TIP

The resting time before carving is very important, so don't be tempted to skip it.

7 Meanwhile, shape the remaining stuffing into walnut-size balls. Arrange on a tray, cover with clear film and chill until 20 minutes before the pork is cooked. Then add the stuffing balls to the roasting tin and baste them with the cooking juices from the meat.

8 To make the apple sauce, peel, core and chop the apples, then place in a small pan with the cider or water and cook for 5–10 minutes, stirring occasionally, or until very soft. Beat well or process in a blender or food processor to make smooth apple sauce. Beat in the butter and sugar, adding a little more sugar to taste, if required. Reheat the apple sauce just before serving, if necessary.

9 Carve the joint into thick slices. If the crackling is very hard, you may find it is easier to slice the crackling off the joint first, before carving the meat, then cut the crackling into serving pieces using poultry shears or a heavy, sharp chef's knife or cleaver. Serve the pork with the crackling, stuffing balls, apple sauce and a selection of seasonal vegetables.

SOMERSET CIDER-GLAZED HAM

William the Conqueror introduced cider making to England from Normandy in 1066. This wonderful old West-Country ham glazed with cider is traditionally served with cranberry sauce and is ideal for Christmas or Boxing Day.

SERVES EIGHT TO TEN

INGREDIENTS

- 2kg/4½lb middle gammon joint
- 1.3 litres/2¼ pints/5⅔ cups medium-dry cider
- 1 large or 2 small onions
- about 30 whole cloves
- 3 bay leaves
- 10 black peppercorns
- 45ml/3 tbsp soft light brown sugar
- bunch of flat leaf parsley, to garnish

For the cranberry sauce

- 350g/12oz/3 cups cranberries
- 175g/6oz/¾ cup soft light brown sugar
- grated rind and juice of 2 clementines
- 30ml/2 tbsp port

1 Weigh the ham and calculate the cooking time at 20 minutes per 450g/1lb, then place it in a large casserole or saucepan. Stud the onion or onions with 5–10 of the cloves and add to the casserole or pan with the bay leaves and peppercorns.

2 Add 1.2 litres/2 pints/5 cups of the cider and enough water just to cover the ham. Heat until simmering and then carefully skim off the scum that rises to the surface using a large spoon or ladle. Start timing the cooking from the moment the stock begins to simmer.

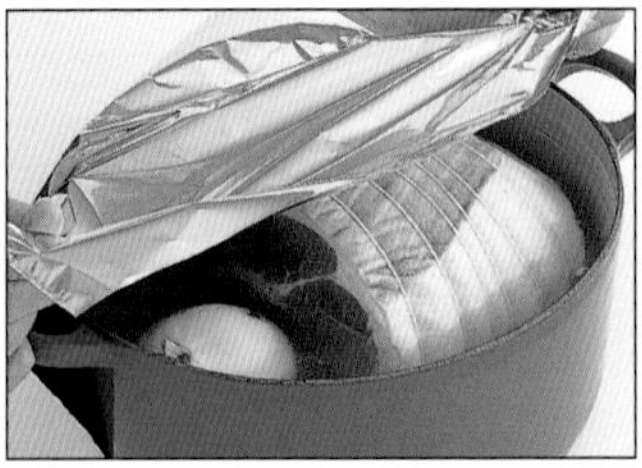

3 Cover with a lid or foil and simmer gently for the calculated time. Towards the end of the cooking time, preheat the oven to 220°C/425°F/Gas 7.

4 Heat the sugar and remaining cider in a pan; stir until the sugar has dissolved.

5 Simmer for 5 minutes to make a dark, sticky glaze. Remove the pan from the heat and leave to cool for 5 minutes.

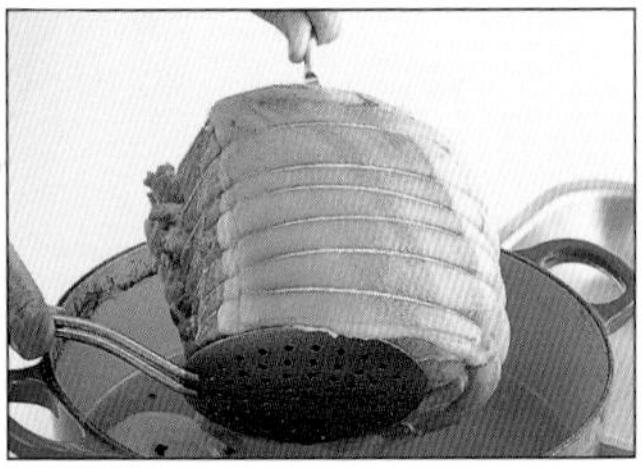

6 Lift the ham out of the casserole or pan using a draining spoon and a large fork. Carefully and evenly, cut the rind from the ham, then score the fat into a neat diamond pattern. Place the ham in a roasting tin or ovenproof dish.

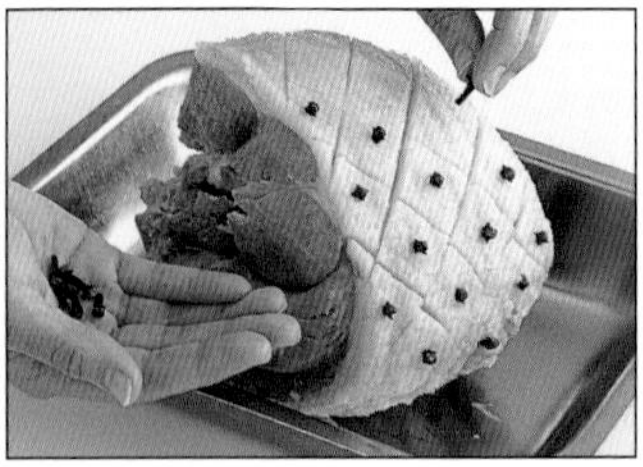

7 Press a clove into the centre of each diamond, then carefully spoon over the glaze. Bake for 20–25 minutes, or until the fat is brown, glistening and crisp.

8 Simmer all the cranberry sauce ingredients in a heavy-based saucepan for 15–20 minutes, stirring frequently. Transfer the sauce to a jug. Serve the ham hot or cold, garnished with parsley and with the cranberry sauce.

COOK'S TIPS

- A large stock pot or preserving pan can be used in place of the casserole or saucepan for cooking the ham.
- Leave the ham until it is just cool enough to handle before removing the rind. Snip off the string using a sharp knife or scissors, then carefully slice off the rind, leaving a thin, even layer of fat. Use a narrow-bladed, sharp knife for the best results – a filleting knife, or a long, slim ham knife would be ideal.

VARIATION

Use honey in place of the soft brown sugar for the glaze and serve the ham with redcurrant sauce or jelly.

Pan-Fried Pork with Thyme and Garlic Risotto

Lean pork chump chops are delicious served with smooth, creamy, but robust, risotto in this quick and contemporary meal.

SERVES FOUR

INGREDIENTS
- 4 large pork chump or loin chops, each weighing about 175g/6oz, rind removed
- 1 garlic clove, finely chopped
- juice of ½ lemon
- 5ml/1 tsp soft light brown sugar
- 25g/1oz/2 tbsp butter
- fresh thyme sprigs, to garnish

For the risotto
- 25g/1oz/2 tbsp butter
- 15ml/1 tbsp olive oil
- 2 shallots, chopped
- 2 garlic cloves, finely chopped
- 250g/9oz/1⅓ cups risotto rice
- 15ml/1 tbsp fresh thyme leaves
- 900ml/1½ pints/3¾ cups boiling pork or chicken stock
- salt and ground black pepper

1 Put the chops in a shallow dish, sprinkle the garlic over. To make the marinade, mix the lemon juice and soft light brown sugar together, and drizzle this over the chops.

2 Turn the chops to coat both sides with the lemon mixture, then cover the dish and leave the chops to marinate in the fridge while making the risotto.

3 To make the risotto, heat the butter with the oil in a large, heavy-based saucepan until foaming. Cook the shallots and garlic gently until the shallots are softened, but not coloured. Add the rice and thyme and stir until the grains are well coated with butter and oil.

4 Add a ladleful of boiling stock and cook gently, stirring occasionally. When all the stock is absorbed, add another ladleful. Continue cooking the risotto in this way until all the stock is absorbed. The secret of a good risotto is to have a pan of simmering stock ready and never to add too much at a time. The whole process should take 25–30 minutes. Season to taste.

5 Cook the chops when the risotto is half cooked. Melt the butter in a large, heavy-based frying pan. Remove the chops from the marinade, allowing the lemon juice to drip off, and fry them for 3–4 minutes on each side.

6 Divide the risotto among four plates and arrange the chops on top. Serve at once, garnished with fresh thyme.

MINI PORK AND BACON PIES

THESE LITTLE PIES CAN BE MADE UP TO A DAY AHEAD OF BEING SERVED AND THEY ARE A GOOD CHOICE FOR A SUMMER PICNIC OR SPECIAL PACKED LUNCH.

MAKES TWELVE

INGREDIENTS
- 10ml/2 tsp sunflower oil
- 1 onion, chopped
- 225g/8oz pork, coarsely chopped
- 115g/4oz cooked bacon, finely diced
- 45ml/3 tbsp chopped mixed fresh herbs, such as sage, parsley and oregano
- 6 eggs, hard-boiled and halved
- 1 egg yolk, beaten
- 20g/¾oz packet powdered aspic
- 300ml/½ pint/1¼ cups boiling water
- salt and ground black pepper

For the hot water crust pastry
- 450g/1lb/4 cups plain flour
- 115g/4oz/½ cup white vegetable fat or lard
- 275ml/9fl oz/generous 1 cup water

1 Preheat the oven to 200°C/400°F/Gas 6. To make the hot water crust pastry, sift the flour into a bowl and add a good pinch each of salt and pepper. Gently heat the fat or lard and water in a large pan until the fat has melted. Increase the heat and bring to the boil.

2 Remove the pan from the heat and pour the liquid into the flour, stirring. Press the mixture into a smooth ball of dough using the back of a spoon – take care as the dough is very hot. When smooth, cover the bowl and set it aside.

3 Heat the oil in a frying pan, add the onion and cook until soft. Stir in the pork and bacon and cook until browning. Remove from the heat and stir in the herbs and seasoning.

4 Roll out two-thirds of the pastry on a lightly floured work surface. Use a 12cm/4½in round cutter to stamp out rounds to line 12 muffin tins. Place a little meat mixture in each pie, then add half an egg to each and top with the remaining meat.

5 Roll out the remaining pastry and use a 7.5cm/3in round cutter to stamp out lids for the pies. Dampen the rims of the pastry bases and press the lids in place. Pinch the edges to seal. Brush with egg yolk and make a small hole in the top of each pie to allow the steam to escape. Bake for 30–35 minutes. Leave to cool for 15 minutes, then transfer to a wire rack to cool completely.

6 Meanwhile, stir the aspic powder into the boiling water until dissolved. Shape a piece of foil into a small funnel and use this to guide a little aspic in through the hole in the top of each pie. Leave them to cool and set, then chill for up to 24 hours before serving.

STIR-FRIED PORK WITH MUSHROOMS

PORK TENDERLOIN IS THE PERFECT CUT FOR STIR-FRYING – IT IS LEAN AND COOKS IN MINUTES WHEN CUT INTO FINE STRIPS.

SERVES FOUR

INGREDIENTS

- 30ml/2 tbsp sesame oil
- 450g/1lb pork tenderloin, cut into fine strips
- 1 onion, halved and sliced
- 1 green chilli, seeded and chopped
- 2 garlic cloves, sliced
- 150g/5oz oyster mushrooms, sliced
- 200g/7oz runner beans or green beans, sliced
- 2 oranges, peeled and cut into segments
- 15ml/1 tbsp clear honey
- 30ml/2 tbsp sherry

To serve

- 350g/12oz egg noodles, cooked
- 30ml/2 tbsp sesame oil

1 Heat the oil in a wok or large frying pan until very hot (almost smoking). Stir-fry the pork in three batches for 2 minutes each, or until crisp. Remove each batch in turn, then add the onion, chilli, garlic, mushrooms and runner beans or green beans. Stir-fry the vegetables for 3–5 minutes.

2 Return the pork to the wok. Add the orange segments, honey and sherry, and cook for a further 2 minutes, stirring frequently.

COOK'S TIP

When stir-frying, cut the ingredients into similar size strips so that they cook evenly and quickly, and prepare all the ingredients before you begin cooking.

3 Prepare the egg noodles in a separate pan or wok. Heat the oil and stir-fry the cooked noodles for 2–3 minutes, or until hot, then divide them among individual warm serving bowls and spoon the pork stir-fry on top. Serve at once.

SWEET-AND-SOUR RIBS OF PORK WITH EGG-FRIED RICE

THIS IS AN ANGLO-AMERICAN TAKE ON CHINESE FOOD – HARDLY AUTHENTIC SICHUAN BUT TERRIFICALLY TASTY NONETHELESS.

SERVES FOUR

INGREDIENTS

- 2 shallots, chopped
- 1 garlic clove, chopped
- 30ml/2 tbsp tomato purée
- 45ml/3 tbsp orange marmalade
- 30ml/2 tbsp light soy sauce
- grated rind and juice of 1 orange
- grated rind and juice of 1 lemon
- 1.5kg/3¼lb meaty pork ribs
- salt and ground black pepper

For the egg-fried rice

- 30ml/2 tbsp sunflower oil
- 6 spring onions, sliced
- 1 red pepper, seeded and chopped
- 175g/6oz/1½ cups peas
- 2 eggs, lightly beaten
- 350g/12oz/1⅔ cups long grain rice, cooked

1 Preheat the oven to 200°C/400°F/Gas 6. Mix the shallots, garlic, tomato purée, marmalade, soy sauce, orange and lemon rind and juice in a pan. Bring to the boil, stirring all the time, then simmer until reduced to a syrupy glaze. Season with salt and pepper.

2 Arrange the pork ribs in a roasting tin. Drizzle the glaze over the ribs and bake for 30–40 minutes, turning occasionally and basting with the glaze.

3 Meanwhile prepare the egg-fried rice. Heat the oil in a large frying pan and cook the spring onions, pepper and peas until just tender. Add the lightly beaten eggs and cook until they are just beginning to set, then beat vigorously. Add the cooked rice and cook, stirring often, until piping hot.

4 Serve the rice on individual warmed plates, topped with the well-browned and glazed pork ribs.

NOISETTES OF PORK WITH CREAMY CALVADOS AND APPLE SAUCE

THIS DISH GIVES THE IMPRESSION OF BEING FAR MORE DIFFICULT TO PREPARE THAN IT REALLY IS, SO IT IS IDEAL AS PART OF A FORMAL MENU TO IMPRESS GUESTS. BUTTERED GNOCCHI OR GRIDDLED POLENTA AND RED CABBAGE ARE SUITABLE ACCOMPANIMENTS.

SERVES FOUR

INGREDIENTS

- 30ml/2 tbsp plain flour
- 4 noisettes of pork, about 175g/6oz each, firmly tied
- 25g/1oz/2 tbsp butter
- 4 baby leeks, finely sliced
- 5ml/1 tsp mustard seeds, coarsely crushed
- 30ml/2 tbsp Calvados
- 150ml/¼ pint/⅔ cup dry white wine
- 2 Golden Delicious apples, peeled, cored and sliced
- 150ml/¼ pint/⅔ cup double cream
- 30ml/2 tbsp chopped fresh parsley
- salt and ground black pepper

1 Place the flour in a bowl and add plenty of seasoning. Turn the noisettes in the flour mixture to coat them lightly.

2 Melt the butter in a heavy-based frying pan and cook the noisettes until golden on both sides. Remove from the pan and set aside.

3 Add the leeks to the fat remaining in the pan and cook for 5 minutes. Stir in the mustard seeds and pour in the Calvados, then carefully ignite it to burn off the alcohol. When the flames have died down pour in the wine and replace the pork. Cook gently for 10 minutes, turning the pork frequently.

4 Add the sliced apples and double cream and simmer for 5 minutes, or until the apples are tender and the sauce is thick, rich and creamy. Taste for seasoning, then stir in the chopped parsley and serve at once.

Carbonara Abruzzi

In Italy, a dish served alla carbonara comes with a sauce made from eggs, olive oil, cream and strips of bacon. The name is taken from a nineteenth-century secret society, the purpose of which was to achieve a united Italy, with members disguised as charcoal burners (carbonari) working in the forest of Abruzzi.

SERVES FOUR

INGREDIENTS

- 500g/1¼lb spaghetti
- 30ml/2 tbsp olive oil
- 450g/1lb unsmoked back bacon rashers, cut into strips
- 1–2 garlic cloves, finely chopped
- 2 eggs, beaten
- 300ml/½ pint/1¼ cups single cream
- 25g/1oz Parmesan cheese, coarsely grated, plus extra for serving
- 30ml/2 tbsp chopped fresh parsley
- salt and ground black pepper

COOK'S TIP

This dish cools very quickly, so warm the serving bowls in advance and serve the pasta immediately it is cooked. It also overcooks very easily so, if you have guests, make sure that they are seated and ready to eat before you add the egg mixture to the spaghetti.

1 Cook the spaghetti in a very large saucepan of boiling salted water for about 10 minutes, or according to the packet instructions, until *al dente*: tender but with a bit of bite.

2 Meanwhile, heat the oil in a large, heavy-based frying pan (it must be large enough to hold the cooked spaghetti). Cook the bacon and garlic for about 10 minutes, stirring frequently, or until the bacon is golden. Drain the spaghetti.

3 Beat the eggs, cream, Parmesan and pepper. Add the hot spaghetti to the bacon and mix well. Pour in the egg mixture and cook for about 1 minute, turning the spaghetti all the time using tongs or a spoon and fork. Do not overcook the mixture or the eggs and cream will curdle.

4 Serve at once, spooned into warmed, shallow bowls and scattered with a little Parmesan and chopped parsley.

Pork and Bacon Rillettes with Onion Salad

Rillettes is potted meat, the most famous of which is made in Tours, France from pork and ham. This version makes a great starter, delicious snack or light meal.

SERVES EIGHT

INGREDIENTS
- 1.8kg/4lb belly of pork, boned and cut into cubes (reserve the bones)
- 450g/1lb rindless streaky bacon, finely chopped
- 5ml/1 tsp salt
- 1.5ml/¼ tsp freshly ground black pepper
- 4 garlic cloves, finely chopped
- 2 fresh parsley sprigs
- 1 bay leaf
- 2 fresh thyme sprigs
- 1 fresh sage sprig
- 300ml/½ pint/1¼ cups water
- crusty French bread, to serve

For the onion salad
- 1 small red onion, halved and finely sliced
- 2 spring onions, cut into matchstick strips
- 2 celery sticks, cut into matchstick strips
- 15ml/1 tbsp freshly squeezed lemon juice
- 15ml/1 tbsp light olive oil
- ground black pepper

1 In a large bowl, mix the pork, bacon and salt. Cover and leave at room temperature for 30 minutes. Preheat the oven to 150°C/300°F/Gas 2. Stir the pepper and garlic into the meat. Tie the herbs together to make a bouquet garni and mix this into the meat.

2 Spread the meat mixture in a large roasting tin and pour in the water. Place the bones from the pork on top and cover tightly with foil. Cook for 3½ hours.

3 Discard the bones and herbs, and ladle the meat mixture into a metal sieve set over a large bowl. Allow the liquid to drain through into the bowl, then turn the meat into a shallow dish. Repeat until all the meat is drained. Reserve the liquid. Use two forks to pull the meat apart into fine shreds.

4 Line a 1.5 litre/2½ pint/6¼ cup terrine or deep, straight-sided dish with clear film and spoon the shredded meat into it. Strain the reserved liquid through a sieve lined with muslin and pour it over the meat. Leave to cool. Cover and chill in the fridge for at least 24 hours, or until the rillettes has set.

COOK'S TIP

Ask the butcher to bone and chop the pork and to let you have the bones because they contribute an excellent flavour to the rillettes.

5 To make the onion salad, place the sliced onion, spring onions and celery in a bowl. Add the freshly squeezed lemon juice and light olive oil and toss gently. Season with a little freshly ground black pepper, but do not add any salt as the rillettes is well salted.

6 Serve the rillettes, cut into thick slices, on individual plates with a little onion salad and thick slices of crusty French bread and unsalted butter.

MUFFINS WITH BACON, EGGS AND QUICK HOLLANDAISE SAUCE

THIS MAKES A TERRIFIC CELEBRATION BREAKFAST, IDEAL FOR BIRTHDAYS, ANNIVERSARIES OR OTHER DAYS WHEN YOU WANT TO SET OUT WITH A SMILE ON YOUR FACE. YOU WILL NEED A BLENDER OR FOOD PROCESSOR TO MAKE THE SPEEDY VERSION OF HOLLANDAISE SAUCE.

SERVES FOUR

INGREDIENTS
- 350g/12oz rindless back bacon rashers
- dash of white wine vinegar
- 4 eggs
- 4 English muffins
- butter, for spreading
- salt and ground black pepper

For the hollandaise sauce
- 2 egg yolks
- 5ml/1 tsp white wine vinegar
- 75g/3oz/6 tbsp butter

1 Preheat the grill and cook the bacon for 5–8 minutes, turning once, or until crisp and brown on both sides.

2 Fill a large frying pan with water and bring to the boil. Add the vinegar and regulate the heat so that the water simmers. Crack the eggs into the water and poach them for 3–4 minutes, or slightly longer for firm eggs.

3 Split and toast the muffins while the eggs are cooking. Spread with butter and place on warmed plates.

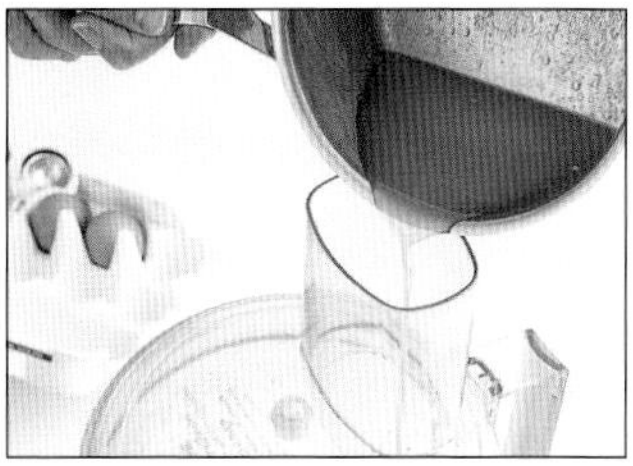

4 To make the hollandaise sauce, process the egg yolks and white wine vinegar in a blender or food processor. Melt the butter. With the motor still running, very gradually add the hot melted butter through the feeder tube. The hot butter cooks the yolks to make a thick, glossy sauce. Switch off the machine as soon as all the butter has been added and the sauce has thickened. Season to taste.

5 Arrange the bacon on the muffins and add a poached egg to each. Top with a spoonful of sauce and grind over some black pepper. Serve immediately.

COOK'S TIPS

Eggs that are a week or more old will not keep their shape when poached so, for the best results, use very fresh free-range organic eggs. To make sure that you don't break the yolk, crack the eggs into a cup before carefully adding them to the gently simmering water.

Sausages, Cured Meats and Offal

Richly flavoured, and extremely good to eat, sausages and offal are used to create some of the tastiest dishes in the world. Cassoulet de Languedoc and Devilled Kidneys are classic dishes, but this chapter also includes modern meal ideas, such as Crunchy Salad with Black Pudding. A little goes a long way, too, when flavourful cured meats are used for cooking. They can be used as the main ingredient in a dish, or combined with other meats or poultry as a flavour enhancer. The recipes in this chapter are light and modern, easy to shop for and quick to prepare and cook. There are wonderfully warm salads, tasty starters and appetizers, speedy snacks and simple, yet stunning dinner-party dishes.

Mediterranean Sausage and Pesto Soup

This hearty soup makes a satisfying one-pot meal that brings the summery flavour of basil to midwinter meals. Thick slices of warm crusty bread make the perfect accompaniment.

SERVES FOUR

INGREDIENTS

- 15ml/1 tbsp olive oil, plus extra for frying
- 1 red onion, chopped
- 450g/1lb smoked pork sausages
- 225g/8oz/1 cup red lentils
- 400g/14oz can chopped tomatoes
- 1 litre/1¾ pints/4 cups water
- oil, for deep-frying
- salt and ground black pepper
- 60ml/4 tbsp pesto and fresh basil sprigs, to garnish

1 Heat the oil in a large pan and cook the onion until softened. Coarsely chop all the sausages except 1 and add them to the pan. Cook for about 5 minutes, stirring, or until the sausages are cooked.

2 Stir in the lentils, tomatoes and water, and bring to the boil. Reduce the heat, cover and simmer for about 20 minutes. Cool the soup slightly before pureéing it in a blender. Return the soup to the rinsed-out pan.

3 Cook the remaining sausage in a little oil in a small frying pan for 10 minutes, turning it often, or until lightly browned and firm. Transfer to a chopping board or plate and leave to cool slightly, then slice thinly.

4 Heat the oil for deep-frying to 190°C/375°F or until a cube of day-old bread browns in about 60 seconds. Deep-fry the sausage slices and basil briefly until the sausages are brown and the basil leaves are crisp.

5 Lift them out using a draining spoon and drain on kitchen paper.

6 Reheat the soup, add seasoning to taste, then ladle into warmed individual soup bowls. Sprinkle with the deep-fried sausage slices and basil and swirl a little pesto through each portion. Serve with warm crusty bread.

ITALIAN SAUSAGES WITH PANCETTA AND BEANS

VARIATIONS ON THE THEME OF SAUSAGE AND BEAN STEW ARE FOUND IN MOST COUNTRIES AS AN INEXPENSIVE, EASY AND HEARTY PEASANT DISH. BAKED POTATOES OR CREAMY MASHED POTATOES ARE AN EXCELLENT ACCOMPANIMENT FOR THE STEW.

SERVES FOUR

INGREDIENTS

- 15ml/1 tbsp sunflower oil
- 12 Italian spicy fresh pork sausages
- 50g/2oz pancetta, chopped
- 2 onions, quartered
- 2 garlic cloves, crushed
- 1 red pepper, halved, seeded and sliced
- 2 × 400g/14oz cans chopped tomatoes
- 400g/14oz can cannellini beans, drained and rinsed
- salt and ground black pepper

VARIATION

Use beef or lamb sausages in place of the pork sausages, substitute chopped leeks for the onions and add a finely chopped and seeded red chilli along with the pepper. Serve with polenta.

1 Pour the sunflower oil into a flameproof casserole and add the sausages and pancetta. Cook over a medium heat for about 10 minutes, turning the sausages and pancetta occasionally, or until the pancetta is crispy and the sausages are golden brown. Be careful to moderate the heat – if it is too fierce the sausages will burst. Use a draining spoon to remove the sausages and pancetta from the casserole and set aside.

2 Discard any excess fat and add the onions and garlic. Cook for about 5 minutes over a high heat, stirring frequently. Add the pepper and cook for 2–3 minutes.

3 Replace the sausages and pancetta and stir in the tomatoes and beans. Heat until simmering, then cover and simmer for about 20 minutes, stirring occasionally. Season to taste.

Cassoulet de Languedoc

There are many regional variations of this classic French casserole of sausage, beans and assorted meats, each widely different from the next according to its town of origin. In Languedoc alone, the towns of Toulouse, Castelnaudary and Carcassonne all claim to be the historical home of the authentic cassoulet.

SERVES EIGHT

INGREDIENTS

- 225g/8oz/1¼ cups dried haricot beans, soaked for 24 hours
- 2 large onions, 1 cut into chunks and 1 chopped
- 1 large carrot, quartered
- 2 cloves
- small handful of parsley stalks
- 225g/8oz lean gammon, in one piece
- 4 duck leg quarters, split into thighs and drumsticks
- 225g/8oz lean lamb, trimmed and cubed
- 2 garlic cloves, finely chopped
- 75ml/5 tbsp dry white wine
- 175g/6oz cooked Toulouse sausage, or garlic sausage, skinned and coarsely chopped
- 400g/14oz can chopped tomatoes
- salt and ground black pepper

For the topping

- 75g/3oz/1½ cups fresh white breadcrumbs
- 30ml/2 tbsp chopped fresh parsley
- 2 garlic cloves, finely chopped

1 Drain and thoroughly rinse the beans, then place them in a large saucepan and add the onion cut into chunks, carrot, cloves and parsley stalks. Pour in enough cold water to cover the beans completely and bring to the boil.

2 Boil the beans for 10 minutes, then reduce the heat, cover and simmer for 1½ hours, or until the beans are tender. Skim off any scum that rises to the surface and top up with boiling water as necessary. Drain the cooked beans, reserving the stock; discard the onion, carrot, cloves and parsley stalks.

3 Put the gammon into a pan and cover with cold water. Bring to the boil, reduce the heat and simmer for 10 minutes. Drain and discard the water, leave until cool enough to handle, then cut the meat into chunks. Preheat the oven to 150°C/300°C/Gas 2.

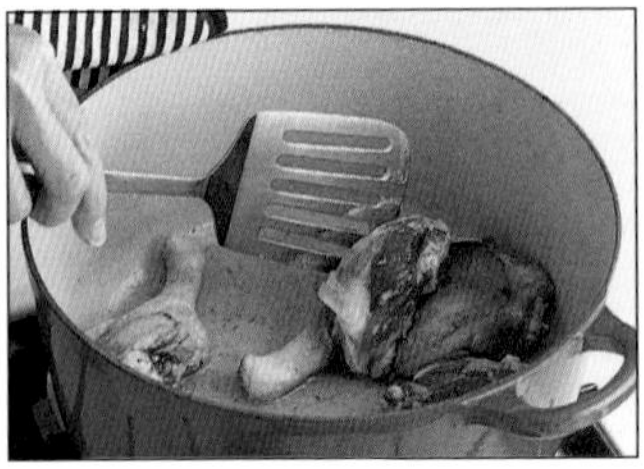

4 Heat a large, flameproof casserole and cook the duck portions in batches until golden brown on all sides. Use a draining spoon to remove the duck portions from the casserole, set aside. Add and brown the trimmed and cubed lamb in batches, removing each batch and setting aside.

5 Pour off the excess fat from the casserole, leaving about 30ml/2 tbsp. Cook the onion and garlic in this fat until softened but not coloured. Stir in the wine and remove from the heat.

6 Spoon a layer of beans into the casserole. Add the duck, then the lamb, gammon, sausage, tomatoes and more beans. Season each layer as you add the ingredients. Pour in enough of the reserved stock to cover the ingredients. Cover, and cook in the oven for 2½ hours. Check occasionally to ensure the beans are covered, add more stock if necessary.

7 Mix together the topping ingredients and sprinkle over the cassoulet. Cook, uncovered, for a further 30 minutes.

Pork and Leek Sausages with Mustard Mashed Potato and Onion Gravy

Long, slow cooking is the trick to remember for good onion gravy as this reduces and caramelizes the onions to create a wonderfully sweet flavour. Do not be alarmed at the number of onions – they reduce dramatically in volume during cooking.

SERVES FOUR

INGREDIENTS
- 12 pork and leek sausages
- salt and ground black pepper

For the onion gravy
- 30ml/2 tbsp olive oil
- 25g/1oz/2 tbsp butter
- 8 onions, sliced
- 5ml/1 tsp caster sugar
- 15ml/1 tbsp plain flour
- 300ml/½ pint/1¼ cups beef stock

For the mash
- 1.5kg/3¼lb potatoes
- 50g/2oz/¼ cup butter
- 150ml/¼ pint/⅔ cup double cream
- 15ml/1 tbsp wholegrain mustard

1 Heat the oil and butter in a large saucepan until foaming. Add the onions and mix well to coat them in the fat. Cover and cook gently for about 30 minutes, stirring frequently. Add the sugar and cook for a further 5 minutes, or until the onions are softened, reduced and caramelized.

2 Remove the pan from the heat and stir in the flour, then gradually stir in the stock. Return the pan to the heat. Bring to the boil, stirring, then simmer for 3 minutes, or until thickened. Season.

VARIATION

Pesto and garlic mash is also good with sausages. Instead of the mustard, add 15ml/1 tbsp pesto, 2 crushed garlic cloves and a little olive oil.

3 Meanwhile, cook the potatoes and the pork and leek sausages. First, cook the potatoes in a saucepan of boiling salted water for 20 minutes, or until tender.

4 Drain the potatoes well and mash them with the butter, double cream and wholegrain mustard. Season with salt and pepper to taste.

5 While the potatoes are cooking, preheat the grill to medium. Arrange the sausages in a single layer in the grill pan and cook for 15–20 minutes, or until cooked, turning frequently so that they brown evenly.

6 Serve the sausages with the creamy mash and plenty of onion gravy.

VENISON SAUSAGES WITH RED WINE GRAVY AND POLENTA

STRONGLY FLAVOURED, MEATY SAUSAGES ARE DELICIOUS WITH ROBUST RED WINE AND ASSERTIVE SHIITAKE MUSHROOMS. SERVE WITH PLENTY OF POLENTA TO MOP UP THE DELICIOUS GRAVY.

SERVES FOUR

INGREDIENTS

- 15ml/1 tbsp sunflower oil (optional)
- 12 venison or wild boar sausages
- 2 leeks, sliced
- 2 plump cloves garlic, sliced
- 225g/8oz/3¼ cups shiitake mushrooms, quartered
- 15ml/1 tbsp plain flour
- 600ml/1 pint/2½ cups red wine
- 30ml/2 tbsp chopped mixed fresh herbs, such as flat leaf parsley and marjoram
- salt and ground black pepper

For the polenta

- 750ml/1¼ pints/3 cups water
- 175g/6oz/1½ cups instant polenta
- 50g/2oz/¼ cup butter

1 Pour the oil, if using, into a large frying pan, add the sausages and cook over a medium heat for 15–20 minutes, turning frequently.

2 Add the leeks, garlic and mushrooms and mix well. Cook the vegetables for 10–15 minutes, or until the leeks are soft and beginning to brown.

3 Sprinkle in the flour and gradually pour in the wine, stirring and pushing the sausages around to mix the flour and liquid smoothly with the leeks.

4 Bring slowly to the boil, reduce the heat and simmer for 10–15 minutes, stirring occasionally, or until the wine sauce is smooth and glossy.

5 Meanwhile, cook the instant polenta. Pour the water into a saucepan and add a little salt, then bring it to the boil. Sprinkle in the polenta, stirring all the time, and cook for 4–5 minutes, stirring constantly, or until thick and smooth. Remove the pan from the heat and beat in the butter with seasoning to taste.

6 Season the red wine sauce with salt and pepper to taste and scatter the herbs over the sausages. To serve, put a large ladleful of polenta into each serving dish or deep plate (soup plates or pasta dishes are ideal) and top with the sausages, leeks and sauce.

DUCK SAUSAGES WITH SPICY PLUM SAUCE

Rich duck sausages are best baked in their own juices rather than flashed under the grill. Creamy mashed sweet potatoes and spicy plum sauce complement and contrast with the richness of the sausages.

SERVES FOUR

INGREDIENTS
- 8–12 duck sausages

For the sweet potato mash
- 1.5kg/3¼lb sweet potatoes, cut into chunks
- 25g/1oz/2 tbsp butter
- 60ml/4 tbsp milk
- salt and ground black pepper

For the plum sauce
- 30ml/2 tbsp olive oil
- 1 small onion, chopped
- 1 small red chilli, seeded and finely chopped
- 450g/1lb plums, stoned and chopped
- 30ml/2 tbsp red wine vinegar
- 45ml/3 tbsp clear honey

1 Preheat the oven to 190°C/375°F/Gas 5. Arrange the duck sausages in a single layer in a large, shallow ovenproof dish and bake, uncovered, for 25–30 minutes, turning the sausages two or three times during cooking, to ensure that they brown and cook evenly.

2 Meanwhile, put the sweet potatoes in a saucepan and pour in enough water to cover them. Bring to the boil, reduce the heat and simmer for 20 minutes, or until tender. Drain and mash the potatoes, then place the pan over a low heat. Stir frequently for about 5 minutes to dry out the mashed potato. Beat in the butter and milk, season.

3 Heat the oil in a small pan and fry the onion and chilli gently for 5 minutes. Stir in the plums, vinegar and honey, then simmer gently for 10 minutes.

4 Serve the freshly cooked sausages with the sweet potato mash and piquant plum sauce.

Chunky Sausage Rolls

Old-fashioned sausage rolls, made with good-quality sausagemeat, have a fabulous flavour which their bought alternatives cannot match. These rolls are just right for a packed lunch.

MAKES TWELVE

INGREDIENTS
- 225g/8oz/2 cups plain flour
- 2.5ml/½ tsp English mustard powder
- 115g/4oz/½ cup butter
- 15g/½oz Parmesan cheese, finely grated
- 40ml/8 tsp iced water
- 450g/1lb good-quality sausagemeat
- 5ml/1 tsp chilli sauce, garlic sauce or chutney
- beaten egg, to glaze

1 Preheat the oven to 190°C/375°F/Gas 5. Sift the flour and mustard powder into a bowl. Rub in the butter until the mixture resembles fine breadcrumbs and stir in the cheese. Mix in enough iced water to bind the crumbs into a soft, but not sticky, dough. Wrap the dough in clear film and chill.

2 Mix the sausagemeat with the chilli sauce, garlic sauce or chutney, and divide it into 12 equal portions. Shape each portion into a sausage measuring about 7.5cm/3in long.

VARIATION

To make cocktail sausage rolls, cut each large roll into 4 small slices, making 48 in all. Bake the mini sausage rolls for about 10 minutes, or until cooked through.

3 Roll out the pastry to a 20 × 45cm/8 × 18in rectangle and cut into 12 rectangles. Place a sausage in the middle of each, brush the edges of the pastry with water and roll it over the sausage to enclose it completely. Place on a baking sheet with the joins underneath. Chill for 10 minutes. Brush the sausage rolls with beaten egg and bake for 20 minutes, or until golden and cooked. Serve warm or cold.

Toad-in-the-Hole

This is one of those dishes that is classic comfort food – remembered as a childhood favourite and perfect for lifting the spirits on cold days. Use only the best sausages for this grown-up version which has chopped chives added to the batter.

SERVES FOUR TO SIX

INGREDIENTS
- 175g/6oz/1½ cups plain flour
- 30ml/2 tbsp snipped fresh chives (optional)
- 2 eggs
- 300ml/½ pint/1¼ cups milk
- 50g/2oz/¼ cup white vegetable fat or lard
- 450g/1lb Cumberland sausages or good-quality pork sausages
- salt and ground black pepper

VARIATION

For a young children's supper, omit the chives from the batter and cook cocktail sausages in patty tins until golden. Add the batter and cook for 10–15 minutes, or until puffed and golden.

1 Preheat the oven to 220°C/425°F/Gas 7. Sift the flour into a bowl with a pinch of salt and pepper. Make a well in the centre of the flour. Whisk the chives, if using, with the eggs and milk, then pour this into the well in the flour. Gradually whisk the flour into the liquid to make a smooth batter. Cover and leave to stand for at least 30 minutes.

2 Put the fat into a small roasting tin and place in the oven for 3–5 minutes. Add the sausages and cook for 15 minutes. Turn the sausages twice during cooking.

3 Pour the batter over the sausages and return to the oven. Cook for about 20 minutes, or until the batter is risen and golden. Serve at once.

Pan-Fried Calf's Liver with Crisp Onions

Sautéed or creamy mashed potatoes go well with fried calf's liver. Serve a salad of mixed leaves with plenty of delicate fresh herbs, such as fennel, dill and parsley, to complement the simple flavours of this main course.

SERVES FOUR

INGREDIENTS

- 50g/2oz/¼ cup butter
- 4 onions, finely sliced
- 5ml/1 tsp caster sugar
- 4 slices calf's liver, each weighing about 115g/4oz
- 30ml/2 tbsp plain flour
- 30ml/2 tbsp olive oil
- salt and ground black pepper
- parsley, to garnish

1 Melt the butter in a large, heavy-based pan with a lid. Add the onions and mix well to coat with butter. Cover the pan with a tight-fitting lid and cook gently for 10 minutes, stirring occasionally.

2 Stir in the sugar and cover the pan. Cook the onions for 10 minutes more, or until they are soft and golden. Increase the heat, remove the lid and stir the onions over a high heat until they are deep gold and crisp. Use a draining spoon to remove the onions from the pan, draining off the fat.

3 Meanwhile, rinse the calf's liver in cold water and pat it dry on kitchen paper. Season the flour, put it on a plate and turn the slices of liver in it until they are lightly coated in flour.

COOK'S TIP

Take care not to cook the liver for too long as this may cause it to toughen.

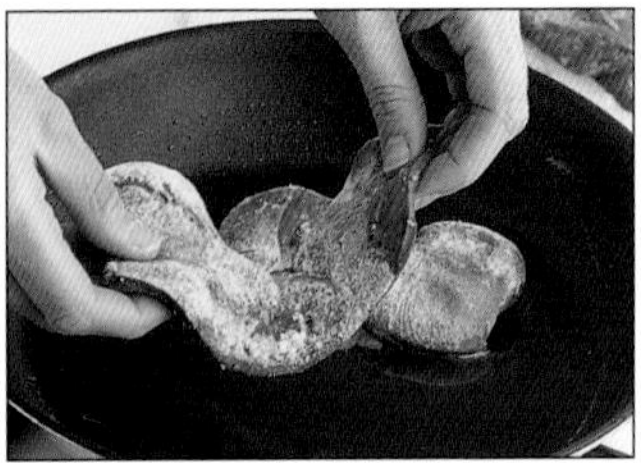

4 Heat the oil in a large frying pan, add the liver and cook for about 2 minutes on each side, or until lightly browned and just firm. Arrange the liver on warmed plates, with the crisp onions. Garnish with parsley and serve with sautéed or mashed potatoes.

LAMB'S LIVER AND BACON CASSEROLE

BOILED NEW POTATOES TOSSED IN LOTS OF BUTTER GO WELL WITH THIS SIMPLE CASSEROLE. THE TRICK WHEN COOKING LIVER IS TO SEAL IT QUICKLY, THEN SIMMER IT GENTLY AND BRIEFLY. PROLONGED AND/OR FIERCE COOKING MAKES LIVER HARD AND GRAINY.

SERVES FOUR

INGREDIENTS
- 30ml/2 tbsp sunflower oil
- 225g/8oz rindless unsmoked back bacon rashers, cut into pieces
- 2 onions, halved and sliced
- 175g/6oz/2⅓ cups chestnut mushrooms, halved
- 450g/1lb lamb's liver, trimmed and sliced
- 25g/1oz/2 tbsp butter
- 15ml/1 tbsp soy sauce
- 30ml/2 tbsp plain flour
- 150ml/¼ pint/⅔ cup chicken stock
- salt and ground black pepper

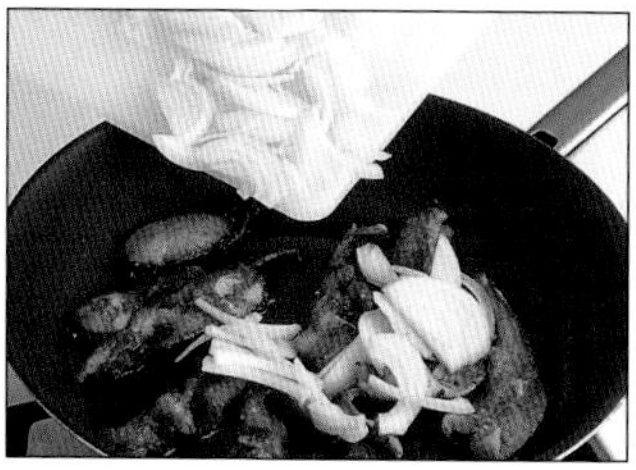

1 Heat the oil in a frying pan and fry the bacon until crisp. Add the onions to the pan and cook for about 10 minutes, stirring frequently, or until softened. Add the mushrooms to the pan and fry for a further 1 minute.

2 Use a draining spoon to remove the bacon and vegetables from the pan and set aside. Add the liver to the pan and cook over a high heat for 3–4 minutes, turning once to seal the slices on both sides. Remove the liver from the pan and keep warm.

3 Melt the butter in the pan, add the soy sauce and flour and blend together. Stir in the stock and bring to the boil, stirring until thickened. Return the liver and vegetables to the pan and heat through for 1 minute. Season with salt and pepper to taste, and serve at once with new potatoes and lightly cooked green beans.

CRUNCHY SALAD WITH BLACK PUDDING

Black pudding is a type of sausage enriched with blood and flavoured with spices. In Britain it is thought of as a Lancashire speciality, but similar sausages are also found all over Europe. Fried until crisp, slices of black pudding are extremely good in salad, particularly with crunchy bread croûtons and sweet cherry tomatoes. Serve this salad in bowls or shallow soup plates.

SERVES FOUR

INGREDIENTS
- 250g/9oz black pudding, sliced
- 1 focaccia loaf, plain or flavoured with sun-dried tomatoes, garlic and herbs, cut into chunks
- 45ml/3 tbsp olive oil
- 1 cos lettuce, torn into bite-size pieces
- 250g/9oz cherry tomatoes, halved

For the dressing
- juice of 1 lemon
- 90ml/6 tbsp olive oil
- 10ml/2 tsp French mustard
- 15ml/1 tbsp clear honey
- 30ml/2 tbsp chopped fresh herbs, such as coriander, chives and parsley
- salt and ground black pepper

1 Dry-fry the black pudding in a large, non-stick frying pan for 5–10 minutes, or until browned and crisp, turning occasionally. Remove the black pudding from the pan using a draining spoon and drain on kitchen paper. Set the black pudding aside and keep warm.

2 While the black pudding is cooking, cut the focaccia into chunks. Add the oil to the juices in the frying pan and cook the focaccia cubes in two batches, turning often, until golden on all sides. Drain the focaccia on kitchen paper.

3 Mix together the focaccia, black pudding, lettuce and cherry tomatoes in a large bowl. Mix together the dressing ingredients and season with salt and pepper. Pour the dressing over the salad. Mix well and serve at once.

VARIATION

If you are unsure of black pudding, then try this recipe with spicy chorizo or Kabanos sausages instead. Cut them into thick diagonal slices before cooking. Use another crusty bread, such as ciabatta for the croûtons, if you prefer.

DEVILLED KIDNEYS ON BRIOCHE CROÛTES

THE EXPRESSION "DEVILLED" DATES FROM THE 18TH CENTURY. IT WAS USED TO DESCRIBE DISHES OR FOODS THAT WERE SEASONED WITH HOT SPICES GIVING A FIERY FLAVOUR THAT WAS ASSOCIATED WITH THE DEVIL AND THE HEAT OF HELL.

SERVES FOUR

INGREDIENTS

- 8 mini brioche slices
- 25g/1oz/2 tbsp butter
- 1 shallot, finely chopped
- 2 garlic cloves, finely chopped
- 115g/4oz/1½ cups mushrooms, halved
- 1.5ml/¼ tsp cayenne pepper
- 15ml/1 tbsp Worcestershire sauce
- 8 lamb's kidneys, halved and trimmed
- 150ml/¼ pint/⅔ cup double cream
- 30ml/2 tbsp chopped fresh parsley

1 Preheat the grill and toast the brioche slices until golden brown on both sides, and keep warm.

2 Melt the butter in the pan until it is foaming. Add the shallot, garlic and mushrooms, then cook for 5 minutes, or until the shallot is softened. Stir in the cayenne pepper and Worcestershire sauce and simmer for about 1 minute.

3 Add the kidneys to the pan and cook for 3–5 minutes on each side. Finally, stir in the cream and simmer for about 2 minutes, or until the sauce is heated through and slightly thickened.

4 Remove the brioche croûtes from the wire rack and place on warmed plates. Top with the kidneys. Sprinkle with chopped parsley and serve immediately.

COOK'S TIPS

If you can't find mini brioches, you can use a large brioche instead. Slice it thickly and stamp out croûtes using a 5cm/2in round cutter. If you prefer, the brioche croûtes can be fried rather than toasted. Melt 25g/1oz/2 tbsp butter in a frying pan and fry the croûtes until crisp and golden on both sides. Remove from the pan and drain on kitchen paper.

Chicken Liver Pâté

This is one of the simplest pâtés to make and it tastes excellent with crisp melba toast.

SERVES FOUR

INGREDIENTS
- 115g/4oz/½ cup butter
- 4 shallots, finely chopped
- 2 garlic cloves, finely chopped
- 225g/8oz chicken livers, rinsed and trimmed
- 30ml/2 tbsp dry sherry
- 300ml/½ pint/1¼ cups double cream
- salt and ground black pepper

To garnish
- fresh herbs, such as thyme, bay leaves and parsley
- lemon or orange slices

COOK'S TIP

Don't overcook the livers or they may harden and become grainy in texture. When cooked, they should be still very slightly pink in the centre.

1 Melt half the butter in a large frying pan. Add the shallots and garlic, and cook until softened but not coloured. Add the chicken livers and stir over a medium heat for 8–10 minutes, or until they are just firm and cooked through.

2 Purée the chicken liver mixture in a blender with the remaining butter and sherry, transfer to a bowl.

3 Lightly whip the cream until it stands in soft peaks, then fold it into the chicken liver mixture with seasoning to taste. Spoon the pâté into a serving dish and chill until set.

4 Serve spoonfuls of the pâté on large plates, garnished with fresh herbs and slices of lemon or orange. Serve with melba toast or warm crusty bread.

Haggis Tartlets with Bashed Neeps and Tatties

Haggis is the traditional Scottish sausage of highly spiced lamb's offal bound with oatmeal, packed into a lamb's stomach ready for gentle poaching. The casing is not eaten, but split open so that the filling can be scooped out. These days synthetic casings are used as well as the traditional paunch, but since this is not eaten, it does not make any difference other than to the appearance.

SERVES EIGHT

INGREDIENTS
- 450g/1lb haggis
- 3 filo pastry sheets, each about 30 × 20cm/12 × 8in, thawed if frozen
- 25g/1oz/2 tbsp butter, melted
- 90ml/6 tbsp whisky
- salt and ground black pepper

For the bashed neeps
- 1 large swede, cut into chunks
- 45ml/3 tbsp double cream
- 50g/2oz/¼ cup butter

For the tatties
- 900g/2lb potatoes, cut into chunks
- 60ml/4 tbsp double cream
- 50g/2oz/¼ cup butter
- large pinch of grated nutmeg

1 Cook or reheat the haggis according to the packet instructions. Preheat the oven to 190°C/375°F/Gas 5.

2 Cut each sheet of filo pastry into six 15cm/6in squares. Brush eight sections of a muffin tin with melted butter and line each with a filo square. Brush with butter and place a second piece of pastry on top. Bake for 5–7 minutes, or until crisp and pale golden.

3 To make the neeps and tatties, cook the swede and potato in separate pans of boiling salted water for 20 minutes, or until tender. Drain and mash separately with cream and butter. Season to taste and add a little nutmeg to the potatoes.

4 Split the cooked haggis open and use a teaspoon to scoop out the mixture, dividing it among the filo tartlet cases. Moisten each tartlet with a generous amount of whisky and serve at once with the bashed neeps and tatties.

PARMA HAM WITH POTATO RÉMOULADE

RÉMOULADE IS A CLASSIC PIQUANT DRESSING BASED ON MAYONNAISE. THE TRADITIONAL FRENCH VERSION IS FLAVOURED WITH MUSTARD, GHERKINS, CAPERS AND HERBS, BUT SIMPLER VARIATIONS ARE SEASONED ONLY WITH MUSTARD. LIME JUICE BRINGS A CONTEMPORARY TWIST TO THIS RECIPE FOR A CREAM-ENRICHED DRESSING.

SERVES FOUR

INGREDIENTS

- 2 potatoes, each weighing about 175g/6oz, quartered lengthways
- 150ml/¼ pint/⅔ cup mayonnaise
- 150ml/¼ pint/⅔ cup double cream
- 5–10ml/1–2 tsp Dijon mustard
- juice of ½ lime
- 30ml/2 tbsp olive oil
- 12 Parma ham slices
- 450g/1lb asparagus spears, halved
- salt and ground black pepper
- 25g/1oz wild rocket, to garnish
- extra virgin olive oil, to serve

1 Put the potatoes in a saucepan. Add water to cover and bring to the boil. Add salt, then simmer for about 15 minutes, or until the potatoes are tender, but do not let them get too soft. Drain thoroughly and leave to cool and then cut into long, thin strips.

2 Beat together the mayonnaise, cream, mustard, lime juice and seasoning in a large bowl. Add the potatoes and stir carefully to coat them with the dressing.

3 Heat the oil in a griddle or frying pan and cook the Parma ham in batches until crisp and golden. Use a draining spoon to remove the ham, draining each piece well. Cook the asparagus in the fat remaining in the pan for about 3 minutes, or until tender and golden.

4 Put a generous spoonful of potato rémoulade on each plate and top with several slices of Parma ham. Add the asparagus and garnish with rocket. Serve at once, offering olive oil to drizzle over.

CHICKEN BREASTS WITH SERRANO HAM

THIS MODERN SPANISH DISH IS LIGHT AND VERY EASY TO MAKE. IT LOOKS FABULOUS, TOO.

SERVES FOUR

INGREDIENTS

- 4 skinless, boneless chicken breasts
- 4 slices Serrano ham
- 75g/3oz/6 tbsp butter
- 30ml/2 tbsp chopped capers
- 30ml/2 tbsp fresh thyme leaves
- 1 large lemon, cut lengthways into 8 slices
- a few small fresh thyme sprigs
- salt and ground black pepper

COOK'S TIP

This dish is just as good with other thinly sliced cured ham, such as prosciutto or Parma ham, in place of the Serrano ham.

1 Preheat the oven to 200°C/400°F/Gas 6. Wrap each chicken breast loosely in clear film and beat with a rolling pin until slightly flattened. Arrange the chicken breasts in a large, shallow ovenproof dish, then top each with a slice of Serrano ham.

2 Beat the butter with the capers, thyme and seasoning until well mixed. Divide the butter into quarters and shape each into a neat portion, then place on each ham-topped chicken breast. Arrange 2 lemon slices on the butter and sprinkle with small thyme sprigs. Bake for 25 minutes, or until the chicken is cooked through.

3 To serve, transfer the chicken portions to a warmed serving platter or individual plates and spoon the piquant, buttery juices over the top. Serve at once, with boiled new potatoes and steamed broccoli or mangetouts. Discard the lemon slices before serving, if you prefer.

Prosciutto and Mozzarella Parcels on Frisée Salad

Prosciutto is Italian for ham, probably the most famous of which (to non-Italians) is Parma ham. The name is a variation on PRESCIUTTO *which means, literally, dried beforehand. The types of prosciutto vary according to the particular curing process used.*

SERVES SIX

INGREDIENTS
- a little hot chilli sauce
- 6 prosciutto crudo or Parma ham slices
- 200g/7oz mozzarella, cut into 6 slices
- 6 filo pastry sheets, each measuring 45 × 28cm/18 × 11in, thawed if frozen
- 50g/2oz/¼ cup butter, melted
- 150g/5oz frisée salad, to serve

COOK'S TIP
Parma ham is readily available, usually along with at least one other type of prosciutto, but visit a good Italian delicatessen and you will find a choice of regional hams.

1 Preheat the oven to 200°C/400°F/ Gas 6. Sprinkle a little of the chilli sauce over each slice of prosciutto crudo or Parma ham. Place a slice of mozzarella on each piece of ham, then fold the ham around the cheese to enclose the slices completely.

2 Brush a sheet of filo pastry with a little melted butter and fold it in half to give a double-thick piece measuring 23 × 14cm/9 × 5½in. Place a ham and mozzarella parcel on the middle of the pastry and brush the remaining pastry with a little butter, then fold it over to enclose the ham and mozzarella in a neat parcel. Place on a baking sheet with the edges of the pastry underneath and brush with a little butter. Rcpcat with the remaining parcels and pastry sheets.

3 Bake the filo parcels for 15 minutes, or until the pastry is crisp and evenly golden. Arrange the salad on six plates and add the parcels. Serve at once.

Smoked Chicken with Peach Mayonnaise in Filo Tartlets

These are attractive and, because smoked chicken is sold ready cooked, they require the minimum of culinary effort. The filling can be prepared a day in advance and chilled, but do not fill the pastry cases until you are ready to serve them or they will become soggy.

MAKES TWELVE

INGREDIENTS
- 25g/1oz/2 tbsp butter
- 3 sheets filo pastry, each measuring 45 × 28cm /18 × 11in, thawed if frozen
- 2 skinless, boneless smoked chicken breasts, finely sliced
- 150ml/¼ pint/⅔ cup mayonnaise
- grated rind of 1 lime
- 30ml/2 tbsp lime juice
- 2 ripe peaches, peeled, stoned and chopped
- salt and ground black pepper
- fresh tarragon sprigs, lime slices and salad leaves, to garnish

1 Preheat the oven to 200°C/400°F/ Gas 6. Melt the butter in a small pan. Brush 12 small individual tartlet tins with a little of the melted butter. Cut each sheet of filo pastry into 12 equal rounds large enough to line the tins, allowing enough to stand up above the tops of the tins.

2 Place a round of pastry in each tin and brush with a little butter, then add another round of pastry. Brush each with more butter and add a third round of pastry.

3 Bake the tartlets for 5 minutes, or until the pastry is golden brown. Leave in the tins for a few moments before transferring to a wire rack to cool.

4 Mix the chicken, mayonnaise, lime rind and juice, peaches and seasoning. Chill this chicken mixture for at least 30 minutes, or up to 12 hours. When ready to serve, spoon the chicken mixture into the filo tartlets and garnish with tarragon sprigs, lime slices and salad leaves.

PASTA SALAD WITH SALAMI

THIS SALAD IS SIMPLE TO MAKE AND IT CAN BE PREPARED IN ADVANCE FOR A PERFECT STARTER OR, SERVED IN MORE GENEROUS QUANTITIES, TO MAKE A SATISFYING MAIN COURSE.

SERVES FOUR

INGREDIENTS

- 225g/8oz pasta twists
- 275g/10oz jar charcoal-roasted peppers in oil
- 115g/4oz/1 cup stoned black olives
- 4 sun-dried tomatoes, quartered
- 115g/4oz Roquefort cheese, crumbled
- 10 slices peppered salami, cut into strips
- 115g/4oz packet mixed leaf salad
- 30ml/2 tbsp white wine vinegar
- 30ml/2 tbsp chopped fresh oregano
- 2 garlic cloves, crushed
- salt and ground black pepper

1 Cook the pasta in a large saucepan of boiling salted water for 12 minutes, or according to the instructions on the packet, until tender but not soft. Drain thoroughly and rinse with cold water, then drain again.

2 Drain the peppers and reserve 60ml/4 tbsp of the oil for the dressing. Cut the peppers into long, fine strips and mix them with the olives, sun-dried tomatoes and Roquefort in a large bowl. Stir in the pasta and peppered salami.

3 Divide the salad leaves among 4 individual bowls and spoon the pasta salad on top. Whisk the reserved oil with the wine vinegar, oregano, garlic and seasoning to taste. Spoon this dressing over the salad and serve at once.

VARIATION

Use chicken instead of the salami and cubes of Brie in place of the Roquefort.

WARM SALAD OF BAYONNE HAM AND NEW POTATOES

WITH A LIGHTLY SPICED NUTTY DRESSING, THIS WARM SALAD IS AS DELICIOUS AS IT IS FASHIONABLE, AND AN EXCELLENT CHOICE FOR INFORMAL ENTERTAINING.

SERVES FOUR

INGREDIENTS

- 225g/8oz new potatoes, halved if large
- 50g/2oz green beans
- 115g/4oz young spinach leaves
- 2 spring onions, sliced
- 4 eggs, hard-boiled and quartered
- 50g/2oz Bayonne ham, cut into strips
- juice of ½ lemon
- salt and ground black pepper

For the dressing

- 60ml/4 tbsp olive oil
- 5ml/1 tsp ground turmeric
- 5ml/1 tsp ground cumin
- 50g/2oz/⅓ cup shelled hazelnuts

1 Cook the potatoes in boiling salted water for 10–15 minutes, or until tender, then drain well. Cook the beans in boiling salted water for 2 minutes, drain.

2 Toss the potatoes and beans with the spinach and spring onions in a bowl.

3 Arrange the hard-boiled egg quarters on the salad and scatter the strips of ham over the top. Sprinkle with the lemon juice and season with plenty of salt and pepper.

4 Heat the dressing ingredients in a large frying pan and continue to cook, stirring frequently, until the nuts turn golden. Pour the hot, nutty dressing over the salad and serve at once.

VARIATION

Replace the potatoes with a 400g/14oz can mixed beans and pulses. Drain and rinse the beans and pulses, then drain again. Toss lightly with the green beans and spring onions.

CHORIZO WITH GARLIC POTATOES

A classic tapas recipe, this simple dish can be served in small quantities as a snack or, as here, in slightly larger proportions for a starter. The name tapas is derived from tapa, a lid, traditionally used by Spanish barmen to cover glasses of cold fino or manzanilla sherry to prevent flies from settling in the drink. The lid usually took the form of a saucer of small canapés or a small portion of a tasty dish to be enjoyed with the sherry.

SERVES FOUR

INGREDIENTS

- 450g/1lb potatoes
- 3 eggs, hard-boiled and quartered
- 175g/6oz chorizo sausage, sliced
- 150ml/¼ pint/⅔ cup mayonnaise
- 150ml/¼ pint/⅔ cup soured cream
- 2 garlic cloves, crushed
- salt and ground black pepper
- 30ml/2 tbsp chopped fresh coriander, to garnish

VARIATION

To give this dish a more piquant flavour, add about 15ml/1 tbsp finely chopped cornichons and 4 finely chopped anchovy fillets. If coriander isn't available, then use 15ml/1 tbsp fresh marjoram instead.

1 Cook the potatoes in a saucepan of boiling salted water for 20 minutes, or until tender. Drain and leave to cool.

2 Cut the potatoes into bite-size pieces. Place them in a large serving dish with the eggs and chorizo sausage, and season to taste with salt and pepper.

3 In a small bowl, stir the mayonnaise, soured cream and garlic together with seasoning to taste, then spoon this dressing over the potato mixture.

4 Toss the salad gently to coat the ingredients with dressing, then sprinkle with chopped coriander to garnish.

POTATO AND PEPPERONI TORTILLA

Cooked potatoes are delicious with spicy pepperoni in a thick Spanish-style omelette. Salad and crusty bread are excellent accompaniments.

SERVES FOUR

INGREDIENTS

- 30ml/2 tbsp olive oil
- 225g/8oz potatoes, cooked and cut into cubes
- 75g/3oz pepperoni, sliced
- 3 spring onions, sliced
- 115g/4oz Fontina cheese, cut into cubes
- 115g/4oz/1 cup frozen peas, thawed
- 6 eggs
- 30ml/2 tbsp chopped fresh parsley
- salt and ground black pepper

COOK'S TIP

If you do not have the confidence to invert the tortilla and replace it in the pan, simply finish cooking it under a preheated grill for 5–8 minutes, or until just set.

1 Heat the oil in a non-stick frying pan and add the potatoes, pepperoni and spring onions. Cook over a high heat for about 5 minutes, stirring occasionally, then stir in the cheese and peas.

2 Beat the eggs with the parsley and seasoning, then pour the mixture over the ingredients in the frying pan. Cook gently for about 10 minutes, or until the egg mixture is golden underneath.

3 When the mixture has almost set, cover the pan with a large plate and carefully invert the pan and its cover to turn out the tortilla. Slide the tortilla back into the pan and continue cooking for a further 10 minutes, or until browned underneath.

4 Turn out the tortilla on to a large, flat platter and serve hot or warm, cut into slices. Alternatively, leave until cold.

Bresaola and Rocket Pizza

Although the Armenians initiated the idea of topping flattened dough with savoury ingredients before baking it, it was the Italians – the Neapolitans in particular – who developed the pizza in the 1830s.

SERVES FOUR

INGREDIENTS

- 150g/5oz packet pizza base mix
- 120ml/4fl oz/½ cup lukewarm water
- 225g/8oz/3¼ cups mixed wild mushrooms
- 25g/1oz/2 tbsp butter
- 2 garlic cloves, coarsely chopped
- 60ml/4 tbsp pesto
- 8 slices bresaola
- 4 tomatoes, sliced
- 75g/3oz/⅓ cup full-fat cream cheese
- 25g/1oz rocket

1 Preheat the oven to 200°C/400°F/Gas 6. Tip the packet of pizza base mix into a large mixing bowl and pour in enough of the water to mix to a soft, not sticky, dough.

2 Turn out the dough on to a lightly floured surface and knead for about 5 minutes, or until smooth and elastic. Divide the dough into two equal pieces, knead lightly to form two balls, then pat out the balls of dough into flat rounds.

3 Roll out each piece of dough on a lightly floured surface to a 23cm/9in round and transfer to baking sheets.

4 Slice the wild mushrooms. Melt the butter in a frying pan and cook the garlic for 2 minutes. Add the mushrooms and cook over a high heat for about 5 minutes, or until the mushrooms have softened but are not overcooked.

5 Spread pesto on the pizza bases, to within 2cm/¾in of the edge of each one. Arrange the bresaola and tomato slices around the rims of the pizzas, then spoon the cooked mushrooms into the middle.

6 Dot the cream cheese on top of the pizzas and bake for 15–18 minutes, or until the bases are crisp and the cheese just melted. Top each pizza with a handful of rocket leaves just before serving. Serve at once.

COOK'S TIP

If you are in a hurry, buy two ready-made pizza bases instead of the pizza mix and bake for 10 minutes.

ROASTED VEGETABLE AND GARLIC SAUSAGE LOAF

STUFFED WITH CURED MEAT AND ROASTED VEGETABLES, THIS CRUSTY COB LOAF MAKES A COLOURFUL CENTREPIECE FOR A CASUAL SUMMER LUNCH. SERVE WITH FRESH GREEN SALAD LEAVES.

SERVES SIX

INGREDIENTS
- 1 large cob loaf
- 2 red peppers, quartered and seeded
- 1 large leek, sliced
- 90ml/6 tbsp olive oil
- 175g/6oz green beans, blanched and drained
- 75g/3oz garlic sausage
- 2 eggs, hard-boiled and quartered
- 115g/4oz/1 cup cashew nuts, toasted
- 75g/3oz/⅓ cup soft cheese with garlic and herbs
- salt and ground black pepper

1 Preheat the oven to 220°C/425°F/ Gas 7. Slice the top off the loaf using a large serrated knife and set it aside, then cut out the soft centre, leaving the crust intact. Stand the crusty shell on a baking sheet.

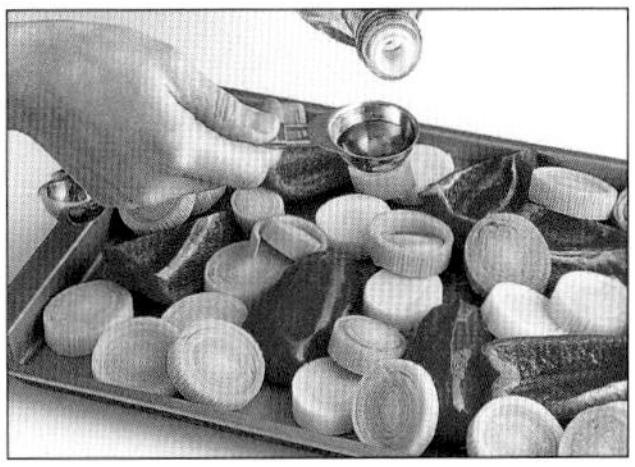

2 Put the peppers and leek in a roasting tin with the oil and cook for 25 minutes, turning occasionally, or until the peppers have softened.

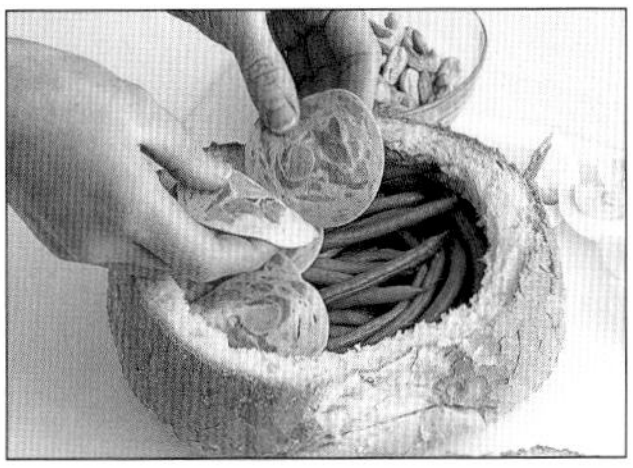

3 Spoon half of the pepper mixture into the bottom of the loaf, pressing it down well with a spoon. Add the green beans, garlic sausage, eggs and cashew nuts, packing the layers down well. Season each layer before adding the next. Dot the soft cheese over the filling and top with the remaining peppers.

4 Replace the top of the loaf and bake it for 15–20 minutes, or until the fillling is warmed through. Serve at once, cut into wedges or slices.

VARIATION

You can use a variety of different-shaped loaves, such as a large, uncut sandwich loaf, for this recipe. Hollow out the loaf and fill as above, then cut into slices.

COOK'S TIP

Don't throw away the soft centre of the loaf. It can be made into breadcrumbs and frozen for use in another recipe.

POULTRY

Chickens and poussins, turkeys, ducks, geese and guinea fowl are domesticated birds, specially reared for the pot. They are at their best cooked simply, and all make delicious and healthy meals. This section opens with a classic recipe for Roast Chicken with Madeira Gravy and Bread Sauce and includes the quintessential French dish Coq au Vin, but there are also light, summery recipes such as Escalopes of Chicken with Baby Vegetables, and Chicken with Tarragon Cream. Guinea Fowl is cooked with a creamy whisky sauce, while duck is prepared in a fresh, tart plum sauce, and there are salads, too – the most spectacular, a divine recipe that combines lightly dressed leaves with poached eggs and skewers of crisply cooked duck.

Roast Chicken with Madeira Gravy and Bread Sauce

This is a simple, traditional dish which tastes wonderful and makes a perfect family meal. Roast potatoes and seasonal green vegetables, such as Brussels sprouts stir-fried with chestnuts, are delicious with roast chicken.

SERVES FOUR

INGREDIENTS
- 50g/2oz/¼ cup butter
- 1 onion, chopped
- 75g/3oz/1½ cups fresh white breadcrumbs
- grated rind of 1 lemon
- 30ml/2 tbsp chopped fresh parsley
- 30ml/2 tbsp chopped fresh tarragon
- 1 egg yolk
- 1.5kg/3¼lb oven-ready chicken
- 175g/6oz rindless streaky bacon rashers
- salt and ground black pepper

For the bread sauce
- 1 onion, studded with 6 cloves
- 1 bay leaf
- 300ml/½ pint/1¼ cups milk
- 150ml/¼ pint/⅔ cup single cream
- 115g/4oz/2 cups fresh white breadcrumbs
- knob of butter

For the gravy
- 10ml/2 tsp plain flour
- 300ml/½ pint/1¼ cups well-flavoured chicken stock
- dash of Madeira or sherry

1 Preheat the oven to 200°C/400°F/Gas 6. First make the stuffing. Melt half the butter in a saucepan and fry the onion for about 5 minutes, or until softened but not coloured.

2 Remove the pan from the heat and add the breadcrumbs, lemon rind, parsley and half the chopped tarragon. Season with salt and pepper, then mix in the egg yolk to bind the ingredients into a moist stuffing.

VARIATION
Cocktail sausages, which have been wrapped in thin streaky bacon rashers make a delicious accompaniment to roast chicken. Roast them alongside the chicken for the final 25–30 minutes cooking time.

3 Fill the neck end of the chicken with stuffing, then truss the chicken neatly and weigh it. To calculate the cooking time, allow 20 minutes per 450g/1lb, plus 20 minutes.

4 Put the chicken in a roasting tin and season it well with salt and pepper. Beat together the remaining butter and tarragon, then smear this over the bird.

5 Lay the bacon rashers over the top of the chicken (this helps stop the light breast meat from drying out) and roast for the calculated time. Baste the bird every 30 minutes during cooking and cover with buttered foil if the bacon begins to overbrown.

6 Meanwhile, make the bread sauce. Put the clove-studded onion, bay leaf and milk in a small, heavy-based saucepan and bring slowly to the boil. Remove the pan from the heat and leave the milk to stand for at least 30 minutes so that it is infused with the flavouring ingredients.

7 Strain the milk into a clean pan (discard the flavouring ingredients) and add the cream and breadcrumbs. Bring slowly to the boil, stirring continuously, then reduce the heat and simmer gently for 5 minutes. Keep warm while you make the gravy and carve the chicken, then stir in the butter and season to taste just before serving.

8 Transfer the chicken to a warmed serving dish, cover tightly with foil and leave to stand for 10 minutes.

9 To make the gravy, pour off all but 15ml/1 tbsp fat from the roasting tin. Place the tin on the hob and stir in the flour. Cook the flour for about 1 minute, or until golden brown, then gradually stir in the stock and Madeira or sherry. Bring to the boil, stirring all the time, then simmer for about 3 minutes until thickened. Add seasoning to taste and strain the gravy into a warm sauceboat.

10 Carve the chicken and serve it at once, with the stuffing, gravy and hot bread sauce.

COOK'S TIP
To keep chicken moist during roasting, some recipes suggest cooking the bird on its sides, turning it halfway through cooking, and others place the breast down. Covering the top of the breast with rashers of bacon and adding foil to prevent this from overcooking is easier and more effective.

ESCALOPES OF CHICKEN WITH BABY VEGETABLES

THIS IS A QUICK AND LIGHT DISH – IDEAL FOR SUMMER, WHEN IT IS TOO HOT TO SLAVE OVER THE STOVE FOR HOURS OR TO EAT HEAVY MEALS. FLATTENING THE CHICKEN BREASTS THINS THE MEAT AND ALSO SPEEDS UP THE COOKING.

SERVES FOUR

INGREDIENTS

- 4 skinless, boneless chicken breasts, each weighing 175g/6oz
- juice of 1 lime
- 120ml/4fl oz/½ cup olive oil
- 675g/1½lb mixed baby potatoes, carrots, fennel (sliced if large), asparagus and peas
- sea salt and ground black pepper
- sprigs of fresh flat leaf parsley, to garnish

For the tomato mayonnaise

- 150ml/¼ pint/⅔ cup mayonnaise
- 15ml/1 tbsp sun-dried tomato paste

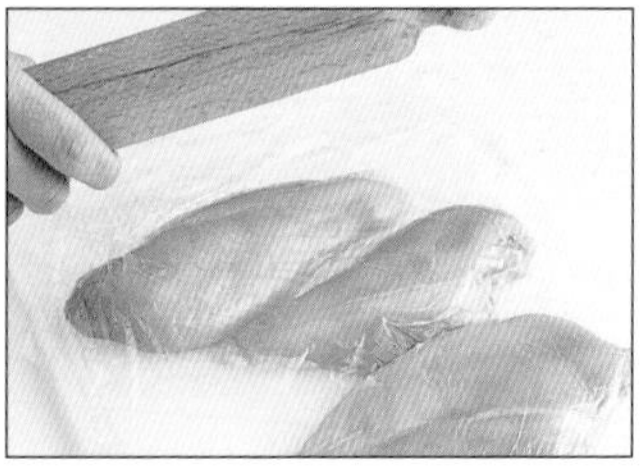

1 Lay the chicken breasts between two sheets of clear film or greaseproof paper and use a rolling pin to beat them flat until they are evenly thin. Season the chicken with salt and pepper and sprinkle with the lime juice.

2 Heat 45ml/3 tbsp of the oil in a frying pan or griddle pan and cook the chicken escalopes for 10–12 minutes on each side, turning frequently.

3 Meanwhile, put the potatoes and carrots in a saucepan with the remaining oil and season with sea salt. Cover and cook over a medium heat for 10–15 minutes, stirring frequently. Add the fennel and cook for a further 5 minutes, stirring frequently. Finally, add the asparagus and peas and cook for 5 minutes more, or until all the vegetables are tender.

4 To make the sauce, mix together the mayonnaise and sun-dried tomato paste in a small bowl. Spoon the vegetables on to a warmed large serving platter or individual plates and arrange the chicken on top. Serve the tomato mayonnaise with the chicken and vegetables. Garnish with sprigs of flat leaf parsley.

COOK'S TIP

Any combinations of baby vegetables can be used. The weight is for prepared vegetables (they are usually sold trimmed). Adjust the cooking time or the order in which they are added to the pan according to how long the chosen vegetables take to cook, for example add root vegetables first, before quick-cooking courgettes, mangetouts, French beans or similar ingredients.

COQ AU VIN

THIS FRENCH COUNTRY CASSEROLE WAS TRADITIONALLY MADE WITH AN OLD BOILING BIRD, MARINATED OVERNIGHT IN RED WINE, THEN SIMMERED GENTLY UNTIL TENDER. MODERN RECIPES USE TENDER ROASTING BIRDS TO SAVE TIME AND BECAUSE BOILING FOWL ARE NOT READILY AVAILABLE.

SERVES SIX

INGREDIENTS
- 45ml/3 tbsp light olive oil
- 12 shallots
- 225g/8oz rindless streaky bacon rashers, chopped
- 3 garlic cloves, finely chopped
- 225g/8oz small mushrooms, halved
- 6 boneless chicken thighs
- 3 boneless chicken breasts, halved
- 1 bottle red wine
- salt and ground black pepper
- 45ml/3 tbsp chopped fresh parsley, to garnish

For the bouquet garni
- 3 sprigs each of fresh parsley, thyme and sage
- 1 bay leaf
- 4 peppercorns

For the beurre manié
- 25g/1oz/2 tbsp butter, softened
- 25g/1oz/¼ cup plain flour

1 Heat the oil in a large, flameproof casserole and cook the shallots for 5 minutes, or until golden. Increase the heat, add the bacon, garlic and mushrooms and cook for a further 10 minutes, stirring frequently.

2 Use a draining spoon to transfer the cooked ingredients to a plate, then brown the chicken portions in the oil remaining in the pan, turning them until they are golden brown all over. Return the shallots, garlic, mushrooms and bacon to the casserole and pour in the red wine.

3 Tie the ingredients for the bouquet garni in a bundle in a small piece of muslin and add to the casserole. Bring to the boil, reduce the heat and cover the casserole, then simmer for 30–40 minutes.

4 To make the beurre manié, cream the butter and flour together in a small bowl using your fingers or a spoon to make a smooth paste.

5 Add small lumps of this paste to the bubbling casserole, stirring well until each piece has melted into the liquid before adding the next. When all the paste has been added, bring back to the boil and simmer for 5 minutes.

6 Season the casserole to taste with salt and pepper and serve garnished with chopped fresh parsley and accompanied by boiled potatoes.

Chicken and Asparagus Risotto

Use thick asparagus, as fine spears overcook in this risotto. The thick ends of the asparagus are full of flavour and they become beautifully tender in the time it takes for the rice to absorb the stock.

SERVES FOUR

INGREDIENTS

- 50g/2oz/¼ cup butter
- 15ml/1 tbsp olive oil
- 1 leek, finely chopped
- 115g/4oz/1½ cups oyster mushrooms, sliced
- 3 skinless, boneless chicken breasts, cubed
- 350g/12oz asparagus
- 250g/9oz/1¼ cups risotto rice
- 900ml/1½ pints/3¾ cups boiling chicken stock
- salt and ground black pepper
- Parmesan cheese curls, to serve

1 Heat the butter with the oil in a pan until the mixture is foaming. Add the leek and cook gently until softened, but not coloured. Add the mushrooms and cook for 5 minutes. Remove the vegetables from the pan and set aside.

2 Increase the heat and cook the cubes of chicken until golden on all sides. Do this in batches, if necessary, and then replace them all in the pan.

3 Meanwhile, discard the woody ends from the asparagus and cut the spears in half. Set the fine tips aside. Cut the thick ends in half and add them to the pan. Replace the leek and mushroom mixture and stir in the rice.

4 Pour in a ladleful of boiling stock and cook gently, stirring occasionally, until the stock is absorbed. Continue adding the stock a ladleful at a time, simmering until it is absorbed, the rice is tender and the chicken is cooked.

COOK'S TIP

Use a cheese slicer or vegetable peeler to pare thin curls off a large piece of fresh Parmesan cheese.

5 Add the fine aspargus tips with the last ladleful of boiling stock for the final 5 minutes and continue cooking the risotto gently until the asparagus is tender. The whole process should take about 25–30 minutes.

6 Season the risotto to taste with salt and lots of freshly ground black pepper and spoon it into individual warm serving bowls. Top each bowl with curls of Parmesan, and serve.

CHICKEN WITH TARRAGON CREAM

THE ANISEED-LIKE FLAVOUR OF TARRAGON HAS A PARTICULAR AFFINITY WITH CHICKEN, ESPECIALLY IN CREAMY SAUCES SUCH AS THE ONE IN THIS FAVOURITE FRENCH BISTRO-STYLE DISH. SERVE SEASONAL VEGETABLES AND BOILED RED CAMARGUE RICE WITH THE CHICKEN.

SERVES FOUR

INGREDIENTS

- 30ml/2 tbsp light olive oil
- 4 chicken supremes, each weighing about 250g/9oz
- 3 shallots, finely chopped
- 2 garlic cloves, finely chopped
- 115g/4oz/1½ cups wild mushrooms (such as chanterelles or ceps) or shiitake mushrooms, halved
- 150ml/¼ pint/⅔ cup dry white wine
- 300ml/½ pint/1¼ cups double cream
- 15g/½oz mixed fresh tarragon and flat leaf parsley, chopped
- salt and ground black pepper
- sprigs of fresh tarragon and flat leaf parsley, to garnish

COOK'S TIP

Boneless chicken breasts could be used in place of the chicken supremes.

1 Heat the light olive oil in a large frying pan and add the chicken supremes, skin-side down. Cook for 10 minutes, turning the chicken twice, or until it is a golden brown colour on both sides.

2 Reduce the heat and cook the chicken breasts for 10 minutes more, turning occasionally. Use a draining spoon to remove the chicken breasts from the pan and set aside.

3 Add the shallots and garlic to the pan and cook gently, stirring, until the shallots are softened but not browned. Increase the heat, add the mushrooms and stir-fry for 2 minutes, or until the mushrooms just start to colour.

4 Replace the chicken, nestling the pieces down into the other ingredients, and then pour in the wine. Simmer for 5–10 minutes, or until most of the wine has evaporated.

5 Add the cream and gently move the ingredients around in the pan to mix in the cream. Simmer for 10 minutes, or until the sauce has thickened. Stir the chopped herbs into the sauce with seasoning to taste. Arrange the chicken on warm plates and spoon the sauce over. Garnish with sprigs of tarragon and flat leaf parsley.

Stuffed Chicken in Bacon Coats

A simple cream cheese and chive filling flavours these chicken breasts and they are beautifully moist when cooked in their bacon wrapping. Serve jacket potatoes and a crisp, fresh green salad as accompaniments.

SERVES FOUR

INGREDIENTS
- 4 skinless, boneless chicken breasts, each weighing about 175g/6oz
- 115g/4oz/½ cup cream cheese
- 15ml/1 tbsp snipped chives
- 8 rindless unsmoked bacon rashers
- 15ml/1 tbsp olive oil
- ground black pepper

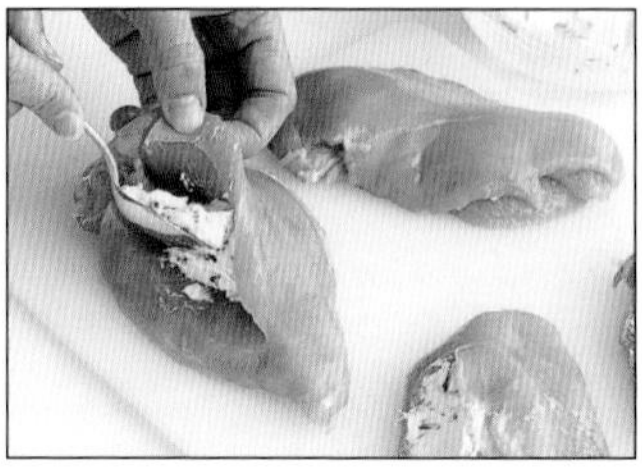

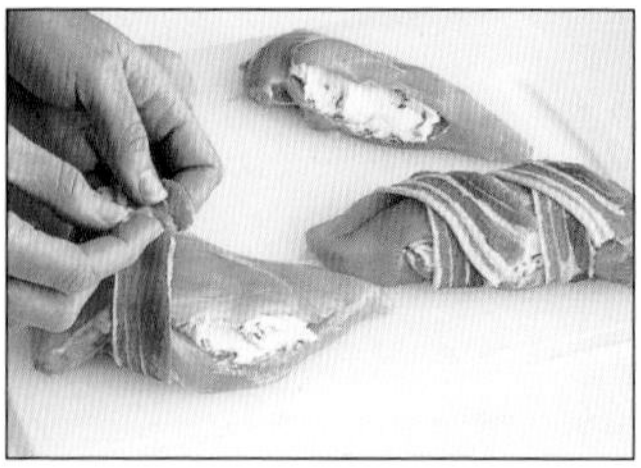

1 Preheat the oven to 200°C/400°F/Gas 6. Using a very sharp knife, carefully make a horizontal slit from the side into each chicken breast (the cheese is going to be stuffed in each slit).

2 To make the filling, beat together the cream cheese and chives. Divide the filling into four portions and, using a teaspoon, fill each slit with some of the cream cheese. Push the sides of the slit together to keep the filling in.

3 Wrap each breast in two rashers of bacon and place in an ovenproof dish. Drizzle the oil over the chicken and bake for 25–30 minutes, brushing occasionally with the oil. Season with black pepper and serve at once.

Southern Fried Chicken

Colonel Sanders opened the first of thousands of "finger lickin' good" Kentucky Fried Chicken restaurant franchises in 1955, after his own roadside restaurant had to close for lack of custom when passing traffic was diverted on to a new highway. This is a low-fat interpretation of the original deep-fried dish, which is now an international fast food favourite. Serve with potato wedges to complete the meal.

SERVES FOUR

INGREDIENTS
- 15ml/1 tbsp paprika
- 30ml/2 tbsp plain flour
- 4 skinless, boneless chicken breasts, each weighing about 175g/6oz
- 30ml/2 tbsp sunflower oil
- salt and ground black pepper

For the corn cakes
- 200g/7oz sweetcorn kernels
- 350g/12oz mashed potato, cooled
- 25g/1oz/2 tbsp butter

To serve
- 150ml/¼ pint/⅔ cup soured cream
- 15ml/1 tbsp snipped chives

COOK'S TIP
To make the mashed potato, cook the potatoes in boiling salted water for about 20 minutes until tender, then drain well. Add a little milk and mash until smooth.

1 Mix the paprika and flour together on a plate. Coat each chicken breast in the seasoned flour.

2 Heat the oil in a large frying pan and add the floured chicken breasts. Cook over a high heat until a golden brown colour on both sides. Reduce the heat and continue cooking for a further 20 minutes, turning once or twice, or until the chicken is cooked right through.

3 Meanwhile, make the corn cakes. Stir the sweetcorn kernels into the cooled mashed potato and season with plenty of salt and pepper to taste. Using lightly floured hands, shape the mixture into 12 even-size round cakes, each about 5cm/2in in diameter.

4 When the chicken breasts are cooked, use a draining spoon to remove them from the large frying pan and keep hot. Melt the butter in the pan and cook the corn cakes for 3 minutes on each side, or until golden and heated through.

5 Meanwhile, mix together the soured cream with the chives in a small bowl to make a dip. Transfer the corn cakes from the frying pan to serving plates and top with the chicken breasts. Serve at once, offering the soured cream with chives on the side.

TANDOORI CHICKEN

THE WORD TANDOORI REFERS TO A METHOD OF COOKING IN A CHARCOAL-FIRED CLAY OVEN CALLED A TANDOOR. IN NORTHERN INDIA AND PAKISTAN, A WIDE VARIETY OF FOODS ARE COOKED IN THIS TYPE OF OVEN, BUT IN WESTERN COUNTRIES THE METHOD IS MOST POPULAR FOR CHICKEN. WARM NAAN BREAD AND MANGO CHUTNEY MAY BE OFFERED WITH THE CHICKEN AND RICE.

SERVES FOUR

INGREDIENTS
- 30ml/2 tbsp vegetable oil
- 2 small onions, cut into wedges
- 2 garlic cloves, sliced
- 4 skinless, boneless chicken breasts, cut into cubes
- 100ml/3½fl oz/⅓ cup water
- 300g/11oz jar tandoori sauce
- salt and ground black pepper
- fresh coriander sprigs, to garnish

To serve
- 5ml/1 tsp ground turmeric
- 350g/12oz/1⅔ cups basmati rice

1 Heat the oil in a flameproof casserole. Add the onions and garlic, and cook for about 3 minutes, or until the onion is beginning to soften, stirring frequently.

2 Add the cubes of chicken to the casserole and cook for 6 minutes. Stir the water into the tandoori sauce and pour it over the chicken. Bring to the boil, then reduce the heat and simmer for 10 minutes, or until the chicken pieces are cooked through and the sauce is slightly reduced and thickened.

3 Meanwhile, bring a large saucepan of lightly salted water to the boil, add the turmeric and rice and bring back to the boil. Stir once, reduce the heat to prevent the water from boiling over and simmer the rice for 12 minutes, or according to the time suggested on the packet, until tender.

4 Drain the rice well and serve with the tandoori chicken on warmed individual serving plates, garnished with sprigs of fresh coriander.

COOK'S TIP

You will find jars of ready-made tandoori sauce in large supermarkets.

THAI CHICKEN CURRY

THIS FLAVOURFUL AND FRAGRANT, CREAMY CURRY IS QUITE SIMPLE TO MAKE EVEN THOUGH IT INCLUDES A VARIETY OF INTERESTING INGREDIENTS.

SERVES SIX

INGREDIENTS
- 400ml/14oz can unsweetened coconut milk
- 6 skinless, boneless chicken breasts, finely sliced
- 225g/8oz can bamboo shoots, drained and sliced
- 30ml/2 tbsp fish sauce
- 15ml/1 tbsp soft light brown sugar

For the green curry paste
- 4 green chillies, seeded
- 1 lemon grass stalk, sliced
- 1 small onion, sliced
- 3 garlic cloves
- 1cm/½in piece galangal or fresh root ginger, peeled
- grated rind of ½ lime
- 5ml/1 tsp coriander seeds
- 5ml/1 tsp cumin seeds
- 2.5ml/½ tsp shrimp or fish sauce

To garnish
- 1 red chilli, seeded and cut into fine strips
- finely pared rind of ½ lime, finely shredded
- fresh Thai purple basil or coriander, coarsely chopped

To serve
- 175g/6oz/scant 1 cup Thai jasmine rice
- pinch of saffron strands

1 First make the green curry paste: put the chillies, lemon grass, onion, garlic, galangal or ginger, lime rind, coriander seeds, cumin seeds and shrimp or fish sauce in a food processor or blender and process until they are reduced to a thick paste. Set aside.

2 Bring half the coconut milk to the boil in a large frying pan, then reduce the heat and simmer for about 5 minutes, or until reduced by half. Stir in the green curry paste and simmer for a further 5 minutes.

3 Add the finely sliced chicken breasts to the pan with the remaining coconut milk, bamboo shoots, fish sauce and sugar. Stir well to combine all the ingredients and bring the curry back to simmering point, then simmer gently for about 10 minutes, or until the chicken slices are cooked through.The mixture will look grainy or curdled during cooking, but do not worry as this is quite normal.

4 Meanwhile, prepare the garnish and set aside. Add the rice and saffron to a pan of boiling salted water. Reduce the heat and simmer for 10 minutes, or until tender. Drain the rice and serve it with the curry, garnished with the chilli, lime rind and basil or coriander.

Glazed Poussins

Golden poussins make an impressive main course and they are also very easy to prepare. A simple mushroom risotto and refreshing side salad are suitable accompaniments.

SERVES FOUR

INGREDIENTS
- 50g/2oz/¼ cup butter
- 10ml/2 tsp mixed spice
- 30ml/2 tbsp clear honey
- grated rind and juice of 2 clementines
- 4 poussins, each weighing about 450g/1lb
- 1 onion, finely chopped
- 1 garlic clove, chopped
- 15ml/1 tbsp plain flour
- 50ml/2fl oz/¼ cup Marsala
- 300ml/½ pint/1¼ cups chicken stock
- small bunch of fresh coriander, to garnish

VARIATION

To give the poussins extra flavour, stuff each poussin before roasting with a quartered clementine and one or two garlic cloves, then skewer the legs with sprigs of fresh rosemary.

1 Preheat the oven to 220°C/425°F/Gas 7. Heat the butter, mixed spice, honey and clementine rind and juice until the butter has melted, stirring to mix well. Remove from the heat.

2 Place the poussins in a roasting tin, brush them with the glaze, then roast for 40 minutes. Brush with any remaining glaze and baste occasionally with the pan juices during cooking. Transfer the poussins to a serving platter, cover with foil and stand for 10 minutes.

3 Skim off all but 15ml/1 tbsp of the fat from the roasting tin. Add the onion and garlic to the juices in the tin and cook on the hob until beginning to brown. Stir in the flour, then gradually pour in the Marsala, followed by the stock, whisking all the time. Bring to the boil and simmer for 3 minutes to make a smooth, rich gravy.

4 Transfer the poussins to warm plates or a platter and garnish with coriander. Offer the gravy separately.

Spatchcock Poussins with Herbes de Provence Butter

Spatchcock is said to be a distortion of an 18th-century Irish expression "dispatch cock" for providing an unexpected guest with a quick and simple meal. A young chicken was prepared without frills or fuss by being split, flattened and fried or grilled.

SERVES TWO

INGREDIENTS
- 2 poussins, each weighing about 450g/1lb
- 1 shallot, finely chopped
- 2 garlic cloves, crushed
- 45ml/3 tbsp chopped mixed fresh herbs, such as flat leaf parsley, sage, rosemary and thyme
- 75g/3oz/6 tbsp butter, softened
- salt and ground black pepper

VARIATIONS

Add some finely chopped chilli or a little grated lemon rind to the butter.

1 To spatchcock a poussin, place it breast down on a chopping board and split it along the back. Open out the bird and turn it over, so that the breast side is uppermost. Press the bird as flat as possible, then thread two metal skewers through it, across the breast and thigh, to keep it flat. Repeat with the second poussin and place the skewered birds on a large grill pan.

2 Add the chopped shallot, crushed garlic and chopped mixed herbs to the butter with plenty of seasoning, and then beat well. Dot the butter over the spatchcock poussins.

3 Preheat the grill to high and cook the poussins for 30 minutes, turning them over halfway through. Turn again and baste with the cooking juices, then cook for a further 5–7 minutes on each side.

Citrus Chicken Salad

This zesty salad makes a refreshing change from rich food. It is a good choice for a post-Christmas buffet, when cooked turkey can be used instead of chicken.

SERVES SIX

INGREDIENTS

- 120ml/4fl oz/½ cup extra virgin olive oil
- 6 boneless chicken breasts, skinned
- 4 oranges
- 5ml/1 tsp Dijon mustard
- 15ml/3 tsp clear honey
- 300g/11oz/2¾ cups white cabbage, finely shredded
- 300g/11oz carrots, peeled and finely sliced
- 2 spring onions, finely sliced
- 2 celery sticks, cut into matchstick strips
- 30ml/2 tbsp chopped fresh tarragon
- 2 limes
- salt and ground black pepper

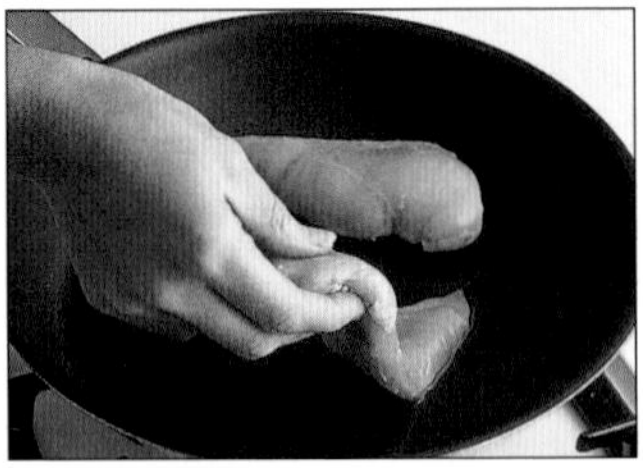

1 Heat 30ml/2 tbsp of the oil in a large, heavy-based frying pan. Add the chicken breasts to the pan and cook for 15–20 minutes, or until the chicken is cooked through and golden brown. (If your pan is too small, cook the chicken in two or three batches.) Remove the chicken from the pan and leave to cool.

2 Peel two of the oranges, cutting off all pith, then cut out the segments from between the membranes and set aside. Grate the rind and squeeze the juice from 1 of the remaining oranges and place in a large bowl. Stir in the Dijon mustard, 5ml/1 tsp of the honey, 60ml/4 tbsp of the oil and seasoning to taste. Mix in the cabbage, carrots, spring onions and celery, then leave to stand for 10 minutes.

3 Meanwhile, squeeze the juice from the remaining orange and mix it with the remaining honey and oil, and tarragon. Peel and segment the limes, as for the oranges, and lightly mix the segments into the dressing with the reserved orange segments and seasoning to taste.

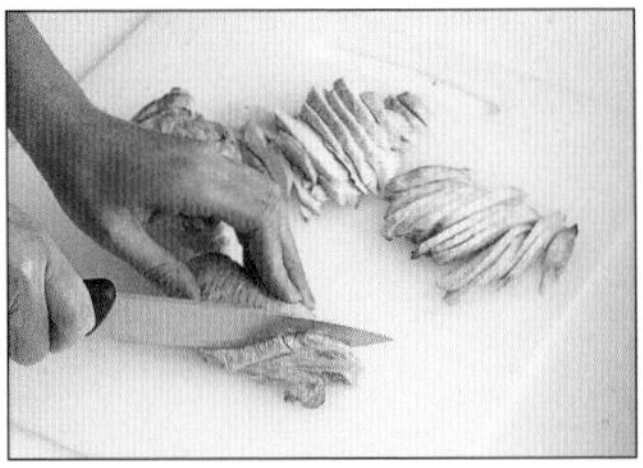

4 Slice the cooked chicken breasts and stir into the dressing. Spoon the vegetable salad on to plates and add the chicken mixture, then serve at once.

VARIATION

For a creamy result, mayonnaise, crème fraîche or soured cream can be used to dress the chicken instead of the orange, oil and honey mixture.

Guinea Fowl with Whisky Cream Sauce

Served with creamy sweet potato mash and whole baby leeks, guinea fowl is superb with a rich, creamy whisky sauce.

SERVES FOUR

INGREDIENTS
- 2 guinea fowl, each weighing about 1kg/2¼lb
- 90ml/6 tbsp whisky
- 150ml/¼ pint/⅔ cup well-flavoured chicken stock
- 150ml/¼ pint/⅔ cup double cream
- 20 baby leeks
- salt and ground black pepper
- fresh thyme sprigs, to garnish
- mashed sweet potatoes, to serve

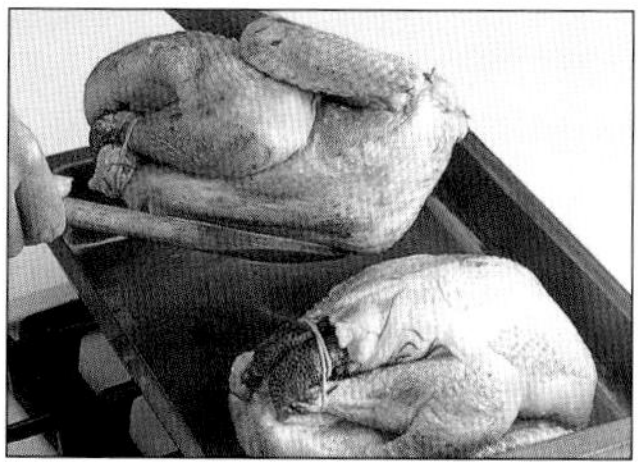

1 Preheat the oven to 200°C/400°F/ Gas 6. Brown the guinea fowl on all sides in a roasting tin on the hob, then turn it breast uppermost and transfer the tin to the oven. Roast for about 1 hour, until the guinea fowl are golden and cooked through. Transfer the guinea fowl to a warmed serving dish, cover with foil and keep warm.

2 Pour off the excess fat from the tin, then heat the juices on the hob and stir in the whisky. Bring to the boil and cook until reduced. Add the stock and cream and simmer again until reduced slightly. Strain and season to taste.

3 Meanwhile, trim the leeks so that they are roughly the same length as the guinea fowl breasts, then cook them whole in boiling salted water for about 3 minutes, or until tender but not too soft. Drain the leeks in a colander.

4 Carve the guinea fowl. To serve, arrange portions of mashed sweet potato on warmed serving plates, then add the carved guinea fowl and the leeks. Garnish with sprigs of fresh thyme, and season with plenty of freshly ground black pepper. Spoon a little of the sauce over each portion and serve the rest separately.

VARIATION

If you don't like the flavour of whisky, then substitute brandy, Madeira or Marsala. Or, to make a non-alcoholic version, use freshly squeezed orange juice instead.

TURKEY AND CRANBERRY BUNDLES

After the traditional Christmas or Thanksgiving meal, it is easy to end up with lots of turkey leftovers. These delicious filo pastry parcels are a marvellous way of using up the small pieces of cooked turkey.

SERVES SIX

INGREDIENTS

- 450g/1lb cooked turkey, cut into chunks
- 115g/4oz/1 cup Brie, diced
- 30ml/2 tbsp cranberry sauce
- 30ml/2 tbsp chopped fresh parsley
- 9 sheets filo pastry, 45 × 28cm/18 × 11in each, thawed if frozen
- 50g/2oz/¼ cup butter, melted
- salt and ground black pepper
- green salad, to serve

1 Preheat the oven to 200°C/400°F/Gas 6. Mix the turkey, diced Brie, cranberry sauce and chopped parsley. Season with salt and pepper.

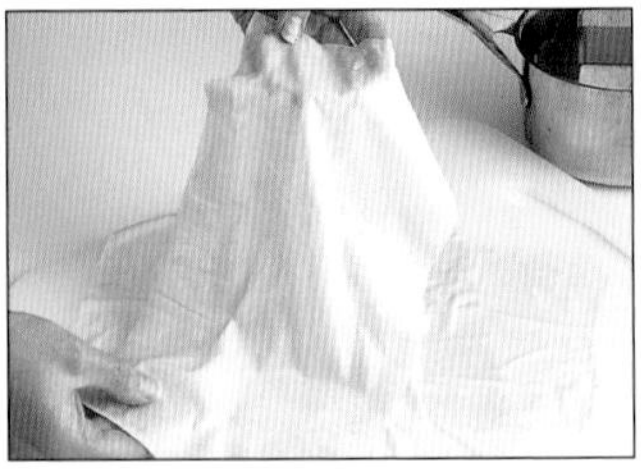

2 Cut the filo sheets in half widthways and trim to make 18 squares. Layer three pieces of pastry together, brushing them with a little melted butter so that they stick together. Repeat with the remaining filo squares to give six pieces.

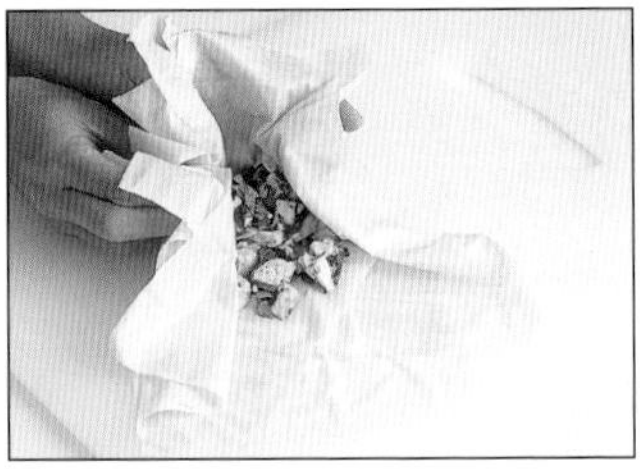

3 Divide the turkey mixture among the pastry, making neat piles on each piece. Gather up the pastry to enclose the filling in neat bundles. Place on a baking sheet, brush with a little melted butter and bake for 20 minutes, or until the pastry is crisp and golden. Serve hot or warm with a green salad.

VARIATIONS

These little parcels can be made with a variety of fillings and are great for using up left-over cooked meats. To make Ham and Cheddar Bundles, replace the turkey with ham and use Cheddar in place of the Brie. A fruit-flavoured chutney would make a good alternative to the cranberry sauce. Alternatively, to make Chicken and Stilton Bundles, use cooked chicken in place of the turkey and white Stilton instead of Brie. Replace the cranberry sauce with mango chutney.

Turkey Lasagne

This easy meal-in-one pasta bake is delicious made with cooked turkey pieces and broccoli in a rich, creamy Parmesan sauce.

SERVES FOUR

INGREDIENTS

- 30ml/2 tbsp light olive oil
- 1 onion, chopped
- 2 garlic cloves, chopped
- 450g/1lb cooked turkey meat, finely diced
- 225g/8oz/1 cup mascarpone cheese
- 30ml/2 tbsp chopped fresh tarragon
- 300g/11oz broccoli, broken into florets
- salt and ground black pepper

For the sauce

- 50g/2oz/¼ cup butter
- 30ml/2 tbsp flour
- 600ml/1 pint/2½ cups milk
- 75g/3oz/1 cup freshly grated Parmesan cheese
- 115g/4oz no pre-cook lasagne verdi

1 Preheat the oven to 180°C/350°F/Gas 4. Heat the oil in a heavy-based saucepan and cook the onion and garlic until softened but not coloured. Remove the pan from the heat and stir in the turkey, mascarpone and tarragon, with seasoning to taste.

2 Blanch the broccoli in a large saucepan of salted boiling water for 1 minute, then drain and rinse thoroughly under cold water to prevent the broccoli from overcooking. Drain well and set aside.

COOK'S TIP

This is a delicious way of using up any cooked turkey that is left over after Christmas or Thanksgiving celebrations. It is also especially good made with half ham and half turkey.

3 To make the sauce, melt the butter in a saucepan, stir in the flour and cook for 1 minute, still stirring. Remove from the heat and gradually stir in the milk. Return to the heat and bring the sauce to the boil, stirring continuously. Simmer for 1 minute, then add 50g/2oz/⅔ cup of the Parmesan and plenty of salt and pepper.

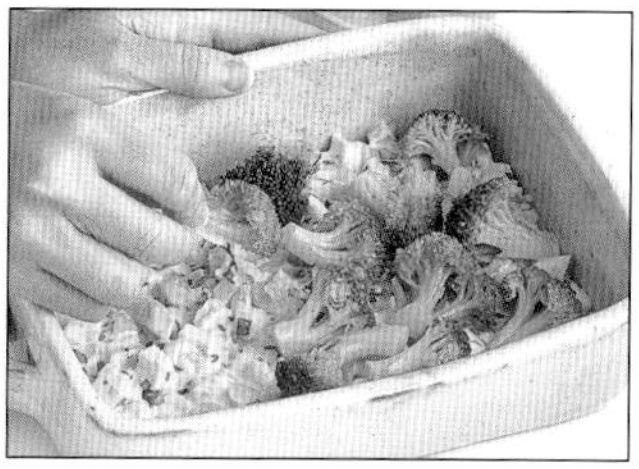

4 Spoon a layer of the turkey mixture into a large, shallow baking dish. Add a layer of broccoli and cover with sheets of lasagne. Coat with cheese sauce. Repeat these layers, finishing with a layer of cheese sauce on top. Sprinkle with the remaining Parmesan and bake for 35–40 minutes.

Turkey Patties

Minced turkey makes deliciously light patties, which are ideal for summer meals. The recipe is a flavourful variation on a classic burger and they can also be made using minced lamb, pork or beef. Serve the patties in split and toasted buns or pieces of crusty bread, with chutney, salad leaves and chunky fries.

SERVES SIX

INGREDIENTS
- 675g/1½lb minced turkey
- 1 small red onion, finely chopped
- grated rind and juice of 1 lime
- small handful of fresh thyme leaves
- 15–30ml/1–2 tbsp olive oil
- salt and ground black pepper

VARIATIONS
Minced chicken or minced pork could be used instead of turkey in these burgers. You could also try chopped oregano, parsley or basil in place of the thyme, and lemon rind instead of lime.

1 Mix together the turkey, onion, lime rind and juice, thyme and seasoning. Cover and chill for up to 4 hours to allow the flavours to infuse, then divide the mixture into six equal portions and shape into round patties.

2 Preheat a griddle pan. Brush the patties with oil, then place them on the pan and cook for 10–12 minutes. Turn the patties over, brush with more oil and cook for 10–12 minutes on the second side, or until cooked through.

DUCK WITH PLUM SAUCE

THIS IS AN UPDATED VERSION OF AN OLD ENGLISH DISH, WHICH WAS TRADITIONALLY SERVED IN THE LATE SUMMER AND EARLY AUTUMN WHEN VICTORIA PLUMS ARE BEAUTIFULLY RIPE.

SERVES FOUR

INGREDIENTS
- 4 duck quarters
- 1 large red onion, finely chopped
- 500g/1¼lb ripe plums, stoned and quartered
- 30ml/2 tbsp redcurrant jelly
- salt and ground black pepper

COOK'S TIP
It is important that the plums used in this dish are very ripe, otherwise the mixture will be too dry and the sauce will be extremely tart.

VARIATIONS
If you can't locate red onions, then use a white onion instead. Fine cut orange marmalade makes a tangy alternative to the redcurrant jelly.

1 Prick the duck skin all over with a fork to release the fat during cooking and help give a crisp result, then place the portions in a heavy frying pan, skin-sides down.

2 Cook the duck pieces for 10 minutes on each side, or until golden brown and cooked right through. Remove the duck from the frying pan using a draining spoon, and keep warm.

3 Pour away all but 30ml/2 tbsp of the duck fat, then stir-fry the onion for 5 minutes, or until golden. Add the plums and cook for a further 5 minutes, stirring frequently. Add the redcurrant jelly and mix well.

4 Replace the duck portions and cook for a further 5 minutes, or until thoroughly reheated. Season with salt and pepper to taste before serving.

STIR-FRIED DUCK WITH PINEAPPLE

THE FATTY SKIN ON DUCK MAKES IT IDEAL FOR STIR-FRYING: AS SOON AS THE DUCK IS ADDED TO THE HOT PAN THE FAT IS RELEASED, CREATING DELICIOUS CRISP SKIN AND TENDER FLESH WHEN COOKED. STIR-FRIED VEGETABLES AND NOODLES MAKE THIS A MEAL IN ITSELF.

SERVES FOUR

INGREDIENTS

- 250g/9oz fresh sesame noodles
- 2 duck breasts, thinly sliced
- 3 spring onions, cut into strips
- 2 celery sticks, cut into matchstick strips
- 1 fresh pineapple, peeled, cored and cut into strips
- 300g/11oz mixed vegetables, such as carrots, peppers, beansprouts and cabbage, shredded or cut into strips
- 90ml/6 tbsp plum sauce

1 Cook the noodles in a saucepan of boiling water for 3 minutes. Drain.

2 Meanwhile, heat a wok. Add the duck to the hot wok and stir-fry for about 2 minutes, until crisp. If the duck yields a lot of fat, drain off all but 30ml/2 tbsp.

3 Add the spring onions and celery to the wok and stir-fry for 2 minutes more. Use a draining spoon to remove the ingredients from the wok and set aside. Add the pineapple strips and mixed vegetables, and stir-fry for 2 minutes.

4 Add the cooked noodles and plum sauce to the wok, then replace the duck, spring onion and celery mixture.

5 Stir-fry the duck mixture for about 2 minutes more, or until the noodles and vegetables are hot and the duck is cooked through. Serve at once.

COOK'S TIP

Fresh sesame noodles can be bought from large supermarkets – you'll find them in the chiller cabinets alongside fresh pasta. If they aren't available, then use fresh egg noodles instead and cook according to the instructions on the packet. For extra flavour, add a little sesame oil to the cooking water.

WARM DUCK SALAD WITH POACHED EGGS

THIS SALAD LOOKS SPECTACULAR AND TASTES DIVINE, AND MAKES A PERFECT CELEBRATION STARTER OR, ACCOMPANIED BY WARM CRUSTY BREAD, A LIGHT LUNCH OR SUPPER DISH.

SERVES FOUR

INGREDIENTS

- 3 skinless, boneless duck breasts, thinly sliced
- 30ml/2 tbsp soy sauce
- 30ml/2 tbsp balsamic vinegar
- 30ml/2 tbsp groundnut oil
- 25g/1oz/2 tbsp unsalted butter
- 1 shallot, finely chopped
- 115g/4oz/1½ cups chanterelle mushrooms
- 4 eggs
- 50g/2oz mixed salad leaves
- salt and ground black pepper
- 30ml/2 tbsp extra virgin olive oil, to serve

1 Toss the duck in the soy sauce and balsamic vinegar. Cover and chill for 30 minutes to allow the duck to infuse in the soy sauce and vinegar. Meanwhile, soak 12 bamboo skewers (about 13cm/5in long) in water to help prevent them from burning during cooking.

2 Preheat the grill. Thread the duck slices on to the skewers, pleating them neatly. Place on a grill pan and drizzle with half the oil. Grill for 3–5 minutes, then turn the skewers and drizzle with the remaining oil. Grill for a further 3 minutes, or until the duck is cooked through and golden.

VARIATION

Instead of threading the duck strips on to skewers, simply stir-fry in a little oil for a few minutes until crisp and cooked through, then scatter over the salad leaves with the mushrooms.

3 Meanwhile, melt the butter in a frying pan and cook the finely chopped shallot until softened but not coloured. Add the chanterelle mushrooms and cook over a high heat for about 5 minutes, stirring occasionally.

4 Poach the eggs while the chanterelles are cooking. Half fill a frying pan with water, add salt and heat until simmering. Break the eggs one at a time into a cup before tipping carefully into the water. Poach the eggs gently for about 3 minutes, or until the whites are set. Use a draining spoon to transfer the eggs to a warm plate and trim off any untidy white.

5 Arrange the salad leaves on serving plates, then add the chanterelles and skewered duck. Carefully add the poached eggs. Drizzle with olive oil and season with freshly ground black pepper, then serve at once.

MARMALADE-GLAZED GOOSE

SUCCULENT ROAST GOOSE IS THE CLASSIC CENTREPIECE FOR A TRADITIONAL CHRISTMAS LUNCH. RED CABBAGE COOKED WITH LEEKS, AND BRAISED FENNEL ARE TASTY ACCOMPANIMENTS.

SERVES EIGHT

INGREDIENTS
- 4.5kg/10lb oven-ready goose
- 1 cooking apple, peeled, cored and cut into eighths
- 1 large onion, cut into eighths
- bunch of fresh sage, plus extra sprigs to garnish
- 30ml/2 tbsp ginger marmalade, melted
- salt and ground black pepper

For the stuffing
- 25g/1oz/2 tbsp butter
- 1 onion, finely chopped
- 15ml/1 tbsp ginger marmalade
- 450g/1lb/2 cups ready-to-eat prunes, chopped
- 45ml/3 tbsp Madeira
- 225g/8oz/4 cups fresh white breadcrumbs
- 30ml/2 tbsp chopped fresh sage

For the gravy
- 1 onion, chopped
- 15ml/1 tbsp plain flour
- 150ml/¼ pint/⅔ cup Madeira
- 600ml/1 pint/2½ cups chicken stock

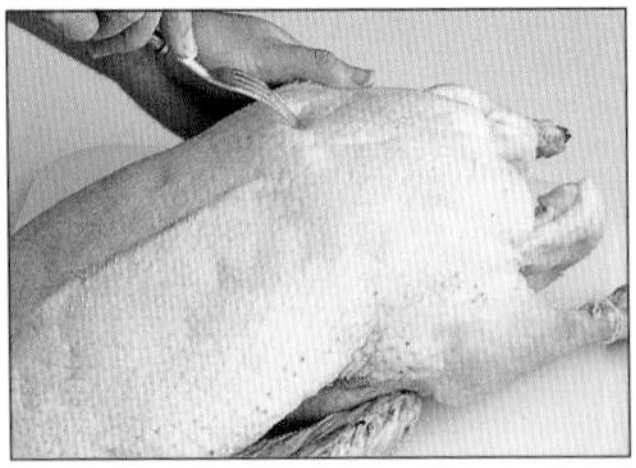

1 Preheat the oven to 200°C/400°F/Gas 6. Prick the skin of the goose all over with a fork and season the bird generously, both inside and out.

COOK'S TIP

Red cabbage goes well with goose. Cook 1 small leek, sliced, in 75g/3oz/6 tbsp butter, add 1kg/2¼lb/9 cups shredded red cabbage, with the grated rind of 1 orange, and cook for 2 minutes. Add 30ml/2 tbsp Madeira and 15ml/1 tbsp brown sugar and cook for 15 minutes.

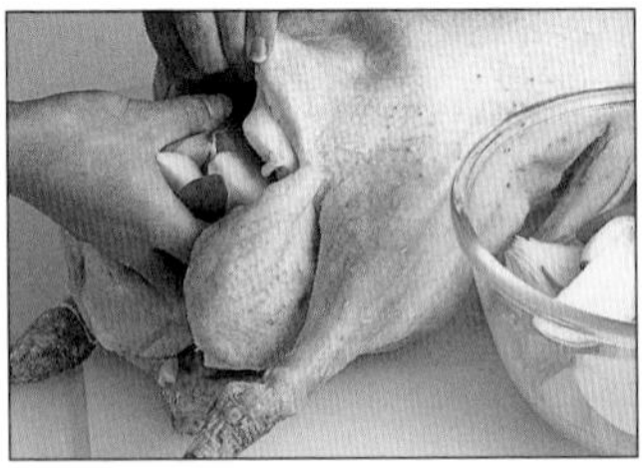

2 Mix the apple, onion and sage leaves and spoon the mixture into the parson's nose end of the goose.

3 To make the stuffing, melt the butter in a large saucepan and cook the onion for about 5 minutes, or until softened but not coloured. Remove the pan from the heat and stir in the marmalade, chopped prunes, Madeira, breadcrumbs and chopped sage.

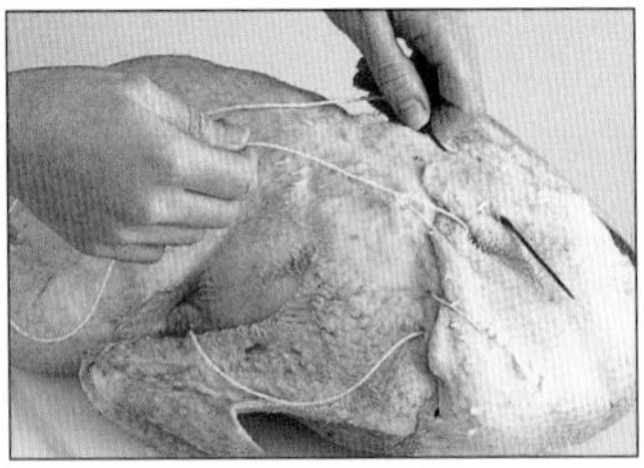

4 Stuff the neck end of the goose with some of the stuffing, and set the remaining stuffing aside in the fridge. Sew up the bird or secure it with skewers to prevent the stuffing from escaping during cooking.

5 Place the goose in a large roasting tin. Butter a piece of foil and use to cover the goose loosely, then place in the oven for 2 hours.

6 Baste the goose frequently during cooking and remove excess fat from the tin as necessary, using a small ladle or serving spoon. (Strain, cool and chill the fat in a covered container: it is excellent for roasting potatoes.)

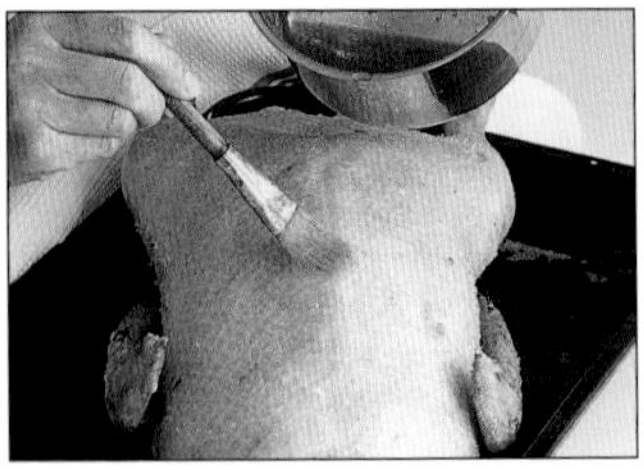

7 Remove the foil from the goose and brush the melted ginger marmalade over the goose, then roast for 30–40 minutes more, or until cooked through. To check if the goose is cooked, pierce the thick part of the thigh with a metal skewer; the juices will run clear when the bird is cooked. Remove from the oven and cover with foil, then leave to stand for 15 minutes before carving.

8 While the goose is cooking, shape the remaining stuffing into walnut-size balls and place them in an ovenproof dish. Spoon 30ml/2 tbsp of the goose fat over the stuffing balls and bake for about 15 minutes before the goose is cooked.

9 To make the gravy, pour off all but 15ml/1 tbsp of fat from the roasting tin, leaving the meat juices behind. Add the onion and cook for 3–5 minutes, or until softened but not coloured. Sprinkle in the flour and then gradually stir in the Madeira and stock. Bring to the boil, stirring continuously, then simmer for 3 minutes, or until thickened and glossy. Strain the gravy and serve it with the carved goose and stuffing. Garnish with sage leaves.

Game and New Meats

Game birds and animals have rich, distinctive flavours and are often cooked to make robust and warming dishes. Traditional dishes abound in this chapter, with classics such as Roast Pheasant, Rich Game Pie and Rabbit with Mustard, but there are also contemporary ideas, such as Grilled Spiced Quail with Mixed Leaf and Mushroom Salad. New meats such as crocodile, kangaroo and buffalo are richly flavoured, yet lean and healthy, and lend themselves to all sorts of cooking methods. Try Roast Stuffed Fillets of Crocodile, crisp deep-fried Goujons of Ostrich with Fries and Lemon Mayonnaise, or griddled Marinated Alligator Steaks with Cajun Vegetables.

ROAST PHEASANT

IN SEASON FROM THE BEGINNING OF OCTOBER BUT AT ITS BEST IN NOVEMBER AND DECEMBER, PHEASANT CONTAINS VERY LITTLE FAT, SO IT IS IMPORTANT TO ENSURE THAT IT STAYS MOIST DURING COOKING. A LAYER OF STREAKY BACON COVERING THE BREAST HELPS THE MEAT STAY SUCCULENT.

SERVES TWO

INGREDIENTS
1 hen pheasant
25g/1oz/2 tbsp butter
115g/4oz rindless streaky bacon rashers
salt and ground black pepper
game chips, to serve

For the stuffing
25g/1oz/2 tbsp butter
1 leek, chopped
115g/4oz peeled, cooked chestnuts, coarsely chopped (see Cook's Tip)
30ml/2 tbsp chopped fresh flat leaf parsley

For the gravy
15ml/1 tbsp cornflour
300ml/½pint/1¼cups well-flavoured chicken stock
50ml/2fl oz/¼cup port

1 Preheat the oven to 190°C/375°F/ Gas 5. Season the pheasant inside and out with plenty of salt and pepper.

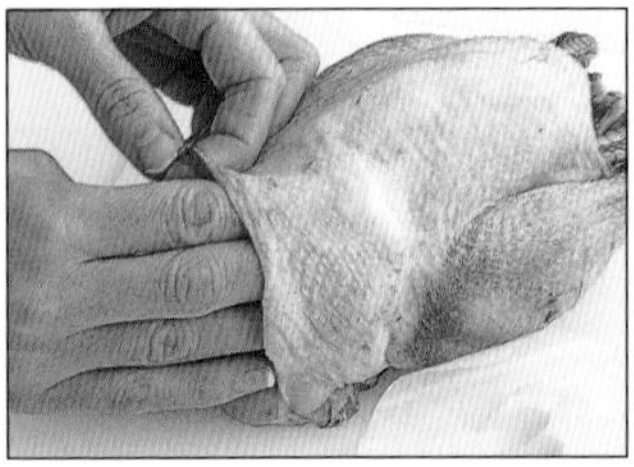

2 Carefully loosen and lift the skin covering the breast and rub the butter between the skin and flesh.

COOK'S TIP
For convenience, it is much easier to use vacuum-packed chestnuts rather than fresh, which are fiddly to peel and cook. Simply rinse the chestnuts thoroughly with boiling water and drain before using. Whole, unsweetened canned chestnuts could be used, but these are fairly dense and much softer than the vacuum-packed version.

3 To make the stuffing, melt the butter in a saucepan and, when foaming, add the leek. Cook for about 5 minutes, or until softened but not coloured. Remove the pan from the heat, and mix in the cooked, chopped chestnuts, parsley and seasoning to taste.

4 Spoon the stuffing into the body cavity of the pheasant and secure the opening with skewers. Arrange the bacon rashers in a lattice pattern over the breast. Place in a roasting tin.

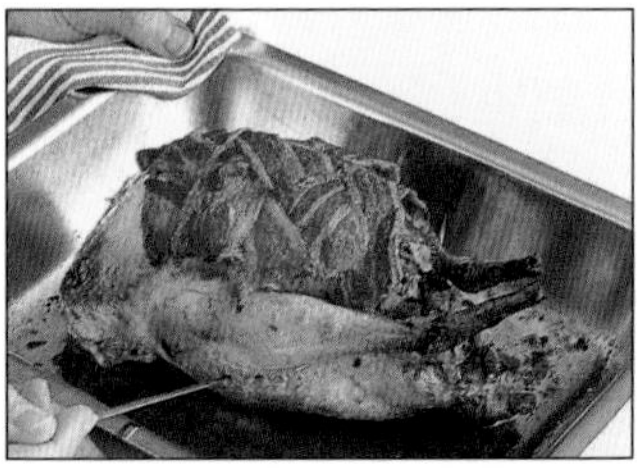

5 Roast the pheasant for 1–1½ hours, or until the juices run clear when the bird is pierced with a skewer in the thickest part of the leg.

6 Remove the pheasant from the oven and cover closely with foil, then leave to stand in a warm place for 15 minutes before carving.

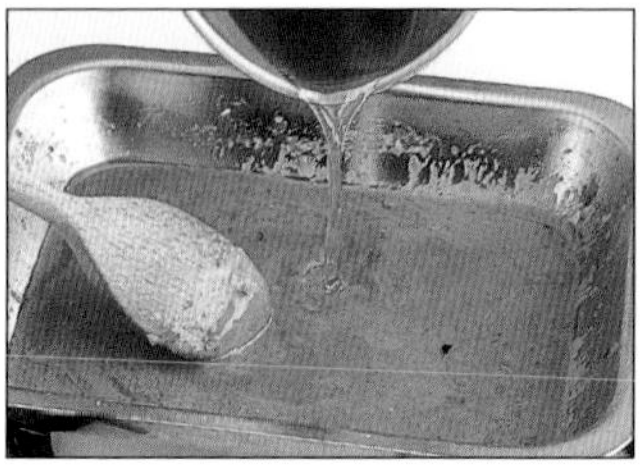

7 Meanwhile, heat the juices in the roasting tin on the hob and stir in the cornflour to form a paste. Gradually pour in the stock and port, stirring continuously. Bring to the boil, then reduce the heat and simmer for about 5 minutes, or until the sauce is slightly thickened and glossy.

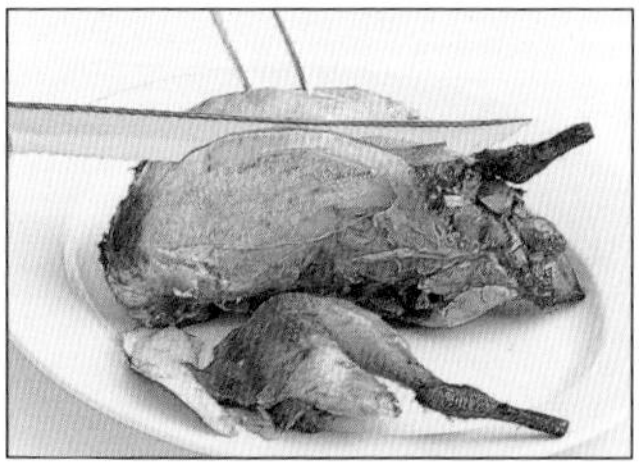

8 Strain the sauce into a sauce boat or serving jug and keep warm while you carve the pheasant, then serve the pheasant with the stuffing and gravy. Crisp, deep-fried matchstick potato chips or classic game chips would make a good accompaniment.

GRILLED SPICED QUAIL WITH MIXED LEAF AND MUSHROOM SALAD

THIS IS A PERFECT SUPPER DISH FOR AUTUMNAL ENTERTAINING. QUAIL IS AT ITS BEST WHEN THE BREAST MEAT IS REMOVED FROM THE CARCASS, SO THAT IT COOKS QUICKLY AND CAN BE SERVED RARE.

SERVES FOUR

INGREDIENTS
- 8 quail breasts
- 50g/2oz/¼ cup butter
- 5ml/1 tsp paprika
- salt and ground black pepper

For the salad
- 60ml/4 tbsp walnut oil
- 30ml/2 tbsp olive oil
- 45ml/3 tbsp balsamic vinegar
- 25g/1oz/2 tbsp butter
- 75g/3oz/generous 1 cup chanterelle mushrooms, sliced, if large
- 25g/1oz/3 tbsp walnut halves, toasted
- 115g/4oz mixed salad leaves

1 Preheat the grill. Arrange the quail breasts on the grill rack, skin-sides up. Dot with half the butter and sprinkle with half the paprika and a little salt.

2 Grill the quail breasts for 3 minutes, then turn them over and dot with the remaining butter, then sprinkle with the remaining paprika and a little salt. Grill for a further 3 minutes, or until cooked. Transfer the quail breasts to a warmed dish, cover and leave to stand while preparing the salad.

COOK'S TIP
Take care when roasting the walnuts as they scorch quickly and will become bitter if over-browned. The best way to roast them is to heat a non-stick frying pan until hot. Add the walnuts and cook for 3–5 minutes, or until golden, turning them frequently.

3 Make the dressing first. Whisk the oils with the balsamic vinegar, then season and set aside. Heat the butter until foaming and cook the chanterelles for about 3 minutes, or until just beginning to soften. Add the walnuts and heat through. Remove from the heat.

4 Thinly slice the cooked quail breasts and arrange them on four individual serving plates with the warmed chanterelle mushrooms and walnuts and mixed salad leaves. Drizzle the oil and vinegar dressing over the salad and serve warm.

Quail Hot-Pot with Merlot and Winter Vegetables

Sweet, slightly tangy, grapes are a classic ingredient for accompanying quail, and here they bring a fresh, fruity flavour to the rich red wine sauce. Creamy mashed potatoes are an excellent accompaniment for the hot-pot.

SERVES FOUR

INGREDIENTS

- 4 quail
- 150g/5oz seedless red grapes
- 50g/2oz/¼ cup butter
- 4 shallots, halved
- 175g/6oz baby carrots, scrubbed
- 175g/6oz baby turnips
- 450ml/¾ pint/scant 2 cups Merlot or other red wine
- salt and ground black pepper

For the croûtes

- 4 slices white bread, crusts removed
- 60ml/4 tbsp olive oil
- fresh flat leaf parsley, to garnish

1 Preheat the oven to 220°C/425°F/ Gas 7. Season the quail and stuff with grapes. Melt the butter in a flameproof casserole and brown the birds. Remove using a slotted spoon and set aside.

2 Add the shallots, carrots and turnips to the fat remaining in the casserole and cook until they are just beginning to colour. Replace the quail, breast-sides down, and pour in the Merlot or other red wine. Cover the casserole and transfer it to the oven. Cook for about 30 minutes, or until the quail are tender.

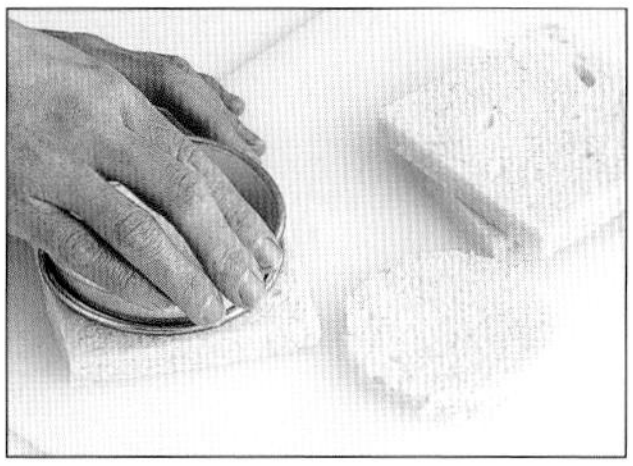

3 Meanwhile, make the croûtes. Use a 10cm/4in plain cutter to stamp out rounds from the bread. Heat the oil in a frying pan and cook the bread until golden on both sides. Drain on kitchen paper and keep warm.

4 Place the croûtes on plates. Use a draining spoon to set a quail on each croute. Arrange the vegetables around the quail, cover and keep hot.

5 Boil the cooking juices hard until reduced to syrupy consistency. Skim off as much butter as possible, then season the sauce to taste. Drizzle the sauce over the quail and garnish with parsley, then serve at once.

PAN-FRIED PHEASANT WITH OATMEAL AND CREAMY MUSTARD SAUCE

Oatmeal is often used for coating fish before pan frying, but it is equally good with tender poultry, game and other meats. Instead of a heavy egg base, sweet, slightly tangy redcurrant jelly is used to bind the oatmeal to the tender pheasant breast fillets.

SERVES FOUR

INGREDIENTS

- 115g/4oz/1 cup medium oatmeal
- 4 skinless boneless pheasant breasts
- 45ml/3 tbsp redcurrant jelly, melted
- 50g/2oz/¼ cup butter
- 15ml/1 tbsp olive oil
- 45ml/3 tbsp wholegrain mustard
- 300ml/½ pint/1¼ cups double cream
- salt and ground black pepper

1 Place the oatmeal on a plate and season it with salt and pepper. Brush the pheasant breasts with redcurrant jelly, then turn them in the oatmeal to coat them evenly.

2 Heat the butter and oil in a frying pan until foaming. Add the oatmeal-coated pheasant breasts and cook over a high heat until golden brown on both sides. Reduce the heat and cook for a further 8–10 minutes.

3 Stir the mustard and cream into the pan, stirring it into the cooking juices. Bring slowly to the boil, then simmer for 10 minutes, or until the sauce has thickened and the pheasant breasts are cooked through.

WILD DUCK WITH OLIVES

Compared to farmed duck, wild duck, which has a brilliant flavour, is worth the extra expense for a special occasion meal. These are quite small birds, so allow two pieces per portion. Mashed parsnips and green vegetables are good with the duck.

SERVES TWO

INGREDIENTS

- 1 wild duck, weighing about 1.5kg/3¼lb, cut into 4 portions
- 1 onion, chopped
- 1 carrot, chopped
- 2 celery sticks, chopped
- 4 garlic cloves, sliced
- 1 bottle red wine
- 300ml/½ pint/1¼ cups well-flavoured game stock
- small handful of fresh thyme leaves
- 2.5ml/½ tsp arrowroot
- 225g/8oz/2 cups stoned green olives
- 115g/4oz passata
- salt and ground black pepper

1 Preheat the oven to 220°C/425°F/Gas 7. Season the duck portions with salt and pepper and place them in a large flameproof casserole.

2 Roast the duck for 20 minutes, then remove the casserole from the oven. Use a draining spoon to remove the duck from the casserole and set aside. Reduce the oven temperature to 160°C/325°F/Gas 3.

3 Carefully transfer the casserole to the hob and heat the fat until it is sizzling. Add the onion, carrot, celery and garlic, and cook for 10 minutes, or until the vegetables are softened. Pour in the wine and boil until it has reduced by about half.

4 Add the stock and thyme leaves, then replace the duck portions in the casserole. Bring to the boil, skim the surface, then cover the casserole and place in the oven for about 1 hour, or until the duck is tender. Remove the duck portions and keep warm.

5 Skim the excess fat from the cooking liquid, strain it and return it to the casserole, then bring it to the boil. Skim the liquid again, if necessary.

6 Mix the arrowroot to a thin paste with a little cold water and whisk it into the simmering sauce. Add the olives and passata and replace the duck, then cook, uncovered, for 15 minutes. Check the seasoning and serve.

GROUSE WITH ORCHARD FRUIT STUFFING

TART APPLES, PLUMS AND PEARS MAKE A FABULOUS ORCHARD FRUIT STUFFING THAT COMPLEMENTS THE RICH GAMEY FLAVOUR OF GROUSE PERFECTLY.

SERVES TWO

INGREDIENTS
- juice of ½ lemon
- 2 young grouse
- 50g/2oz/¼ cup butter
- 4 Swiss chard leaves
- 50ml/2fl oz/¼ cup Marsala
- salt and ground black pepper

For the stuffing
- 2 shallots, finely chopped
- 1 cooking apple, peeled, cored and chopped
- 1 pear, peeled, cored and chopped
- 2 plums, halved, stoned and chopped
- large pinch of mixed spice

1 Sprinkle the lemon juice over the grouse and season it with salt and pepper. Melt half the butter in a large flameproof casserole, add the grouse and cook for 10 minutes, or until browned, turning occasionally. Use tongs to remove the grouse from the casserole and set aside.

2 Add the shallots to the fat remaining in the casserole and cook until softened but not coloured. Add the apple, pear, plums and mixed spice, and cook for about 5 minutes, or until the fruits are just beginning to soften. Remove the casserole from the heat and spoon the hot fruit mixture into the body cavities of the birds.

3 Truss the birds neatly with string. Smear the remaining butter over the birds and wrap them in the chard leaves, then replace them in the casserole.

4 Pour in the Marsala and heat until simmering. Cover tightly and simmer for 20 minutes, or until the birds are tender, taking care not to overcook them. Leave to rest in a warm place for about 10 minutes before serving.

COOK'S TIP

There isn't a lot of liquid in the casserole for cooking the birds – they are steamed rather than boiled, so it is very important that the casserole is heavy-based with a tight-fitting lid, otherwise the liquid may evaporate and the chard burn on the base of the pan.

MARINATED PIGEON IN RED WINE

THE TIME TAKEN TO MARINATE AND COOK THIS CASSEROLE IS WELL REWARDED BY THE FABULOUS RICH FLAVOUR OF THE FINISHED DISH. STIR-FRIED GREEN CABBAGE AND CELERIAC PURÉE ARE DELICIOUS WITH PIGEON CASSEROLE.

SERVES FOUR

INGREDIENTS

- 4 pigeons, each weighing about 225g/8oz
- 30ml/2 tbsp olive oil
- 1 onion, coarsely chopped
- 225g/8oz/3¼ cups chestnut mushrooms, sliced
- 15ml/1 tbsp plain flour
- 300ml/½ pint/1¼ cups game stock
- 30ml/2 tbsp chopped fresh parsley
- salt and ground black pepper
- flat leaf parsley, to garnish

For the marinade

- 15ml/1 tbsp light olive oil
- 1 onion, chopped
- 1 carrot, peeled and chopped
- 1 celery stick, chopped
- 3 garlic cloves, sliced
- 6 allspice berries, bruised
- 2 bay leaves
- 8 black peppercorns, bruised
- 150ml/¼ pint/⅔ cup red wine vinegar
- 150ml/¼ pint/⅔ cup red wine
- 45ml/3 tbsp redcurrant jelly

1 Mix all the ingredients for the marinade in a large dish. Add the pigeons and turn them in the marinade, then cover and chill for 12 hours, turning the pigeons frequently.

VARIATION
If you are unable to buy pigeon, this recipe works equally well with rabbit or hare. Buy portions and make deep slashes in the flesh so that the marinade soaks into, and flavours right to, the centre of the pieces of meat.

2 Preheat the oven to 150°C/300°F/ Gas 2. Heat the oil in a large, flameproof casserole and cook the onion and mushrooms for about 5 minutes, or until the onion has softened.

3 Meanwhile, drain the pigeons and strain the marinade into a jug, then set both aside separately.

4 Sprinkle the flour over the pigeons and add them to the casserole, breast-sides down. Pour in the marinade and stock, and add the chopped parsley and seasoning. Cover and cook for 2½ hours.

5 Check the seasoning, then serve the pigeons on warmed plates and ladle the sauce over them. Garnish with parsley.

Rich Game Pie

Terrific for stylish picnics or just as smart for a formal wedding buffet, this pie looks spectacular when baked in a fluted raised pie mould. Some specialist kitchen shops hire the moulds to avoid the expense of purchasing them; alternatively a 20cm/8in round springform tin can be used.

SERVES TEN

INGREDIENTS
- 25g/1oz/2 tbsp butter
- 1 onion, finely chopped
- 2 garlic cloves, finely chopped
- 900g/2lb mixed boneless game meat, such as skinless pheasant and/or pigeon breast, venison and rabbit, diced
- 30ml/2 tbsp chopped mixed fresh herbs such as parsley, thyme and marjoram
- salt and ground black pepper

For the pâté
- 50g/2oz/¼ cup butter
- 2 garlic cloves, finely chopped
- 450g/1lb chicken livers, rinsed, trimmed and chopped
- 60ml/4 tbsp brandy
- 5ml/1 tsp ground mace

For the hot water crust pastry
- 675g/1½lb/6 cups strong plain flour
- 5ml/1 tsp salt
- 115ml/3½fl oz/scant ½ cup milk
- 115ml/3½fl oz/scant ½ cup water
- 115g/4oz/½ cup lard, diced
- 115g/4oz/½ cup butter, diced
- beaten egg, to glaze

For the jelly
- 300ml/½ pint/1¼ cups game or beef consommé
- 2.5ml/½ tsp powdered gelatine

1 Melt the butter in a small pan until foaming, then add the onion and garlic, and cook until softened but not coloured. Remove from the heat and mix with the diced game meat and the chopped mixed herbs. Season well, cover and chill.

2 To make the pâté, melt the butter in a saucepan until foaming. Add the garlic and chicken livers and cook until the livers are just browned. Remove the pan from the heat and stir in the brandy and mace. Purée the mixture in a blender or food processor until smooth, then set aside and leave to cool.

3 To make the pastry, sift the flour and salt into a bowl and make a well in the centre. Place the milk and water in a saucepan. Add the lard and butter and heat gently until melted, then bring to the boil and remove from the heat as soon as the mixture begins to bubble. Pour the hot liquid into the well in the flour and beat until smooth. Cover and leave until cool enough to handle.

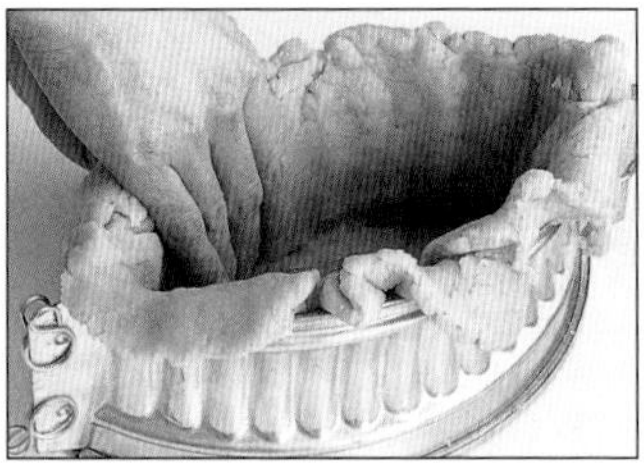

4 Preheat the oven to 200°C/400°F/Gas 6. Roll out two-thirds of the pastry and use to line a 23cm/9in raised pie mould. Spoon in half the game mixture and press it down evenly. Add the pâté and then top with the remaining game.

5 Roll out the remaining pastry to form a lid. Brush the edge of the pastry lining the tin with a little water and cover the pie with the pastry lid. Trim off excess pastry from around the edge. Pinch the edges together to seal in the filling. Make 2 holes in the centre of the lid and glaze with egg. Use pastry trimmings to roll out leaves to garnish the pie. Brush with egg.

6 Bake the pie for 20 minutes, then cover it with foil and cook for a further 10 minutes. Reduce the oven temperature to 150°C/300°F/Gas 2. Glaze the pie again with beaten egg and cook for a further 1½hours, keeping the top covered loosely with foil.

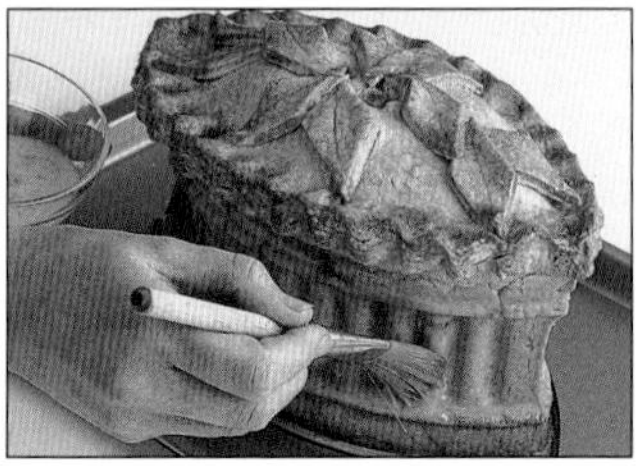

7 Remove the pie from the oven and leave it to stand for 15 minutes. Increase the oven temperature to 200°C/400°F/Gas 6. Stand the tin on a baking sheet and remove the sides. Quickly glaze the sides of the pie with beaten egg and cover the top with foil, then cook for a final 15 minutes to brown the sides. Leave to cool completely, then chill the pie overnight.

8 To make the jelly, heat the game or beef consommé in a small saucepan until just beginning to bubble, whisk in the gelatine until dissolved and leave to cool until just setting. Using a small funnel, carefully pour the jellied consommé into the holes in the pie. Chill until set. This pie will keep in the fridge for up to 3 days.

Medallions of Venison with Herby Horseradish Dumplings

Venison is lean and full-flavoured. This recipe makes a spectacular dinner party dish – it gives the appearance of being difficult to make but is actually very easy.

SERVES FOUR

INGREDIENTS
- 600ml/1 pint/2½ cups venison stock
- 120ml/4fl oz/½ cup port
- 15ml/1 tbsp sunflower oil
- 4 × 175g/6oz medallions of venison
- chopped parsley, to garnish
- steamed baby vegetables, such as carrots, courgettes and turnips, cooked, to serve

For the dumplings
- 75g/3oz/⅔ cup self-raising flour
- 40g/1½oz beef suet
- 15ml/1 tbsp chopped fresh mixed herbs
- 5ml/1 tsp creamed horseradish
- 45–60ml/3–4 tbsp water

1 First make the dumplings: mix the flour, suet and herbs and make a well in the middle. Add the horseradish and water, then mix to make a soft but not sticky dough. Shape the dough into walnut-sized balls and chill in the fridge for up to 1 hour.

2 Boil the venison stock in a saucepan until reduced by half. Add the port and continue boiling until reduced again by half, then pour the reduced stock into a large frying pan. Heat the stock until it is simmering and add the dumplings. Poach them gently for 5–10 minutes, or until risen and cooked through. Use a draining spoon to remove the dumplings from the pan.

3 Smear the oil over a non-stick griddle, heat until very hot. Add the venison, cook for 2–3 minutes on each side. Place the venison medallions on warm serving plates and pour the sauce over. Serve with the dumplings and the vegetables, garnished with parsley.

VENISON PIE

THIS IS A VARIATION ON COTTAGE PIE AND THE RESULT USING RICH VENISON IS PARTICULARLY TASTY – A SPECIAL TREAT. SERVE WITH LIGHTLY STEAMED GREEN VEGETABLES.

SERVES SIX

INGREDIENTS
- 30ml/2 tbsp olive oil
- 2 leeks, trimmed and chopped
- 1kg/2¼lb minced venison
- 30ml/2 tbsp chopped fresh parsley
- 300ml/½ pint/1¼ cups game consommé
- salt and ground black pepper

For the topping
- 1.5kg/3¼lb mixed root vegetables, such as sweet potatoes, parsnips and swede, coarsely chopped
- 15ml/1 tbsp horseradish sauce
- 25g/1oz/2 tbsp butter

VARIATION

This pie can be made with other minced meats, such as beef, lamb or pork. If leeks aren't available, then use a large onion and chop coarsely.

1 Heat the oil in a saucepan. Add the leeks and cook for about 8 minutes, or until softened and beginning to brown.

2 Add the minced venison to the pan and cook for about 10 minutes, stirring frequently, or until the meat is well browned. Stir in the chopped parsley, consommé and seasoning, then bring to the boil, cover and simmer for about 20 minutes, stirring occasionally.

3 Meanwhile, preheat the oven to 200°C/400°F/Gas 6 and prepare the topping. Cook the vegetables in boiling, salted water to cover for 15–20 minutes. Drain and mash with the horseradish sauce, butter and pepper.

4 Spoon the venison mixture into an ovenproof dish and top with the mashed vegetables. Bake for 20 minutes, or until piping hot and beginning to brown.

SPICY VENISON CASSEROLE

BEING LOW IN FAT BUT HIGH IN FLAVOUR, VENISON IS AN EXCELLENT CHOICE FOR HEALTHY, YET RICH, CASSEROLES. CRANBERRIES AND ORANGE BRING A FESTIVE FRUITINESS TO THIS SPICY RECIPE. SERVE WITH SMALL JACKET POTATOES AND GREEN VEGETABLES.

SERVES FOUR

INGREDIENTS
- 30ml/2 tbsp olive oil
- 1 onion, chopped
- 2 celery sticks, sliced
- 10ml/2 tsp ground allspice
- 15ml/1 tbsp plain flour
- 675g/1½lb stewing venison, cubed
- 225g/8oz fresh or frozen cranberries
- grated rind and juice of 1 orange
- 900ml/1½ pints/3¾ cups beef or venison stock
- salt and ground black pepper

1 Heat the oil in a flameproof casserole. Add the onion and celery and fry for about 5 minutes, or until softened.

2 Meanwhile, mix the ground allspice with the flour and either spread the mixture out on a large plate or place in a large plastic bag. Toss a few pieces of venison at a time (to prevent them becoming soggy) in the flour mixture until they are all lightly coated.

3 When the onion and celery are softened, remove from the casserole using a draining spoon and set aside. Add the venison pieces to the casserole in batches and cook until browned and sealed on all sides.

4 Add the cranberries, orange rind and juice to the casserole along with the beef or venison stock, and stir well. Return the vegetables and all the venison to the casserole and heat until simmering, then cover tightly and reduce the heat. Simmer for about 45 minutes, or until the venison is tender, stirring occasionally.

5 Season the venison casserole to taste with salt and pepper before serving.

VARIATION

Farmed venison is increasingly easy to find and is available from good butchers and many large supermarkets. It makes a rich and flavourful stew, but lean pork or braising steak could be used in place of the venison, if you prefer. You could also replace the cranberries with pitted and halved ready-to-eat prunes and, for extra flavour, use either ale or stout instead of about half the stock.

HARE POT PIES

THE FULL, GAMEY FLAVOUR OF HARE IS PERFECT FOR THIS DISH; HOWEVER, BONELESS VENISON, RABBIT, PHEASANT OR ANY OTHER GAME MEAT CAN BE USED IN THIS RECIPE. A LARGE PIE CAN BE MADE INSTEAD OF INDIVIDUAL POT PIES, IF YOU PREFER.

SERVES FOUR

INGREDIENTS
- 30ml/2 tbsp olive oil
- 1 leek, sliced
- 225g/8oz parsnips, sliced
- 225g/8oz carrots, sliced
- 1 fennel bulb, sliced
- 675g/1½lb boneless hare, diced
- 30ml/2 tbsp plain flour
- 60ml/4 tbsp Madeira
- 300ml/½ pint/1¼ cups game or chicken stock
- 45ml/3 tbsp chopped fresh parsley
- salt and ground black pepper

For the topping
- 450g/1lb puff pastry, thawed if frozen
- 1 egg yolk, beaten, to glaze

1 Heat the olive oil in a large, flameproof casserole, add the sliced leek, parsnips, carrots and fennel and cook for about 10 minutes, stirring frequently, or until the vegetables are softened. Use a draining spoon to remove the vegetables from the casserole and set aside.

2 Add the hare to the casserole in batches and stir-fry over a high heat for 10 minutes, or until browned. When all the meat is browned, return it to the pan. Sprinkle in the flour and stir in the Madeira and stock. Return the vegetables to the casserole with the seasoning and parsley. Heat until simmering, then cook for 20 minutes.

3 Preheat the oven to 220°C/425°F/Gas 7. Spoon the hare mixture into four individual pie dishes. Cut the pastry into quarters and roll out on a lightly floured work surface to cover the pies, making the pieces larger than the dishes. Trim off the excess pastry and use the trimmings to line the rim of each dish. Dampen the pastry rims with cold water and cover with pastry lids. Pinch the edges together to seal in the filling. Brush with beaten egg yolk and make a small hole in the top of each pie to allow steam to escape.

4 Bake for 25 minutes, or until the pastry is risen and golden. If necessary, cover the pastry with foil after 15 minutes to prevent it from overbrowning.

RABBIT WITH MUSTARD

THIS CLASSIC DISH IS GOOD WITH BUTTERED PASTA OR POLENTA.

SERVES FOUR

INGREDIENTS
- 4 large rabbit portions
- 15ml/1 tbsp wholegrain mustard with honey
- 30ml/2 tbsp olive oil
- 1 onion, chopped
- 1 celery head, coarsely chopped
- 1 red pepper, seeded and chopped
- 15ml/1 tbsp plain flour
- 450ml/¾ pint/scant 2 cups chicken stock
- 300ml/½ pint/1¼ cups dry white wine
- salt and ground black pepper
- 30ml/2 tbsp chopped fresh parsley, to garnish

VARIATION
Mildly aniseed-flavoured fennel can be used in place of the celery in this dish. Chop it coarsely and add to the casserole with the onion.

1 Make deep cuts in the rabbit portions using a sharp knife. Spread them liberally with the mustard and leave to stand while cooking the vegetables.

2 Heat the olive oil in a large, flameproof casserole. Cook the chopped onion, celery and red pepper for 5 minutes, or until they are just beginning to soften. Use a draining spoon to remove the vegetables from the casserole and set aside.

3 Cook the rabbit portions in the casserole for 5 minutes on each side, or until deep golden in colour. Return the vegetables to the casserole and stir in the flour, stock and wine. Season.

4 Bring to the boil, cover and simmer for about 35 minutes. Remove the lid and continue simmering for 10 minutes, or until the rabbit is tender. Taste for seasoning and serve garnished with the chopped fresh parsley.

RABBIT WITH RED WINE AND PRUNES

THIS IS A FAVOURITE FRENCH DISH AND IS OFTEN FOUND ON THE MENUS OF SMALL COUNTRY RESTAURANTS. IT IS DELICIOUS SERVED WITH SAUTÉED POTATOES.

SERVES FOUR

INGREDIENTS
- 8 rabbit portions
- 30ml/2 tbsp vegetable oil
- 2 onions, finely chopped
- 2 garlic cloves, finely chopped
- 60ml/4 tbsp Armagnac or brandy
- 300ml/½ pint/1¼ cups dry red wine
- 5ml/1 tsp soft light brown sugar
- 16 ready-to-eat prunes
- 150ml/¼ pint/⅔ cup double cream
- salt and ground black pepper

VARIATION
Chicken can also be cooked in this way. Use 4 chicken drumsticks and 4 thighs in place of the rabbit portions.

1 Season the rabbit portions liberally with salt and pepper. Heat the vegetable oil in a large, flameproof casserole and fry the rabbit portions in batches until they are golden brown on all sides.

2 Remove the browned rabbit portions from the casserole, add the chopped onion and garlic, and cook, stirring occasionally, until the onion is softened.

3 Return the rabbit to the casserole, add the Armagnac or brandy and ignite it. When the flames have died down, pour in the wine. Stir in the sugar and prunes, cover and simmer for 30 minutes.

4 Remove the rabbit from the casserole and keep warm. Add the cream to the sauce and simmer for 3–5 minutes. Season to taste and serve at once.

MARINATED WILD BOAR WITH MUSHROOMS

WILD BOAR TASTES LIKE RICH, GAMEY BEEF. HERE IT IS COOKED SLOWLY, WITH LOTS OF SHIITAKE MUSHROOMS AND STOUT, TO MAKE A WONDERFULLY SUCCULENT CASSEROLE.

SERVES FOUR

INGREDIENTS
- 900g/2lb lean wild boar, trimmed and diced
- 2 large onions, chopped
- 3 garlic cloves, chopped
- 900ml/1½ pints/3¾ cups stout
- 60ml/4 tbsp sunflower oil
- 450g/1lb/6½ cups shiitake mushrooms, halved
- 15ml/1 tbsp plain flour
- 5ml/1 tsp freshly ground black pepper
- 30ml/2 tbsp redcurrant jelly
- 30ml/2 tbsp chopped fresh parsley
- salt

VARIATION
Shiitake mushrooms have a wonderfully strong flavour. If you prefer a milder taste, then use a mixture of chestnut, oyster and button mushrooms.

1 Put the boar in a large, shallow china or glass dish with the onions, garlic and stout. Marinate for at least 2 hours, stirring occasionally. Strain the meat and onions, reserving the stout.

2 Heat the oil in a large, flameproof casserole and fry the meat with the onion and garlic in batches until browned. Set the meat aside. Add the mushrooms a handful at a time, adding more when the previous batch have reduced in volume.

3 Mix the flour with a little of the reserved marinade to make a smooth paste. Return the meat to the casserole and pour in the stout with the flour paste. Mix well and bring the casserole slowly to the boil.

4 Reduce the heat and simmer for 1 hour, stirring occasionally. Add the pepper with salt to taste, the redcurrant jelly and the parsley. Simmer for a further 30 minutes, or until the wild boar is melt-in-the-mouth tender.

SKEWERED WILD BOAR WITH GINGER DIPPING SAUCE

MEAT FROM ITALY, BREAD FROM GREECE AND A DIPPING SAUCE FROM CHINA COME TOGETHER IN THIS DISH THAT IS A GOOD EXAMPLE OF FUSION COOKING, BRINGING TOGETHER THE FLAVOURS AND METHODS OF THREE COUNTRIES.

SERVES FOUR

INGREDIENTS
- 450g/1lb lean wild boar
- 15ml/1 tbsp clear honey
- 50g/2oz/¼ cup butter
- 15ml/1 tbsp dark soy sauce

For the dip
- 2.5cm/1in piece fresh root ginger, peeled and finely chopped
- 30ml/2 tbsp sesame oil
- 60ml/4 tbsp hoisin sauce

To serve
- pitta breads
- shredded iceberg lettuce

1 Soak four bamboo skewers in warm water for about 30 minutes. (This will help prevent them burning.) Cut the wild boar into small, even-size cubes and thread the cubes on to the drained skewers. Preheat the grill to hot.

2 Melt the honey and butter with the soy sauce in a small saucepan, and brush liberally over the wild boar. Cook the skewered meat under the grill, for about 12 minutes, turning frequently, and brushing with extra glaze.

3 Meanwhile, cook the ginger in the sesame oil in a small saucepan for a few minutes. Stir in the hoisin sauce. Remove from the heat.

4 Warm the pitta breads under the grill. Split them, then smear a little of the dip over the inside of each pitta and add some lettuce. Serve with the wild boar skewers and the remaining dip.

GOUJONS OF OSTRICH WITH FRIES AND LEMON MAYONNAISE

FIRM, MEATY OSTRICH MAKES DELICIOUSLY DIFFERENT GOUJONS, ESPECIALLY WHEN SERVED WITH ZESTY LEMON-FLAVOURED MAYONNAISE AND CRUNCHY CHIPS.

SERVES FOUR

INGREDIENTS
- 15ml/1 tbsp plain flour
- 450g/1lb ostrich fillet, cut into fine strips
- 1 egg white, beaten
- 50g/2oz/1 cup fresh white breadcrumbs
- sunflower oil, for deep frying
- 3 large potatoes, cut into thin strips
- grated rind of 1 lemon
- 150ml/¼ pint/⅔ cup mayonnaise
- salt and ground black pepper
- herb salad, to serve

COOK'S TIP
For speed, if you have two suitable pans, cook the potatoes and ostrich goujons separately and simultaneously.

1 Season the flour with salt and pepper and place on a plate or in a shallow dish. Dip the ostrich strips first in the flour, then in the beaten egg white and finally in breadcrumbs. It is easier to do this in batches.

2 Heat the sunflower oil for deep-frying in a large, heavy-based saucepan or deep-frying pan to 190°C/375°F, or until a cube of day-old bread browns in 30–60 seconds.

3 Cook the ostrich goujons in batches for about 5 minutes, or until golden and crisp. Remove from the oil and drain on kitchen paper and keep hot. Reheat the oil and cook the strips of potatoes for about 5–6 minutes, or until crisp and golden. Drain well on kitchen paper.

4 Stir the grated lemon rind into the mayonnaise. Serve the ostrich goujons with the fries and lemon mayonnaise, accompanied by the herb salad.

OSTRICH STEW WITH SWEET POTATOES AND CHICK PEAS

LEAN AND FIRM, OSTRICH MEAT MARRIES WELL WITH THE SOFT-TEXTURED SWEET POTATOES.

SERVES FOUR

INGREDIENTS
- 45ml/3 tbsp olive oil
- 1 large onion, chopped
- 2 garlic cloves, finely chopped
- 675g/1½lb ostrich fillet, cut into short strips
- 450g/1lb sweet potatoes, peeled and diced
- 2 × 400g/14oz cans chopped tomatoes
- 400g/14oz can chick-peas, drained
- salt and ground black pepper
- fresh oregano, to garnish

COOK'S TIP
Steamed couscous is a quick and easy accompaniment to this healthy stew.

1 Heat half the oil in a flameproof casserole. Add the onion and garlic, and cook for about 5 minutes, or until softened but not coloured, stirring occasionally. Remove from the casserole using a draining spoon and set aside. Add the remaining oil to the casserole and heat.

2 Fry the meat in batches over a high heat until browned. When the last batch is cooked, replace the meat and onions and stir in the potatoes, tomatoes and chick-peas. Bring to the boil, reduce the heat and simmer for 25 minutes, or until the meat is tender. Season and serve, garnished with oregano.

ROAST STUFFED FILLETS OF CROCODILE

THIS IS A MARVELLOUS, MODERN DINNER-PARTY DISH. CROCODILE IS A HEALTHY, LOW-FAT MEAT AND COOKED IN THIS WAY, IS EASY TO SERVE AND DELICIOUS TO EAT.

SERVES FOUR

INGREDIENTS

- 2 × 225g/8oz crocodile fillets
- 225g/8oz cooked mixed long grain and wild rice
- 1 leek, finely chopped
- 2 courgettes, finely chopped
- grated rind and juice of 1 lemon
- a little butter
- 45ml/3 tbsp balsamic vinegar
- salt and ground black pepper

VARIATION

Use 450g/1lb alligator fillet, halved, in place of the crocodile fillets.

1 Preheat the oven to 200°C/400°F/ Gas 6. Season the crocodile fillets with coarsely ground sea salt and pepper. Mix together the cooked mixed long grain and wild rice, leek, courgettes and lemon rind.

2 Grease an ovenproof dish with a little butter and lay one crocodile fillet in it. Spoon the rice mixture over the top. Put the other crocodile fillet on top. Press the crocodile fillets together and tie them at regular intervals with fine string to keep the stuffing in place.

3 Pour the lemon juice and balsamic vinegar over, and cover the crocodile with a piece of buttered foil. Roast for 15–20 minutes, or until the crocodile is browned, tender and cooked through.

4 Remove the string and cut the stuffed crocodile into portions. Transfer to warmed plates and serve at once.

MARINATED ALLIGATOR STEAKS WITH CAJUN VEGETABLES

THIS LOUISIANA SPECIALITY MAKES A COLOURFUL – AND FLAVOURFUL – SUPPER DISH.

SERVES FOUR

INGREDIENTS
- 4 alligator steaks, cut from the fillet, each weighing 175g/6oz
- juice of 2 limes
- 1 shallot, sliced
- 1 fresh red chilli, seeded and chopped
- 30ml/2 tbsp soy sauce
- 30ml/2 tbsp sesame oil
- chopped fresh coriander, to garnish

For the Cajun vegetables
- 2 red peppers, halved, seeded and cut into chunks
- 2 orange peppers, halved, seeded and cut into chunks
- 2 red onions, each cut into 6 wedges
- 4 garlic cloves
- 1 green chilli, seeded and chopped
- 30ml/2 tbsp sesame oil
- salt and ground black pepper

1 Trim the alligator steaks so they are similar in size. Put them in a large china or glass dish and add the lime juice, shallot, red chilli, soy sauce and sesame oil. Turn the steaks in the flavouring ingredients and then cover the dish with clear film. Set the steaks aside in a cool place to marinate while cooking the vegetables.

COOK'S TIP
The flavours in this dish are quite robust, so it is best to serve the steaks and Cajun vegetables with something simple like buttered pasta or rice.

2 Preheat the oven to 230°C/450°F/ Gas 8. Mix the chunks of red and orange peppers, onion wedges, garlic and chilli in a large roasting tin. Add the sesame oil and seasoning and toss well.

3 Roast the vegetables in the preheated oven for about 30 minutes, stirring them occasionally to prevent them from sticking to the tin.

4 Preheat a non-stick griddle pan or frying pan until very hot. Remove the alligator steaks from the marinade using a draining spoon and cook them in the hot pan for 8–10 minutes on each side, or until cooked through. Brush the steaks with marinade occasionally to keep them moist during cooking. Serve the steaks with the Cajun vegetables, garnished with chopped coriander.

KANGAROO WITH TAMARIND CHILLI SAUCE

BUTTERED NOODLES AND A LIGHTLY DRESSED MIXED GREEN LEAF SALAD ARE GOOD ACCOMPANIMENTS FOR RICH, DENSE KANGAROO STEAKS IN A SIMPLE SPICY SAUCE.

SERVES FOUR

INGREDIENTS

- 4 kangaroo steaks, each weighing about 175g/6oz
- buttered noodles and salad, to serve
- parsley, to garnish

For the sauce

- 15ml/1 tbsp chilli sauce
- 45ml/3 tbsp tamarind paste
- 15ml/1 tbsp clear honey
- 50g/2oz/¼ cup butter

COOK'S TIP

Tamarind paste is available from South-east Asian food stores, and you may also find it in some large supermarkets.

1 Preheat the grill to high. To make the sauce, mix together the chilli sauce, tamarind paste and clear honey in a small bowl. Melt the butter in a small saucepan over a low heat, then pour the butter into the bowl and blend into the sauce until it is smooth.

2 Arrange the kangaroo steaks on a grill rack and brush the sauce liberally over them. Grill the steaks for 3–5 minutes, then turn them and brush with the remaining sauce. Cook the steaks for a further 3–5 minutes, then serve with noodles and salad. Garnish with parsley.

BUFFALO STEAKS WITH HORSERADISH CREAM

THE FLAVOUR OF BUFFALO IS VERY LIKE THAT OF BEEF SO, NOT SURPRISINGLY, IT GOES EXTREMELY WELL WITH HORSERADISH CREAM – ONE OF THE CLASSIC BEEF ACCOMPANIMENTS.

SERVES FOUR

INGREDIENTS
- 4 buffalo steaks, each weighing about 150g/5oz
- 25g/1oz/2 tbsp butter
- 15ml/1 tbsp sunflower oil
- salt and ground black pepper
- a few whole chives, to garnish
- mixed salad leaves, to serve

For the horseradish cream
- 15ml/1 tbsp freshly grated horseradish (or to taste)
- 115g/4oz/½ cup crème fraîche
- 15ml/1 tbsp snipped fresh chives

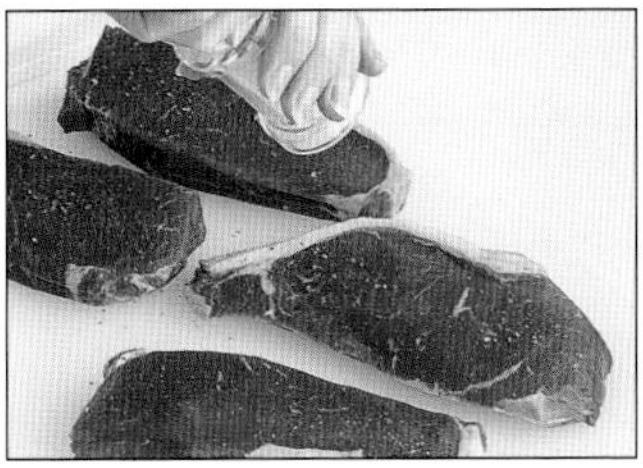

1 Season the steaks on both sides with salt and plenty of ground black pepper. Heat the butter and oil in a large frying pan until sizzling. Add the steaks and cook for 3–4 minutes on each side, turning once.

2 Meanwhile, make the horseradish cream. Mix the horseradish, crème fraîche and snipped chives in a small bowl. Serve the steaks with a dollop of horseradish cream, garnish with chives and serve with a mixed leaf salad.

SHOPPING INFORMATION

United Kingdom
Butchers' Shops

R. Allen and Co.
117 Mount Street
London W1Y 6HX
Tel: 020 7499 5831

A. Crombie and Son
97–101 Broughton Street
Edinburgh EH1 3RZ
Tel: 0131 556 7643

Frank Godfrey Limited
7 Highbury Park
London N5 1QJ
Tel: 020 7226 2425

Harrods Food Hall
87 Brompton Road
London SW1X 7XL
Tel: 020 7730 1234

Harvey Nichols Food Hall
109–125 Knightsbridge
London SW1X 7RJ
Tel: 020 7235 5000

Ilford Kosher Meats
7 Beehive Lane
Ilford, London R61 3R6
Tel: 020 8554 3238

Jefferies
42 Coombe Road
Norbiton, Kingston
Surrey KT2 7AS
Tel: 020 8546 0453

C. Lidgate
110 Holland Park Avenue
London W11 4UA
Tel: 020 7727 8243

Loon Fung Supermarket
42–44 Gerrard Street
London W1V 7LP
Tel: 020 7437 7332

MacBeth's
11 Tolbooth Street
Forres, Morayshire
Grampian 1V36 1PH
Tel/Fax: 01309 672254

Macsween
120 Bruntsfield Place
Edinburgh EH10 4ES
Tel: 0131 229 1216

Morawski (Polish delicatessen)
157 High Street
London NW10 4TR
Tel: 020 8965 5340

O'Hagan's Sausage Shop
Delling Lane
Bosham, Nr Chichester
PO18 8NN
Tel: 01243 574833

Randalls
113 Wandsworth Bridge Road
London SW6 2CE
Tel: 020 7736 3426

Randall & Aubin (specialize in French cuts of meat)
14–16 Brewer Street
London W1R 3FS
Tel: 020 7287 4447

Rias Altas (Spanish delicatessen)
97 Frampton Street
London NW8 8NA
Tel: 020 7262 4340

SW7 Meat Emporium
19 Bute Street
London SW7 3EY
Tel: 020 7581 0210

Selfridges
400 Oxford Street
London W1A 1AB
Tel: 020 7629 1234

Simply Sausages
Hart's Corner
341 Central Markets
Farringdon Street
London EC1A 9NB
Tel: 020 7329 3227

Mail Order

Barrow Boar
Foster's Farm
South Barrow, Yeovil
Somerset BA22 7LN
Tel: 01963 440315
Fax: 01963 440901
Email: sales@barrowboar.co.uk

Gamston Wood Ostriches
Gamston Wood Farm
Upton, Retford
Notts DN33 ORB
Tel: 01777 838 858
Email: sales@gamstonwoodostriches.co.uk
Web site: www.gamstonwoodostriches.co.uk
(also at Borough Market, Southwark, London SE1 on Friday and Saturday)

Goodman's Geese
Goodman Bros.
Walsgrove Farm
Great Witley
Worcester WR6 6JJ
Tel: 01299 896272
Fax: 01299 896889
Web site: www.getme.co.uk/goodman'sgeese

Donald Russell Direct (traditionally reared meat)
Freepost SCO 4131
Harlaw Road
Inverurie
Aberdeenshire AB51 4ZL
Tel: 01467 629666
Fax: 01467 629434
Email: info@donaldrussell.co.uk

Cooking Equipment

Divertimenti
45–47 Wigmore Street
London W1H 9LA
Tel: 020 7935 0689
139 Fulham Road
London SW3 6SD
Tel: 020 7581 8065

Information Services

Meat and Livestock Commission
Winterhill House
Snowdon Drive
Milton Keynes
Bucks MK6 1AX
Tel: 01908 677577
Fax: 01908 609826

Traditional Farmfresh Turkey Association
Tel: 01323 899802
Fax: 01323 899583
(for details of nearest stockist)

Australia

Meat & Livestock Australia Limited
PO Box 4129
Sydney NSW 2001
Tel: (02) 9463 9333
Fax: (02) 9463 9393
Web site: www.mla.com.au

Australian Poultry Industries Association
PO Box 579
North Sydney NSW 2059
Tel: (02) 9929 4077
Fax: (02) 9925 0627

National Meat Association
Level 2
Albany Street
Crows Nest NSW 2060
Tel: (02) 9906 3769
Fax: (02) 9438 5144

Penny's Butchery
880 Military Road,
Mosman NSW 2088
Tel: (02) 9969 3372

A C Butchery
174 Marion Street,
Leichhardt NSW 2040
Tel: (02) 9569 8687

BIBLIOGRAPHY

The Book Of Ingredients by Philip Dowell and Adrian Bailey (Mermaid, 1983)

A Concise Encyclopedia Of Gastronomy by André L Simon (Penguin, 1983)

Le Cordon Bleu Techniques & Recipes: Meat by Jeni Wright and Eric Treuille (Cassell, 1998)

Le Cordon Bleu Techniques & Recipes: Poultry, Game & Eggs by Jeni Wright and Eric Treuille (Cassell, 1998)

The Diner's Dictionary by John Ayto (Oxford University Press, 1993)

English Food by Jane Grigson (Penguin, 1993)

Food by Clarissa Dickson Wright (Ebury, 1999)

The Food Chronology by James Trager (Aurum Press, 1996)

Food In England by Dorothy Hartley (Futura, 1985)

Fresh Ways With Beef & Veal (Time Life Books, 1986)

Fresh Ways With Lamb (Time Life Books, 1986)

Fresh Ways With Pork (Time Life Books, 1986)

Fresh Ways With Poultry (Time Life Books, 1986)

Game Cookery by Nicola Cox (Victor Gollancz, 1989)

The Good Housekeeping Cookery Book (Ebury Press, 1985)

A History Of Food by Maguelonne Toussaint-Samat (Blackwell, 1994)

How To Eat by Nigella Lawson (Chatto & Windus, 1998)

Larousse Gastronomique edited by Robert J Coutine (Paul Hamlyn, 1988)

Ma Cuisine by Auguste Escoffier translated by Vyvyan Holland (Hamlyn, 1984)

Mastering The Art Of French Cooking by Simone Beck, Louisette Bertholle and Julia Child (Penguin, 1966)

Meat Course by Sophie Grigson (Network, 1995)

On Food And Cooking by Harold McGee (Allen & Unwin, 1986)

The Oxford Companion To Food by Alan Davidson (Oxford University Press, 1999)

Reader's Digest Complete Guide To Cookery by Anne Willan (Dorling Kindersley, 1989)

Le Répertoire de la Cuisine by Louis Saulnier (Leon Jaeggi, 1982)

The Rituals Of Dinner by Margaret Visser (Penguin, 1993)

Wine by Keith Richmond and Lucy Knox (Hamlyn, 1997)

The World Atlas Of Food edited by Jane Grigson (Mitchell Beazley, 1974)

ACKNOWLEDGEMENTS

Picture Acknowledgements

All photographs are by Craig Robertson and Janine Hosegood, except the following: Steve Moss p7 and 8tl; Sam Stowell p145; Jon Whittaker pp174–175, 195; Cephas Picture Library p6b John Darling, p7t Hervé Champolion, p92b Mick Rock; Anthony Blake Photo Library p20t Jon Sims, p36t Keiran Scott, p46 Anthony Blake, p80t John Sims; Food Features p98b; Planet Earth Pictures p8b Geoff du Feu, p9tr Peter Stephenson, p9b M&C Denis-Huot, p20b Brian Brown; BBC Natural History Unit p6t Eliot Lyons, p9tl George McCarthy, p36b Davis Kjaer; Bruce Coleman Collection p8tr Mark N Boulton47 George McCarthy, p81b Hans Reinhart; p104b Robert Maier, p112t Stephen J Krasemann.

Publisher's Acknowledgements

The publishers would like to thank the following companies who supplied meat, game or poultry for photography: Christina Baskerville of Barrow Boar, Jim and Sue Farr of Gamston Wood Ostriches, Keith Fisher of the Meat and Livestock Commission, and Fayre Game Ltd. We would also like to thank Magimix and Divertimenti for providing specialist cooking equipment for photography.

Authors' Acknowledgements

A book like this is an enormous undertaking and we could not have done it without the help and advice of a lot of people. We would like to thank Chris and Jeremy Godfrey who run the butcher's, Frank Godfrey Ltd in Islington, north London. We have learned a lot about meat by listening to them over the years. We also want to thank Keith Baker of the Meat and Livestock Commission, and Fred Mullion of the Worshipful Company of Butchers.

We want to thank Sarah Lowman for helping us test the recipes and Tina Fenner for keeping us organized; Joanna Farrow, Bridget Sargeson, Annabel Ford and Victoria Walters, the home economists who prepared the food for photography; Helen Trent, the stylist who found the props; Craig Robertson and Janine Hosegood, who took the pictures; Bridget Jones and Susanna Tee, who edited the text; and Linda Fraser for offering us the project in the first place.

INDEX

Notes

Notes

Notes

Notes

Notes

Notes

NOTES

Notes